A HAIR'S BREADTH FROM DEATH

THE MEMOIRS OF HAMPARTZOUM MARDIROS CHITJIAN

Memoirs of a survivor
of the Armenian Genocide

Gomidas Institute

London

A Gomidas Institute publication. This book was first printed in 2004 by Taderon Press in association with the Gomidas Institute.

Reprinted with permission. 2021

ISBN 978-1-909382-62-6

For more information and updates about this work please visit our website.

Gomidas Institute
42 Blythe Rd.
London W14 0HA
United Kingdom
www.gomidas.org
info@gomidas.org

In memory of my beloved wife
a survivor from Malatya
Ovsanna Piloyan Chitjian,
and
the one and half million innocent martyrs
of the Turkish genocide of Armenians

Աչքս գրեաց ՏԷն կախայ ՏԷ
Ականջս լ ատՏԷն
ՍիրկՍ յիկարացա ՏԷ աշկա լԷն
Կը ՐոՐ ՑՐայ ՑամիՐԷն

My eyes are frightened from what they have seen
My ears from what they have heard
My heart has weakened from the past
and trembles from what is yet to come.

TABLE OF CONTENTS

PHOTOGRAPHS AND ILLUSTRATIONS

ACKNOWLEDGEMENTS

I would like to express my appreciation and acknowledgement for the suggestions and moral support given to me by Dr. J Michael Hagopian, Hilmar Kaiser, Peter Abajian, Adrene Grigorian and Lena Kaimian while preparing these memoirs.

Particular thanks and appreciation go to Seda Maronyan for writing the Armenian rendition of these memoirs, and undertaking the task of compiling the list of 300 letters, most of which were written by my dad during the period between 1919-1923. Without her dedication this book would not have been written.

Finally, I would like to add the following credits for the photographs, Kevork Yerevanian's *A Story of Charsanjak*, Tracy Atkison's *"The German, the Turk and the Devil made a Triple Alliance"*, Theresa Huntington Ziegler's *"Great Need over the Water"*, Boghos Jafferian's *Farewell Kharpert*, Charles Chitjian for the photo of his grandmother and mother, Olga Kuludjian for the photograph of her mother Zaruhy Mishmeeshian, Joanne Saver for the specific location of Perri, the Poochigian Archives: www.geocities.com/poochfamily/homeland2, Seda Maronyan for the hand drawn illustrations and maps.

PREFACE

As far back as I can remember, one of the most joyous moments my parents had were the social visits with their *yergeeratzees,* survivors of the Turkish atrocities in 1915. Everyone relished sharing fond memories of their childhood. That is when I first recognized *Yergeer** was *a very special place*—a place where everything not only was dearly cherished and in many ways were different from what they presently had. Relatives and friends were more warm-hearted and compassionate. Apricots, *toot* (mulberries), grapes, plums, watermelon were much tastier. Even the air and water were different! They all took much pleasure recalling what they once had. I could not understand why they had left such a place. The Armenians had lived on that land for 3,000 years. They were the first nation to adopt Christianity as their national religion. Ancient ruins and relics remain scattered throughout the landscape in present day Turkey. Why could they not go back to their ancestral birthplace—to their *yergeer?*

By the time I was ten years old, I became aware that these joyous memories *quickly* led into a sadder mood. Their tears perturbed me. I could not understand how they *all* share *a common sad memory of their childhood*—happiness switched to grief and sorrow. Eyes were filled with tears. *Sov* (Starvation), *Charrt and Godoradz* (Genocide) were three words continuously repeated. Words I could not comprehend at that early age. I knew, however, those words elicited pain and heartache. **They had lost everything they once cherished.** The Turks were responsible for the murder, separation and break-up of their families. My father was left alone, an orphan. He had to fend for his survival. I soon began to empathize about the horror of being left alone, an orphan—a terrifying fear that still lurks in my psyche…

At some point in my adulthood, I realized my father's anguish was swelling with pain and disbelief. The years were passing by and the Armenian Genocide committed by the Turks against its own subjects remains **unaddressed**—a position that defies the very moral fiber and fundamental principles of free democracies worldwide: For whom is there justice? Where is the Truth?[†]

It is hard to remember a day when my father does not recall some aspect of his youth. I rejoice with him when I listen to his cherished memories during his childhood in Perri. Unfortunately, he mostly recalls some aspects of the *Charrt.*

---

* Historically *Yergeer* refers to all the villages, towns and cities located in Western Armenia (Greater Armenia)—now occupied by Turkey.

† He was outraged every time he recalled the statement "gentleman Turk" made by a U.S. president early on during the Cold War.

These moments have always created a sense of *helplessness* within my gut. There was *no one* to help him. If I could not help him during those turbulent years, then I *must* help him *now*. That is what I have attempted to do during the entirety of *my* lifetime. Unfortunately, no matter how much I try, the feeling of loss and pain never ceases within himself. My father is 102.

In 1975, I never would have thought that the activities of the mini-class with my ten to twelve year old students along with their parents and with the teachers in the school district's Ethnic Studies Program would *stimulate and prompt* my father to embark upon writing his memoirs. This, however, was a task he had mentally entertained for years. He was very concerned the Genocide and its consequences would be forgotten and buried just as our innocent one and a half million martyrs lay on the wasteland of Turkey. Although, he enthusiastically began and diligently wrote 50 pages of a basic framework about the six years of him living a *dog's life,* the pain of remembering and recording became too much for him even though he was *only* seventy-four years old when he first attempted to undertake that task. Remembering and writing was much *too* difficult for him to assume on his own. Thus, the project was left unfinished. However, throughout the following years, he sporadically continued to write about specific issues that touched his heart and mind.

Shortly after the loss of his beloved wife Ovsanna in May 1998, twenty-five years later, he became more determined to complete the task of writing his memoirs that he had started years earlier. It was only by chance we found someone who understood and was capable to fulfil my father's requirements. No part of his text was to be *changed, modified or deleted.* His vocabulary and spelling should be kept in tact. As much as possible, he wanted to preserve the *specific dialect and idiosyncrasies* he had acquired in his youth—when and where his saga took place.

It was an incredible *chance encounter* that brought Seda Maronyan to us. She had the respect and will to acquiesce to my father's stipulations. As their work got underway, I was delighted to hear my father's words were being recorded. Listening to Seda read his words was almost as dear as listening to my father relating his saga. His story was here forever…

However, it did not take long for me to realize not only I but also any one else who could not read Armenian would not have access to *his* story and the inhuman atrocities of the Armenian Genocide. Therefore, an *English version* became necessary. I had to assume the task of writing the English version, because we already had experienced much difficulty finding an appropriate person to write my father's memoirs according to his specifications without modification. Although, I took great caution to *maintain the essence* of my father's original text, I was not able to fully capture the emotional impact and nuances of the pain and grief expressed in his own words in the Armenian. It is nearly impossible to literally translate emotional and allegorical passages from Armenian into English! Thus a deliberate *simple* style was used to reflect the contents and emotions *as true* as possible. With that point in mind, I handled the spelling of Armenian, Turkish, and Kurdish names and words in two ways. When I felt there *was* a generally accepted spelling of a word, I kept that spelling. For words that were not common nor had an established spelling, I used the basic American English phonetic spelling as much as possible. It was imperative that I keep my father's pronunciation—with the hope we kept his dialect the way he learned in Perri and Kharpert, alone. There are at least seven different spellings of Kharpert. Perri could have been spelled Perry, Pery or Peri. I chose Perri because that was the way my father spelled it in Armenian. *Even at the age of 102 plus, my father is very clear and alert with what he did and did not say. He is very critical that he be repeated as to what he said, that is what he experienced.*

Seda and I used *four sources* to compile his memoirs: his initial fifty page memoirs, his sporadically written papers, his oral dictation which was the greatest source, and the letters he had received from his nephew which gave us the exact date for particular events as well as a few names of people he had forgotten.

I had one more advantage, *my own* memory of the numerous times I had heard his experiences. I have acquired an awareness of his feelings on his outlook on life. I have always marvelled at his keen memory. Throughout the years, I *never* heard the details of any one of his accounts waiver. At any given time, he may remember new and different situations and put aside a few, but the *specific details never changed.*

The format of his initial Foreword which he wrote twenty-five years ago was maintained throughout his saga. He relates his story in the first person, talks to his reader and intermittently weaves out of his past into the present, interjecting his present day commentary and emotions. *The Past is so much a part of his present—* the impact and implications of the aftermath of the Genocide are intertwined in his psyche, mind and soul—the past is *always* with him!

He unfolded the episodes that took place in Part II chronologically for us. He used no notes, enthusiastically his saga just *poured* out from within—*it was waiting to be recorded!* During the two year period that it took us to write his saga, recalling painful images began to take its toll upon him. As his painful facial expressions deepened, it became more difficult to witness—delving any deeper was avoided. It is a pity I had not assumed this responsibility years earlier.[*]

All of Part I was elicited from him by Seda and myself. There was a bit of reluctance on his part that we dwelled *too* much on that area, in fear it would detract from Part II. This segment was remembered as a blend of memories of his life before the death of his mother and grandfather as seen through the eyes of the young naïve eight year old boy and his life of that of a thirteen year old youth with daily chores and cherished memoirs of his school years. As he unfolds a specific memory, he may not bring complete closure to that incident. I feel so much was

---

[*] I am "positive" there is a wealth of pertinent information locked within his soul!

left out, despite how much we encouraged him to *remember more*. Was this lack of recollection due to fatigue since he was ninety-eight years old when we started the project and he just did not remember, or are there hidden memories too painful to surface—or both?

Parts II and III overall followed his hand-written words plus oral dictation and the letters. From time to time, he recalled a new incident. A *hidden* experience unfolded. Some memories were frivolous, others were more significant. These recollections suggest there is so much more stored in his memory. However, the real *impact* of his pleasant and painful recollections is fully understood only when observed with his facial and body gestures, the tone of his voice, and the tears that well up in his eyes. Only then can you *really* understand the devastation that the Genocide had on his soul and mind for eighty-eight years. Therefore, the true essence of his state was not fully captured and that was unfortunate. That could only have been fully accomplished through an audiovisual medium.

At the age of 102 plus, his single wish is to see justice for Armenians—"is there a God that recognizes human rights for ALL of His people?"

> *At the height of the 1915 Genocide, Talaat Pasha (the mastermind of the Genocide) rebuffed Henry Morgenthau, the U.S. Ambassador to Turkey during that period. "It is no use for you to argue. We have already disposed of three-quarters of the Armenians. There are none left in Bitlis [William Saroyan's birthplace], Van and Erzeroum. The hatred between the Turks and the Armenians is now so intense that we have got to finish with them. If we do not they will plan their revenge."*

At that same time, the United States Government commissioned the collection of sacks filled with Armenians bones? What did our government do with those bones? The U.S. archives are filled with evidence. The world knows and continues to do nothing as they had done in 1915. If the Armenian Genocide had been justly resolved in 1915, that part of the world would be in peace today. Today's problems in the world are a continuation of yesterday's greed and self-serving actions.

The world will never be at peace when "man's inhumanity to man" is repeatedly denied. *Justice* is felt universally. *It can not be denied to some and enjoyed by others!*

Lesson to be learned! When historical events continue to repeat themselves empires come and go!

Zaruhy Sara Chitjian
Dec., 2003

FOREWORD

I am a *survivor* of the Turkish atrocities committed against the Armenian nation. My name is Hampartzoum Chitjian. I was born in Ismiel in 1901. If you have not witnessed atrocities such as this, then read with patience and listen with compassion to what I, the author, have written about my suffering, my reflections, and feelings about my first statements. Please listen to what I have said, and then try to understand what I have experienced.

To be more exact, I am one of the *victims*, who miraculously escaped from the barbaric, incomprehensible inhumane acts in history conspired by the Ottoman Government in 1915. One never survives from a Genocide. You may escape *physically*, but your mind and soul are tormented forever. If you have been in an inferno, you are *scarred* for life.

My eyes have been terrified from all that they have seen and likewise, my ears from all that they have heard—atrocities I witnessed for six years. My heart has become weary and worn out from the past and *tremors* with fear for the future of Armenia and the Armenians.

If the celestial hope and light doesn't remain lit upon the Armenians, if God doesn't help us, we will live our lives with remorse and fear, gradually becoming extinct.

From the malicious Turks, I have heard on several occasions, "If only we had the Armenians' final realization." They meant to say the Armenians were now divided from within, but fear for the future when they should unite.

Will we see our demise from the Turks or from within? Unity within our people is our only salvation and hope for achieving our national goals and aspirations.

In 1915, the unmerciful God turned his back on the Armenians. He left the Armenians with unbearable days—the one nation that supported Him the most, the first nation that adopted Christianity. Yet, he allowed the Turks to perpetrate the most barbaric heinous acts against humanity and *attempted* to completely annihilate the whole nation. Why?

We lost our mothers, fathers, brothers, sisters—more than one and a half million Armenians. And more devastating, we lost all our *historical* homeland—a homeland deeply rooted in our culture, traditions and our souls. What a loss for humanity. This nation and her people had so much more to offer the world.

Fortunately, with the help of God the memories of my childhood up to the tender age of thirteen, going on fourteen, are frozen deeply in my mind and soul.

Now, at the age of one hundred two, in the year 2003, I am still able to vividly relish and enjoy the images of my youth. A life so cherished and so greatly missed.

As I witnessed the vicious destruction of my family, home and *Yergeer,* I fortuitously was able to protect a small fraction of all that was dear to me—the precious images that have nourished my heart and soul for over eighty-eight years. Not a day goes by when I don't recall a glimpse of my immediate surroundings, my precious family, teachers, classmates, the abundant springs, the rushing waters of the Perri River, the delicious sweet taste of *toot* and grapes... the homeland of my soul, my *Yergeer.* The historical homeland of my ancestors, the culture and traditions of a people dating back three thousand years. The yearning in my heart never ceases.

I don't know how my mind and soul integrated all of my experiences, allowing me to cope and endure the subsequent pain and suffering inflicted by the Turkish atrocities, which were discreetly planned and barbarically executed. As I lived one day at a time, from incident to incident, I must have learned how to store each new terrifying incident as far back in my mind as possible, and prepared myself for the next moment. . . *to survive!*

Only when I found freedom and had established myself amidst safe surroundings, did these tightly stored images begin to emerge in my nightmares and at the brink of all my daily thoughts for the rest of my life. I never learned how to cope with those images. **They have haunted and tormented me eternally... at this age and time of my life, the pain and torment have intensified for I have not seen reparation, nor justice. My soul will only rest in peace when these two have been met.**

Akh, akh this is life for an Armenian. Not only does he become weary by reliving his saga. Maybe so does the reader or perhaps God as well!

I would first like you to become familiar with where I lived and how I lived before it was all brutally taken from me.[*] Perri was the principal town, a *kiughakaghak,* in the county of Charsanjak which was in the southeastern area of the Derseem District in the province of Kharpert, which had 365 villages. Thus, it was northeast of the city of Kharpert, (60-80 miles,) a walking distance of four days. Pertahk was midway between Kharpert and Perri, a distance of two walking days. Pahloo was southeast of Perri a walking distance of one day. The town was an agricultural settlement which was built on the slope of a hill along the Perri River. Perri was divided into six districts (*taghs*) of which five were inhabited. We lived in the Gahmarr Aghpiur Tagh.

The Perri River ran through Perri and merged with the Yeprahd (Euphrates) River. The terrain of Perri and its environment is very mountainous, covered with hillsides and valleys. Because of the heavy rains and snowfalls, the harsh winters

[*]   Joanne Saver, "Poochigian archives" http://*www.geocides.com/poochfamily/home/ and2.htm*

are long and extremely cold and there is an abundance of springs, waterfalls, rivers and streams. These water sources facilitated much of our lifestyle, as did the rich earth.

My dear reader,

*As you vicariously embark upon the journey of my saga, please empathize with compassion and cherish with your heart and soul all that I had and all that I lost forever. If you feel the pain I endured as I survived one of the darkest days in history, then you will understand my state of mind during the past eighty-eight years—the remaining years of my life. . . **You never survive from a Genocide.***

Hampartzoum Mardiros Chitjian
(1976)

PART 1

My Life in Perri Before the Charrt

My Cherished Homeland

Yehrgeeres

Perri
before the
1915 *Chart* - Genocide

K. Yerevanian

1. FAMILY INTRODUCTION

As much as I can remember, the atmosphere in our household was compassionate, cordial and tender. Harsh words and actions were absent. Yet, at the same time, the elders in my family were not outgoing or demonstrative. They were restrained and reserved with their words and actions, and somber with their emotions. They were *keenly aware* of their political subjugation under the rule of the infidel Turk. Always fearing for their personal welfare, livelihood and bodily harm. Their minds were never at peace. Joy and laughter were cherished memories in my childhood that came with very simple experiences and very few special celebrations.

My name is Hampartzoum Chitjian, the son of Mardiros and Tervanda. We were six brothers. The eldest was Bedros, followed by Mihran, Kaspar my twin, myself, Kerop and Nishan, the youngest. There was an approximate five-year difference between the boys. I also had three sisters, Zaruhy, who was the first born child, Sultahn and my half sister Yeranouhi, the youngest child. Altogether, my father had nine children.

My paternal grandfather, Toros, lived with us along with his youngest daughter, Aghavni. His eldest daughter, Marinos, lived with her husband in Medzgerd. They never had children. Because it took more than one walking day to Medzgerd, we did not see much of her.

Our total lifestyle reflected the staunch faith in Christianity practiced both by my father and my grandfather, more so than any of the other parents in my school. They were in prayer night and day. They were true believers. So much so, that when a community member became ill, Kaspar and I were called to their bedside to read to them from the Bible. Because we were only eight to nine years old and unscathed by the ways of the world, they believed we had healing powers. Kaspar enjoyed reading to the sick. He felt more capable, because he was a better reader. However, we always went together, because he was afraid to go alone. Since we were called often, we felt we were of some benefit. That made us feel good.

We not only practiced Christian doctrine; we also observed Christian ethics. We were very respectful and responsible for each other. As much as each family member was able, he willingly fulfilled his particular chores and responsibilities. At age ninety-two, my grandfather was the only one without a chore. Although he was in relatively good health, he only had to look after himself. We all loved and respected him dearly. He was the king of our family.

Upon entering the house, my father always acknowledged his father with a courteous bow, a kiss on his hand, the hands raised to the forehead and then lowered with another kiss. The gesture meant that my grandfather's words and wishes were paramount in the family. While my father was a heavy smoker, out of respect, he never smoked in front of his father who was a non-smoker. In a manner typical of Armenian brides at that time, my mother never spoke to my father in front of his father, even though she had borne his eight children.

Our household was modest, simple and humble. We never felt the lack of anything. We were content with whatever my father was able to provide for us. Unfortunately, I do not have a more vivid recollection of my mother. I remember her being very reserved, with medium height, olive complexion, dark hair and dark eyes. In that respect, I took after her, as did my older brother Mihran, my younger brother Kerop and my sister Zaruhy. My mother's head was always covered with a scarf that not only hid her hair, but also most of her face. I never once saw her whole face, her eyes were always sad... *Meghk!* (a sigh of sorrow)

She was in charge of all of the household chores and the care of the younger children. In those days women's chores were *much harder* than those of the men were. My Aunt Aghavni and two sisters, Zaruhy and Sultahn, were always helping with one household chore or another. They worked from the time they awoke to the time they went to sleep.

My mother had eight children. All were about two to three years apart from each other. She nursed them all. However, when my twin brother and I were born, she did not have the strength to nurse both of us. I was the first born by about fifteen minutes. I was larger and healthier. Thus she allowed another woman, who had just lost a newborn, to nurse me. For about a year, I was taken to that woman several times a day to be nursed. Kaspar had perfect teeth. To the day he died at the age of eighty-two, he had all his teeth with no cavities. In our later years, I was envious of him whenever I saw him bite into an apple. I had my first tooth pulled at age seventeen and by the time I was in my seventies I had dentures. I attribute that difference to the fact Kaspar was nursed by my mother for several years (up to the age of six). In addition, he had her gentle temperament and was more endearing and charming than me.

Whenever my mother directly interacted with any of the older male family members she lowered her scarf even more. Consequently, I don't have a clear image of my mother's face. It must have been a *tender face,* because she always treated us lovingly.

What I do remember most about my mother were the many times I found her alone with tears flowing down her face. I knew she was reliving the atrocious moments when her mother, brothers and she witnessed the barbaric Turks viciously beheading her beloved, innocent father in the 1895 massacres in

Vasgerd. Her father tried to stop Turks from plundering their house—all that they had! The pain of that wretched moment was etched in her soul forever. *Her tears never stopped...*

She had four brothers. They were all farmers. They owned a large piece of land on which they grew wheat. That land was near the *galls,* the area where wheat was threshed. Only her youngest brother, Mardiros Mooradian, had two sons. His eldest son Setrag was a year older than my brother Bedros. His youngest son was Hmahyag. He was a couple of years younger than I was. They were my only cousins. I had no cousins from my father's side, even though he had two sisters.

While I always sympathized with my mother when she was consumed with those devastating memories from the age of eight, *it never occurred to me that one day I, too,* would be afflicted with the *same painful existence* caused by the same beastly Turks for the rest of my life...tormented forever!

My father, *Chitjee Mardiros,* on the other hand, was tall with a fair complexion and reddish brown hair. He had a long moustache of the same color, each end curled over an ear. Along with his large dark eyes, long dark eyelashes, which curled up, and his reddish brown eyebrows, he had a very distinguished look. He was a *very impressive,* handsome man. Bedros, my oldest brother, my twin Kaspar, my youngest brother Nishan and my sister Sultahn all had my father's features.

My father's general facial expressions were, however, also reserved and guarded like my mother's. They were both preoccupied with the existing illusive external conditions. I, of course, was not fully aware of the *real* danger in which we were living, even though we were all aware of the precarious conditions the Armenians had always endured, compared to the Turks and Kurds, who lived in Perri.

My father was the sole provider for thirteen people. His craft was very laborious and time consuming. From early morning to late evening he was involved with the *guhdavs* (muslin), from printing, to repairing or making new designs on his wood blocks, to replenishing his colored dyes.

I was keenly aware of my father's staunch religious faith. *The faith that ultimately God would protect the Armenians* and his family. With my subsequent treacherous experiences, my pain was compounded because I lived to witness the betrayal of my father's faith in God. Where was God? How could He turn His back on those who adamantly believed in Him? How could He allow such an unconscionable act?

My grandfather, on the other hand, had a more tranquil and cheerful disposition. He always instilled a sense of joy in his grandchildren. As the eldest member of the family, he was the head of the household. He assumed the burden of setting the mood of our daily lives. He was always telling us stories and fables to teach, discipline and amuse us. He too had a majestic stature, especially for his age. He was a little taller than my father. He too had broad shoulders and a husky body. I remember him as having beautiful white hair and bushy eyebrows complementing his fair complexion and dark eyes. He too was a very handsome man. From what I had heard, at some point my great-grandfather emigrated from Bolis to Dikranagerd. And sometime later my grandfather emigrated to Ismiel where we lived side by side in three adjoining houses. We lived in the middle house. Distant relatives, *gerdastan,* seven generations removed, lived on either side. Alexan Amo, a *fedayee* (a freedom fighter), and his wife, Altoon Bahgee, were on one side and Der Nerses and his family on the other side. When I was about one to two years old, my father moved away from Ismiel and settled in Perri.

As a child, I was more active and adventurous than Kaspar. Consequently, I was more mischievous. Thus, my grandfather spent more time with me. That special one-on-one time together nurtured a strong bond between us. His words of wisdom, anecdotes and fables gave me pleasure and comfort. Those impressions and memories consoled me not only in my childhood, but even more so during the most horrific experiences I was yet to encounter. He definitely molded the backbone of my character and strengthened my ingenuity. Whenever necessary, I was always able to fall back on some tale or advice to console, guide or even humor me with the immediate situation I was facing. Now, even in my twilight years, I still relish the pleasure and comfort he passed on to me. *Perhaps that is what kept me alive for so long.* The bond between grandfather and grandson is never forgotten—there were some things the Turks could not destroy!

While I had developed a special bond with my grandfather, Kaspar developed a special bond with my father. We grew up feeling that was a natural experience, and we never developed negative attitudes towards each other. There is one incident I remember well when my father and grandfather had Kaspar and me engage in wrestling when we were no more than four to five years old. The victor would receive five walnuts and two more if he pinned down his opponent. Since I was larger, I usually won and collected more walnuts. Therefore, from time to time my father would trip my leg with his foot to allow Kaspar to win and collect walnuts.

Unfortunately, I never knew any of my other grandparents.

2. NEIGHBORHOOD AND NEIGHBORS

This is all that I can remember of the image of my immediate neighborhood and layout of our house.

Our block was situated on a narrow street about ten to twelve feet wide. The houses were one to two stories high on both sides of the narrow cobblestone street.

An *ahroo* (channel) ran through the center of the street. The "Gahmarr *Aghpiur* (Fountain)" was the source of its water. The channels splintered into two branches at *Mewsahlah Dahsh* (Moslem burial rock) and passed by the kiln. One branch led to the shopping centers. The other branch came towards our house and continued on down towards the Yermoian's house. The channel was made on two levels. The bottom channel carried the toilet waste away from the houses. The top channel which was not coverd carried away the street debris.

There was one empty lot on the corner of our block. The first house on our block was Varteeg Bahgee's house, which was the only two-story house on our side. Her son had gone to America to avoid the Turkish draft. Her daughter-in-law lived with her, as well as her brother Giragos, his wife and their young daughter, Vartouhi. Alexan Amo was Varteeg Bahgee's older brother. Our one story house was next.

Voskereech Baghdazar, a goldsmith, who was on our right, had an eleven-year-old son. They didn't socialize much with others. Next to him were the only two Turkish families on our block. First was Gooree Oso's house and the next house belonged to Karahmeen Esh. They were both elderly

K. Yerevanian

Gahmarr Aghpiur

Map of Perri

(Kevork Yerevanian, *The Story of Charsanchak*)

Korr Mamo's Gardens

Arkhaj gardens

Gol
Spring ■

Government
building

Kiln

Potters
Wheel

Gahmarr
Spring

Blacksmith
Shop

Korr Mamoe's
House ■

Ouraghian Fahroon

Pahklava Poor

Mishmeshian

Shoe Shop

Shops

Shops

Minaret

Police
Station ■

Turkish
School

Road leading
to School

Mewsahlah
Dash

Nalbandian

Khazanchee
Mardiros

Vosgerich
Mardiros

Meynazar

channel

Areef Effendi

Mid-Wife

Karameen
Esh

Gooree
Oso

Vosgerich
Bagbdasar

Our
House

Ago-Ebo

Crazy
Boy

Bandazian

Varteeg
Bahgee

channel

Aghsah
Bahchee
Marobian

Kevork
Noroian's house

Bedros
Yermoyan

Antaramian's
House

Road leading to School →

Galls

Threshing Fields

Hmahyag's
house

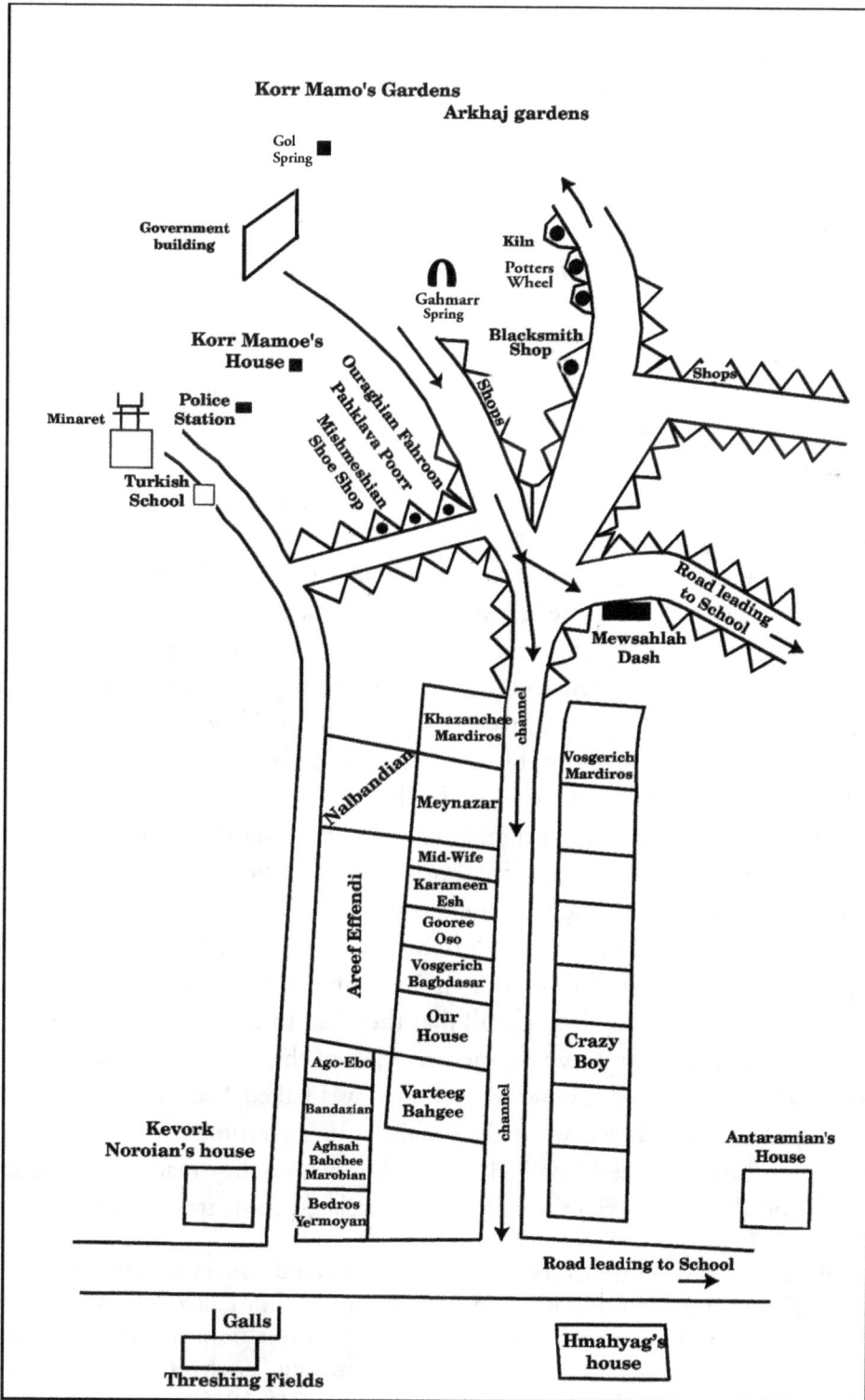

Map of my immediate neighborhood (relative distance)

couples, and each one owned a donkey that they rented out. Next came the *tayag* (mid-wife) and her daughter. She once had a dog without hind legs that she sold for five dollars. Maynazar lived next to her. He had a very tall handsome son, Avedis, around fifteen to sixteen years old. He was always well dressed and brazenly strutted around the neighborhood.

The last house on the block on the corner belonged to Khazanchee Mardiros. He sold fine fabrics in the *shoogah* (marketplace). He was well to do and was the moneylender in the community; therefore, he had the means to send his daughter, Aghavni, to school.

I can't recall as much about our neighbors who lived across the street from us. I only remember the family who lived in the house directly across from ours. That was the family whose son had lost his mind while he was in America and became known as the "crazy boy."[*]

The last house on their corner belonged to Vaskertzee Mardiros. His house was directly across from Khazanchee Mardiros. He too was well to do, and he also had a daughter named Aghavni who attended school. I think both girls were about the same age—they might have been a year younger than me.

We bought our milk, cheese and yogurt from Vaskertzee Mardiros. Every morning, I went to his house to buy freshly made yogurt. If the yogurt was sold out, I took home milk and we made our own yogurt. Vaskertzee Mardiros kept about five to ten cows in his stable at night, his *naghergee* (shepherd) took them out to graze along the hillsides during the day.

The shopping centers began right after Vaskertzee Mardiros' house. There was a variety of about one hundred fifty shops that sold fine silk, woolen fabric, and fine clothing and shoes. Candles, matches, and cigarette paper. A variety of grains, sesame, hemp, and cotton came from Itchmeh; china, utensils and other imports, such as our lantern were brought from Germany. Because I didn't have much opportunity to shop, I don't know all that they had to offer.

Not too far from our house on the street left of the *Mewsahlah Dahsh* was the Ourakhian's *fahroon* (bakery) where *pakhlava* was baked and sold. Next to them was the *poorr* (where bread was baked mainly for government officials). On the same street the Mishmeeshians had a shoe shop where they made and sold shoes in Perri and the nearby vicinities. They were related to us from my father's side.

---

[*] On January 5, 2003 we received a letter from Edward Antaramian (from Kenosha, Wisconsin) inquiring if I knew his family. It didn't take long for me to remember the Antaramians who lived across the street from us, several houses from the "Crazy Boy." I remember Assadour, Jivan and Parrahvon who was a couple of years younger than me. After the *Charrt* of 1915-1916, while I lived with Korr Mahmoe, I spotted Parrahvon on the streets in Perri. He was a very tall and handsome boy. Parrahvon was Edward's cousin.

The Mishmeeshians were four brothers who lived together with their respective families in one large house that was located behind the church. If I remember correctly, their names were Ohan, Abraham, Kaspar and Marsoub. Kaspar and Marsoub were teachers at our school. At some time, Marsoub was transferred to another school. I do, however, remember their visits to our house. Their house was built on two different parcels of land. Each parcel was directly opposite of one another across the road that led behind the church up towards the mountain. They utilized both parcels into one large house. The first floor of each parcel faced the other across the road. The top levels of both sides were linked over the road. This created the semblance of a bridge over the road. I have never seen another house built with that design.

The *Mewsahlah Dahsh,* the Moslem burial rock, where the dead were brought for prayer before being buried was right in the middle of all of the shops in the center of town. A crowd of people was always bustling around this area. At that particular point the main road splintered into three main streets.

To the right, one road led to our church and school grounds. The middle road led to the *Arkhaj Baghchah* (mulberry grove), and to the blacksmith shop. A little further down was the *bardahghnah* (kiln) and potter's wheel. A large assortment of shapes and sizes of pottery was made and sold there. Torros Malkhasian's father was our potter. He made all the pottery for Perri and nearby villages. Torros was my classmate. He lived near Hagop Holipigian who lived in a beautiful house on the hillsides a distance behind the church. The third road led towards the Gahmarr *Aghpiur,* the government building, police station, the Turkish school and the minaret.

The empty corner lot next to Varteeg Bahgee's house and the two empty lots behind her house were good places for the boys to play games. I have good memories playing there with my classmates when we had free time.

Bedros Yermoian lived on the corner adjacent to the empty lot behind our block. His father owned the *tzeetzeeyank* (millstone). Next to his house, behind our house was Aghsah Bahgee's house. She lived there with her two small daughters. Her husband had fled to America to avoid the wrath of the Turkish army.

Next to her house was the Bandazian's house. Several families lived there together. Of all the family members, only one son, Guyzahg, survived. (In the early 1920s, he worked in Kaspar's market in Los Angeles for a short period of time.)

Next to the Bandazian's house was a subterranean house, the only subterranean house in Perri that I remember. Ago-Ebo lived there with his Armenian wife and son Levon.

Areef Effendi's house, a huge two-story house, was next door. It was directly behind several houses—ours, Voskereech Baghdazar's, Gooree Oso's, Karahmeen Esh's and the midwife's. The only thing I knew about him was that he was both a prominent and wealthy Turkish official. We played handball against his wall from our rooftop.

The Nalbandians, our blacksmith, lived next to Areef Effendi. They had two sons, Higaz and Khosrov. Higaz was a husky boy and one of the weaker students in Mihran's class. Khosrov was older, a good student, and popular. I last saw him in Haleb (Aleppo), where he was working for a newspaper reporting the local news.

Kevork Noroian, my best friend, lived right across from the *galls,* where wheat was threshed. The *galls* (threshing area) were a distance from our house, right behind the Yermoian's house. The wheat and vegetable fields were next to the *galls.* Farmers in that area lived in small houses. Many of them raised hens and roosters. I specifically remember the distinct, beautiful colors of the dark reddish-brown feathers and their lush red combs and wattles as they strutted around with their tails held high. They were, however, messy birds. Their loud shrill "cockadoodle doo" could be heard in the mornings all the way to our house!

My cousin, Hmahyag, lived in that area, as did his three uncles. All four of the Mooradian brothers were farmers. The road passing by their house also led to our school. Sometimes we used this route to walk to school, and sometimes we took the route passing *Mewsahlah Dahsh.* The Eoksouzian's lived on the same street right across from the Protestant Church, which was half way between our house and the school.

3. DESCRIPTION OF HOUSE

Our house was fenced off from the street by a thick wall about ten feet high and fifteen inches wide. All of the houses on our street, as well as the houses across from us, had these walls. As you walked down our street, all you saw were the walls. Homes were completely hidden behind these walls.

Along the wall, in front of each house, was a wooden door that led into the *torrtah* (courtyard). As you entered our *torrtah,* the right half was enclosed on three sides. Immediately to the right of the door was the toilet. The toilet, a small enclosed area, was placed close to the outside wall and above the channel running under the street.

On that side of the *torrtah,* we had a hearth that was used to heat water in *bighintz* (copper) tubs used for our bathing, washing clothes and *guhdavs* (muslin). Several empty tubs used for household needs were stored along the opposite wall under the windows. Two of the largest tubs filled with water for this purpose were also placed along this same wall. It was my responsibility to make sure those tubs were always filled with water. We stored firewood along the wall, adjacent to the goldsmith's house next to the hearth. The women were able to work in that area of the *torrtah* throughout the year, because it was enclosed on three sides.

The left half of the *torrtah* facing the *toeneer doon* was the open courtyard. There wasn't a wall between the *torrtah* and the *toeneer doon*—it was open. In the left corner of the *toeneer doon,* a ladder lead up to the rooftop. The *toeneer* was behind the ladder. It was a large under ground clay pit made especially for baking bread. Every house had a *toeneer.*

Sitting mats were placed on the floor along the wall adjacent to Varteeg Bahgee's house in the *toeneer doon.* Whenever we had guests, we sat in that area.

Further in towards the rear of the *toeneer doon* was my father's work area. There was ample room for his work—a table, benches, tubs for the dyes, tools and the *guhdavs.*

Behind his work area was the *akhor* (stable) which was closed off with a wall. It had a door facing the *toeneer doon.* To my recollection, we only used the stable to house one hen.

The eggs were primarily for my grandfather. When fried in butter, they were easy for him to eat—he had lost all of his teeth. There was something like a box where the hen would perch, and in my younger years, I liked to sit next to it and gently pet the hen's head. As I recited:

Partial view of my block

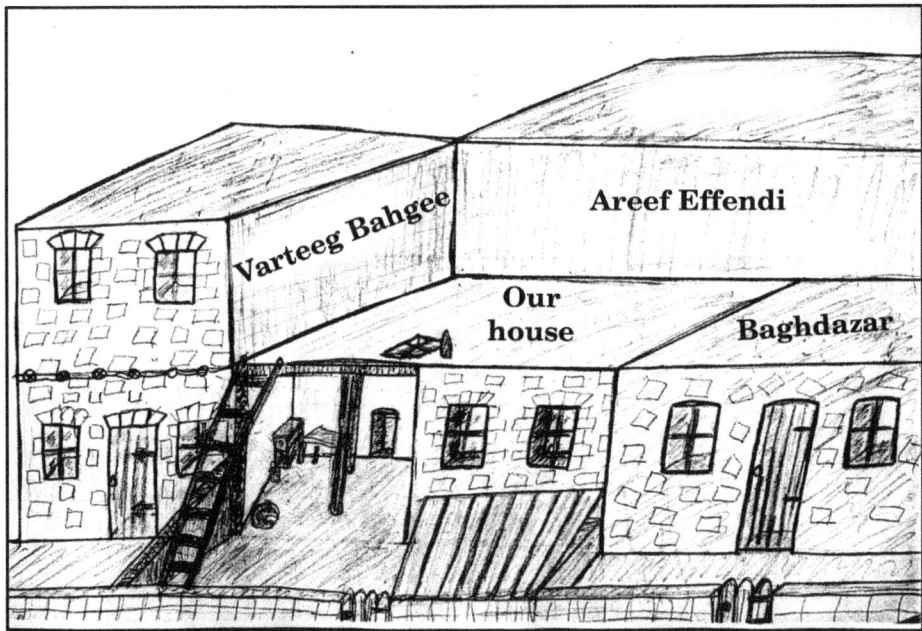

Exterior view of my house

Joo Joo kunatzeer.

Ahghan yehgher havgeet goozeh.

Havgeet chee gah, kehz guh morteh!

Chick, Chick go to sleep.

Your master has come for eggs.

You will be killed if there are no eggs!

Shortly after, it would lay an egg and then jump away. At Easter time, my sister boiled about a dozen eggs in yellow onion skins, and we each got one. After my grandfather died, we no longer kept the hen.

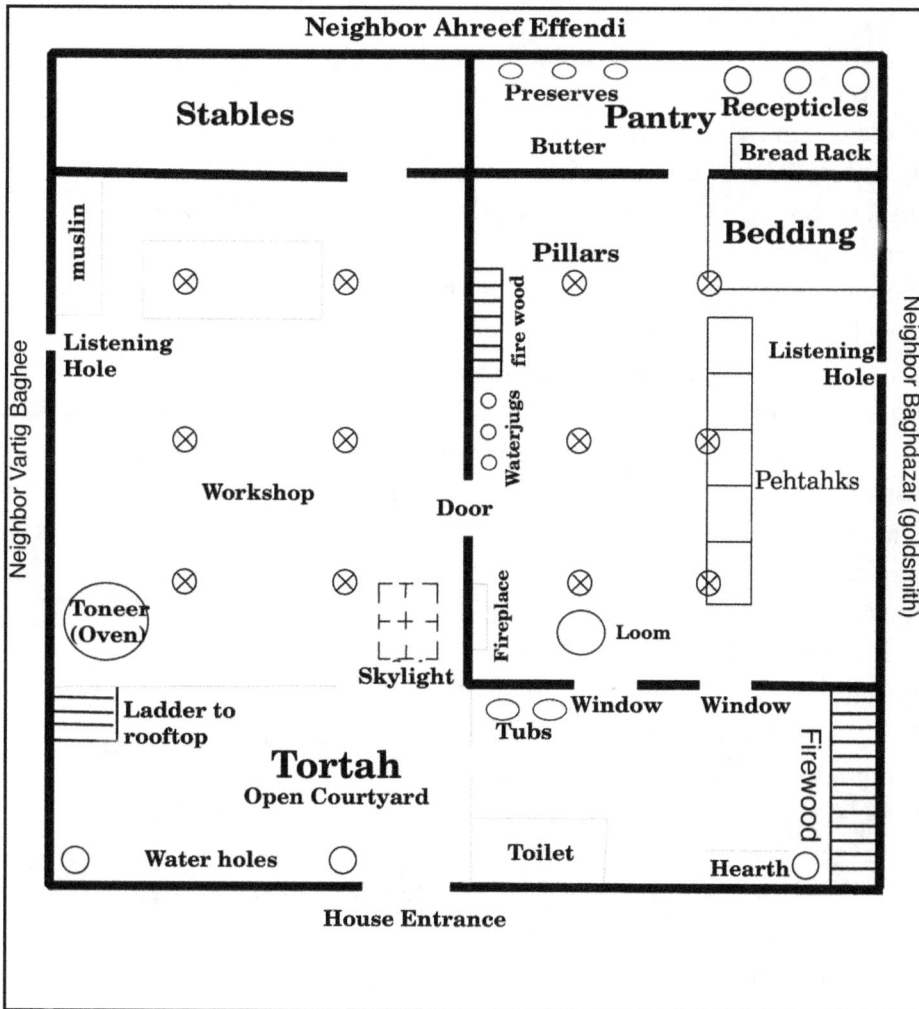

The floor plan of our house

The heavy roof of our house was held up by twelve evenly spaced pillars. A thick wall separated the *toeneer doon* from the family quarters. Towards the front right corner of the ceiling there was a skylight in the *toeneer doon*.

The entry door into the family quarters was in between the first two pillars along the wall separating the family quarters and the *toeneer doon*. As you entered from the *toeneer doon*, the fireplace was towards the right-hand corner. It was a built-in fireplace with a chimney that extended about two feet above the rooftop. The embers in the fireplace assured a constant source of fire at all times. Even during the hot summer months, we never allowed the embers to burn out. Matches sold in the marketplace were considered to be expensive. Thus if for some reason, the embers did burn out, we borrowed embers from the neighbors.

The adjacent wall facing the enclosed *torrtah* had the only two windows in the house. Our weaving loom *(horr)* was placed between them.

The *pehtahks* (containers) ran down the center of the room, dividing the family quarters into two areas. During the day the bedding was stored in the back corner next to the pantry, behind the *pehtahks*.

Pehtahks (containers) were placed on wooden stands. We had several in which we stored flour and various grains. They all had the same width and depth. The width was about three feet and the depth about four feet. The tallest was about six feet and held our flour. Subsequently, they gradually decreased in height. The various grades of bulghur were stored in the next tallest, followed by *zehzahts* (raw whole wheat) and *vosb* (lentils).

On the wall adjacent to the goldsmith's wall, behind the *pehtahks* was a hole about six inches wide and about three feet above the ground. There was an identical hole directly opposite to the wall adjacent to Varteeg Bahgee's house. These holes within the houses were a means to communicate with neighbors. Neighbors alerted each other of pending emergencies and dangers by talking to each other through the holes.

Our *khuzehn* (pantry) was located in the back to the right of the stable. It was separated from our living quarters by a wall. It too had a door in the middle of that wall. Our entire foodstuff was stored there in large *gahrahs'* (terra cotta), some were larger than others. The largest *gahrahs* held my father's brandy and wine. The *godes* held the preserves, pickles, dried fruits, mulberries, raisins and sweet butter. The bread rack hung to the right of the door.

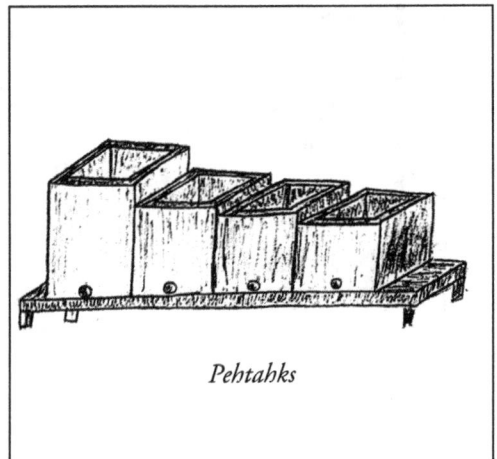

Pehtahks

We kept a pile of firewood for the fireplace along the wall adjacent to the *toeneer doon.* Along the same wall there were four (water jugs) *goosh* for drinking and cooking purposes.

There were four doors throughout the entire house, and they were made of wood. We only had one wooden key that locked the door on the outside wall door. The two windows and the skylight were made of glass. The wooden flooring throughout the entire house was covered with a thick layer of gray clay smoothed over firmly with the *logh,* a roller. The walls of the house were made of very thick adobe bricks, *karpeej.* The thickness of the walls insulated the house very efficiently, both during the bitter cold winters and during the hot summer. Because our winters were so cold, however, we also had to have a *sobah* (wooden stove). We set up the *sobah* as soon as the cold weather began and took it down when the weather began to warm up. The *sobah* was placed in the family quarters near the fireplace. Its pipes were connected to the chimney above the fireplace.

To avoid the possibility of flooding, the floor of the *torrtah* on both sides were a few inches lower than the floor of the rest of the house, creating a slant toward the street. There were holes along the edge strategically placed that allowed the rainwater and snow to drain away into the channel running beneath the *torrtah's* floor. Although there was no roof covering, rainwater and melting snow did not collect in the *torrtah.* This is as much as I can remember about the layout of our house, as well as our neighborhood, in Perri.

4. LAND RESOURCES AND CUSTOMS

SOIL

The hillsides of Perri were very rich with several different types of soil and clay.

A dark gray soil was used on all rooftops. The surface of our wooden roof was packed about six to eight inches thick with the gray soil. The soil was padded firmly with a *logh*. Therefore, at the beginning of each winter, repairs were made in cracks or damaged areas. Then it was padded down firmly again with the *logh*, preparing the roof to withstand the heavy weight of that year's snowfall.

We also had a particular adobe to make the *karpeej* for the walls of the house inside and out. The thickness of the walls of our house, about eighteen inches, helped to keep the house cool during the hot summer months and warm during the bitter cold winter months. The adobe was mixed with *herrt* (chaff) and then poured into wooden frames to form the desired sizes and shapes of the bricks then set in the sun to bake. They dried into a reddish color. The *pehtahks,* rectangular shaped containers, were made with that same adobe. The size of those bricks was much smaller.

We also had several different types of clay. Each clay was used for a particular purpose, accommodating our various needs.

From western Perri we had *gaghgee* (white powdery clay). It had a sweet aroma. When mixed with water, it served as a white paint. The inside and outside walls and the floor of the house and the *pehtahks* were painted with this white clay.

We had dark clay with a nice scent that we used for bathing and washing clothes. It lathered and cleansed similar to our present-day soaps.

Since Perri was very rich with various types of clay it was well known for the production of pottery. Our various pottery receptacles were made with clay that had to be fired in a kiln. When fired, it turned into a reddish color. The *bardahghnah* (kiln) was in the *shoogah* (marketplace). Torros Malkhasian's father not only made all of our pottery; he also provided pottery for the nearby villages.

On the hillsides, we also had a soil similar to fine sand. It was a soft, clean soil called *arrtarr hogh*. Newborn infants were swaddled on that soil, called *konedagh*. Routinely, the soil was cleaned and warmed to keep the infant dry and comfortable.

We had sturdier gray clay, similar to cement, that was used for the *galls* where wheat was threshed. The surface of each *gall* covered an area about 30' by 30'. A thick layer of the clay was spread on the ground and padded down firmly. The same clay was used for the *serrgahns* where mulberries were dried. The *serrgahn* was not as thick as the *gall*. This same clay was also used for the floors in the houses. All of these surfaces were smoothed over with a *logh*.

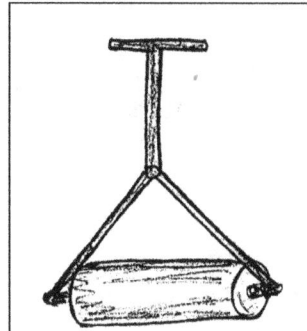

Logh

POTTERY AND CONTAINERS

We had a variety of receptacles in different shapes and sizes. The size and shape of each container denoted how the pottery was used. The *parch* (water pitcher) had a spout and handle. Salt was mixed into the clay, causing it to sweat, thereby keeping the water cool. This clay was found near the banks of the Perri River. The sides of the pitcher were thinner than those of other receptacles—they were almost translucent, similar to glass. A *goozh* (jug) had thicker sides. It had one or two handles on either side. They were made in various sizes and shapes for specific purposes. My father stored his wine and brandy in a *gahrahs*, the largest container with the thickest sides that was four to five feet deep and three feet wide. *Godes* were about half the size of the *gahrahs*. My mother stored a variety of pickles and preserves in *godes*.

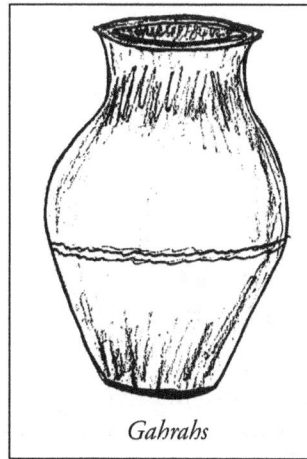

Gahrahs

Butter was made in a *khnotzee* (churn) which had a unique shape and held about five gallons. We used our *khnotzee* primarily to make *tahn* (yogurt drink). When not in use, the *khnotzee* hung from the ceiling behind the *pehtahks*.

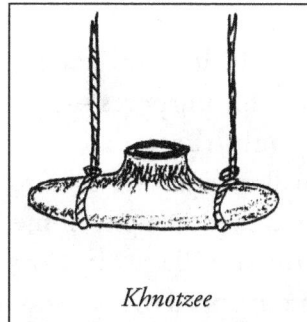

Khnotzee

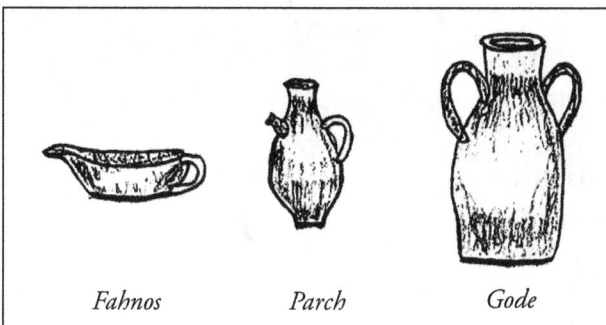

Fahnos   *Parch*   *Gode*

Goozh

There was a spout with a lid near the bottom of each *pehtahk* that allowed the grain to pour out when needed. The *pehtahks* were arranged in the house so that they served as a partition within the family quarters.

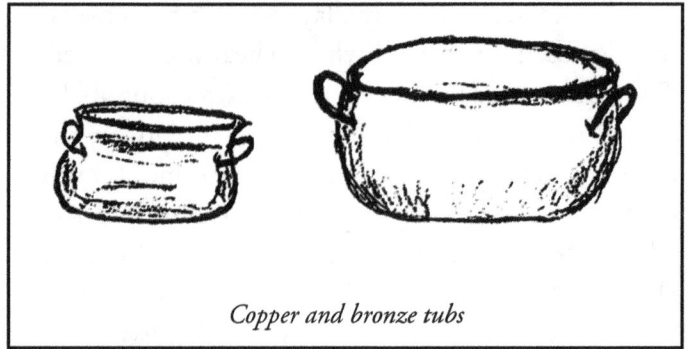

Copper and bronze tubs

We also had several copper and bronze tubs that were kept in the *torrtah*.

Another device used to carry or store particular items was the *chuhkhun*. A square piece of cloth made from muslin or wool in various sizes. Anything that had to be carried or stored was placed in the center of the square and then the corners of the square were folded over the top. Our bags, (*doebrahgs* and *byoosahgs*) were made with muslin.

DEEGS and KAYLAHGS

Since clay receptacles were breakable and impractical for carrying because of their weight, *deegs* were used to transport goods, especially liquids. *Deegs* were made of cleaned out sheep or lambskin. All the openings except one were tightly tied so it was completely airtight and watertight. Skins of different sizes were used for different purposes—I saw them used on only three different occasions. Smaller *deegs* were used to hold butter. My father brought home butter from Kurdish villages in *deegs*. The *deegs* were strapped over the donkey's back as he walked home. Our drinking water at school was brought in a *deeg*. The Kurdish vendors also used *deegs* to sell *tahn* from house to house.

Much larger skins were used to make *kaylahgs* (rafts). Before closing the last opening, air was blown into the skin to inflate it like a balloon. At that

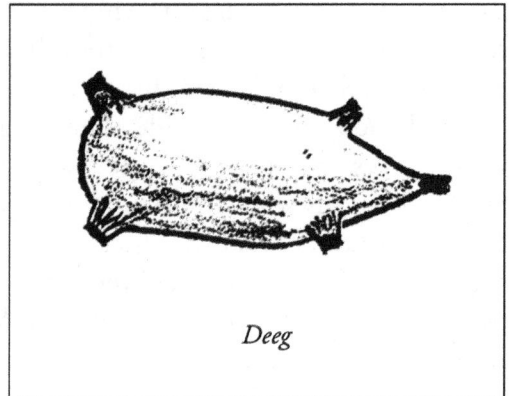

Deeg

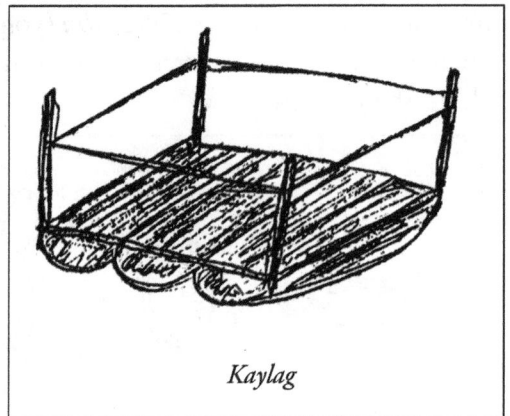

Kaylag

point, the opening was sealed making it airtight. Finally, several *deegs* were fastened together. The size and number of *deegs* used determined the size of the *kaylahg*. Flat boards were fastened to the surface of the *deegs*. Two poles were placed on the front and back ends, allowing the owner and passengers to hold on.

The rafts were used to cross the many rivers throughout that area of Turkey. The owner used a paddle to guide the raft to the other side of the river. He charged a small fee for each crossing. He located himself at the safest area along the riverbanks where most people wanted to cross in order to go from one village to another. The ride crossing the river was risky depending on the weather and the current of the river. A large *kaylahg* was able to support the weight of six people and a small load.

TREES

Perri's mountains were lush, covered with a rich variety of plants and trees. They generously served the needs of the people: from a variety of uses in construction, such as the frames, rooftops, and columns for buildings, to everyday uses, such as firewood.

There was also an abundance of shrubs and bushes. The *mehsheh* (poplar) tree was used for many purposes. It was not too tall—about six to seven feet—and grew everywhere. It had a long, thin but sturdy trunk. Some homes and gardens were lined with *mehsheh* trees on all four sides for protection from intrusions. The

Mehsheh (Poplar)

Ouri (Willow)

stark threshing sound of their leaves alerted us of the presence of intruders. Since they propagated easily and quickly, they were commonly used for firewood and as sticks for one purpose or another.

Ouree (willow) trees also grew throughout this region. The breadth and fullness of the drooping branches made them very accessible. They also had a variety of uses, but I used them primarily to make my baskets. Their pliable branches allowed me to swiftly weave baskets when I needed one in a hurry.

Baskets were another means for carrying goods. They were relatively easy to make and were free because they were made with the branches of willow trees, which grew abundantly along the riverbanks. Their one drawback was that they were not very durable. From time to time, they broke, especially when we hauled fresh grapes home from our *baghchah,* because the grapes were heavy. So I had to either quickly repair a loose spot or make a new one.

Again, the size and shapes of the baskets varied according to their intended use. The baskets for grapes were about four feet deep and three feet wide, while another basket could be one foot deep and two feet wide. Or, a flat basket could be ten inches deep and a yard wide.

In the 1980s, I surprised myself when I made a few baskets with ivy vines from my backyard. The ivy vines were not a good substitute for the willow branches. The baskets not only did not look as nice as my original baskets, but the vines were much harder to manipulate. Before I used to make a basket within a couple of hours. Now these took me over two weeks to make and with a lot more effort. However, I had the satisfaction of knowing that I still had maintained my skill after the passing of so many years. I had made so many baskets during my youth.

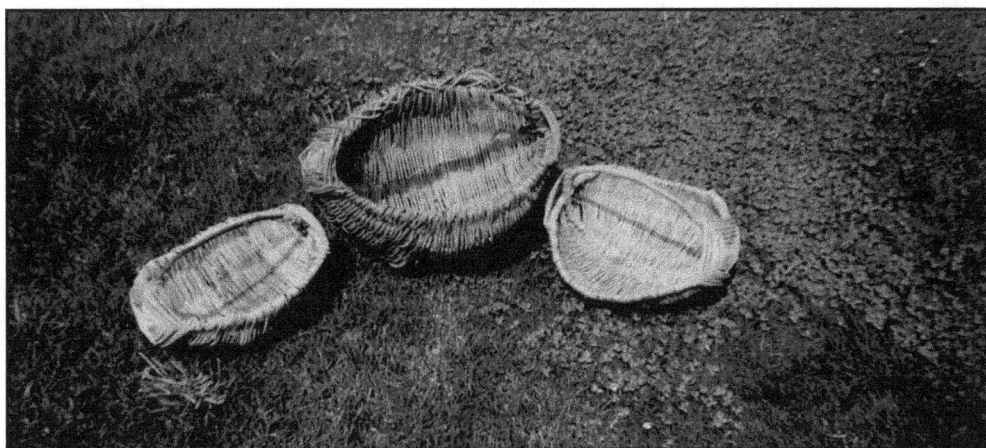

These are a few of the baskets I made (cir. 1980s)

I still remember how to make baskets (cir. 1999)

GALLS, CHAGHATS, TZEETZEEYANK, YERGAHNK

Farmers took bundles of their freshly cut wheat and barley to the nearby *galls* to thresh. They stacked the bundles three feet deep with the grain pointing towards the center of the *gall*. Then they fastened a *gahn* (wooden board) to the harness of their ox. The bottom of the board was covered with sharp protruding stones.

The farmer stood in the center of the *gall* and with his *mahsoosah*, a long stick with a sharp nail at one end, he prodded his ox to slowly circle the *gall*, round and round. As the ox slowly dragged the board over the wheat, the grain separated from the husk.

Simultaneously, the husk and stalks were shredded into small pieces called *herrt* (chaff). As the wind blew the *herrt* off the *gall*, it formed piles on the ground. The *herrt* was used primarily for animal feed, but it also had many other uses. All the *herrt* produced belonged to the farmer.

The piles of grain however, had to be left on the *gall* until they were taxed. The farmer was allowed to take his share after a Turkish official tagged the pile of grain with an official flag and took their share. The farmer was lucky if he got thirty percent of the wheat. Even with such *exorbitant taxation*, Armenians were still able to provide a comfortable existence for themselves. They were diligent and relentless workers.

Prior to 1915, there were about eight hundred Armenian families and one hundred Turkish and a few Kurdish families living in Perri. The Armenians' standard of living was much higher than that of the Turks. The Armenians were the artisans, professionals, merchants, farmers and producers.

That is exactly why the Turks sporadically raided and plundered Armenian homes and businesses. Finally, in 1915, they decided to take everything and stopped all progress and achievements made by the Armenians. They filled their homes with Armenian goods and possessions. They stockpiled what was left over in the Armenian churches and the abandoned large Armenian homes.

It took a couple of years for the Turks to completely deplete the laboriously produced foodstuff. By 1917, when all Armenians were either slaughtered or driven off their ancestral homelands, the Turks themselves experienced famine in the interior regions. They no longer had a source to plunder and confiscate and were too inept to provide for themselves.

I often wonder why the U.S. government allows the Turks to indulge themselves with various means of international blackmail. Perhaps God was rewarding them to use their sword instead of their brawn and conscience! Why else would super powers of the twenty first century concede to their will while they have never acknowledged their barbaric treatment of their innocent citizens? Unfortunately, after their last attack, the Armenians were forever driven off their historical homelands.

The *chaghahts* (flourmills) were generally built in the vicinity of the *galls*. However, they had to be near a waterfall or a source of swift flowing water. That was their source of energy. As far as I can remember, the only mill in Perri lay in ruins, destroyed by the Turks years earlier during one of their rampages against the Armenians. Therefore, flour was ground in nearby villages, brought back, and sold house to house by vendors

Likewise, the whole raw wheat was sold by vendors. After my father bought wheat, he took it to the *tzeetzeeyank* (millstone) to have the bran removed from the kernel. Wheat was used in several ways, but mostly for flour, bulghur and *zehzahts* (raw whole grain wheat).

The *tzeetzeeyank* consisted of two huge flat stones, each with a smooth surface. The base stone was five feet by four feet. The top stone was somewhat smaller and was pulled by a donkey. As the donkey circled the *tzeetzeeyank,* round and round, the bran separated from the kernel.

The *tzeetzeeyank* was also used to extract oil from sesame and hemp seeds. There was one area on the base stone that slightly slanted downward and there was a thin groove from the center to the edge. The groove allowed the oil to drain off more easily when sesame or hemp seeds were pressed for their oil. Sesame oil was used in various foods; it had a taste everyone liked. Hemp oil had a peculiar smell and it had various uses. It not only was used as cooking oil; it had medicinal uses as well as fuel when needed.

The *yergahnk* was somewhat similar to the *tzeetzeeyank,* but much smaller. Every household had one to grind bulghur. The base stone was about thirty inches wide and six inches deep. The top piece was a bit smaller. There was a hole in the center with a cylindrical handle to turn the top surface over the base, round and round, by hand. The handle also had an adjustable gauge so the wheat could be ground into different grades. The *yergahnk* was used frequently by my mother, aunt and sisters to grind other foods as well.

We also had a mortar vessel with a pestle to grind *zehzahts*. The powdery base made a very special *kufta—topeeg, meecheenkee kufta*. This was especially made for the church dinner on the Wednesday that fell in the middle of Lent.

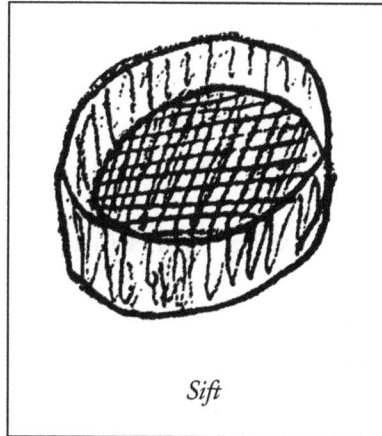

Sift

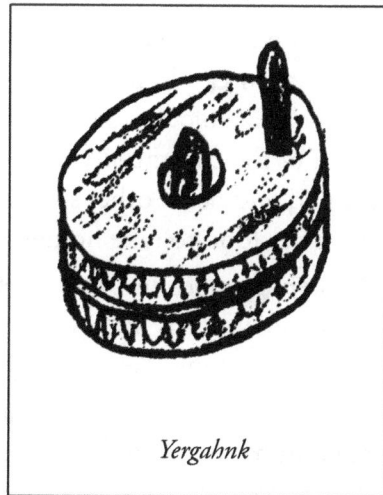

Yergahnk

5. SOCIAL LIFE

There were no jails in Perri. There was only one police station with a small detention room where culprits were taken for questioning. For less serious offences, there was a trial of sorts at the church. If the wrongdoer was considered very offensive, he was ostracized from the city. He was relocated in another area and never allowed to return. The fear of the shame that fell upon his family kept everyone in check. We did not need a jail.

Likewise there were no homeless people in Perri. Everyone, young or old had somewhere to call home. There was only one family, a mother with a daughter about ten years old, who didn't have the means to be completely self-supporting. The rest of the community assisted them. Once a week, the little girl came to our house and said her mother sent her regards and blessings to our house. As she left, we gave her food to take home; everyone else helped her in a similar manner.

Affluent families among us were not pretentious. Their wealth was only evident by their possessions and positions in the community. They were generally as modest as everyone else.

There were no inns or restaurants in Perri. Whenever someone was passing through or happened to have lost their way, even if they were a total stranger who needed to rest for that day, they went to the church. Someone there would direct him to a home they felt was capable of accommodating the stranger. Everyone thought it was a great honor and welcomed the guest into their houses. When they were ready to leave, the host gave the traveler a loaf of bread and sent him on his way.

SOCIAL OCCASIONS

Since we had only relatively recently moved to Perri from Ismiel and my father was wrapped up with his work, we didn't have many opportunities for social events. We interacted mainly with our immediate neighbors on our block, relatives and classmates. Therefore, I have very little recollection of festive celebrations or holidays. I mainly remember all of my teachers and classmates at school whom I dearly cherished.

From time to time the Mishmeeshians visited our house. I used to feel very proud that one of our teachers at school was a relative. When we needed shoes, we went to their shop. We were fitted for size and within a few days we went back to pick up the shoes. I was always fascinated with the process of making shoes. It seems they had a particular tool for each specific step of the process.

When major events took place in school in 1913, the community at large had their traditional picnic in spring when the mulberries were beginning to ripen. Each family took a particular dish or two to share with others. There was music, dancing, and singing. Children played their own games or mingled with the adults. Everyone had a joyous time.

One picnic was held in the Khraj Baghchah on the east side of town. The setting there was more beautiful with colorful flowers and green brush that concealed the mulberry trees. There were many gushing springs in that area. Everyone dressed up for that picnic. The picnic held in the Arkhaj Baghchah was on the west side. Even though the activities were similar, the scenery was not as nice and there weren't as many springs in that area. More or less the same people attended that picnic, but they dressed in more ordinary attire.

During this time, the workload and financial burden continued to drain my father's strength and soul. He never stopped worrying about how he was going to overcome all of his misfortunes. Luckily, I was getting older, larger and strong enough to assume Mihran's chores along with mine.

CLOTHING

Like all of the other boys, I wore a *zuhboon,* a distinct dress like outerwear worn by both girls and boys from childhood to the age of twelve. It was a loose, wide garment down to the ankle, with a large pocket in front. Then, like the men, the older boys wore a trouser called a *shalvar* with a loose fitting shirt. Most of the men also wore *meeltahns,* long vests that came down to their knees.

Zuhboon

From the age of twelve and above, boys and men wore a *kodee,* a waistband about ten inches wide and two yards long. It wrapped around the waist three to four times and was worn primarily to prevent injuries since most men engaged in laborious and strenuous tasks. It also helped the men to keep a straight posture and a flat stomach. Boys and men wore woolen socks that came up to their kneecaps and *yehmahnee* shoes. They also had leather slip-ons

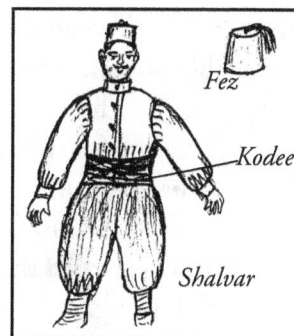

Fez

Kodee

Shalvar

similar to today's men's slip-ons. My grandfather wore that type of shoe. My father, brother and I always wore *yehmahnees.*

The women and older girls wore plain traditional dresses that were relatively loose fitting. The hem of their skirts came down to their ankles. They had long aprons and a *yahzmah* (scarf) tied around their heads. They too wore woven stockings.

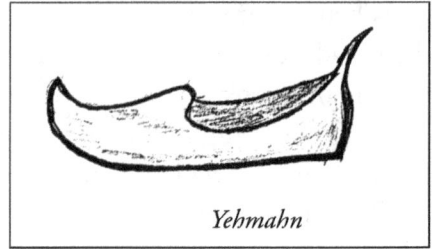

Yehmahn

The women also had two basic styles of shoes. For everyday, in the house they wore a backless open toe *pabooj* (slipper). For special social occasions they wore *konedourahs* (a pump with a two to three inch heel). I remember when we went on our picnics in the Khraj Baghchah the women wore *konedourahs.* Even my aunt and sisters wore such shoes. Infants and young children wore knitted woolen socks that had leather soles.

Most of our clothing was made from cotton muslin. Many homes had their own

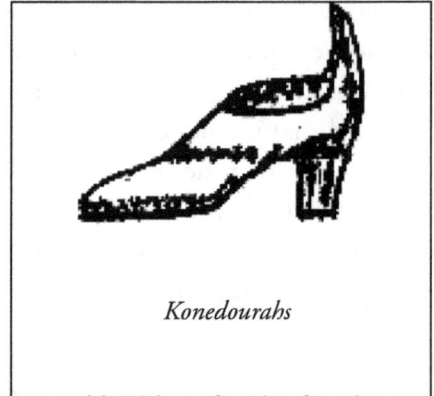

Konedourahs

looms and wove all the fabric needed for clothing and bedding for the family. Not only did almost everyone sew their own clothing by hand, they also spun their own yarn from raw cotton and raw wool. My sister, Sultahn, was very skillful using an *eeleeg* (spindle). Sultahn spun our wool and cotton yarn; she also wove our woolen and cotton muslin. My grandfather used a *karrehmahn,* different from a spindle, to spin a very fine thread. I remember watching my grandfather doing such work. It wasn't strenuous, and it helped him pass the time.

To the best of my knowledge, there was only one tailor in Perri. Finer fabrics in silk and wool were sold in the *shoogah* when they were available and they were very expensive. They were used by the wealthy for special social occasions. Clothing did not mark class distinction— no one felt inferior when they wore simple clothing.

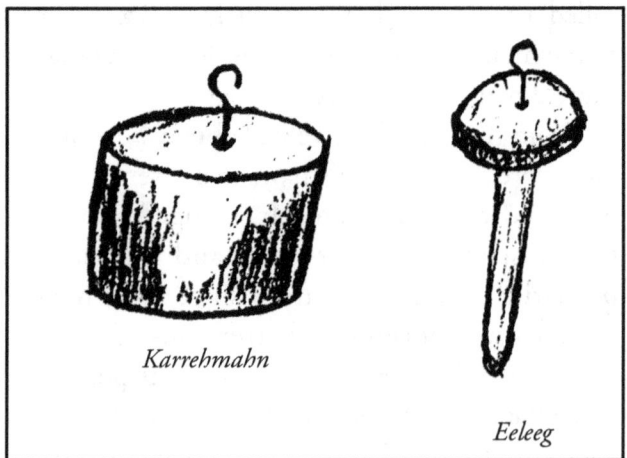

Karrehmahn

Eeleeg

SOURCE OF LIGHT

In the evenings our main source of light came from our kerosene lantern which had beautifully color designed glass sides and hung on the center column in the family quarters. If we ran out of kerosene, hemp oil took its place. In the evenings, it lit up the room enough so that my father was able to work on his tools, the women could work on their needlework, and we did our homework. The fire in the fireplace also enhanced the light in our house.

We used candles whenever we needed light outside of the house in the evenings. The *fahnos* (candleholder) kept the candle upright and prevented it from extinguishing. The candles were made from bee's wax. They were relatively inexpensive and were sold at the *shoogah* (marketplace).

Years later, making candles from bee's wax was a skill I utilized when I wandered from village to village and was always fortunate to find a job and a place to sleep in the *akhor* (stable). During the evenings, I had to work in the dark. Whenever I had a little money and felt I could afford to buy wax, I made my own candles. Since matches were too expensive for me, I had a difficult time finding a way to light the candles. Most of the time I relied on the moonlight and stars. The stars in Kharpert seemed to be brighter than those in the sky over Los Angeles.

MAKING PURCHASES

We purchased more than half of our household needs from the *charjees* (vendors) who came to our house. For most purchases we used currency, but there were situations where an exchange of goods was made. The Kurd who delivered our firewood received two loaves of bread in exchange for a huge bundle of firewood that lasted for a couple of months. If he was a *keervah* (reliable Kurdish friend), we gave him pickled peppers with its juice, a treat greatly appreciated by everyone.

Often when my father delivered the *guhdavs* in the Kurdish areas, he was given several *deegs* filled with butter in exchange for his labor. If we had more butter than we needed, he used some of the butter in exchange for another item or food. For some items we went directly to where they were made or produced. For example, we always bought our milk and yogurt from our neighbor down the block and our pottery ware was purchased at the *bardahghnah.* Not much of our needs were bought from the *shoogah.* If we did need to shop at the marketplace, routinely my father or brothers would go. The women in my family never went to the *shoogah.*

FOLK MEDICINES

For years I was aware of "Kaspar's *mahlahmat*" (embarrassment). From birth, he was physically weak and as much as I can recall, I was protective of him. I knew he felt badly and concerned that he wet himself whenever he was under stress. We knew he couldn't control his mishaps. He helped with light chores as much as he could, and we never expected more from him.

Once a year there was a church service on "The Day of *Mahlahmats*" when the priest prayed over those who had a chronic medical problem that caused an embarrassment. When we came home from church, Kaspar and I went on our rooftop. I lit a circle of candles, and he walked around them several times as I read passages from the Bible. We tried to find a remedy for his condition.

We even took baths in the *Togh Aghpiur*. That spring had cloudy, ice cold water and was used for healing purposes. As we splashed ourselves in the water and shivered, we prayed. Before we left, we hung a piece of our clothing on a nearby brush and made a wish. Those springs were along the nearby hillsides. Years later in 1922 in Los Angeles, when Kaspar had his bad kidney removed we learned the cause for his weakness. As far as I know, he did not have any complications living with only one kidney for the rest of his life.

Since we didn't have a doctor in Perri, we relied on our clergymen and respected teachers to suggest a remedy for our medical problems. They were considered to be learned people. When I was seven years old and was playing hide-and-seek, I fell off our rooftop and injured my head. Immediately, tobacco was placed on my wound. Ever since then, I have had an indentation in that spot on my forehead. When my mother was attacked by a swarm of bees, the raw skin of a newly sacrificed lamb was covered over her head to cure her wound. In both cases, we made a complete recovery. Unfortunately, not all remedies or advice were helpful.

When my stepmother accidentally stepped one foot into a cauldron filled with boiling hot garbanzos, her pain was unbearable. Her woolen stockings meshed with her burned skin. The quickest advice came from one of our most highly esteemed teachers, Baron Hovannes Eoksouzian. His suggestion was to pour salt on her burns. The results were disastrous, and it took quite a while for her foot to heal. I really felt sorry for her.

I used to hear about remedies such as the oil from grape seeds and hemp seeds had medicinal uses. Hemp oil was more available than the grape seed oil.

6. WOMEN'S WORK

Every morning after breakfast, my father began to work on his daily tasks in the *toeneer doon,* my grandfather would leave to go to church, and we would leave for school. The women were already busy with their chores. Some chores were daily routines and some were seasonal. They busily worked endlessly throughout the whole day. Their work was not only time consuming but very laborious. From early spring to late fall, a variety of preparations had to be made for the long harsh winters. The women's work was never done.

Before we woke, my mother had made our breakfast, which was usually a hot *chorrbah* (soup or broth). Sultahn and my Aunt Aghavni attended to the bedding for the whole family twice each day. We did not have European furniture—we slept on the floor. Each mattress was always placed in a particular spot on the floor in the same semicircular pattern in front of the fireplace. First a *pahlahs,* a woven mat made from goat's hair or *khuseer* (a straw mat) was placed on the floor. Then a *kehcheh,* a mat made with pressed cotton, was laid down. On top of that was the *doeshag,* the mattress that was made with a muslin bag stuffed with raw lamb's wool. That was covered with a woven cotton sheet. Finally, there was the *angogheen,* a lamb's wool comforter. The next morning, each piece was picked up in reverse order. There were seven individual mattresses to be picked up and set out each day. During the day our bedding was stored in a corner next to the pantry behind the *pehtahks.* We all doubled up on a mattress. I slept with Kerop, Kaspar slept with my aunt, Bedros with Mihran, Sultahn with Nishan, my mother and father had theirs, my grandfather and Zaruhy each had their individual mattresses.

Starting in spring, when the mulberries ripened, a variety of preserves (*rojeeg* and *bastegh*) were made with the mulberry juice. Mixed with a flour base, the mulberries were cooked into a sweet *mahlez* (paste). *Rojeeg* and *bastegh* were dried on the rooftop for three to four days, depending on the warmth and intensity of the sun. My favorite preserve was *kasmahjah* made with dried mulberries. The dried mulberries were ground with our *yergahnk* making a sweet sticky flour, *tooteh ahlour.* That was then firmly packed into a *tapsee,* a tray twenty-four inches wide and one and one-half inches deep. Nothing else was added. It, too, was dried on the rooftop. After a day or two, when it was half done, it was ready to be cut into diamond pieces similar to *pakhlava.* It took another few days to dry in the hot sun and become a sweet, crispy treat. These were lined in *godes* and stored in the pantry so we could enjoy them throughout the winter months. I still yearn for that sweet

Baking toneer hatz

taste as it melted in my mouth. There is nothing else like it. Another favorite treat we made with our *yergahnk* was a paste from ground sesame seeds similar to peanut butter. I loved to sneak in and swipe away the freshly ground, soft, sweet smelling sesame with my finger and run off before Sultahn could stop me.

About every three months, my mother baked bread. It was a flat round cracker bread about twenty to twenty-four inches in diameter. The bread was baked in the *toeneer* located in a spacious corner in the *toeneer doon.* Almost every house had one, and everyone baked their own *toeneer hatz* or *chorr hatz* (dry, cracker bread).

The day before the bread was to be baked my mother and aunt prepared enough dough to last three months. The dough was placed in a muslin sack and set in our wooden tub. Kaspar and I helped knead the dough. We wore *mahs,* a special pair of socks that had a thin leather sole and for several minutes we stomped on the bag, kneading the dough with our feet. From time to time, we flipped the bag over to make sure the dough was evenly kneaded.

Once kneaded, the dough was removed from the sack and set aside allowing it to rise overnight. At the same time, logs were lit in the *toeneer,* allowing enough time for the logs to burn to a particular ember. By morning, the sides of the *toeneer* were nice and hot, ready to bake the bread. My mother and aunt then divided the dough into smaller batches.

On bread baking day, we hired a woman who came to our house to do the actual baking. She sat on the floor close to the edge of the *toeneer.* As my mother and aunt rolled out pieces of dough on round wooden boards, the hired woman consistently slapped one piece on the inside wall of the *toeneer* and plucked another out, one piece after another. All three women worked very quickly in unison.

From time to time the women stopped to add a new log in the pit. They rested until the embers were at the right stage. Then they resumed their routine. The whole process always took two days. It was a strenuous job, especially for the hired woman who was hired for forty *parah* (cents). I felt sorry for her.

The baked bread was stacked on a special rack that hung in the *khuzehn*

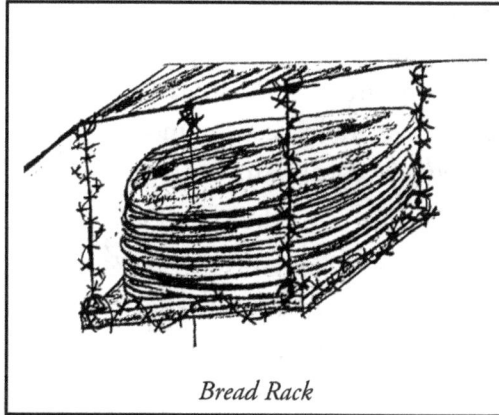

Bread Rack

(pantry). Our household cat was helpful in warding off rodents, as were thorns from a particular plant from the hillsides that were laced around the rack. For days, the sweet aroma of the freshly baked bread lingered around the house, both inside and outside. I can still smell that sweet aroma.

On the last day, while the *toeneer* was still hot, my mother always made *kashkahg* or *hereezah* in a large cauldron that fitted inside the pit. The dish was made with *zehzahts* (whole-wheat grain), butter and shredded lamb. We always looked forward to that treat. It melted in your mouth. We used our hearth to bake another bread (*beeleek*) which was thicker and softer, similar to a flat loaf of bread. Both breads were used equally throughout the year. Every year, in late fall, *khavourmah* was made also in the hearth. The cubed lamb's meat was stewed in its own fat for hours in a copper *khahzahn* (large cauldron about thirty inches wide and twenty-four inches deep) until the meat was extremely tender and shredded with ease. Two to three large *godes* were then filled and stored in the *khuzehn*. This supply also lasted throughout the winter. I liked it best when it was heated in its own fat and rolled in *toeneer hatz.**

From late spring, we bought a variety of fruits and vegetables from the gardens where they were grown, stalls where they were sold in the marketplace, or from the vendors who came to the house. What we did not use at the time was pickled, dried or preserved in some manner. Each day or so, a new task was undertaken.

Towards the end of summer and early fall, everyone worked with an assortment of grains. We used bulghur the most. My father bought raw wheat for bulghur directly from the farmer. The women worked with it in several stages: First, the grain was cleaned from extraneous bits of debris. Then, it was washed and boiled

* "Toneer hatz" was eaten dry, much like a cracker, or before serving it was slightly sprinkled with water to soften the consistency.

in the large tubs over the hearth in the *torrtah*. Next, it was hauled up to the rooftop bucket by bucket to dry. My father took the boiled dry grain to Yermoian to be hulled with his *tzeetzeeyank*. The hulled grain was brought back and dried once more on the rooftop. The women ground it with our *yergahnk*. In this final stage, the ground wheat was sifted with two different strainers separating the grain into three grades, coarse, medium and fine. The bulghur was finally stored in the *pehtahks* according to the grade.

Flour on the other hand was purchased from vendors who came to the house and stored in the largest *pehtahk*.

During this season, they also dried yogurt. Yogurt was whipped about an hour as it swiftly swung from side to side in the *khnotzee,* then it was set in porous bags to drain. When it was completely skimmed to a solid consistency, it was rolled into balls and set out to dry on the rooftop. The process took about four to five days. During the cold bitter months, the *chortahn* (dried yogurt) was mixed with *zehzahts,* making a delicious *tahn ahbour* (yogurt soup).

Another laborious summer chore was to wash the raw wool stuffing inside the mattresses and the comforters. The wool was washed in the *torrtah* and dried on the rooftop. The size and weight of these covers made it an arduous task to wash and haul up to the rooftop to dry. The next day, the dry wool was whipped with a strong twig from the *Mehsheh* tree. This process fluffed up the matted wool, making it much softer and warmer during the cold winter nights. The final stage was to refill both the mattress and the comforter with the raw wool. They were quilted to prevent the wool from bunching up. Since this was such a difficult and time consuming task, the many mattresses and comforters were not washed every year—alternating one or two one year and the following year another couple were done.

Sultahn spent most of her time spinning wool and cotton to make yarn using an *eeleeg* and the *horr* (loom) to weave the fabric for our *charshahf* (sheets) and other various needs. She also was very skilled in embroidery with fine threads. She took the time to embroider beautiful colorful designs along the sides of our knee-high socks, around the buttonholes of our *meeltahns* (vests) and on the front of our shirts. I really appreciated those beautiful designs and her generous kindheartedness towards all of us.

Most of our clothing was hand sewn by the women. I don't recall who made what in particular. But I do remember how much I marvelled and appreciated what Sultahn was able to accomplish. She did all of those chores without a complaint, even though she had contracted polio at a very young age of three to four years, leaving her left arm bent up towards her chest. Despite her handicap, she always had a happy disposition, laughing and making jokes with us. She was a very beautiful girl—she and Nishan resembled my father. Like them, she was also fair.

As you see, the women worked from morning until they went to sleep at night. Their work was never completed. During the cold winter days and evenings, they brought out some form of needlework. Winters were extremely cold with much snow, rain and wind. We were snowed in for weeks at a time and had to be prepared for several months.

As I look back, I can only marvel at the extent of work these women accomplished—responsibilities taken for granted! *Meghk!*

7. FATHER'S WORK

My father was an artisan. He hand painted designs on plain *guhdavs* (cotton muslin) which were woven mainly by men. In Turkish such a person was called a *chit'chee*. Chitjian, our surname, comes from that word.

In early spring his Armenian and Kurdish customers brought their plain muslin and specified the design and colors they wished printed on it. The more elaborate the design and the more colors requested influenced the price of his labor. This craft was both very laborious and time consuming.

The printed muslin was used for women's everyday dresses and men's shirts and *shalvahrs* (pants), children's *zuhboons* (dress), Moslem prayer mats, bedding covers and other items.

As soon as the muslin was brought in, my father washed it in a solution, which he made with the leaves and buds from the *suhmagh* plant. The process not only cleaned the muslin, but also set the fabric to prevent further shrinkage. The washing and drying all took place in the *torrtah*.

The art of printing the *guhdavs* was difficult and time consuming. He worked on the *guhdavs* from early spring through late summer. He had two basic tools. One was the *gaghabar* (a wood block) with an etched on design. My father created his own designs and etched them on the wood blocks. He had hundreds of designs and wood blocks with which to work. He continuously created new ones and repaired or replaced old ones. Sharp points protruded on each of the four corners of the wood block to help align the design in an exact pattern as he progressively lifted and placed the *gaghabar* down throughout the whole length of the muslin. Each piece was about five yards long and twenty-four inches wide.

His other tool was the *aljack* (a thick pad made of a soft material). He strapped it on the inside of his right hand from the palm of his hand to his wrist. It was about 8"x3"x2?". He used the *aljack* as he pounded down hard and pressed firmly on the *gaghabar* several times. The *aljack* protected his hand from the constant impact of pounding down on the *gaghabar*.

My father prepared some of the dyes himself and purchased the rest. The two main colors he used were black and red. The black dye was used for the outlines of the design. He made this dye with a solution using rust from old horse and donkey shoes that he got from the blacksmith shop. He reused the shoes for many years. He kept them submerged in water to cause continuous rusting. Whenever he needed a new batch of black dye, he hung the shoes out to rust. He added tree resin, *khezh,* to the rust solution to make the dye colorfast and easier to use. The black design never faded regardless of how often it was washed. The red dye was used in the final stage of the process, which he bought in the marketplace.

As he started to print, he dipped the *gaghabar* into the pan of black dye, brushed off the excess, aligned the pinpoints on the muslin and pounded down hard several times with his right hand. He held and guided the muslin with his left hand. He repeated that process until the printing was completed. At various times he changed his wood block to follow the chosen pattern.

I can still hear my father's voice as he softly sang to himself the melancholy songs that expressed his fears and feelings. Now I, too, feel the very same emotions he struggled with as he firmly pounded on the *gaghabar.*

> *"Lyre resonate your tunes for the whole world to hear,*
> *about the persecuted Armenians, the mortally wounded.*
> *Groan as you cry, with so much affliction, so much evil.*
> *With so much blood, we have shed so many tears.*
> *If our descendants should forget this much grief,*
> *let the whole world dishonor the Armenians..."*

By the end of summer during our school break, he had finished printing all of his orders. Kaspar and I were available to help him. Early one morning, he rented Gooree Oso's donkey, loaded the *guhdavs* on the donkey's back and we headed towards the Perri River, which was a forty-five minute walk from our house. Kaspar and I hung on to each handle of the large copper tub we took with us.

As soon as we reached the river, we gathered sticks and made a fire to boil the *guhdavs* in the tub with the red dye. Then one after the other, we washed out each *guhdav* in the river and spread them out to dry, draped over the large boulders along the riverbank. We pinned all four corners down with smaller rocks so they wouldn't fly away. In the meantime we fed the donkey several times and kept an eye on it so it wouldn't stray.

Finally, towards the end of the long day, we gathered and folded the dry *guhdavs,* loaded them on the donkey's back and headed back home.

Some customers came to our house to pick up their printed *guhdavs.* My father delivered the rest. He rented Gooree Oso's donkey again to deliver to those who lived a distance from our house, covering about ten to fifteen Kurdish villages. Each time he went away for more than a week, he spent the nights at a *keervah's* (a trusted Kurd) house until all of his orders were delivered. That particular Kurd was not only a trustworthy friend, but he was also the leader of his village. There was a close bond between the two men. For many years they had shared a mutual trust and respect for each other.

One day, a Kurd who had so much faith in my father begged him to help him get rid of a pain he had. My father wanted to help but he didn't know what to do. The Kurd insisted my father's prayers might help him. My father knew the Kurds didn't understand Armenian, so he quickly recited, "May the pain in your stomach go to your heart." A week later, the Kurd returned to thank my father for getting him well! My father always felt the Kurds had that much trust in the Armenians and would have been good allies.

I think my father was beginning to train me to go out on my own. When I was barely thirteen years old, one day he took me to a small nearby Armenian village, Havhav. I only remember being given honey and bread. We stayed away for two days but he never told me why we were gone.

On many days and nights my father was caught in strong snow or rainstorms while making deliveries. He would come home soaked to the skin and exhausted even more so, thereby aggravating his existing burdens. I felt sorry for my father. He worked very hard to provide for all 13 of us so that we would have a better life. Strange as it may seem, however, my father never mentioned being attacked or robbed. His activities were very obvious and it was known he had money on him as he returned home. Was he protected by his *keervah?*

8. TYPICAL DAY

Traditionally, we woke up before sunrise, because that was considered Godly. Likewise, it was considered a sin to wake up after the sun had risen. Each person would then begin tending to their respective chores. When my grandfather and father were ready to wash their hands and face, the eldest son prepared to pour water from a pitcher and hand each of them a towel. Consecutively he kissed their hands and took them to his forehead as a sign of respect. Then each of us stood in a row while the next son was ready to pour water for his eldest brother. That procession continued until all of the boys were washed and ready for breakfast. I have no recollection of where and how the women and girls washed. In the meantime my father and grandfather were in light prayer, "May God bless us and give us a fruitful day..."

My mother had a light breakfast ready for us. On cold days we had hot soup. On the other days, we had the *serr* (cream) off the top of freshly made yogurt. Every morning, I purchased freshly made *mahdzoon* (yogurt) from Vaskertzee Mardiros.

Breakfast was not a formal affair. Each person ate at his or her own pace and went on with their personal tasks. My father went into the *toeneer doon* and began his daily work. My grandfather went to church with a piece of *chorr hatz* in his pocket. He had no teeth so he crushed the bread into crumbs and slipped a little at a time into his mouth. He ate his bread as he slowly walked to church. He seemed to enjoy that routine. During the winter months when all of my father's *guhdavs* were delivered, he accompanied my grandfather for the morning services.

Upon hearing the school bells, the older boys left for school. My mother, aunt and sisters were already engaged with their chores. The younger children amused themselves on their own. They were always well behaved, never causing a problem for anyone. They were not allowed to go out of the house alone. When my grandfather returned, he spent time with them. Likewise, none of the women went out without my father. It was not safe for them to do so because of the prevailing Turkish threat against the Armenians.

Familiar *chargees* (vendors) came to the house with their wares so there really was no need for shopping. On those rare occasions when something had to be purchased from the marketplace, my father or older brothers would do the shopping.

At noon during the lunch break at school, we usually came home for a light lunch. We either had *mahdzoon* and bread or bread dunked in pickled hot pepper juice. This was very tasty and it was considered a real treat. Then we rushed back to school for the afternoon session.

At four o'clock we were dismissed from school. Sometimes we went home for an hour, or we stayed and played with our schoolmates until the church opened at five o'clock for the evening services. We were expected to attend that service everyday. Both my father and grandfather were also always there, making certain we were there on time. The women went to church only on holidays and funerals. After a rather lengthy service, we all walked home together.

By the time we got home, it was usually past six o'clock and time for dinner, our main meal of the day. My father and grandfather took their regular places sitting on floor mats on either side in front of the *ojahk* (fireplace). My grandfather's place was always on the left side and my father's was on the right side. The boys had a round table with short legs, and like the others, we also sat on floor mats. The table was placed in between my father and grandfather in front of the fireplace. We knelt around the table and recited the Lord's Prayer. Before we were allowed to get up after dinner, we repeated the Lord's Prayer. I cannot recall where the women ate.

After dinner, we did our homework. If we needed help, my father or grandfather helped us, even though they themselves had no formal education. After finishing our homework, before we went to bed, all of us gathered again around the fireplace. As usual, my father took his place, again on the right and my grandfather, again on the left. The boys gathered in between the two. We recited all twenty-four verses of the *Havadov Khostovaneem* (I Confess With Faith), each reciting at least one verse. Then we knelt on our knees and sang *"Der Voghormia"* (Lord Have Mercy). Each night we finished with a different phrase—hope for world peace, cures for the sick, freedom for Armenians, unity within Armenians, love in the family, protection for departed family members, help for the needy. We concluded with *"Hayr Mer,"* the Lord's Prayer—this whole process lasted for almost two hours every night.

My father ended our prayers by repeating, "Without the will of God, even the leaves on a tree do not move. Knock on God's door. He will open it. Ask and He will give!" I have never seen another true believer like my father. He was a true Christian. Even within the clergy, it is hard to find a person with a pure soul like my father's. My father always taught us to have a pure heart and strong faith like true Christians.

Before we went to sleep, he and my grandfather took turns telling us a story about a prayer. They were both excellent storytellers. They not only added humor to the day for us, but most importantly, they instilled character and faith within my soul forever. That was the most cherished part of the day for me. One such story went something like this:

> One day a muleteer with forty mules was going to a faraway place to sell his wares. On the way robbers pursued him until it got dark. They knew he had a gun so they waited until he went to sleep so they could overcome him and steal his wares.
>
> As the sun set, the muleteer stopped to rest for the night. Before closing his eyes to sleep, the muleteer recited all twenty-four verses of the *Havadov Khostovaneem*.
>
> As he began to recite the first verse, the walls rose and enclosed the muleteer and forty mules. By the time he finished with the twenty fourth verse, the walls were completed, and the muleteer and forty mules were totally safe.
>
> The next morning they continued on with their journey. Each night he would rest and repeat the same prayer. The following morning, they continued on with their journey.
>
> Four nights passed and the robbers were not able to overcome the muleteer.
>
> However, by the fifth night, the muleteer was really very exhausted with all the walking. He still began to say the *Havadov Khostovaneem*, but he was so tired that he fell asleep before he completed all twenty-four verses. He had forgotten to recite the last verse.
>
> The robbers were quick to notice that oversight. It was like an open window. The robbers seized the opportunity and approached the opening. They put up a ladder and started to climb up to it.
>
> The muleteer realized his mistake and quickly started to recite the missing verse. Just at that moment one robber had his foot in the opening, the other had his hands, and the last one had his head in the opening. In the nick of time, the muleteer completed the last verse and the opening closed, killing all of the robbers. The next morning he noticed all of the men were dead and he continued on with his journey.

The story illustrates the power of faith. I, too, had that much faith when I escaped out of Kharpert. Each night I repeated the twenty-four verses of the *Havadov Khostovaneem* with all my soul and faith. In a very short time you will learn from me how protective faith can be.

From the beginning God created good and evil men. Unfortunately, the good gradually has lost its influence in our lives today. And boastfully, the evil men have achieved a position of ninety eight percent in our daily lives. This is my judgment based on what I have heard and seen in life. Maybe God no longer listens to His true followers, since He was unable to reform them. He, too, joined in with the wicked. Gone are my cherished childhood days. How much I yearn for them!

9. BEDROS GOES TO AMERICA, ZARUHY MARRIES

In 1909, the conspiring Turkish government attempted to change the color of its "black shirt" and changed its decree to imply it would treat all Armenians equal with the Turkish citizens. That was a deliberate deception to legally draft Armenian men into the Turkish army.

Armenians, however, were very much aware that their men were being cruelly abused in the Turkish army. All Armenian soldiers were used as forced slave labor, building roads and railways. When they no longer were able to work, completely exhausted from their abuse, they were slaughtered and their bodies were strewn along the roadsides.

Now more than ever, the political atmosphere was getting increasingly ominous. My father and grandfather felt that the worst was yet to come. With all of the turn of events, both my parents and grandfather became very concerned about Bedros who had just turned seventeen and thereby became eligible for the draft.

For all practical reasons, my father was not financially able to send Bedros to America. In addition to going into debt, he would be losing an extra hand that would have eased his workload. But they knew the risk if he stayed. They were also aware of many boys who had fled to America in hopes of escaping enrollment in the Turkish army, or hoping to earn more money to support those who were left behind. From time to time, however, news would come about their deaths, inappropriate relationships and harmful life styles.

My mother was concerned more with the misfortunes the naive, young Armenian boys encountered in America when they were sent abroad alone. She knew they were not ready to be on their own in a strange land without an older relative or friend to guide and protect them from different customs and lifestyles. At that age the boys in Perri were still under the supervision of parents, families, teachers and neighbors. Some boys couldn't handle the abrupt, newly found freedom. There were so many tragic stories about the neighborhood boys who had fled to America for refuge.

The son of one of our neighbors killed himself by jumping off his apartment rooftop. He was distraught over a relationship he had with an American girl in

Chicago. One day his parents received a letter asking if they had money to have their son's body returned to Perri.

Another neighbor, who lived across the street from us, returned home from America mentally deranged. Sporadically, for no apparent reason, he would beat his sisters. He would also walk towards the church, stooping down kissing the cobblestones on the road. His father would have to go after him to take him back home. He always had to keep an eye on his son to make sure he did not hurt himself. He was nicknamed the "crazy boy."

Such stories were very disturbing for everyone. It was not easy for my parents to make the decision to send Bedros to America but they felt they had no other choice. They decided to take the risk and sent Bedros to America because it was more dangerous if he stayed. In addition, to cover his expenses, my father was forced to go into debt, a position he always feared and from which he was never able to recover.

Bedros snuck out of the country with an older distant relative, Dikran Amo (uncle), from Ismiel. The burden of the debt became an additional strain on my father throughout the following years. The separation of her eldest son added on to my mother's sorrow.

Shortly after Bedros left, my eldest sister, Zaruhy, married a Protestant, Boghos Khatunahgian. They had a simple wedding at our house. All that I remember from that day was when Kaspar was told to sit upon Zaruhy's dowry. According to superstition, if a younger brother sat on the bride's dowry, the couple's first born would be a boy. Once Kaspar sat down he wouldn't get off; he teased them until he was given a few cents. The couple lived with his parents in the same area where the Yerevanians lived, a distance from our house.

Unfortunately, Zaruhy's situation did not improve. Boghos had recently converted into the Protestant faith in order to receive a *chooval* (gunnysack) of flour. That was enough to provide his family with enough bread for a year. My father greatly objected to his conversion. Shortly after their marriage, Boghos went to Adana, hoping to find a better job. After he got there, the massacres had started and hundreds of people had been killed. He quickly found a way and fled to America. Zaruhy was left to the mercy of two disagreeable sisters-in-law. They tormented Zaruhy, even though they were much younger. To relieve her from all the badgering, from time to time, my father sent me to bring her home to visit with us for a couple of days. On a few occasions, when he went to Kharpert, he took her to Sako Mahlahsee to visit with her *gunkamayr* (godmother) Juvar.

10. GRANDFATHER AND MOTHER DIE

Within a couple of months of Bedros' departure, we received our first letter from him and learned he had been detained in Marseilles, France. The reality that my mother would never see her eldest son began to take a heavy toll on her. At the same time, in the absence of her eldest daughter, she had to assume additional chores. She also had given birth to her last son Nishan. Her body weakened, and she soon took ill for more than three months.

During that time we got news that Setrag was killed in a job-related accident in America. Setrag was one of her only two nephews. He was a little older than Bedros, and he too had gone to America a couple of years before Bedros.

My mother was previously convinced that when the naive young boys went to America they would be harmed one way or another. Now with this news, my mother's illness was aggravated, and she became even weaker. We will never know if she would have otherwise recovered her strength had she not heard that news.

When we learned about Setrag's death, we also learned more about his job in America. All we previously knew was that he worked for the government and we were impressed that he had found such a good job. With this letter, we learned that he was a gardener in a government compound. Apparently an electrical line fell to the ground. Since he was not familiar with electrical wires, he attempted to move it. The moment he touched the wire he was electrocuted.

While we were all gravely concerned about my mother's illness, early one morning we were awakened and abruptly told my grandfather had died during the night. I couldn't believe the words. I wasn't prepared for that—none of us were. We had all been worrying about my mother…

Now, without any warning, my precious grandfather was gone, the one person who always gave me comfort and emotional strength. The pillar of our family was gone. Although he was ninety-two, I had never seen him ill or complain about a pain. His only physical disability was the loss of his teeth.

I don't remember how he managed to eat, but he did. His favorite pastime was to take a piece of *chorr hatz,* slip it into his pocket and bit by bit crumble it up and put it in his mouth as he strolled in front of our house or towards the shops, socializing with the neighbors along the way. He was respected by all. Additionally, my father honored him by giving him another favorite treat, something easy to eat. My father had a special way of cutting watermelons. He first made several slices all around the length of the watermelon. Each cut went to the center. Then he stood the watermelon up on its base. With a quick, hard whack with the bottom of his fist on the top of the watermelon, the sections opened up like a flower leaving a vertical core, the center of the watermelon—that piece belonged to my grandfather. The boys were all happy with their slices as they went off munching on a very sweet slice. During the season, we always had plenty of watermelons.

He was the king of our family, and now he had died. I was only eight years old. It was a very significant loss for me. That was also the first time I experienced the feeling of deprivation, the yearning for someone or something I really cherished and needed. Previously, I felt I had everything I needed or wanted.

My grandfather had made a great impression on my life, even though I lost him at such a young age. His teachings, along with my father's, molded my character, accomplishments and aspirations for life. I feel very fortunate I had both in my life.

As ill as my mother was, she got up from her sick bed and walked slowly to my grandfather's bedside. With tears in her eyes, she gently cradled his head with her frail hands and softly whispered, "Why didn't you wait just one more day? We both could have gone together?" Then she slowly walked back to her bed. Although they hardly said a word to each other during all those years, there was a strong bond between them.

Following traditional custom, we helped wash my grandfather's body and wrapped him in a shroud in preparation for his burial that took place the same day. A wooden coffin was brought from the church; few neighbors had gathered at our house. Then the men carried the coffin on their shoulders and walked slowly towards the church. Grief stricken, we followed. After the church service, in the same manner, we followed the men towards the new Armenian cemetery that was quite a distance from our home—first down a hill, then up another. We returned home after the burial, exhausted and overwhelmed with sorrow.

Before we went to sleep that night, my mother told Kaspar, "Tomorrow you will bury me." And indeed that very night my beloved mother passed away. We were all already so numb and in a state of shock, the memory of that day blurred in with the previous day. In less than twenty-four hours after the death of my precious grandfather, we laid my beloved mother to rest beside him. While she had been ill for three months, it never entered my mind she would die. None of us knew at the time that would prove to be the genesis of the dreadful days that lay ahead.

The double tragedy in less than two days intensified the grieving process for all of us. Now, two of the most important people in our lives were gone forever. The losses brought the rest of us closer together in our struggles to cope. We accepted our new daily responsibilities. From that day on, Aghavni assumed most of the responsibilities for running the household. She was both concerned and endearing to us. We called her *Bahgee* (sister in Kurdish), which is what my brothers and I also called our two sisters. Mihran had taken on Bedros' responsibilities when he went to America. We called him *Agha Yeghpayr* and likewise, the younger boys all referred to their older brothers by that title. However, Nishan and Kerop had a difficult time phrasing those two words so they called us *"Agha-payr"* and as they got older that title never changed!

My father was completely overburdened emotionally and physically by those losses.

11. FATHER REMARRIES

The double loss of my grandfather and mother numbed my father. He knew we needed additional help with the household chores and the care of my younger brothers. A few months later, he remarried. My stepmother's name was Vartouhi. She was close in age to my father, forty five to fifty years old, and was a pretty woman. She had been previously married and widowed twice. She had a daughter from her first husband who lived in the village of Gotahreech, a village more than a half-day walk from Perri. On one occasion I visited her daughter for three days. With her second husband she had a twenty-year-old son, Hagop, who also lived in Gotahreech. I saw him once when he came to our house. As was the custom, for a widow who remarries, Vartouhi's children remained with their respective paternal families.

My father and Vartouhi soon had a daughter, Yeranouhi. She was a beautiful, playful baby. We all loved her. We rarely left her alone—one person or another was always picking her up and carrying her about. Consequently, she had a hard time learning to walk, even by the time she was three years old.

Unfortunately, my stepmother didn't know how to assume my mother's responsibilities, and that created an even greater burden on my aunt and Sultahn. Now, not only was my mother gone, but my sister Zaruhy as well. The situation alienated both my brother Mihran and me from Vartouhi. I felt especially sorry for Sultahn, because of her physical handicap, I knew the workload was too much for her.

On one occasion, I saw my stepmother, from behind the *pehtahks,* strike Sultahn who whimpered in pain. I was not only surprised, but also extremely upset. Sultahn had always done more than her share of the household chores. We had never before experienced such harsh behavior in our household. I threatened Vartouhi and told her never to touch Sultahn or any of the other younger children again. No more was said of the incident. However, a cool feeling remained between us. I have felt sorry for that ever since.

My father had to support all of us. That wasn't easy because he planned to send all of his sons to school and had to make sure we were well dressed.

We all tried our best to console and support our father. The burdens were continuously mounting on him. Within just a few years, he had lost his eldest son to a foreign country, couldn't get out of debt, lost his first born, Zaruhy, when she married, and had endured the loss of his first wife and father, both of whom had been his moral support and for whom he had been dependent upon.

The constant ominous atmosphere in which we lived was compounded by the effect of those losses. We gradually felt the enormity of his burden that was obvious by his sullen posture. We no longer had our cherished story hour at the end of each day.

Now after our nightly prayers, my father retired early and before he fell asleep, he smoked twenty cigarettes that Aghavni rolled by hand for him—the paper and matches were bought from the *shoogah*—and he drank a flask, a half pint of his own homemade brandy or wine. When he awoke in the morning, the empty flask was near his bedside. There was no sign of ashes from his cigarettes. My aunt told us that he ate the ashes as a cure for his stress and fatigue.

Once a year during the summer months, my father brought home his tobacco from the nearby Kurdish village, Dahnahburran in the Derseem where it was grown. I don't know if he made a trade with his work on the *guhdavs* or if he bought it. He dried the beautiful yellow-green leaves on our rooftops. He strung lines from Varteeg Bahgee's wall to Areef Effendi's wall and draped the leaves over the lines until they dried. These same lines were used for other purposes. I remember they were used to hang *rojeeg* out to dry under the sun.

For the next four years we learned to adjust to the losses and the significant changes that came into our lives. We all continued to try to help and encourage one another.

Major changes were taking place in our school that also affected our home life and community. Fortunately many of those changes helped my father financially. A more optimistic atmosphere replaced the somber religious tone in the village. Picnics were arranged where the whole community attended. Villagers socialized with each other and had joyous afternoons, offering us opportunities to meet people and make new friends. While those changes were greatly appreciated, we still yearned for those no longer living with us. *However, my father never did accept many of the changes. He felt they were too bold and would only antagonize the Turkish ire. He knew the Armenians were not ready for a confrontation.*

12. MIHRAN GOES TO AMERICA

In 1913 the political climate was steadily getting worse. Mihran turned seventeen and once again my father had to decide what was best to do for his son. Although he felt Bedros was safe in Chicago, he was concerned about the freedom of his lifestyle. He couldn't understand why Bedros wasn't able to help pay off his debt. After four years Bedros still didn't have a good paying job. Now he alone had to decide what to do with Mihran. What would be best for him? Would he have a better life in Perri or would he be safer in America?

He was more concerned about Mihran's fate because he never forgot how he almost lost Mihran when he was just an infant. During the time when they were living in Ismiel and while he was away on a job, my mother and grandfather were left alone with Zaruhy, Bedros, Sultahn and Mihran who was only a few days old. One day a Kurdish neighbor advised my mother to gather up her children quickly, leave the house and hide in the hills for three to four hours. He warned her that some rogue Kurds were planning an attack to plunder Armenian homes. The Turkish officials not only didn't stop those Kurds; they encouraged them to inflict as much pain as possible on the Armenians to create animosity between the two minorities to further the Turkish design.

The Kurd warned her that if she stayed, there would most likely be a confrontation, and she would be risking her life and that of her children. My mother agreed with him and decided to take his advice. She felt she wouldn't be able to handle all four children who were less than six years old, so she quickly wrapped Mihran tightly in his *kondagh* (swaddling clothes) and placed him out of sight near the *toeneer* to help keep him warm since she didn't know how long they would have to stay away from the house. With a prayer for God's protection, she left him. Carrying the other three children, she and my grandfather fled from the house and ran up to the hills to hide. Several hours later, when they returned, she discovered that the house had been completely ransacked. Most of their belongings, from preserved foods to bedding, were gone.

But most alarming, the baby was not in sight. He was not where she had left him. Only when he began to cry, did they discover him in the *toeneer* where he must have fallen. Luckily the embers were cold, and he was not hurt. That was Mihran's fate as an infant. What would it be now? Would he have better luck in America?

Even though he was losing another helping hand and again would be deeper in debt, my father decided to send Mihran to join Bedros in America. He hoped Mihran would find a good job and would be able to send money back to help pay off his debt but that never happened either. The first letter we received from Mihran disclosed how difficult it was for him to find a job. Both he and Bedros were having a difficult time surviving on what little they were earning.

My father became concerned about his sons' lifestyle. It bothered him that they showed no concern for the family that was left behind in Perri. It wasn't the debt that really bothered him. He worried why his sons had not found adequate jobs, since they were strong, healthy and capable men, yet they never sent one cent to help their family—their lifestyle in American was his main concern.

The workload and financial burdens continued to drain my father's strength and soul. He never stopped worrying about how he was going to overcome his misfortunes. Luckily I was getting older and larger. Now I was strong enough to assume Mihran's chores along with mine. My father also made me his assistant.

Below are excerpts from two different letters reflecting my father's concerns regarding their situation in Turkey.[*]

1914 July 6, Perri: My father's letter to Dikran:

...In several letters I have explained our difficulties. Now I find it redundant to write in detail what our situation is going to become. Our situation is pitiable. I think you understand the burden of our twenty-two voskee (gold pieces) debt. I also just bought wheat for four voskees and asked you for help, but you didn't answer me about that. Dikran, didn't you write that when you receive the reply about the eleven voskees, you would write to me? What happened? Have pity on me... I write to you on a regular basis what is needed, and when you read what I have written to you, answer me, so that I can be at ease...

1914, December 20, Perri: My father's letter to his sons

...In regards to the family, we are barely getting by within our means. Everything is still expensive but wheat is still cheap. For example, an eolcheck (bushel) of bulghur is worth fifteen ghooroosh and yesterday I made an exchange for two eolchechs of wheat. It's been some time since we boiled our bulghur...

---

[*]   These original letters were kept by my brother Bedros and were given to me by his son Levon.

Excerpt of letter dated 6 July 1914

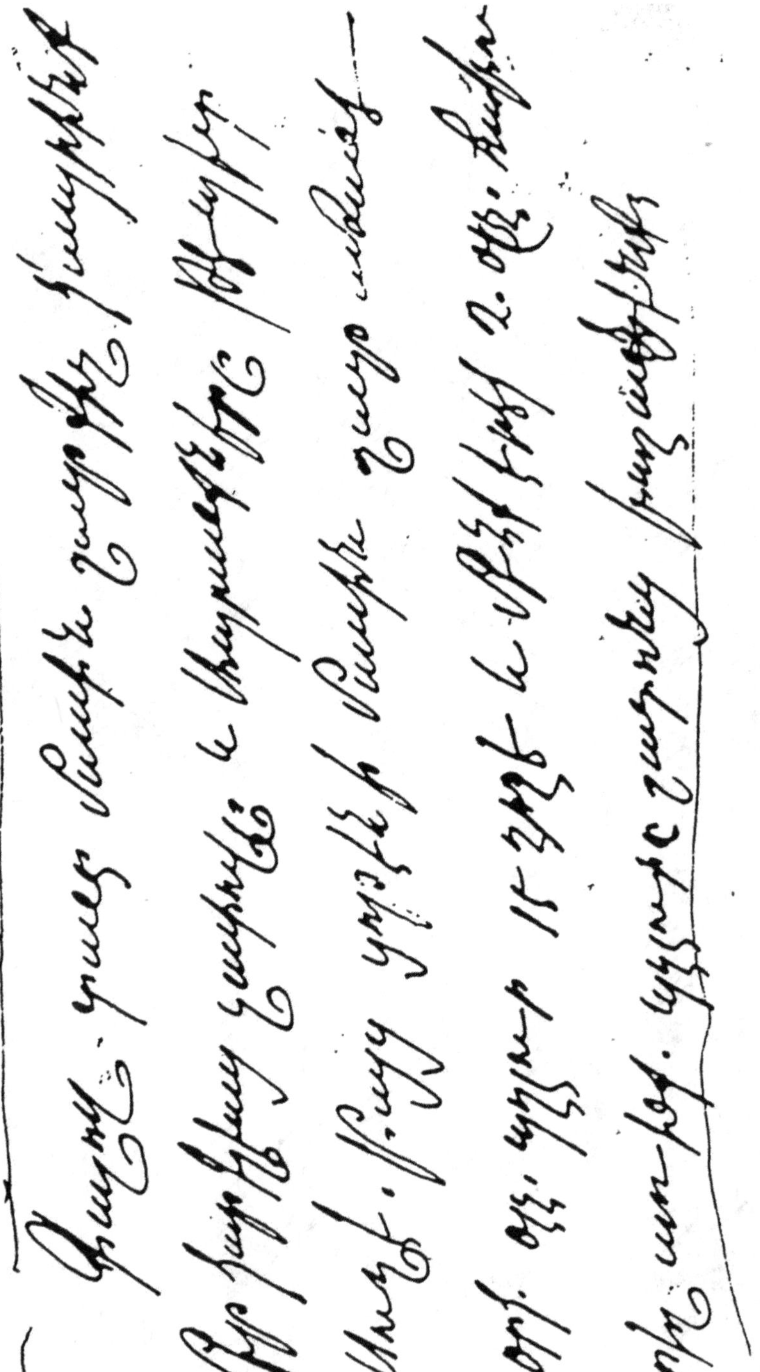

Excerpt of letter dated 20 December 1914

13. MY CHORES

Starting from age ten, I was given specific chores. Kaspar wasn't physically able to help with strenuous and laborious tasks. As soon as I was strong enough, it was my sole responsibility to make sure we always had fresh water in the house. I had to walk fifteen minutes to the Gahmarr Spring several times each day, carrying two three-gallon clay jugs *(goozh)* that I filled with water and returned home. On occasion, the jugs would break and had to be replaced.

I had to make sure we had water at all times in both areas. We stored water in two large tubs in the *torrtah* that was used for bathing and washing clothes. Inside the family quarters, we also had four jugs that we used for drinking and cooking. Each jug held two to four gallons of water. Even though I usually made three to four trips a day to the spring, whenever necessary, I made extra trips.

Gradually, I began to assume the responsibility to greet out guests. Throughout the year, whenever a guest or one of my father's customers came to our house, I greeted and invited them into our *torrtah*. I served them *tahn* and bread or pickled peppers with their juice—everyone considered this a treat. If they couldn't continue on their journey that day, they had dinner with us and were allowed to sleep over for the night. We had extra bedding for guests that I would set up in our *toeneer doon.* The next morning, after breakfast, I gave them a snack as they left. On rainy days or nights, whenever someone who was wet from the rain came to the house, I would have him sit in front of our hearth in the *torrtah* while I dried his clothing. My father felt a guest was God's gift to us, and we welcomed them gladly and treated them with respect. We felt it was an honor and a privilege to have a stranger, Armenian or Kurd, come into our house.

Right after Mihran left, I took over most of his chores and whatever heavy task the women could not do became my responsibility. At the same time I started to help my father in the *baghchah*. My father's vineyard and mulberry grove were quite a distance from our house. It was more than an hour's walk. It was situated between two valleys at the base of the Arkhaj Mountains, along the banks of the Perri River, which flowed near the road going towards Pertahk and Kharpert. It was an ideal setting for our vineyard and trees. The heavy snowfalls and rains abundantly irrigated the grounds naturally during our long harsh winters. We had only one nice spring in our vineyard.

On the eastern slopes in the *Khraj Baghchah* there were many larger springs. The fruit ripened later and was sweeter than ours. In addition, there was a variety of nut trees such as walnuts and almonds. But I mostly coveted the extremely tasty mushrooms.

There were three separate vineyards side by side in between that stretch of the valley. My father's vineyard was in the middle. To the right of us was the Der Garabedian's vineyard—his was the largest. On the left, was the Apelian's vineyard. That land was cared for by Apelian's widow and daughter and their hired help, who was also the *baghbanjee* (overseer of the garden). The *baghbanjee* oversaw all three gardens night and day from intruders. My father aspired to buy her land for the asking price of seven dollars, but he felt obligated to first pay off his existing debts. She had ladyfinger grapes that were larger and sweeter than ours. When you ate them, your fingers stuck together as if they were covered with honey.

For a few years, in the 1960s, the *baghbanjee's* widow and daughter were our neighbors in Los Angeles.

All three families had mulberry trees planted a distance of ten to fifteen feet parallel to the banks of the Perri River. There was a line of willow trees right on the bank of the river throughout that area.

Mulberries began to ripen in late spring. By early summer they were ready to be picked. Picking mulberries was my first big responsibility for the year.

A month before they ripened, I had to water the trees. My father had about ten to twelve trees. They were a good thirty feet tall with trunks three feet in diameter. I made about four trips to the Perri River using our five-gallon pail to water each tree. Even though the channels and springs provided enough water to irrigate the vineyards, there was not a sufficient supply of water for the trees. The vineyards started from the base of the foothills and went up the hillsides.

In between the mulberry trees and the vineyards, a distance about fifteen feet, everyone had a *serrgahn* (clay floor). The surface of the *serrgahn* was about fifteen feet long and twelve feet wide. This was the floor where the mulberries were spread out to dry.

All three families worked together to pick and dry their mulberries. We started with the Der Garabedians' trees, then ours, and the Apelians' were last. It took three boys working together to get the fruit picked. Hampartzoum, one of my school friends who was a few years younger than me, helped his father. Together we held the corners of a heavy sheet about nine feet by ten feet, and the Apelians' hired hand, who was older, climbed the trees and shook the branches so that the ripened mulberries dropped onto the sheet. Once the sheet was full, we carried it over to the *serrgahn*, spread out the mulberries, and then went back for more. Once the *serrgahn* was filled, covered with mulberries from end to end, we went on to pick the fruit from our trees. When our *serrgahn* was totally covered, we went on to the Apelian's trees.

It took about two to three days for the mulberries to dry. At that point we went back to repeat the process. But first we gathered the dry mulberries in our baskets. My basket for this task was about two feet wide and two feet deep. Dried mulberries were relatively light. I'd carry the basket home over my shoulder. This routine of picking and drying the mulberries had to be repeated four to five different times over a period of two to three months for the year's crop. Meanwhile, within that period, I would go back several times a week to pick fresh mulberries for the family. Everyone at home looked forward to that treat because they were extremely sweet and tasty. We had both the large and small white mulberries. The large mulberries were the size of your index finger, but the smaller mulberries were sweeter. They were as sweet and sticky as honey! I still savor the taste—there is nothing like it!

By the time that task was completed, it was early fall and the grapes were ripening. Each family picked their own grapes. My father hired Gooree Oso to help us pick the grapes and we used his donkey to carry them home because fresh grapes were heavy. We filled two large baskets about three feet wide and four feet deep, gradually tapering at the bottom. We secured a basket on each side of the donkey and walked home. We made several such trips a day.

Buried Hehvenk

We also preserved fresh grapes by burying them in the ground by making a *hehvenk*. I dug about three holes in different sites throughout the vineyard to avoid detection. Each hole was about four to five feet deep and three feet wide and lined with fresh leaves and vines. Then, I made a *hehvenk* by braiding together three of the longest vines bearing the largest number of bunches. I tied each *hehvenk* to a strong branch from a *Mehsheh* tree and lowered it into a hole. Each end of the branch was secured on the opposite sides of the hole allowing the *hehvenk* to hang in the middle of the hole. Finally, I covered each hole with a screen made of vines, leaves and dirt. I tried to disguise the surface of the hole to ward off thieves—not everyone had vineyards and occasionally someone would break into the *hehvenk* as a prank. The buried grapes stayed fresh until the holiday season and it was a nice treat for the whole family.

The grapes we brought home were used in a variety of ways. Some were eaten fresh, some were dried for raisins, and some were made into preserves. However,

A hehvenk from my garden grapes

most of the grapes were used by my father to make wine and brandy. We ate the red sweet grapes, the sweet green grapes similar to the Muscat grapes called *tutmoog* and the sweetest grape, a yellow-green, large ladyfinger called *aghbunkehree*—my favorite!

My father used the *gogeskraw* (large black grapes) and the large green grapes to make wine and brandy. Although they were very large and juicy, they were not very sweet.

Kaspar and I helped my father squeeze the grapes for his wine and brandy. We put the grapes in a porous bag, tightly tied the bag and placed it in our wooden tub. The tub was about four feet deep, five feet wide, and six feet long. It had no leaks. Kaspar and I stomped on the bag with our clean bare feet until all of the juice was squeezed out with the pulp remaining in the bag. That process was repeated several times. Even though Kaspar wasn't very strong, we had a great time sharing that chore. We really had fun! The tub was cleaned well each time, as it was used for several other purposes.

We made several such trips each day.

When we finished, my father took over. I don't recall what he did next, nor do I remember how he made his mulberry brandy.

By far the most difficult chore for me was leveling our rooftops. At the end of fall, just before the heavy snow and rainy season each year, the topsoil on our rooftop had to be padded down firmly and smoothed over with the *logh* to prevent leakage. The *logh* was a smooth, cylindrical stone about twenty four inches long and twenty inches wide. It was pushed much like a manual lawn mower. The *logh* was large, heavy and difficult to maneuver. The rooftop was built with a slight slant to allow the rain and snow to drain off readily. As I pushed the *logh*, the momentum created by the slope pulled on me and required a lot of strength to control. The thought of being dragged off the edge with the *logh* always haunted me. I could have easily slid off and fallen to the ground with the *logh* landing on top of me. I was barely twelve when I took over that demanding chore.

14. GAMES AND FUN ACTIVITIES

When I was not in school or busy doing one of my chores, I was involved with one physical activity or another. On Saturday afternoons, when we had only half a day of school Mihran and I spent many enjoyable hours with our classmates. Mihran was the top athlete in most of the activities. Kaspar usually did not participate; he stayed home and worked on homework.

I remember three games we played using a ball. The balls were extremely hard and had a good bounce, since they were made of tightly wound wool yarn. The larger ball, the size of a large grapefruit, was used in a game where it was slammed against the wall of Areef Effendi's house. The game was similar to handball. One team of three boys stood at arm's length from each other a few feet away from the wall. The other team with three boys took their place behind that team. A member from the team in the back would go in the middle of the front team and slam the ball against the wall. Members from both teams attempted to get possession of the ball. The team possessing the ball the majority of the time won the game.

Another game involved two or more players using a smaller ball, the size of a small orange. One boy would bounce the ball at his side. While making a complete turn on his right foot, he would try to catch the ball before it bounced again. At the same time his opponent would also try to catch the ball. The person who caught the ball the greatest number of times won the game.

The third game I remember using the same smaller ball, a player would bounce the ball once, and before it hit the ground, he would

Mehsheh Sticks

spin around. The player with the greater number of spins to a bounce won the game. Most of us got six or seven spins to a bounce. Those who were really good made twelve to fifteen spins within one bounce.

We used branches from the *mehsheh* tree for a few of our games. For one game we used two sticks about twelve inches long. Using both hands, we held the sticks in front of our chest in a cross position. With a flick of a finger, the horizontal stick would shoot off. The boy whose stick shot the greatest distance won the game.

In another game we also used two sticks, one stick was twelve inches long called *chuhbookh* and the other about three feet long was called *chatleek*. Both ends of the shorter stick were whittled into a sharp point like the tip of a fountain pen. Similar to the first game, the sticks were held in front of the chest in a 'cross' position and with a flick of the finger, the shorter stick would shoot off. After the stick landed on the ground, the pointed end not touching the ground was firmly whacked with the longer stick. Again, the shorter stick went flying through the air and the boy whose stick went the farthest won.

In another game two boys confronted each other. Each boy held on to both ends of a stick about two feet long at chest level. Each opponent tried to unbalance the other by hitting his opponent's stick with his own. The player who lost his balance and fell to the ground lost the game.

Using small lamb anklebones or *jan,* we played a couple of different games. The object of the game was to see how far it would fly along the ground using a special technique to flip the bone with your fingers. We had discovered that the heavier the bone, the farther it flew through the air. Sometimes a boy would cheat by drilling a small hole on the wide side of the bone and filling it with lead.

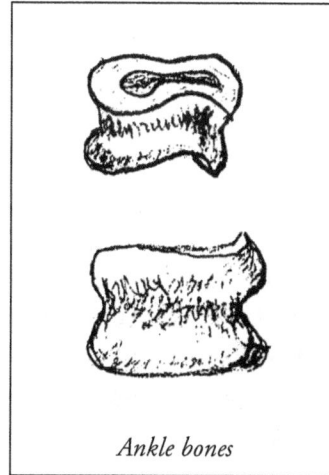

Ankle bones

Using the same bones, we had another game. All four sides of the bone were given a name. One side was called a *bag* (a king) and its opposite side was called a *kogh* (a thief). On the other two sides were a *khoja* (a wise man) and an *esh* (jackass). The bone was thrown on the ground like a die. You were given the name of the side of the bone that faced up. If two or more bones were used, you had additional names. A little story was created with the various names that faced up. More bones were used to allow more story line possibilities. The more creative we were, the more fun we had.

Another game played was on Easter morning, when Sultahn boiled eggs in yellow onion skins, turning them into a dark reddish brown color. As she handed an egg to each of us, we would check the durability of both ends of the eggshell. A tap on our front teeth with the egg was a good test to see if it was a "winner."

There was a particular skill for cupping an egg firmly yet gently in your right hand allowing enough space for your opponent to hit the top of your cupped egg. If your fingers were placed just right, your opponent would miss making contact with the egg. Then it would be your turn to try to hit his egg following the same rules. If the egg cracked on one side, you then turned it around and your opponent would try to hit that end as well. If both ends cracked, you lost your egg to the opponent. If, however, one side didn't crack, you had a chance to hit your opponent's egg. There was a 50/50 chance you could crack both ends of your opponent's egg with the one good end of yours.

Mihran was one of the boys who liked to play pranks on others. He knew where to find tar on the banks of the Perri River. He skillfully blew out the contents of an egg and sealed each end with tar, so that an unsuspecting opponent never had a chance to win. We played both at home with other family members, as well as at church after Easter services with our classmates.

We had another easy game where we tossed a handful of walnuts towards a hole in the ground three to four inches deep with a ten-inch diameter. Standing about three to four feet away, we each flung about twelve to fifteen walnuts. If an even number fell into the hole, we kept the walnuts. If there was an odd number, we didn't get to keep any.

We also played *ach guhbook* (hide and seek). It was while playing this game that I tripped on a gutter nail on our rooftop and fell to the ground, gashing the left side of my forehead. I was about seven years old. We also played "leap frog." We jumped over one to three boys at a time.

A more aggressive game was to unbalance and knock down our opponent while we held one foot up behind our back with our hand from the opposite side of our body. Then with our free arm, held up and bent in front of our chest, we pushed on the opponent's free arm. We confronted each other until one of us fell and was thereby defeated. This was one of my favorite games.

Some days at school we raced with each other just to see who was able to run the fastest and the farthest. We usually ran down to the river, along the riverbank or towards the empty fields. To test our endurance, we ran in a triangular fashion, starting from the church, down to the river, and back up to the foothills and finally back to the church. Most of this run was going up the sides of the mountains. That was hard! It was a long and steep climb.

On a few occasions I went to the *galls* where the boys played a game on the hard smooth surface. We used *sahls* (two flat, hard stones) the size of the palm of my hand. We placed one *sahl* on the *gall*. Then, from quite a distance, we aimed the other *sahl* towards the first one. The object of the game was to see who could hit the first *sahl* and make it slide the farthest. The player who moved their first *sahl* the farthest won the game.

During the last couple of years, along with the major changes beginning in our school, we also started to do physical exercises once a week in the girls' classroom. In addition, two rings were hung from a chain, and we were taught various skills using the rings. Tops where also introduced to the boys. We wound the string around the top, flung it down on a flat surface and watched it spin. We eagerly looked forward to all new activities they brought in.

When the first winter snow began to fall, we were not allowed to play in it. We were allowed to go out only after the second storm covered the old snow when the snow was considered to be cleaner. The first thing we did was to run out and bring in a clean batch of snow, and quickly pour mulberry *shuroob* (syrup) over it. The whole family enjoyed the treat.

During school recess, we had several activities playing in the snow. Invariably we would start by throwing snowballs at each other. Then when the snow froze on the hillside, we were able to slide towards the river, sitting on a small mat. That was great fun.

As the snow deepened, we made snowmen. We rolled a ball of snow down towards the river. It got bigger and bigger as it rolled down the hillside. Every snowman had its own distinctive look. I would make a snowman for Nishan and Kerop at home after I shoved the snow off our rooftop into the street. They had fun playing with it.

The snow soon became so deep that it would block the exterior door to our house. Many times it piled up to our rooftop. To protect our roof from the heavy weight of the snow, the neighbors across the street and I would shovel the snow off our rooftops into the street. At some point the street was impassable. Thus, the only way out of the house was to use our ladder and walk across the rooftops. Snow on the larger roads were cleared off to permit easier and safer travel. That was how we walked to school during the cold winter months.

At the tail end of winter and the onset of spring, we went out looking for mushrooms and a variety of grasses. The very first to blossom were the *baumbohzz* (grass). It had a pinkish white flower that blossomed only at that time of year. As we picked the pinkish flowers, we ate them to our hearts' content and then gathered as many as we could to take home. I had a *doebrahg* (a cloth bag) to carry whatever I collected to take home. Everyone liked them and the more we ate, the more we wanted.

These were followed by mushrooms. The mushrooms were really beautiful when they were just beginning to sprout through the dark soil. Their budding white heads along the brown hillside could be detected from a distance, just before the sunshine reached them and darkened in color. We gathered them as quickly as possible, using a *zehmehlee* (small pocketknife), because everyone preferred them when they were still white. Whenever we took the *zehmehlee*, however, my parents worried if we took too long getting back home, fearing we might have gotten into some mischief. The mushrooms varied in size, the smallest were three to four inches in diameter and the largest ten to twelve inches in diameter. They were about one and one half inches thick. I've never tasted mushrooms since that came close to their wonderful taste.

Right at the end of the *baumbohzz* and mushroom season, the *gangarr,* another type of grass began to sprout over the hillsides. They were not as abundant as the *baumbohzz,* and the supply varied from one season to the next. During a sparse season, what few we found were eaten raw. The boys would satisfy their appetites and then pick a basketful to take home for the family. During the abundant years, we had more than enough to take home to be dried for winter dishes. Luckily the lean years were few and far in between.

The *gangarr* plant was a type of grass that grew in clumps the size of my hand. The clump consisted of several stalks about five to six inches long and the width of a finger. Small leaves ran along the sides of the stalk. The leaves were pulled away, only the stalk was eaten. It had a sweet, soft taste of its own. It was eaten raw or cooked. These plants were found on the hillside between Ismiel and Perri where the spring's waters gushed up so swiftly that you couldn't stoop down to drink it. You had to cup your hands to scoop up the water to drink it. The temperature of the air strangely effected the water. During the winter months it seemed to be warm and during the summer months it seemed cold. Our teachers explained it as a type of an illusion. In the summer months we hunted for *madooda,* a root with an irregular shape and the size of an egg. They had a sweet taste as we chewed on a mouthful until the juice was gone.

Swimming was one of my favorite pastimes, however, we were only allowed to swim in the rivers when they were safe and calm enough for swimming. When I was about ten years old, Mihran taught me how to swim on my back and to increase my speed while swimming on my stomach by paddling my arms and legs. I became a good swimmer using either stroke. I enjoyed every moment I was in the water. I had to be careful, however, when we went into the river, as we never knew when the current would be so forceful that we would not be able to get out. Each year someone lost his life in the rapids or undercurrent. My parents were always warning us about those dangers. There really were not too many good or safe days for swimming.

During three to four months of the year the rivers were frozen so thick that a heavily laden donkey could walk across them. Then, as spring approached, it took another four to five months for the ice to completely thaw. That was the most dangerous time to be near the rivers.

We started to fish only after it was safe. We had a special *tohrr* (net), which was as large as a sheet that we used for fishing. It was sewn up at the sides to look much like a large sack with a drawstring around the opening. We made a large hole in the ice and submerged our net into the river. Within minutes fish would be caught. We never allowed the net to fill up completely because it would be too heavy for us to pull out. We were afraid the ice would crack under us, and we would fall in. The amount of fish we caught was sufficient for our family's needs. Those who caught more sold their catch to those who, for one reason or another, didn't fish, so there was plenty for everyone.

During the summer, I fished with my friends for fun—we fished only for ourselves. We bought a particular plant seed, crushed it, put a little piece into flour dough and rolled it into pea size balls. We threw a handful of these balls into the river. As soon as the fish swallowed one, they became disoriented and floated to the surface. We grabbed them immediately with our cupped hands and chopped off their heads to prevent the possibility of poisoning because they had already turned a yellowish color. We immediately made a fire and roasted our catch. This was a fun time activity spent with my buddies. At that point in my life, I liked to eat fish.

Our favorite fish was the *alla'baulakh*—it had a large red stomach. Unfortunately, they were very rare in our part of the river. On a few occasions, we went up the river closer towards Ismiel where they were more abundant. We had to be extremely careful near those waters because it was so clear that it was very difficult to gauge the depth of the river. We could have easily gone in over our heads, so we were always reluctant to fish there—it was too dangerous for us.

15. SCHOOL DAYS BEFORE DASHNAG CHANGES

My father worked hard and did his best to send all six of his sons to school to get a good education as a means for us to have a better life. He did not want any of his sons to pursue his craft. If he had the means, he would have also sent his daughters to school. He believed they too would have had better lives with an education.

He did his best to impress upon us the value of a good education. Attending school was a privilege. I have always felt indebted to him for the sacrifices he made for my education. How many parents today make sacrifices to send six sons to a good private school in the United States?

My father paid for our tuition, books and supplies. There even was a fee for our drinking water, which was delivered to the school in a *deeg* and then transferred into a *gode*. The *gode* held about five to ten gallons and sat on a table near the door of the girls' classroom. There was a spout near the bottom of the *gode*.

Our school and church was one large complex on a hillside overlooking the Perri River. The church was on the ground floor. The girls' classroom was on the second level. The boys' two classrooms were on the third level, adjacent to a larger room that was used as additional classrooms, and for town hall meetings and community social affairs.

About two hundred students were enrolled. The girls had only one classroom and one teacher, because only a few girls from the more affluent families attended. The boys had three rooms plus the use of the all-purpose room. We had five teachers. I only remember the names of four of the teachers: Baron (Mister) Kaspar and Baron Marsoub Mishmeeshian (two of Mayrig Zaruhy's uncles); and two other brothers, Baron Armenag and his older brother Baron Hovannes Eoksouzian, who was known as a strict disciplinarian. We had one principal, Arshag Baronian (we called him "*Effendi* Arshag") and the *dundess* (the custodian), Vartan Noroian. We had nicknamed him "Vartan *Chortahn*" and used to tease him.

Vartan Chortahn, bellem kez tuhnehm torrtahn
Kaylehreh kahn vraht gahrtahn!

Vartan Chortahn, I will wrap you up and put you in the courtyard.
The wolves will come and read your eulogy!

K. Yerevanian

Baron Eoksouzian, his wife and daughter

He was very strict. "May your roots be cursed!" he would exclaim as his ruler came down on our knuckles!

One of the custodian's major responsibilities was to ring the church bells. There were different rhythms for respective occasions. The most rapid rhythm was for school: ding, ding, ding (a series of seven rapid dings). The rhythm for church services was moderate: ding-dong, ding-dong, ding-dong (again, a series of seven ding-dongs). The third and slowest rhythm was for burials, alerting the people that someone had died and would be buried that day. A slow piercing sound— dong, dong, dong (a series of seven dongs) was also used to alert the village of a pending emergency. Another one of his chores included going to a student's house to check out the reason for their absence.

Kaspar and I were seven years old when we started school. Bedros took us the first day as we eagerly walked by his side. Mihran who was one class ahead of us walked with us. Mihran had been held back a few years in this school because his progress in Ismiel, where he started his education, had not met the school's standards.

Sometime during the first few days, the teacher hung a *karrehtaghdagh* (slate) around our necks. With a piece of *gahveej* (chalk), we began to write the Armenian alphabet and our numerals. We were each given a *byoosahg* (cloth bag) that fastened with a button in which we carried our books, papers, and other supplies. We swung it by our side as we proudly walked back and forth to school.

Kaspar and I were each given five *para* (cent) a week for our school supplies such as pencils, replacements tips for our ink pen, rulers, erasers, and paper. We purchased such items from our *shoogah*. They were imported primarily from Germany. We had to be frugal with our allowance.

The school day began in the large all-purpose room on the third level where both the girls and boys gathered together. We began each day with a daily prayer. We all sang our nationalistic songs and were careful not to provoke the Turkish ire. Finally, roll call was taken. As each name was called, we responded with *"Nerrgah"* (present). First, the girls were dismissed to their classroom. Then, the boys were dismissed to their respective classrooms. We all walked quietly and orderly. The students were very well behaved because they all felt education was a privilege—education was not compulsory.[*]

Both students and parents held teachers in high esteem and treated them with much respect. Likewise, teachers were sincerely concerned about the education of their students and were well trained in their respective subject matter. The basic subjects were very similar to those taught currently in public schools in the United States. Teachers reinforced the values and lifestyle the students were being taught at home. In addition, they were taught Christianity. From my personal perspective, I feel our teachers did a better job when I was in school in Perri than

---

[*]   There were no public schools.

teachers today, despite all of the modern advantages and advances in technology. Perri's educational system should be respected. It is a tragedy that it was brutally destroyed.

The school day was eight hours long. Each period was forty-five minutes. After two periods of instruction, we had a morning recess. During our thirty-minute morning recess, we played games and sometimes had a bite to eat. After recess, we had two more periods of instruction. Following the morning session, we had a one-hour lunch break. Those who lived relatively nearby went home for lunch; otherwise, they ate their lunch at school and played with their friends. Again, the session after lunch had four periods with an afternoon recess break after the first two periods. During the recess breaks the boys played along the hillsides while the girls played on the rooftop of the church.

When school was dismissed at four o'clock, most students stayed to play until the church opened for evening services. My father and grandfather made a point of joining us in church every day. After an hour-long service, we all walked home together.

Parents and teachers actively worked as a team to make sure we learned and were well behaved. Several times a year, the principal and parents were invited into a classroom during oral examinations. My father normally did not have the opportunity to attend, so family friends reported our class progress to him when they visited our house. My parents were both proud and happy that Kaspar and I were the top students in our class. Consequently, we felt compelled to study even harder. This was one way we were able to do something important for them.

Teachers and parents jointly determined the means of punishment when students misbehaved. Even if they misbehaved at home, the school reprimanded students in accordance with the parent's instructions. Sometimes a student was reprimanded both at home and at school. I cannot remember my parents hitting any of us, but I do remember once when Bedros took a letter to school stating that Mihran, Kaspar and I had misbehaved. Mihran was always getting into trouble. He taunted my sister, hardly listened to my parents, and stole raisins from the *khuzehn*. On this one occasion, we were all involved and were caught. However, I do not remember what we had done. Bedros' letter was read in front of the whole school during the opening activities in the morning. We were first given a small lecture about our misbehavior, then our punishment was decided based on the severity of our misdeed. For that particular offense, the three of us received four swats with a ruler on the palm of both hands.

Another day, on a Sunday afternoon, five of us went into the vineyards to play cards, something we knew was forbidden. Since we were not playing for money, we were not concerned about being caught and felt none of us would snitch. Unbeknown to us, Mihran Eoksouzian, the teacher's son, had seen us and told his father. The next morning all five of us were called up to the front of the class, and once again we were each given four swats on our palms. Each time I was hit, I gave out a yell, *"vagh vagh"* ("poor me, poor me"). When Kaspar's turn came up for the swats, the teacher noticed he had wet his pants and took mercy on him. Kaspar was not punished.

I also remember when Baron Eoksouzian gave me swats on my clenched knuckles. He struck down hard with the blunt end of his ruler—I remember how much that hurt, but I do not remember what I did wrong. While I believe in mild forms of discipline, I do not believe in such harsh methods. They are cruel and unnecessary.

On one hot day, Baron Hovannes' three-year-old nephew, apparently became afraid his uncle would punish him, as he had punished the older boys. He ran off into the vineyards. After the entire community searched for hours, my brother Mihran finally found him. He had died from heat exhaustion. Consequently the whole community was terribly upset and up in arms. They all felt reprimand should not be so cruel.

Mihran was the top student in his class in the academic subjects, as well as in all physical activities. He always won the games he played. He was nicknamed "Yehgav" (here he comes). I used to feel proud when I was referred to as Yehgav's brother. Nobody dared to bully me.

In 1915, I had just entered into the fourth level. I had barely covered six and a half years of schooling. From my experiences and achievements, I now feel that my education was the equivalent to that of a high school graduate or more.

The most successful graduates from the sixth level who had the financial means were qualified to attend Yeprahd (Euphrates) College. Yeprahd College, located in Upper Kharpert, was primarily a teacher's college built by American missionaries in the 1880's.

Our school did not have desks—we sat on floor mats. There was a straight row of mats, the top student sat at the front of the classroom and the weakest student sat in the back. After every examination the sitting arrangement was reassigned according to the test scores.

Being a twin gave me the opportunity to sit at the front of the classroom with Kaspar who was the top scholar at our grade level. Although I came in second, occasionally I scored higher than Kaspar and sat in the front seat on my own merit.

Students were placed in classrooms according to the number of years they had attended and test results, not according to their age. Thus, the age level varied within any given grade level. If a student didn't pass the final examinations, he would have to repeat that grade level again.

Kaspar was better in math and sometimes, I had to force him to help me with my homework. He resented that because I spent too much time playing instead of studying. Sometimes I had to be a little forceful before he gave in and helped me.

I was stronger in language and history classes. In 1915, I knew more English than I knew Turkish. We had lessons in both languages, but I never cared for Turkish. I particularly enjoyed learning English.

We were taught the English alphabet and how to read, write and speak simple English phrases. I remember the fun we had with the phrase, "Run, mouse, run—the cat is going to catch you!" My wife, Ovsanna, learned the same phrase while in Malatya. Her education didn't surpass a few months of kindergarten.

At the age of twelve, I felt very proud that I was able to write a few words in English in my letters to Bedros. Little did I know at the time that I would subsequently spend most of my life in America or all too soon I would realize how helpful that little bit of knowledge of English would become as I escaped out of Turkey and found my freedom.

I always regret the fact my coveted education, my most cherished opportunity, was viciously snatched away from me. I never found the opportunity again to finish my education.

Our school was about a fifteen-minute walk from our house. Along the way we invariably encountered a classmate since we all heard the church bells ring at the same time. Young boys passing by older men on the street would have to stop, greet the man with a hello and give a kiss on his hand as they acknowledged each other. Boys couldn't walk on the street with their hands in their pockets, nor could they eat or drink while walking on the street. During the winter months, the boys were required to pick up logs for the fireplace in both the boys' and the girls' classrooms.

I knew all of the boys at school by name. Younger or older, none of us discriminated with whom we played in or out of school. I played with whoever was available when I had time. We all got along with one other. However, I did have one very close special friend and classmate, Kevork Noroian. We were classmates from the first day we entered school. We had similar likes and dislikes and academically we both did very well. His parents were relatively well to do. They owned several cows and in addition to selling milk, they made and sold butter, yogurt and cheese. Every morning his mother spread *serr,* the cream off the top of freshly made yogurt, on a piece of bread, rolled it up and wrapped it. Kevork would give it to me during our morning recess. That gesture always made me feel a little special, knowing his mother was kind enough to think about me. To this very day I have a small bowl of yogurt with honey before going to sleep and Kevork always comes to mind.

Another classmate, Bedros Yermoian, showed me a couple of new things. He was a little younger than I was. He was born in America but his parents had returned to Perri when he was about seven to eight years old. He brought a box of *Crayolas* from America with him. He colored all of his drawings with a variety of beautiful colors. It seemed like a fun thing to do. He allowed some of us to try out the *Crayolas,* a treat I never forgot. He didn't live too far from my house. One day he invited me to his house to show me how his father worked on the *tzeetzeeyank* where my father had our wheat hulled. Bedros surprised all of us with his impressions of their life in America and why his father returned to Perri. We were embarrassed to hear what he said about the lax attitude and behavior of the girls. He was happy his parents decided to return to Perri.

One day another classmate brought orange peels to share with us at school. The aroma was a novelty, as it was so strong and sweet. We all liked it, even though we had never seen or eaten an orange before. It was something new for all of us. Those of us who were fortunate enough to get a little piece of the orange peel felt special. We protected it very carefully. We put it in between the pages of one of our books, and for several weeks we enjoyed that unique fragrance as we opened our book. The first time I saw and ate a whole orange was when Kerop and I reached Beirut. As I remembered, the oranges not only had a nice scent, but they were very tasty as well.

Hampartzoum Der Garabedian and I also would find time to look around for bamboo-like grass along the riverbank while we were drying mulberries in our *baghchah.* We would make about three to four holes on a stalk about ten inches and pretended we had a *doo-dook* (Armenian flute). Then we made our own music, but we were both too shy to share this talent with others.

Although I don't remember the year, I do remember one particular day. In the middle of the afternoon while I was playing on our rooftop when *suddenly* the sky became completely dark. We were left in complete darkness. The elders wondered if it was "the end of the world." Everyone rushed to church for an explanation. Was this a message from God?

Gradually it began to lighten. I don't recall if we were given an explanation of what took place. My wife also remembered that the same incidence took place in Malatya.

SCHOOL ROSTER
NAMES OF MALE STUDENTS

Middle – 2nd Grade

1. Krikor Samerjian
2. Khosrov Nalbandian
3. Alexan Hovhannesian
4. Karekin Yermoian
5. Jivan Boyajian
6. Khosrov Ourfalian
7. Paravon Jizmejian

Middle – 1st Grade

1. Karekin Yerevanian
2. Nigoghos Tanielian
3. Kevork Yerevanian
4. Isahak Assadourian
5. Levon Gopoian
6. Khachadour Harutunian
7. Baghdasar Bandazian
8. Garabed Vasgerdtsian
9. Mardiros Bandazian
10. Hovhannes Bandazian
11. Kevork Poochigian
12. Assadour Antaramian
13. Ghazar Harutunian

Elementary – 2nd Grade

1. Hagop Holopigian
2. Vahan Bandazian
3. Levon Chakmakjian
4. Avedis Kzirian
5. Manoug Poochigian
6. Sarkis Noroian
7. Mihran Chitjian
8. Dikran Meynazarian
9. Ghevont Bandazian
10. Nshan Ourakhian
11. Bedros Bedrossian
12. Avedis Meynazarian
13. Higaz Nalbandian
14. Hagop Kendoian
15. Armenag Tatoian
16. Melidos Mazmanian
17. Jivan Marabanian
18. Boghos Poochigian
19. Misak Maghakian

Elementary – 1st Grade

1. Toros Malkhasian
2. Vahan Tatoian
3. Bedros Yermoian
4. Mardiros Ananigian
5. Kevork Noroian
6. Hampartzoum Chitjian
7. Kaspar Chitjian
8. Hmahyag Mouradian
9. Grigor Manoukian
10. Souren Melidosian
11. Mardiros Yenovkian
12. Khachadour Yezigian
13. Vartan Hagopian
14. Armenag Eoksuzian
15. Melkon Terzian
16. Mihran Mikaelian
17. Levon Melidosian
18. Nshan Marabanian
19. Mihran Mirakian

Preparatory – 3rd Grade

1. Levon Pashajughian
2. Avedis Hagopian
3. Mesrob Yerevanian
4. Kegham Bandazian
5. Hrant Melidosian
6. Mekhsi Noroian
7. Hamprtsm D. Garabedian
8. Mihran Eoksuzian
10. Dikran Noroian
11. Donabed Vartanian
12. Hovhannes Yezigian
13. Zakar Zakoian
14. Ghevont Yezigian
15. Arsen Souqkiasian
16. Samuel Megerdichian
17. Hagop GhorgKevork

Preparatory – 2nd Grade

1. Hajibeg Tertsakian
2. Mihran Bandoian
3. Jivan Antaramian
4. Dikran Chakalmazian
5. Mihran Chakmakjian
6. Howvhannes Khelejian
7. Levon Arakelian
8. Tateos Kazanjian
9. Khoren Pashajughian
10. Manoug Chulfayan
11. Garabed Khachadourian
12. Krikor Eoksuzian

Preparatory – 1st Grade

1. Mardiros Toroian
2. Vartan Kazanjian
3. Markar Hakalmazian
4. Ghazar Echgulian
5. Ghevont Gagoian
6. Boghos Poochigian
7. Hagop Hakalmazian
8. YJivan Gagoian
9. Harutiun Meynazarian
10. Harutiun Vasgertsian
11. Mardiros Sousoulian
12. Mihran Gopoian
13. Zadour Krikorian
14. Levon Yerevanian
15. Levon Mishmeeshian
16. Boghos Mishmeeshian
17. Yervant Chakmakjian
18. Kaghep Paghdasarian
19. Gorun Vasgertsian
20. Asadour Manuelian
21. Krikor Khachigian
22. Dikran Donigian
23. Yeghishe D. Garabedian
24. Khosrov Kouzoian
25. Yervant Yerevanian
26. Gorun Hagopian
27. Yervant Mikaelian
28. Isahag Garabedian
29. Harutiun Chakmakjian
30. Mardiros Mikaelian
31. Yeghishe D. Nerssian
32. Movses Marabanian
33. Nerses D. Nersesian

NAMES OF FEMALE STUDENTS

Middle – 1st Grade

1. Zarouhi Kreghian
2. Yeranouhi Emrshadian
3. Badaskhan Holopigian
4. Mariam Apelian
5. Keghanush Meynazarian
6. Aghavni Marabanian
7. Kohar Tatoian
8. Sultan Kevorkan

Preparatory – 3rd Grade

1. Mariam Marabanian
2. Aghavni Kasbarian
3. Zarouhi Pashajoughian
4. Zarouhi Choragian
5. Annavart Kreghian
6. Azniv Gopoian
7. Yeghisapet Takessian
8. Arousiag Chakmakjian

Elementary – 1st Grade

1. Nevart Yermoian
2. Arpine Marabanian
3. Dzaghig Tavitian
4. Mariam Gagoian
5. Vartouhi Kassabian
6. Sultan Bantazian
7. Payladzou Topjian
8. Mariqa Kheshdoian

Preparatory – 3rd Grade

1. Armine Poochigian
2. Azniv S.K. Chakmakjian
3. Azniv S.K. Chakmakjian
4. Mariam Chakmakjian
5. Yester Hakalmazian
6. Khatoun Meynazarian
7. Arousiag Poochigian

Preparatory – 2nd Grade

1. Armine Poochigian
2. Anna Noroian
3. Khatoun Semerjan
4. Azniv Poochigian
5. Arousiag Takesian
6. Yeghisapet Pashalian
7. Hasmig Hovnanian
8. Gohar Yezigian
9. Baydzar Emrshadian
10. Araxi Tatoian
11. Araxi Bouloudian

Preparatory – 1st Grade

1. Anna Ourakhian
2. Araxi Emrshadian
3. Araxi Hakalmazian
4. Zarouhi Kreghian
5. Araxi Baghdigian
6. Arshaluys Marabanian
7. Aghavni Noroian
8. Anna Boghosian
9. Anna Mouseghian
10. Aghavni Poochigian
11. Arousiag Yermoian
12. Satenig Bezirgenian
13. Aghavni Bidagian
14. Nazeli Yermoian
15. Vartuhi Guiragosian
16. Vartuhi Antaramian
17. Yeghisapet Noroian
18. Terviz Meynazarian
19. Arshaluys Eoksuzian
20. Lousin Yermoian
21. Arshaluys Gopoian
22. Altun Berberian
23. Altun Pashajoughian
24. Yeghisapet Yermoian
25. Vartanush Aghzigian
26. Vartuhi Gagoian
27. Siranoush Bouloudian
28. Vartuhi Eoksouzian
29. Zabel D. Garabedian
30. Arousiag Terzian
31. Yester Garabedian
32. Azniv Bedrosian
33. Arousiag Eoksouzian
34. Azniv Deroian

We certify to the fact that 196 students have attended the co-ed schools in Perri, and to the authenticity of the signatures in the parents' section of this book.

Deacon	Pastor	Secretary
K. Holopigian	A. Nigoghosian	G. Poochigian

President A. Bouloudian
Vice-Prelate Fr. Boghos Garabedian

(These lists have been reproduced from Kevork Yerevanian's book *History of the Armenians of Charsanjak*)

16. SCHOOL AFTER THE DASHNAGS 1912-1915

Some time during my fourth year in school, a community organization, *Perritzeeneroon Meeatzial Meeootiun* (United Perri Society), began to sponsor our school, because Perri was the custodial, political and national center of Charsanjak. The organization was founded in America by emigrants from Perri.

They immediately initiated major changes. They remodeled the classrooms, raised teachers' salaries and brought in a variety of new books. We no longer had to pay tuition or pay for school supplies, books, and paper. They even paid for our drinking water and during the winter the boys did not have to bring in wood for the classroom fireplaces.

I liked the new desks the most. Two desk tops were connected together. The desktops had a slight slant, making writing a little easier. There was a special groove to hold our pen and pencil and an inkwell at the right upper corner. The desktop lifted, and there was a drawer for our books and papers. We had three to four rows of desks in the room—as more students enrolled, more desks were brought in. Each row had four sets of desks.

The top scholar no longer sat in the front seat. Instead, we were seated by height with the shorter students in front and the taller students at the back. However, because Kaspar and I were twins, we were again allowed to sit next to each other even though I was somewhat taller.

A large round clock that was set and wound by hand was hung up on a wall in the all-purpose room. Before that, most of the male teachers had pocket watches, which they pulled out to read from time to time. We never had a clock or pocket watch at home.

Within the year, starting from the middle grades, the boys no longer wore *zuhboons* to school. Like the older boys, we started to wear *shalvahrs* and shirts. My father made sure we were properly dressed. He bought our shirts from the *shoogah*.

Admired by all the students.
I used to give her rose water.

K. Yerevanian

My most admired teacher, Anahid Rahanian and son Armenag

From the very beginning our Christian names were changed to secular names by the new teachers. Kaspar became Massis and I became Papken. Although we and our parents accepted this practice, we used those names only in the classroom by the teachers and principal. We maintained our Christian names at home and outside of the classroom. Religion no longer was taught during school hours, but we still attended church services after school.

An attempt was made to integrate the girls and boys into the same classroom. However, there were many disruptions and in a short period of time, we were separated again.

The new principal's wife, Anna Rahanian, a Perritzee, was the new teacher for girls. She also taught math and English to boys in the fifth and sixth level. She not only was pretty, but everyone liked her very much. I really looked forward to her classes. Occasionally, I gathered beautiful flowers with nice fragrances from the hillsides and made perfume for her. I put the flowers in a glass and set it under the hot sun for two to three days. A fluid with a nice fragrance gathered in the bottom of the glass and when I had enough, I took it to her. She always graciously accepted the gift, and thanked me with a nice smile. That made me very happy.

When they changed the method of reprimand, we were not sure if we preferred the old or the new form of punishment. No longer were swats on the palm, knuckles, or elsewhere allowed. Instead, the culprit was sent to the girls' classroom. A tag was hung around his neck, on which his fault was written and he was made to stand in a corner. Depending on the severity of the offense, he might also have had to stand with one leg bent up behind him. If it were a serious offense, he would also have to raise his opposite arm up for a couple of hours. Most boys decided they preferred the old system of punishment. No boy wanted the humiliation of being sent to the girls' classroom.

Our new school principal, Soghomon Effendi, a Khughitzee (from the village of Khughee), was a tall, husky man. With pride and confidence he lectured the Dashnagtsagan (Armenian Revolutionary Federation) doctrine to us:

> *"It's enough crying with tears and anguish. God has given us intelligence, legs and arms to defend ourselves, our families and our nation."* Now, only Christian ethics were taught, because it was necessary to heighten our awareness to awaken the students' mind of their abusive subjugation. *"It is time to free ourselves from the Turkish bondage. For centuries, for six hundred years, we have cried. Who has heard us? Perhaps God's ears have deafened! How many oceans of tears has He brought upon us? With our churches filled to capacity, the worshipers pray with their hearts, hoping to be spared from prosecution by a blood-thirsty government that believes only to slaughter its citizens—an ill-tempered government that has absolutely no virtues!*
>
> *Armenians are isolated from the civilized world. We have no firearms. Unprotected, we have to rely solely on our Christian prayers, God, and our own physical strength. For centuries we have built churches and schools. We have given no thought to our defense and survival, even though we are surrounded by the beastly Turk!"*

In the mornings, we were no longer cautious. We sang patriotic songs loudly and boldly. The teachers showed pictures of our patriotic heroes and leaders.[*] We no longer said our morning prayers before being dismissed for classes. Instead, we stretched out our hands to have them checked for cleanliness on both sides, along with our nails that had to be short and clean.

---

[*]   Unwittingly they made many mistakes.

Although our Christian faith was not waning, we began to accept the ideal of rebelling against the tyrannical Turkish governmental laws. The teachers taught songs that reinforced those ideas. Guns were the only force we could use to protect ourselves and regain our freedom.

To this idea, I add, not only did we need guns; first we had to unite. Without national unity, we would remain in bondage forever. We were too few in numbers. One hand does not make a sound by itself in the air. Two hands compel people to listen. *Discord,* **the most unforgiving mistake made by my people, has caused 600 years of bondage and persecution. Being subjugated under tyrannical despots, our prayers were not enough, guns were not enough. We needed unity of purpose and action!**

Starting in 1915, the unbearable omen, the most unimaginable fears our forefathers bore took place for the last time.

On one seemingly uneventful day, we were warned that our classrooms would be searched for revolutionary material. All of our patriotic literature and songbooks were promptly buried under the school's wooden floors. We were all cautioned to be careful.

Kaspar and I secretly kept our books that we cherished so much. We decided to bury them under the floor of our stable where we felt we could be more protective of them. When it seemed safe again, we could easily retrieve them. To this day, I wonder if they are still where we put them.

LAST SONG

The following day we no longer sang our Armenian patriotic songs. Instead Baron Marsoub taught us a new song and told us not to forget it. Without frightening us, he gave us spiritual solace for what was looming in our midst. He didn't say another word or give an explanation. It was an allegorical tongue twister. It kept our minds focused on the words. Without hestitation nor losing the rapid ryhthm I have not forgothen a single line!

> *Kehnahtzehk dehsehk ov eh gehrehr aykeen*
> *Kehnahtzeenk dehsahnk aydzn eh gehrehr aykeen*
> *Aydzn oo aykeen mehz Pareegentahn, Tzez Paree Zahdeeg*
>
> *Kehnahtzehk dehsehk ov eh gehrehr aydzeen*
> *Kehnahtzeenk dehsahnk kayln eh gehrehr aydzeen*
> *Kayln oo aydzuh, aydzn oo aykeen*
> *Mehz Pareegentahn, Tzehz Paree Zahdeeg*

Kehnahtzehk dehsehk ov eh gehrehr kayleen
Kehnahtzeenk dehsahnk soorn eh gehrer kayleen
Soorn oo kayluh, kayln oo aydzuh, aydzn oo aykeen
Mehz Pareegentahn, Tzehz Paree Zahdeeg

Kehnahtzehk dehsehk ov eh gehrehr sooruh
Kehnahtzeenk dehsahnk zhankun eh gehrehr sooruh
Zhankn oo sooruh, soorn oo kayluh, kayln oo ayzduh, ayzdn oo aykeen
Mehz Pareegentahn, Tzehz Paree Zahdeeg

Kehnahtzehk dehsehk ov eh gehrehr zhankuh
Kehnahtzeenk dehsahnk yughn eh gehrehr zhankuh
Yughn oo zhankuh, zhankn oo sooruh, soorn oo kayluh, kayln
oo aydzuh, aydzn oo aykeen
Mehz Pareegentahn, Tzehz Paree Zahdeeg

Kehnahtzehk dehsehk ov eh gehrehr yughuh
Kehnahtzeenk dehsahnk mougn eh gehrehr yughuh
Mougn oo yughuh, yughn oo zhankuh, zhankn oo sooruh,
soorn oo kayluh, kayln oo aydzuh, aydzn oo aykeen
Mehz Pareegentahn, Tzehz Paree Zahdeeg

Kehnahtzehk dehsehk ov eh gehrer mouguh
Kehnahtzeenk dehsahnk gahdoon eh gehrehr mouguh,
gahdoon oo mouguh, moughn oo yughuh, yughn oo zhankuh,
zhankn oo sooruh, soorn oo kayluh, hayln oo aydzuh,
aydzn oo aykeen
Mehz Pareegentahn, Tzehz Paree Zahdeeg

Kehnahtzehk dehsehk ov eh dahrehr gahdoon
Kehnahtzeenk dehsahnk harsn eh dahrehr gahdoon
Harsn oo gahdoon, gahdoon oo mouguh, mougn oo yughuh
Yughuhn oo zhankuh, zhankn oo sooruh, soorn oo
Kayluh, kayln oo aydzuh, aydzn oo aykeen,
Mehz Pareegentahn, Tzehz Paree Zahdeeg

Kehnahtzehk dehsehk ov eh dahrehr harsuh
Kehnahtzeenk dehsahnk pehsan eh dahrehr harsuh
Pehsan oo harsuh, harsn oo gahdoon, gahdoon oo mouguh, mougn oo yughuh,
yughn oo zhankuh, zhankn oo sooruh, soorn oo kayluh, kayln oo
aydzuh, aydzn oo aykeen
Mehz Pareegentahn, Tzehz Paree Zahdeeg

* * *

Go see who has eaten the fields
We went and saw the goat had eaten the fields
The goat and the fields
Happy Thanksgiving for us, a Happy Easter for you

Go see who has eaten the goat
We went and saw the wolf had eaten the goat
The wolf and the goat, the goat and the fields
Happy Thanksgiving for us, a Happy Easter for you

Go see who has eaten the wolf
We went and saw the sword had eaten the wolf
The sword and the wolf, the wolf and the goat,
the goat and the fields
Happy Thanksgiving for us, a Happy Easter for you

Go see who has eaten the sword
We went and saw the rust had eaten the sword
The rust and the sword, the sword and the wolf, the wolf and the
goat, the goat and the fields
Happy Thanksgiving for us, a Happy Easter for you

Go see who has eaten the rust
We went and saw the oil had eaten the rust
The oil and the rust, the rust and the sword, the sword and the wolf,
the wolf and the goat, the goat and the fields
Happy Thanksgiving for us, a Happy Easter for you

Go see who has eaten the oil
We went and saw the mouse had eaten the oil
The mouse and the oil, the oil and the rust, the rust and the sword, the
sword and the wolf, the wolf and the goat, the goat and the fields
Happy Thanksgiving for us, a Happy Easter for you

Go see who has eaten the mouse
We went and saw the cat had eaten the mouse
The cat and the mouse, the mouse and the oil, the oil and the rust,
the rust and the sword, the sword and the wolf, the wolf and the goat, the
goat and the fields
Happy Thanksgiving for us, a Happy Easter for you

Go see who has taken the cat
We went and saw the bride had taken the cat
The bride and the cat, the cat and the mouse, the mouse and the oil,
the oil and the rust, the rust and the sword, the sword and the wolf, the
wolf and the goat, the goat and the fields
Happy Thanksgiving for us, a Happy Easter for you

Go see who has taken the bride
We went and saw the groom had taken the bride
The groom and the bride, the bride and the cat, the cat and the mouse,
the mouse and the oil, the oil and the rust, the rust and the sword, the
sword and the wolf, the wolf and the goat, the goat and the fields
Happy Thanksgiving for us, a Happy Easter for you

(Pareegehntan is considered the Armenian's Thanksgiving/Shrovetide. It
is a festive celebration the Sunday before Ash Wednesday where family
and friends gather. A time for confession and absolution...)

The next day, the school was closed. The male teachers and clergymen were taken to the government building for questioning. They were released to convince the people to comply with the orders that all guns and weapons be surrendered to government officials within five days.

The church became our meeting hall. Our two priests, one *vartabed* (celibate priest), six teachers and about ten to fifteen of our most informed community men formed a committee to address the issue.

Among the men there was a lawyer, Bulood Apkar. He was highly respected both by Armenians and Turkish officials. He spoke Turkish fluently and was a chairman in a Turkish government position. There was Mehshedee Avehdoe who was a well-known, courageous *fedayee* (freedom fighter). He was a tall, husky man who always dressed as a *fedayee* with his sword at his side and his dagger in his waistband. For several years he lived hidden in the hills and very cautiously attended the meetings. He was born in Ismiel in 1868 and his given name was Avedis Ghazanjian. He was godfather to Kaspar and me. I felt proud and important that he was my godfather even though I can't recall he ever came to our house in Perri.

One of the priests, Der Krikor Garabedian, was Hampartzoum Der Garabedian's uncle. The other priest, Der Boghos, was a tall handsome man with fair complexion. He was husky and had a large stomach. He was the only member who insisted the Armenians should turn in their guns and knives to the Turkish government. He felt that would appease the government and assure our safety.

As soon as the meetings were over, he and his assistant threw a gunnysack over their shoulders, held a cross high in front of them, and went around pressuring

Armenians to turn in whatever could be *taken* as a weapon. Those families who did not own a gun, like my dear wife's father in Malatya, felt if they secretly bought a gun or knife and turned it in, the Turks would be appeased, and they felt they would be spared. That proved to be a terribly erroneous assumption.

Within days, Der Boghos became more concerned about the welfare of his family. As the situation worsened for the Armenians, he became a *mullah* (Islamic religious figure). He thought the act might insure his safety, along with that of his family. His reactions reminded me of the following anecdote:

> *In a thick forest the trees noticed a man approaching them with an ax. Suspecting he was coming to chop them down, they quickly informed each other of the pending danger. One tree quickly exclaimed to the other trees. "The man is not at fault. The handle on his ax is one of us..."* If there is a turncoat amongst us, the enemy will be victorious.

Eventually, his conversion to Islam did not help him because he was also friendly with the Kurds. The Turks questioned his loyalties when the Kurds from the Derseem rose up against the Turks. He, too, was slaughtered.

On the other hand, Der Krikor was thin, short and very intelligent. He insisted that we not turn in our guns and knives. He felt that, if the situation worsened, we would need everything we had for our self-defense. *Fedayee* Avehdoe, all the teachers and community members felt strongly that we should not turn in our guns and knives. It was their opinion that, whether or not we turned in our guns, the Turks had already planned our demise.

Several boys my age were chosen to serve as errand boys. It was our duty to deliver food to the men who spent the entire day and evenings in the church meetings. We also delivered messages to those who needed to be kept informed and could not attend the meetings. I was so proud and happy that my father chose me for that very important job, even though I had not yet turned fourteen. The meetings went on for five days and nights. I went every day and listened carefully to the debates. I had to listen attentively, because I had to sit at the back of the church. Our church was huge and had the capacity to hold the total population of Perri. There were two large metal doors, one for the men's entrance and another for the women's entrance. Thus I was quite a distance from the men who were up front near the altar. The other boys and I got an easy earful only when their voices rose with emotion.

When I came home each night, my father would ask, "What did this or that priest say? What did the teachers say? What did *Fedayee* Avehdoe say?" After I answered all of his questions, thoughtfully and very perturbed he would always repeat, "The Turks are going to eat our heads! Our leaders are not united with their decisions!"

K. Yerevanian

Fedayee Avedis Ghazanjian "Mehshedee Avedoe"
(Ismiel, 1868-1915)

1915 ԹՒ
ՊԱՐՈՆ ՆԵԿՈՂՈՍ
ԱՍԱՑՈՐ
ՄԵՐ ԴՊՐ
ՑԱՓԻ ԵՐՐ
ԿԱՐԴՒ Ն
ԿՐԱԿ ՄԱՏԱ
ՑՈՒԱԾ
ՍԻՐ ԵՐԵՒ

K. Yerevanian

*In 1915 the Turks closed our school. This was the first murder I wit-
nessed. I cried when I saw his crushed head in a pool of blood.
Remembering this crushes my soul".*

Reverend Assador Neegoghosian and his wife.

Before the meeting came to a close, our *vartabed* had vanished. It was said he
snuck away and headed towards Kharpert to alert the people as to what was
happening in Perri. We never saw or heard from him again.

Right after our last meeting adjourned, the school bells rang and all of the older
boys rushed over to the church. We were all horrified to learn what had just been
discovered at the Protestant church. Reverend Assador Neegoghosian's body was
found lying in a pool of blood, his skull crushed open. Another neighbor who had
been brutally attacked but purposefully left alive was found next to him. He was
left as a warning to the rest of us of what was yet to come. The Reverend was the
first of many Armenians I would subsequently witness who had been brutally
victimized by the Turkish wrath. After that day we never saw any of our male
teachers, principal, committee members, or Mehshedee Avehdoe.

All of the new changes had been deeply disturbing to my father. He knew we
were not ready to provoke the Turks, because we were not organized nor prepared.
He constantly repeated, "If we are not careful, they will eat our heads!" While
working, he invariably sang to himself. By the tone of his voice, the melancholy
droning, we sensed his sorrow and relentless concerns. His mournful facial
expression also reflected his fears. He had never gotten over the sudden loss of his
wife, coupled with that of his father. It troubled him also that he had little choice
in sending his two eldest sons to America. Now the ominous signs consumed and

haunted him. I can still feel the pain in his voice as he softly sang and intensely pounded down on his *gaghabar*, arranging the designs on the *guhdavs*:

> *"Lyre resonate your tunes for the whole world to hear,*
> *about the persecuted Armenians, the mortally wounded.*
> *Groan as you cry, with so much affliction, so much evil.*
> *With so much blood, we have shed so many tears.*
> *If our descendants should forget this much grief,*
> *let the whole world dishonor the Armenians..."*

If, at that precise moment the Armenians had all listened, joined with the Kurds and became a united front, I feel we would have achieved something much better than Paradise. We would not have lost our land, our *Yergeer* (homeland). So many lives would have been spared. We would not have had a million and half innocent martyrs! The rest of us would not have been scattered all over the world.

For hundreds of years Armenians had lived with the Turks who had always subjugated, brutalized and plundered them. They should have realized that in order to survive, their only chance was to present a united front against the Turks. They should have planned how they were going to protect themselves against the Turkish onslaught—**we were completely defenseless!**

During my escape and fight for survival, I, myself, came close to the brush of death on several occasions. My survival must have been a miracle, an act of God! But why weren't all of the other martyrs saved by the same means? I have never stopped questioning this dilemma—I have never received a satisfactory answer.

For six hundred years we were under Turkish subjugation and on the onset of the year 1915, the unbearable atrocities began. The Turks not only ate our heads; they devoured our arms and legs. They are still hungry after eighty-eight years. They still want more! God, where are You?

Unfortunately, we Armenians have also remained the same. We seemingly cannot unite. Until now, at the age of one hundred years, I cannot accept the position that some of our clergy and politicians follow as they continue to divide our masses into ineffective splinter groups. May they all stand on their heads!

PART 2

A Hair's Breadth From Death

The Armenian Genocide
1915–1923

"Mazee Chap, Mahee Mode"

17. EARLY SPRING OF 1915

FATHER GOES IN HIDING

These alarming events were taking place at the beginning of spring in 1915, during the time of the year when we customarily cultivated the vineyards after the winter rains and snow had softened the soil.

Early one morning my father awakened me. He wanted me to go along with him to help him dig around the roots of the vines and clear away some rocks. Since our vineyard covered more than three acres, he knew it would take at least two days. I remember vividly on the first day when he enthusiastically buried the new sprigs with the anticipation they would propagate later that spring. I can still hear his very words. With faith and expectation, he exclaimed, "Not this year, but in two years we will have a better and bigger crop of grapes from these vines!" *He was so sure we would benefit from our hard labor we put in on that day.*

There was still an area towards the road that was very rocky. On the second day we worked very hard clearing away those rocks and planted more sprigs. By the day's end it was almost dark and with our task completed we started to walk back home.

When we were halfway home, we encountered a frightened Armenian from Perri running towards a nearby Kurdish village. He stopped only long enough to warn my father. Breathlessly he advised, *"Mardiros Agha, don't go to Perri! The Turks have beaten all of the teachers to death and have exposed their bodies to warn the rest of us. They are going to kill all of us! They are looking for guns. Don't go back—they will kill you too!"*

That alarming news perturbed my father. He was already overwhelmed with his personal problems and weariness. Now this! We were both very tired and hungry. However, without wasting any more time, he firmly clasped my upper arm and instructed me, "My son, go straight home and wait a couple of days until you hear from me!" With those final words, he immediately fled.

With what anguish, with which God? Imagine what was going on through my father's mind. Did he feel God had no mercy? He was such a reverent believer! What good did our daily prayers, *"Havadov Khostovaneem,"* do for us? Every single night we had all stood together around the fireplace with our heads bowed. Each one of us recited a particular verse, imploring God to help us. **What good did that do?**

Without an embrace, my father left me alone and fearful. Together with the man who had warned him, he headed towards Zehree, a Kurdish village. As he disappeared from sight, I ran home as fast as possible to alert the rest of my family about what had happened.

We had no way of knowing that the previous night was to be the last time we would hear my father ask God for compassion and protection for his family. That was the last night he slept in the sanctity of his house with all of us who loved him so much.

None of us had any inkling of what was in store for us and for our nation. I think God has turned his face away from the Armenians who continue to this day to undermine each other for their own personal aspirations.

On that very same day Armenian men had been rounded up. News was spreading that all our influential men were being imprisoned. *All of the Armenian shops were confiscated and converted into makeshift jails.* In a few days, all those jails were filled to capacity. Some men had already been taken into valleys, killed and their bodies dumped into the creeks and ravines. Yet, at the same time, a few men were being released from jail with the pretense that good men would be spared. Word was spreading that the Turks were torturing and killing members of the *Dashnag* Revolutionary Party. In the meantime *moonehdeeks* (town criers) were also shouting in the streets that it was safe for Armenians sequestered in their homes and hiding places to come out.

After two tense and acutely worrisome days, we finally received a letter from my father. It was delivered by his *keervah,* a good Kurdish friend. The letter said, "Load as many *guhdavs* as you can on the donkey. Hampartzoum and Kaspar, come to me. The *keervah* is very trustworthy."

My stepmother immediately sought advice from Varteeg Bahgee, our neighbor. She was older and more informed about what was transpiring. She confirmed the rumor that all of the good men could feel safe and should come out from hiding. Only the *Dashnags* were being rounded up.

Both my stepmother and Varteeg Bahgee agreed that my father was an innocent and good man. It was well known he spent all of his time working to provide for his family and was never involved with *Dashnag* activities. He strongly believed God would protect us as long as we lived a true Christian life.

My stepmother had Kaspar quickly write a reply to my father that we all wanted him to come home, that he shouldn't be afraid because he was a good man and it would be safe for him. The *keervah* took the letter and returned without Kaspar and me, or the *guhdavs.* We waited with great anticipation for our father to come home. We were still too young and too naive to realize what was going on.

WHIMPERING CRIES

Two days later we recognized a knock at the door as that of my father wrapping with his staff. He always carried his staff when he went away from the house, a means of protection from attacking wild dogs or people. With tears and cries we all rushed to greet him. As he entered the house, he went immediately towards the *toeneer doon* without saying a word.

However, before he even had time to take off his *meeltahn* (coat), a *gendarme* (Turkish policeman) knocked loudly on the door. He told my father the government wanted him. He took my father away without allowing him to rest, say anything to us, or have a bite to eat. We were very concerned whether or not he had eaten while in hiding, because he already looked thinner. The gendarmes were on surveillance for those Armenians who were returning home from hiding places in outlining villages...another hoax!

Again, recalling those days of anguish makes me feel we have a God who likes to deceive. I remember reading the script above the altar in our Holy Cross Church in Los Angeles, "Ask and I shall give—knock and I shall open." Lies, lies, lies, again more lies!

My father was a true and faithful believer. He truly believed what he constantly repeated to himself, "Without the will of God, the leaves on the trees do not move." At that very moment we all had such faith. We could not understand what was happening or why. **We feared God and did nothing without prayer.** We were all God-fearing and law-abiding citizens. Yet they took my father to jail. What was his crime? What had this innocent man done? I believe that God turned his face away from those Armenians who perpetuate disunity, those who only think about their own personal gain. What can we expect to transpire? Just ask me. *Armenian offspring, children of grief...*

For the next two days, Kaspar went out to search for our father. We hadn't heard a word of his whereabouts nor what they might have done to him. We didn't know if he was dead or alive. We had to be very cautious about going out because we too might have been caught; we also didn't have much hope of getting any helpful news. It was especially dangerous for me to go out because I was much larger and older looking than Kaspar.

By the third day, however, I finally decided to *take* the risk and join Kaspar in his pursuits to find my father. Together we went to the center of town. We were stunned to discover all the men were behind the locked doors of the makeshift jails. There were more than one hundred fifty shops, all were converted—each was filled to capacity. The men were incessantly beaten with thick wooden boards.

Their piercing cries of pain and despair filtered into the streets. They were being beaten almost to death.

As we came nearer to the blacksmith shop, I heard a painful, unforgettable plea. *"Please, for the love of your God, please don't beat me any more!"* With a pang of dismay I realized it was my father crying out. We quickly approached the door of the building, and I told the guard on duty, *"Chitjeeyeen Oghleen yehm."* ("I am Chitjian's son.") He went in and brought my father to the door, but did not open it. We couldn't see each other. What a pitiful sight! What a wrenching memory! After all these years, remembering that moment is agonizing and difficult to forget. The person who prayed the *Havadov Khostovaneem* daily was my father. The person who planted new grapevines for the coming year was my father. **Now the person crying and whimpering in jail was my father!**

From the other side of the closed door, my father painfully whimpered to us, *"Please bring me a little bit of brandy and take all of the hundred pieces of guhdavs (muslin) to Gooree Oso's house."*

Leaving Kaspar with my father, I ran home as fast as my feet would allow me to bring my father his brandy. When I was halfway there, I came across a sight that to this day causes my body to tremble! I had never seen nor imagined anything so vicious. How could such an act be committed by another human being with a soul? It was, and still is, impossible for me to fathom. Right on my path was the running channel whose source of water was the Gahmarr Fountain. In the middle of the channel was a young man. He was *still alive but half-crazed.* From his cries, it was obvious he was in excruciating pain. The skin on his back had been sliced from his shoulders to his waist and was still hanging from his back. He was purposefully placed so the swift running water splashed against his wounds and thereby intensified his pain and suffering. He was crying out, "If you have a gun, turn it in to the government, so they won't do the same to you!"

I don't remember how, but I continued to run home as fast as I could. My heart was pounding hard. My mind was trying to make sense of my father's imprisonment, his pitiful cries for mercy. I couldn't comprehend what was happening, or why. Why?

I ran into the house, filled a flask with my father's brandy, wrapped something for him to eat, and I ran back as fast as I could. All the way back my mind was still trying to make sense of what was happening. At the same time I was consumed with fear. What was going to happen to us, to my father? Within minutes I was back at the jail with the brandy and food, but to my disappointment, my father did not touch it, even though he was getting weaker.

Before we had time to assess what harm my father was confronting the guard needled us with his staff to leave. We left with great reluctance but only after reassuring my father that we would return the next day. We felt relieved he was still alive, and that gave us hope. However, we were still very frightened and perplexed.

When Kaspar and I returned home, we quickly figured out how we would fulfill our father's orders. Gooree Oso and his wife lived two houses away. My father always used his donkey and considered him to be a good friend, therefore he must have had a good reason for this decision. So once it got dark we quietly carried the *guhdavs* up to the rooftop. Cautiously and quietly we carried them over to Gooree Oso's rooftop and dropped the *guhdavs* one by one into his *torrtah* (courtyard). Since there were over one hundred pieces, it took us two nights to complete the job. Once the last piece was dropped, we were relieved and grateful we had not been caught. At the same time, we were becoming increasingly aware that we were in far greater danger than we had originally imagined.

As always, no one questioned my father's orders. Because we were barely fourteen we did not discuss such matters and feelings with our stepmother, aunt or sisters. I do not know if they too were feeling our dread. Were we all in some form of denial? Why did my father want the *guhdavs* removed from our house? Why? Not knowing the answer intensified our fears.

WAITING FOR FATHER'S RETURN

The next day, while Kaspar and I were getting ready to take brandy and food to my father, we suddenly heard the clanging sound from the back wall. Our neighbor, Varteeg Bahgee, was alerting us that there was a problem. We all ran to the back corner of the house and leaned toward the hole in the wall. As we anxiously listened, we learned early that morning the Turks were yelling from the minaret that they were going to search our whole area to round up the older Armenian boys.

Kaspar and I were panic stricken. Our minds and eyes had been traumatized by the barbaric means the Armenians were being tortured, and we had to figure out a way not to be caught.

Suddenly I remembered it was generally known Varteeg Bahgee did not have boys in her house. Without wasting a moment, Kaspar and I ran into her stable. We each quickly grabbed a large woven basket used for hauling dung or straw, and covered ourselves. We held our breath and prayed that we would not get caught. Suddenly we heard two policemen come in. As they searched around, we heard them say, *"No one is here!"* After they left, we remained covered a little while longer until we felt safe enough to come out and return to our house.

We were still trembling with fear when we returned home. We knew that we had a lucky break. Now, more than ever, we wished our father would come home.

He would know what was going on and would be able to tell us what to do. *For the first time Kaspar and I had experienced the terror of insecurity and the overwhelming fear of being caught.* That terrifying incident alerted us that now we had to be extremely careful when we left the house. We no longer felt safe. *Each day we heard about someone's demise, torture or death.*

It was during that time when Varteeg Bahgee's daughter-in-law was fatally brutalized. She had been left in the care of her mother-in-law after her husband fled to America. She was a very young and beautiful girl who was no more than fifteen or sixteen years old and several months pregnant. Taking advantage of the lawless and vulnerable climate towards Armenians, a Turkish thug had eyed her and forcibly took her to his house.

Soon after, another Turk who had also seen her had the same intentions. Unable to agree who should be the victor, they jointly agreed to amuse themselves by mutilating her. They ripped the unborn baby from her womb. They pierced a stick through the fragile baby's body and stuck it next to the mother's lifeless body that had been strewn in front of the Gol Fountain to compel all the passers by to witness and at the same time, to serve as a special warning for those Armenians who had not turned in guns.

Where was God at that time? Why was this happening? What was happening to us? When was my father coming home?

A few days later, just before noon, once again we heard my father's familiar knock on the door. As we rushed to open the door, he did not let us touch him. We were all distraught. *His work coat was splattered with dry blood, his face was gaunt, and his eyes were consumed with despair.* His posture conveyed utter exhaustion. He was barely able to stand. I will never forget what was to be my last impression of my father. He projected the excruciating pain from the torture he endured for more than a week, as well as the anguish of what was happening to his life, family, and homeland—and the fear of what was yet to come. I could not bear or comprehend what they had done to that husky, handsome man with the beautiful auburn hair and fair complexion. He had lost all semblance of himself. Why did that happen to an innocent, good, God fearing Christian? That was my father! Why? Why?

In front of me was a thin, gaunt, haggard looking man, *an image of my father that would haunt me the rest of my life.* Even though I was barely fourteen, I was old enough to feel the pain of what had happened and also old enough to fear what was yet to ensue!

That pain was eternal—it could never leave my soul. I am now 102 years old and yet I still relive that very moment every night in my nightmares. It is reflected in all my thoughts during the day. How could anyone forget that image? Could you?

Coupled with what the barbaric Ottoman government inflicted upon us, I always wonder if the Armenians who sought to vindicate the Armenian Cause realized the dire consequences of their actions. Did they know how their decisions would affect their people?

It has always been common knowledge among the Armenians that their lives were in a precarious situation because they were a subjugated people. For centuries they had learned to be extremely discreet about how to endure and survive their plight and at the same time, when the "circumstances allowed," they had to be determined to fight for their freedom. **That would only be possible, however, with a united front, with a united commitment and leadership.**

At age fourteen, I couldn't understand what was happening. What was different this time? What was compelling this barbaric government to commit such heinous atrocities? *What consequences were we to endure if the Armenian decision-makers couldn't agree to an effective united course of action? If they continued to confront, betray, and attack each other, did we have a chance to protect ourselves? Could the hundreds of thousands of lives been spared?*

My father's words that have been most memorable to me were, **"They are going to eat our heads if we do not unite with our actions!"** Those were the same words my deceased, beloved wife, Ovsanna, remembered hearing from her father while they lived in Malatya. She was only six years old in 1915. Her father also feared the same consequences if those words were not heeded. *Even though our homeland was occupied, I know thousands of Armenian lives would have been saved and spared from the heinous atrocities if we had retaliated with a united front.*

For six years I grew into my young manhood under those brutal conditions while enduring horrific experiences. I was always aware innocent Armenians were sporadically rounded up to be tortured first and then killed. Even in self-defense the death of one Turk caused the demise of two hundred or more innocent Armenians at one time. Some of those deaths were the consequence of an inept decision made by Armenians. Were those Armenians aware of what was happening in the interior villages and cities?

Many times, I have personally experienced such precarious situations. It was only with the grace of God that I escaped and survived. I have always wondered why I survived and so many did not. Again I remember some of my father's words. "Only with the will of God, do the leaves of trees move." Did I escape only to relate my experiences as a living witness?

If I survived only to witness all that happened, then I claim that the most bitter, *infamous day of 1915* for me was the moment my father returned home from jail and revealed his plan to the family.

A FOREBODING DECISION

Without losing time, without catching his breath, my father quietly and in a seemingly emotionless tone was informing us of his immediate plans. The feeling of urgency was confusing, along with everything else he was telling us.

He had just entered the house after a week or so of imprisonment, abuse, torture and who knows what else. In a voice that was barely audible or plausible, he was now talking about going away again. Everything was going so fast! He did not even give us a chance to embrace him, or to give him his favorite brandy. He did not take a minute to rest. His body, his posture and his face all reflected how exhausted, depressed and tortured he was.

What was the *urgency of leaving?* Where were we going? Why could we not first comfort him? For days we had missed him so much. We were anxiously waiting for the day when he would return home when once again we would all be together. During this crisis, he would be able to make sense of what was happening and tell us what we should do to protect ourselves. That moment flew by so quickly and he still had not said a word to us. It was hard for me to apprehend and absorb what he intended for us to do.

I only clearly understood that his sister, Aghavni, was to marry Ago-Ebo's son, Levon, whose Turkish name was Mahmed. Ago-Ebo was our neighbor for many years. He was an Armenian who had converted to save his life during the 1895 massacres. His Armenian name was Hagop; his Turkish name was Ebraham. He was now called Ago-Ebo and was considered to be both an Armenian and a Turk, *teh Hye, teh Turk.* Unfortunately, under these conditions, many Armenians converted to save their lives. *Only God knows which decision was really beneficial.* Ago-Ebo was a *chorrehbahn;* he made a living by using a donkey to haul goods from one area to another. He also was related to Buhlood Apkar, a lawyer, and therefore usually better informed than most of the villagers about the affairs in our community. Without fail, he was very protective of Armenians and must have had knowledge about my father's fate.

I think he must have advised my father on what to do, probably on his way home from jail. He must have recommended that Aghavni marry his son and remain in Perri so her life would be spared. He must have also recommended that my father *relinquish his four sons at the Turkish school* with the hope their lives would also be spared, just as his had been spared years ago during the 1894–1895 massacres.

Apparently my father respected and decided to abide by Ago-Ebo's advice. **Did he have another choice?** How else could he have saved the lives of his sons? Aghavni did marry Levon and remained in Perri to raise her own family. She accepted this fate and went by the name of Hadiga.

Those were the last moments I had with my father and family—my father; stepmother; Aunt Aghavni; Aunt Marinos, who had returned from Medzgerd to

Deportation, "aksor"

be safer with her brother; Zaruhy, who had returned much earlier because my father was trying to find a trustworthy person to accompany her to America so she could join her husband; my younger sisters, Sultahn and Yeranuhi; and my three brothers, Kaspar, Kerop and Nishan. We all embraced with a foreboding fear... would that be the last time we would ever be together again! There were no tears, nor wails. **Where was God, our ungodly God!**

At some later time, I learned that most of the villagers were mercilessly driven a distance away from Perri to the village of Khazahn Dahrah and to the Gahtzaheen Tsor, a huge gorge in the valley. As innocent souls from infants to the very elderly drew their last breath, their mutilated bodies—some alive, some near death—were dumped into the hollow of the earth. Each victim in succession poured a shovel of God's earth onto his predecessor. The only ones to survive were the young, beautiful girls, who were set aside to be used for the Turks' wanton pleasures. One of these unfortunate girls was my sister, Zaruhy—what happened to the eight hundred Armenian families of Perri?

18. TURKISH SCHOOL

FATHER VANISHED FROM SIGHT

Without hesitating a moment my father took his four sons and walked towards the small *magtab* (Turkish school), leaving the women behind in the house. As we walked, my father did not utter a word. He was completely speechless. I thought he was mute from the cruel beatings and torture he suffered in jail.

No one uttered a word—not a sound was made. We all walked with fear and dismay in our hearts, not knowing what was going to happen to us or what was going to happen to the rest of our family—my sisters, my aunts, and stepmother. *Why* were we separating? In times of crisis the family should stay together. Instead *we* were splitting up and going in different directions. I did not want to part from my father. Why was he taking us to *that* school? I was so afraid. Custom prevailed, then as always. We were taught not to question my father's command. We obediently obliged.

My father walked in front, clasping tightly onto Kaspar's hand. It was in our later years when I found out from Kaspar that my father had spoken as we were walking. My father's last words were that the Turks were going to send him and the women to America to unite with our brothers. At that point Kaspar asked why the boys were going to the Turkish school and not to America with the family. His final reply was, "America for us is the river." Kaspar confessed that he didn't understand his father's last response, and at that point he was more confused than ever. Unfortunately, we were to find out the true meaning of that statement when we heard it repeated so many times in the subsequent months.

I was following from behind, clasping tightly onto the hands of my two younger brothers. Kerop, who was nine, was on one side, and Nishan, who was barely six on the other side trotting alongside us, trying to keep up by walking as fast as his little feet could bear. Their projected fright and bewilderment ran a chill up and down my spine. They too were in shock, much like myself. I still cannot believe how obediently they walked along my side without a cry, without a word. In their innocent minds, had they perceived something ominous was taking place? What a heartbreaking moment! Akh, akh...

We were all too young to fully comprehend what was transpiring. Splitting up the family when all of the Armenians in Perri were picked up, imprisoned and tortured without cause or explanation was more than we could comprehend or bear.

We continued to walk silently. My father's tortured posture showed no emotion or tears. Had his blood turned into *stone?* I could tell from his eyes he was *smoldering* from within. His mind and soul were completely devastated. I am sure he didn't know what to tell us. He feared if he said anything unknowingly it might jeopardize what we might later say or do, and thereby be harmful for us. He was a devout believer in God. He did what he thought was best and left us in the hands of God.

No one knew at that point what was instigating the Turkish wrath. What were their intentions? We were already a subjugated people on our own homeland. This land had been our land. *Our roots were etched throughout the landscape and always will be...*

With their crazed and warped mentality, with no provocation, a Turkish sultan or a Young Turk was capable of performing any form of atrocity. With that understanding, my father did not want to compromise our situation. I am sure that even he had not envisioned the complete annihilation of the Armenians. The word *genocide* was coined in 1945 by Raphael Lempkin to describe the organized campaign to eliminate the Armenians on their own homelands.

THAT DREADFUL BUILDING

As we came to the entrance of the Turkish school we were all dreading and fearful of what was going to happen next! *My father reluctantly let go of our silently crying souls.* He quickly turned around and walked away, leaving us standing alone in the doorway. There were no good byes, nor were there any tears. We were too afraid, so afraid that even our emotions had turned into stone.

We couldn't move or say a word. We were in shock. We just stood there, watching our father fading further and further away from us. He never looked back. We wanted to run to him to catch up with him, but we were nailed to the ground, shaking with fear. Suddenly, we couldn't see him any more. **I never saw my father again.** My beloved father had *vanished. . .*

May whoever says the Turks are a civil people be cursed with the *same* fate that the Turks bestowed upon the Armenians! For eighty-eight years, I have not forgotten that most tragic moment. If I were to live another eighty-eight years, I still could not forget the devastation of "that" moment!

Armenians who escaped the genocide with relative ease, without much pain, torture or loss of family, and may speak kindly of their *Effendi* (sir) or *Khanum* (madam) do not comprehend how much blood and how many lives the Turks sucked from the Armenians.

A nation that survives without relying on its own hard effort must be sly—like Turkey. *It plays a tune on two strings.* It smiles on Russia in the East and on the United States in the West. It laughs and enjoys the benefits from both. Even God continues to help and support them. To this day Turkey has not changed!

Now what can you say? God always seems to support the deeds of the bad, wicked and guilty. So now to whom could we turn? No one. There is no country to help us. *There is no other way but for all Armenians to unite.* Hand in hand we can survive.

Perhaps one day our God will awaken to help us, just as He has done for the Jews. He not only gave them an independent state but also exceptional strength to further their cause. He will continue to give them more because they are *politically united.* Politically they are one. When will the Armenians wake up? When will the Armenians learn? Divided they will never succeed. *Akh, akh* (an expression of sorrow) *that is how we were brutally separated from our beloved father and family— that pain will simmer in my heart eternally.*

Without hesitation, I accepted the responsibility to be in charge. Somehow I felt I should know what my father expected of me—to take charge, to assess what had to be done to protect my brothers, to protect us from harm. The pain and confusion melted together in my gut. I *missed* him already. I *needed* his guidance, his reassurance—the guidance I always had relied on when I was unable to handle a problem.

Being as protective as I could be, I led my brothers into that dreadful building next to the minaret. The four of us stuck closely together, watching and wondering what was going to happen to us—what were they going to do to us? There were already fifteen to twenty other Armenian boys, ages four to sixteen sitting on the floor, some in small clusters, and some alone. A few were lying down on the bare floor because they were sick, while some were crying. We quickly sat down on the floor, huddled closely together to ensure some comfort. Then we waited like the others while looking at each other and our surroundings. The essence of fright and despair permeated throughout the cold, hostile room.

Those who had to go to the bathroom were escorted outside. There were no such facilities. We just went behind the bushes.

Hours later they brought us *bulghur pilaf* that was confiscated from a pillaged Armenian home. However, who knows how old it was? The pot on the floor was swarming with worms. Not one boy touched it. We were all so terrified—that no one felt their hunger. Without mats or blankets, one by one we all fell asleep on the floor, ignoring the early spring cold.

We stayed in that room for two to three days. Armenian boys from four to sixteen were continuously brought in from all of the nearby villages. The group soon grew to more than two hundred... none of them were my classmates. The room was small, and we were all packed in there together. Each day every boy was given only a small piece of bread once in the morning and once in the evening. One of the larger Armenian boys was escorted to the Gahmarr Fountain, and brought back a large jug of water for us to drink.

After the third day we were all transferred to the nearby *zhoghovahran* (Armenian Protestant church hall) which was much more spacious and next to one of my classmate, Sam Ouraghian's large house. He was fortunate—he was not in our group. One of his uncles had converted some years earlier to save his skin. He and his mother went to live with him. His father had fled to America to avoid the Turkish draft. Years later I met his whole family once again in Los Angeles, California. Ironically, they lived across the street from my brother, Mihran, on Sixth Street and Indiana.

As the number of boys in the church rapidly increased, we still did not know why we were there or what was yet to come. Although we were bewildered and confused, the Turks did not yet harm us. It was very hard for the younger boys who were crying out searching for their mothers and fathers. Their cries intensified our own fears.

AN ATTEMPT TO CONVERT

Within a few days we slowly realized what their intentions were for us. They began a very deliberate plan to convert us. We were to become Turkified. *The very first thing they did was to change our Armenian names into Turkish names.* My name was changed to Rooshdee, Kaspar became Rahsheed, Kerop became Hamdee, and Nishan became Nahyeem.

Next they demanded we no longer speak in Armenian. They insisted we speak only in Turkish. Although we were taught Turkish as a second language in school, we never spoke it. Under those dire conditions, I don't remember how quickly we learned to speak Turkish. What surprised me more was how quickly and unconsciously we completely forgot how to speak Armenian, our beloved mother tongue. That was very traumatic for me during the next six years. It was another major loss, almost as significant as losing a family member.

Again that became another harsh demand on the very young. In their state of confusion, still yearning and searching for their devoted and beloved parents, they couldn't meet the unrealistic demands. Their cries, sometimes in a loud shrill, and sometimes in a frightened whimper, still pierce my soul, especially when I recall the harsh slap they received against their frail little faces as they cried for *"Mairig"* *(Mama)* or *"Hairig"* *(Papa)*. The older boys tried to hush their cries and instructed them to say *anna* and *bah-bah,* the Turkish equivalent for mama and papa.

Next they started to teach us their Turkish history. We were taught to say in Turkish:

> *Hurrieyet, autehlet, musehfet——yahshawsoon meeleht.*
> *Osmahnlee yees kardahshleek deer, kahnahneemeese azerlee.*
> *Beer vahtahnah johnlahrr koorban.*
> *Osmahnlee yees kardahshleek deer.*

> *Freedom, Liberty, Fraternity—long live the people.*
> *We are Ottoman, we are brothers, our customs are ancient.*
> *We must devote our lives as a gift towards our country.*
> *We are Ottoman, we are brothers.*

Not only did we memorize those lines, but we also had to repeat them several times a day.

The last thing they tried to change was our faith in Christianity. We had to memorize and recite in Turkish,

> *Leh eellalah, hemdeellah, hawk dour Mehmed rahzoul ohllah.* [*]
> *Mohamed is a saint and his teachings are correct.*

They changed our names, our language; they took our lands and homes. No matter how hard they tried, they did not succeed in changing our faith. What we kept and felt in our minds, hearts and souls was ours to keep. No one was able to alter what I believed, no matter what they made me say or do, no matter what terrifying experiences I yet had to encounter.

Trying to keep up with all the new demands and changes while *maintaining* my own identity was very hard on me. I know the only reason I survived or was spared was because I never lost my faith in the Grace of God. I never lost sight of my father's words, "The leaves of the trees do not move without the will of God." That kept me alive!

For more than two weeks, early in the morning and again in the evening, we were forced to recite their Moslem prayers. One day a *mullah* (religious figure) would come and the next day a *hoja* (teacher) would come to instruct us. At the end of each week, we were tested. Again the younger boys had a difficult time learning all the strange new words. I don't think Kerop or Nishan were ever able to recite the Turkish prayer.

During these sessions I reflected back to when I was about seven to eight years old and used to sing in our church choir. Every Sunday I was dressed in a fancy

[*] From what I remember, this is what they tried to teach us.

white robe which always made me feel very special. I felt like a saint—some of the happiest moments in my childhood. I can still hear our voices…

Vocheench eh Beedoh, Vahsen pahneet
aytoreek, Dahm kes badasghaneetz…
(a prayer in classical Armenian)

ARMENIAN HOMES PILLAGED

By the end of the second week, the older and larger Armenian boys were forced to pillage all of the abandoned Armenian homes during the day. Those houses were bolted shut and tagged with a government seal indicating that the occupants had been taken away by an order from the Turkish government. The properties and all of the contents both within the houses and on the exterior now belonged to them.

In many cases, by the time we entered the houses, Turkish or Kurdish vultures had already ransacked them. It was very painful for us to disturb all the treasured possessions the Armenians had laboriously acquired either by their own personal hard labor or purchased with their hard-earned money. That included all of the beautiful needlework that took hours to create, the tools and equipment used for the family trade, all of the preserved foods from the breads, grains, dried fruits and vegetables, processed meats and honey to the bedding—just to name a few.

We had to shut down our conscience as we hauled everything away from the wealthy Armenian homes. We filled our large *Loosavorchagan* (the Armenian Apostolic) Church from floor to ceiling. With sorrow and remorse, I wondered if those hallowed walls understood what was transpiring as we trampled on the floors, hauling in the bounty from their slaughtered congregation? I had to block out the cherished feelings and memories of sanctity and protection those walls had given me just a few weeks earlier. Were they saddened and confused as I? The sanctuary reflected our pain of abandonment—it understood and forgave us. Once the church was completely filled, we filled Sam Ouraghian's house to its capacity with Armenian possessions. Turkish officials and workers, who escorted and ordered us around, confiscated whatever they wanted and left the rest to be sold for the government.

Even I was lucky a few times pillaging the Armenia homes. I found a few coins, three *khooroosh* (coins) in all, that was worth about thirty cents. I am sure the owners would have preferred them to be of some help to a fellow Armenian than to the barbaric Turks. I left those coins with my Aunt Aghavni for safekeeping. Her house was in the vicinity where we were plundering. One day when I thought no one was following me, I ducked in to see her. Neither one of us had news of what had happened to the rest of our family. I did not dare stay long and quickly left. We were both still in a bewildered state. Neither one of us knew what was happening or why.

Each evening after a long hard day, I was devastated, not so much by the physical beating my body endured hauling the heavy loads on my back, nor the walk back and forth to the church from the houses that were quite a distance away, but by the *mental* anguish—that was most devastating! For me, disturbing someone's home was tantamount to lynching them. That act was against all the scruples my father and grandfather had taught me. Emotionally I had a very difficult time reconciling with that pain. In addition to *that* feeling, I was equally very concerned about Kerop and Nishan's welfare. Left alone, they were too young to fend for themselves. Neither Kaspar nor I was there for reassurance—Kaspar also was engaged with pillaging. Upon my return each evening, I couldn't hug them enough until we departed again the following morning.

While we were going in and out of houses, back and forth to the church, the incessant whimpering and whining of the stray dogs and cats searching for their owners was very unnerving. They were the only living creatures around, aimlessly lurking around their homes, sniffing relentlessly with the hope of finding their owners. I empathized so well with those creatures when I saw them finally give in. They curled up and died quietly in front of their masters' homes. *Their experience was so much like my own six year tribulation as I wandered aimlessly, like a dog, "shan gyank", just to survive and avoid being captured by the Turks, plagued all the while with the concern for the well being of my parents, sisters and brothers—maintaining hope to find them.*

MY FIRST BRUSH FROM DEATH

Three weeks later without warning, about ten o'clock in the morning, three gendarmes entered the Protestant Church before we were taken out to pillage for the day. Without a word they promptly started to separate boys according to their physical size and age. They grouped me with the older and larger boys aged fourteen to seventeen and kept Kaspar, my twin, with the younger boys. Not knowing why we were being separated, I immediately yelled out, protesting that I did not want to be separated from my younger brothers or my twin. "I'm his twin, we are the same age!" I felt I had to protect them, and I was desperate.

Suddenly, I felt a strong grasp on my arm. Immediately, I recognized the voice of Mihran Mirakian, my older brother's classmate. Mihran was also older and larger than I was. He quietly whispered into my ear, "Let him go, he might survive. Quiet down." Because he was older, I thought he must know what was happening so I stopped yelling.

As it turned out, the older boys were separated from the group because they were designated to be killed on that day. The Turks knew the older boys *were not going to convert* and become Turk and therefore would continue to be a threat. The younger boys were easier to convert and train to work in whatever capacity needed. They also had the genes, carrying the skills and characteristics of their forefathers—something coveted by the Turks. The older boys had served their purpose of clearing out all the Armenian houses; now they were no longer needed. Their presence would be more of a problem for the Turks.

All of the larger boys were put in a small room in the back of the church. A guard bolted the door, and we could hear him pacing back and forth. Whenever he heard one of us make a sound, he shouted back, "Don't croak—within a few hours you will be reunited with your parents!"

Meanwhile, inside the room, Mihran Mirakian, the tallest boy among us, immediately noticed the bars on the window, the only opening in the room. He quietly pulled out a pocketknife he had secretly kept and quickly began to chip away the plaster from the bars. One by one they were all loosened and pulled out of the window. Next, he silently grabbed one of the smaller boys. He hoisted the boy upon his shoulder and motioned with his hand for the boy to jump out of the window and run away. No words were exchanged. We moved swiftly. A second and then a third boy were hoisted upon Mihran's shoulders. They too jumped and ran away. I noticed they all ran in the same direction, one after the other. We were moving as quickly and quietly as possible. We could not be heard, nor could we be stopped. We only had one chance to escape. *We knew we were destined to be killed.*

We couldn't avoid making noise as we jumped out and landed on the ground. Apparently the guard heard sounds of scuffling, but he couldn't figure out its cause. Maybe he thought we were thrashing about inside because we had figured out we were going to be slaughtered. Hearing the thud, he kept repeating, "Don't croak now—you will soon be reunited with your parents."

Luckily for us, the ground outside was covered with dung so we landed softly. The drop was about eight to ten feet, but none of us were hurt. Five or six boys had escaped before my turn came. All I remember was how I got on Mihran's shoulders and jumped out from the window. As I landed, it took a few seconds for me to realize that I was not hurt. Then I quickly stood up, looked around, and started to run. I ran as fast as my feet would take me. While running, I made the split decision to run in the opposite direction from the other boys. They ran down towards the river in the valley. The church was higher up on the hillside, so as I ran down, I could see the shops in front of me.

Although I was free, I was very scared and was not sure which direction would be best for me to take. I decided to run towards the middle of town because, in the event any one of us were caught, it would be best if we ran off in different directions so that we would not all be captured at one time. I also hoped that I would run into another Armenian who might be able to tell me what was happening and help me decide what to do next. For some reason the stories my mother used to tell us about the massacres of 1895 and 1896 were creeping up in my thoughts. They were all I had now to guide me in making decisions critical to survive. I knew I had to figure out a way not to get caught—to stay out of sight!

To this day I have not heard about the fate of the other boys. For eighty-eight years I have searched for them to no avail. We all brushed death together. I never saw or heard about Mihran Mirakian again. I owe my life to him. He was from Khooshee and came to our school in Perri because it was larger and had better teachers. I only hope that he too survived and subsequently had a good life.

Whenever I come face to face with God, I will ask, "What was our crime? What had we done at such a tender age to deserve this? I was barely fourteen!" That precise moment meant life or death for me. As I kept on running as fast as I could, I was hoping I would meet up with a Turk with a heart, rather than with Jesus who had completely abandoned us.

Quietly and slowly, trying desperately to avoid being caught, I approached the rock of *Moosehleh Dahsh,* which was in the middle of town and in the middle of the street, with the main shops and businesses on both sides. With the poignant fear of being captured, I was stunned to find there wasn't a soul in sight. Where was everybody? On any given day, the area had always been crowded with people hustling about doing their daily chores, engaged in various shopping tasks and other business needs. Where were they? What had happened to all of the people? The absence of people and the quiet created a very disturbing and haunting atmosphere. That sensation heightened my fears even more.

At that moment it hadn't occurred to me that the people, including my family, had been rounded up and taken to the outskirts of Perri to be slaughtered. I could not have realized at that particular moment what had happened to my father from the time that he came home from jail to when he relinquished us in front of the Turkish school. Nor could I have imagined all that had transpired during those last three weeks. It was too much for my heart and mind to absorb and understand. The enormous destructive consequences were incomprehensible then as they are to this day.

I was further disturbed that there were no more dogs wandering aimlessly in search of their owners. Where were "they" now? Even the dogs were gone! The town was desolate. Once, there were many dogs in Perri. It was like a ghost town and more than ever, very frightening.

As I was cautiously looking around, to my surprise, I suddenly spotted Ago-Ebo, who was now my Aunt Aghavni's father-in-law. He was the only living creature in sight. He was near the *poorr*. I instantly realized he saw me and without a word, motioned to me with his hand to quickly stop and stand still. Then I noticed another man right behind him. Ago-Ebo began to talk with the man who was tall and thin. He had a white cane in his hand. I quickly realized he was blind. He couldn't see me. They were both standing on the other side of the channel.

All at once, crossing over the channel, the Turk headed slowly towards me. Pointing his cane in my direction, and as he got nearer to me, he called out, *"Chitjeeneen Oghlee…* Chitjian's son, come to me!" *I was still frozen to the ground, losing all hope that I was free.* Confused and scared, I slowly walked towards him. I don't know why I didn't run. When he extended his hand towards my neck, I felt he was going to kill me. I broke out in a cold sweat. Should I run? I thought for sure that he was going to choke me. I looked towards Ago-Ebo for help, but he no longer was there. If I made a move causing a commotion, that would attract others who could see me and I would be seized by a ruthless Turkish mob. I remained glued to the ground.

Extending his white cane in front of him, the blind man was standing right next to me. He first padded my head and then quickly reached for my trembling hand and said, *"You are free now and as long as I am alive, no harm will come to you. You are safe. I swear this upon Allah and curse those who would harm you. May they not survive. I knew your father and he was a good man—he is innocent."* Those were his very first words to me. Then he took my arm, and we slowly walked towards his house. I cautiously was letting my guard down and could feel the intensity of my fear waning.

19. LIFE WITH KORR-MAMOE

WHO SENT HIM TO ME?

Korr-Mamoe's house was next to the government building. It was not too far from the minaret, a tower, where the town crier called out their daily prayers and government notices. The original owner of the house was an Armenian who had been a servant for the Turkish *beg*, (the governor of Perri) whose house was next door. After the Armenian owner was driven away with the other village martyrs, government officials gave the house plus its contents and an additional six Armenian gardens to Korr-Mamoe. Each garden was filled with a variety of vegetables and fruit trees—all planted by the previous Armenian owners.

As we entered his house, he repeated, "May those who were responsible for the plight of the Armenians be cursed and damned forever." Affectionately, he brushed his hand over my head several times and reassured me that he knew my father and that he was a good, law-abiding man. Upon hearing that he both knew and liked my father, I began to relax a little bit more. The feeling of anxiety within me slowly began to subside. Maybe I was able to trust him, but at that point did I have a choice?

During my first night with Korr-Mamoe, I didn't dare close my eyes, nor did I let my guard down. I couldn't sleep even though the Turk sitting at my side was trying his best to befriend me. Using soothing and convincing words he tried to regain my trust and my hope. He took care of me like an angel. *How did he come to me? Did Jesus send him to me? Or, did Mohammed send him to me? You decide!*

That man's name was Mohammed. He was a handsome man with light complexion, black hair, and about thirty-five years old. Unfortunately he was blind from birth. He had just the whites of his eyes—no pupil. Thus he was called, Korr-Mamoe, blind Mohammed. When he was angry or afraid, tears flooded down his cheeks.

THE MEMORABLE GARDEN VISIT

The next night and thereafter, I did manage to fall asleep. The second and third nights, I cried out my brothers' names in my dreams. I felt that I had abandoned them—they were left alone. On the third night Korr-Mamoe comforted me again. "Don't cry tonight. Tomorrow I will take you to see your brothers at the church."

The next day he kept his promise. As soon as it got dark, he wrapped up some food in a bundle and we walked to the Protestant Church. There were only about fifty to sixty little boys left. I quickly spotted Kerop, age nine, sitting on the floor. Nishan, age six, had his head on Kerop's lap because he was not feeling well. What a pathetic feeling ran through my body! I was now their eldest brother. I should have been taking care of them and comforting them. How frightened they must have been—How helpless I felt!

Noticing Kaspar was not in sight, I quickly inquired, "Where's Kaspar?" Kerop answered with a distressed gesture; "A Turk took him away yesterday. We are left all alone. There is no one here to care for us." Unconsciously, he made me feel I intentionally abandoned them, and that made me feel both guilty and sad. He was correct. They were too young to care for themselves. Their plight was left in the hands of God. I was their eldest brother on whom they had been taught to rely upon for their safety. Now, neither Kaspar nor I were there at their side during those terrifying days. We couldn't protect them from danger. We couldn't console their anxiety.

Standing at my side in the hostile atmosphere in the church, Korr-Mamoe sympathized with our predicament. *Now, he understood what caused my nightmares and why I never stopped crying.* He tried to comfort the three of us. He told me to feel free to speak to Kerop and Nishan in Armenian. He felt that would comfort them since they had not touched the food we had taken to them. When that did not help either, he offered another generous gesture. He told me to invite them to his garden that was located on the road leading to the Gol Fountain. I gave Kerop the directions and made sure he understood them because he had never gone anywhere on his own before. Since there were only a few of the very young boys left in the church and there wasn't any supervision, we felt Kerop and Nishan would be able to sneak out without being noticed. We told them where to meet us in the morning. Each garden was enclosed with a brick wall six to eight feet high. Each garden had its own wooden key for the gate.

The next morning as soon as we entered the garden, we heard voices softly calling *"Agha-Par."* They had come! Luckily there was no one else around to hear us. They had come undetected by government officials on the road leading to the Gol Fountain.

Korr-Mamoe left me alone with my brothers as I guided them into the garden. *What a moment!* All three of us were alive and together. We could not hug and embrace each other enough. *Tears streamed down our faces. It was a strange feeling of joy, fear, and despair all wrapped up together.*

I quickly offered them the food Korr-Mamoe had brought, hoping it would brighten their sullen expressions. They just nibbled a little on the food. They should have yearned for *this* food with which they were familiar and liked. Even though they only had bread and water for weeks, they expressed no complaint. They were too consumed with the frightful uncertainty of what was going to happen to them. I am sure they hoped I would stay with them!

Once again, I felt helpless and concerned. I couldn't give them any kind of reassurance that I would be able to protect them—I couldn't lift their spirits! They were too young to understand "my" predicament. Not knowing what else to do, I brazenly plucked a beautiful red peach from a tree. We were not familiar with that fruit. We had never seen nor eaten a peach. The previous Armenian owner most likely had brought back a pit when he returned from a trip to America a few years earlier. The tree had only a few pieces of fruit, so I wasn't sure if Korr-Mamoe would mind. I divided the fruit into two pieces giving each brother a half. As I took out the pit, I was surprised to see all the little holes on it. It was not smooth like an apricot pit. I tried to humor them with it. However, it did not change their sullen facial expressions—there were no smiles.

Soon it was time for them to leave and for us to say goodbye. I knew they didn't want to leave. With tears welling up in our eyes and the feeling of pain and despair in our souls, I led them out of the garden gate. Again trying to encourage them, I told them to return the next day at the same time. As I bid them farewell, I cautioned them to make sure they follow the same road back to the church.

We had that wonderful encounter for three days. Each day became harder and harder to separate. The three of us were very mournful because we didn't know what was transpiring or what had happened to our parents or Kaspar?

On the third day and what turned out to be our last day we spent together, they gave me the tragic news that the Turks had told them they were going to America to join their parents. They were still too young to understand what that meant. They did not realize what their fate would be, but I was afraid for them.

The piercing feeling of despair and forlorn, but most of all, the wretched feeling of helplessness was consuming my inner being because I knew I had no way to save nor protect them. I did not know *what our revered Jesus* was going to bestow upon those two innocent youngsters. I just felt so helpless! Nishan never said a word nor made a sound. He was tightly clinging to Kerop. *His eyes told me how frightened and lonely he was*—how could I ever forget his expression of fear, and the confusion of the loss of his parents—where were they?

Not knowing when and if I would ever see them again, the only thing I thought that might have been helpful to say was for them to try to see our Aunt Aghavni. Kerop knew where Ago-Ebo lived—their house was right behind our home. I told Kerop that I had given Aghavni the three coins I had found and told her to give the coins to him and Nishan if she couldn't keep them with her. I hoped they would be able to stay with her. *That* was the only hope I was able to give them. As they were leaving, I picked whatever fruit and vegetables were available in the garden to insure they would have something more than bread and water for a day or two.

Therefore, they left. They disappeared from my life for a second time. *Tragically that was the last time I was to see my precious youngest brother, Nishan.* He was always our favorite brother, partly because he was the youngest and partly because he was very cute with fair hair, fair complexion and dark eyes. He looked so much like my father—he was always well behaved. From birth, he didn't have a chance—beginning with the loss of our mother at such a tender age and now this!

I wonder if those two innocent, naïve boys had realized the risk they took by leaving the church grounds and walking along the unfamiliar path to the garden? They could have lost their way or been cruelly attacked. That was the first time they had walked anywhere on their own. The route was neither easy to follow, nor close, nor safe. I shudder *now* when I think of what could have happened. They were brave to have taken that risk!

AN ENCOUNTER BY CHANCE

About three months later, Korr-Mamoe sent me on a nearby errand. Just as I left the house, I suddenly saw Kaspar across the street from me. He too spotted me at the same moment and eagerly called out in Turkish, *"Rooshdee, come let me give you a piece of pakhlava!"* He had a *tapzee* (tray) of *pakhlava* for his *Effendi* that he had just picked up from the *fahroon.* What a treasured moment! It was the first time we had seen each other since we were separated in the church. During this interim, neither one of us knew what had happened to the other, nor our whereabouts. Refraining from attracting attention to ourselves, we did not embrace and we kept our voices down—our emotions were stifled. We walked along together for a few minutes exchanging information about our mutual circumstances. I learned that a Turk named Meudayee Oomoomee whose job was something like a district attorney had taken him. Neither one of us had any news about our father nor did we know what was happening. We had lost contact with Kerop and Nishan. We were both searching for our father; we still had hope. Before parting, Kaspar cut out a piece of *pakhlava* from the tray for me and at the same time he tried to squeeze the pieces together to conceal his theft. He feared he would be punished if his actions were discovered. That was my first taste of *pakhlava.* With a big sigh of relief, knowing each of us was still alive and unharmed; we parted sadly and reluctantly just as quickly as we had spotted each other!

FRIGHTFUL OCCURRENCES

A few days later Korr-Mamoe wanted to visit his friend in the village of Khooshee. Halfway there, in the Mahlaheen Tsor (ravine) I went into complete shock from what my eyes confronted—*the most atrocious scene a human being could ever encounter.* Hundreds of Armenian bodies were slaughtered, disfigured in all possible heinous ways—men, women old and young—children and babies. No one was spared. Their bodies were scattered and strewn about or piled upon each other. The ravine and both banks of the Perri River were totally covered. The limbs of babies were sticking out here and there. Gradually, I became aware of the putrid odor of the decaying bodies. It was a relatively recent act of madness. My mind was beginning to shut down. I couldn't absorb all that I was witnessing. *If you have not witnessed such atrocities, your mind could never perceive that such savagery could be committed by human beings!*

Suddenly I heard Korr-Mamoe calling me. Even though he couldn't see what I was facing, the stench revealed the horrors to him. He quickly pulled my arm, *"Come, let's get out of here as fast as we can. Don't look around!"* No sooner had he spoken when I spotted my most beloved classmate, Kevork Noroian. The only feature remaining on his face was one eye. It was open and staring straight at me. It reflected the horror and terror he had experienced. His mouth, nose and other eye had been gouged out by a wild vicious beast or worse, a Turk! The pathetic remains of his body were sprawled among the others.

By now I couldn't move—I wanted to vomit. I was barely fourteen. My innocent brain could not accept the depths of the cruel and horrific acts human beings are capable of inflicting upon others.

It had only been a matter of months when Kevork and I were sharing the happy friendship of two classmates growing up. Emotionally I was drained. I couldn't shed a tear. I felt intense pain. From within, my soul was crying fiercely, "Where is God?" *Why? Why?*

Again, I heard Korr-Mamoe calling out a second time for us to move on. We were already late. He tried to console me by saying, *"May God punish those who were responsible for that heinous act."* Still in shock, we continued to walk on, and as we approached the bridge to cross over to Khooshee, *again* a similar scene of carnage accosted my eyes. This time I had to tell Korr-Mamoe why we couldn't cross the bridge. There was a mountain of bodies from the top of the bridge to the bottom of the ravine. Again there were hundreds of bodies piled upon each other from one end of the bank of the river to the other—some headless, some with their guts hanging out... just try to forget this image! *Akh, akh...*

From the degree of decay I knew this was a more recent slaughter than the first we had witnessed. There was one pathetic difference here. There were many more remains of babies. That intensified my existing distress. At the same moment it

Yerevanian

Innocent Armenian corpses were piled from the top of the Moosooree Bridge (Perri) to the bottom of the river. **Just try to forget that image!**

was dawning on me *what* had happened to all of the people of Perri—there were more than eight hundred Armenian families, but my mind was not ready to accept this heinous act. What happened to them? Was that their fate? They were innocent citizens—they were human beings! Why? Why?

Again Korr-Mamoe made us quickly move on. Because we were unable to cross over the bridge, again he was forced to take an alternate route. We continued to walk on until we finally reached his friend's house. Korr-Mamoe went in to visit with his friend. It was not my place to enter, so I sat outside by the door. While waiting, I tried to cope with all that I had just witnessed. One's mind has no way of comprehending such beastly acts. Within a short period of time, I recalled an incident that I had heard about a couple of years earlier when I was in this vicinity.

With the supervision of a couple of teachers, Kaspar and I had joined a group of schoolmates to help dig up headstones from the old abandoned Armenian cemetery that was on this same road to Khooshee. Because there were no living descendants of those buried there, the clergy from nearby villages were making use of those head stones. At the same time, our principal, Soghomon Effendi, also felt that since the stones were the right size and shape, they could easily be used in his plans to enlargen the school. Enrollment was increasing rapidly because the school no longer was a financial burden on the parents, and therefore additional classrooms were desperately needed. While we were selecting gravestones, we heard the tale about the wealthy Kurd, Darah Bahshee, who had two sons and owned a large piece of land in this area:

> *Since he was aging, Darah Bahshee thought the right time had come for him to divide the land in half, giving each son one half. But he had a problem because there was only one source of water to irrigate the crops on both parcels. To solve his problem, Darah Bahshee devised a plan so each son would have equal access to the water on alternate days. He, himself, rejoiced with his solution because he felt certain the plan would prevent quarreling between the two boys. However, his greedy son decided to take advantage of the other. He found a way to completely stop the water from going to his brother's land. When the second brother realized what had happened, he gathered a few of his friends to help him retaliate against his greedy brother. Together they captured his greedy brother and held his head down on a boulder while his friends crushed his brother's skull with a large rock.*

The villagers were outraged with the vicious brother who took revenge. They put him on a wagon and paraded him around so everyone would show their disgust by cursing upon him. The Turkish officials allowed the charade to take place because they knew that area was near the Armenian villages, and this would be another way to create hostility between the Kurds and the Armenians.

Sure enough, when the wagon strolled through the Armenian communities, the people showed their disgust and horror upon the vicious brother for his beastly act. The condemned brother yelled back, "Don't look at me like that! One day I will be set free, and I will slaughter all you Armenians!"

While I was waiting for Korr-Mamoe, I felt that the Kurd was finally getting his revenge against the Armenians. Only such a crazed mind could carry out such a fiendish retaliation that he took against his own brother.

On our way back home, Korr-Mamoe took another route hoping that I wouldn't be subjected to those horrific incidents again. Korr-Mamoe was a Turk, but he was concerned about my feelings and he tried to protect me. I was always appreciative of that gesture. He too was disgusted with what his own superiors had done to the Armenians.

A few days later, we encountered another tragic incident revealing the Turks' intention to torture and annihilate the Armenians. While Korr-Mamoe and I were on an errand, we were accosted with yet another incomprehensible sight.

Three Armenian men had been tied together at the waist and were left hanging by their ankles from a tree, their stiff headless bodies dangled. The gruesome sight was left for the sole purpose of terrorizing the few remaining Armenians. *What did those butchers want?* Why had they become so vicious toward the Armenians? Every time I saw one of those incidents, I was torn apart from within. *My internal pains were aggravated and my hatred intensified.*

During the time when I lived with Korr-Mamoe, these were a few incidents that affected me profoundly which have remained clear in my memory.

"I am not afraid of hell.
My life has passed through hell.
After suffering for so long, I am only
afraid of what is yet to come!"

CLASSMATES BRIEFLY SPARED

Once when Korr-Mamoe sent me to the *shoogah* (marketplace) to buy something, I ran into Torros Malkhasian, a former classmate. His father was the owner and potter of the *bardahkhanah* (the kiln) where the pottery was made, fired and sold. We were both caught in the grip of an unexpected moment. He started to tell me how his whole family was unmercifully killed and that he was spared for the sole purpose to continue making pottery for the needs of the Turkish government. He showed me several pieces he had made himself and were ready to be fired in the kiln. Even though several months had passed since his father had last fired pottery, the fire in the kiln was still burning. That was the last time I saw Torros.

On several other occasions I saw another neighbor's son, Avedis Maynazar. As before he was still well dressed and walked with the same air of smugness, *chahlehmov*; his head was held up high. He was still a very handsome boy. One day when I was alone and we had a short encounter, he confided in me that he had accepted the Moslem faith. There seemed to be no sense of guilt. That was the path of survival he had chosen. I never did learn what happened to his family.

> *Keemee kee Moosoolmahn sahyarsagh*
> *Khachee khoynoundahn chuhkarr*
> *(Turkish)*

> *Voroon vor Moosoolmahn guh-hahshvenk*
> *Khachuh tzotzehn geh-lah*
> *(Armenian)*

> *Whomever we think charades as a Moslem*
> *A cross slips out from underneath his bosom*
> *(English)*

I can't recall how I absorbed those sordid experiences, and endured the pain I experienced daily. As I lived one day at a time, instinctively, survival was my only priority. I must have learned how to store each new terrifying incident as far back in my mind as possible and prepared myself for the next moment. Only when I found my freedom and had established myself with safe surroundings, did those tightly stored images begin to emerge and unravel. To this day they reoccur in my nightmares and for eighty-eight years have been at the brink of all my daily thoughts. My family and friends can attest to this. I never learned how to cope with those images. *They haunt me eternally.*

PILLAGING WITH KORR-MAMOE

I stayed with Korr-Mamoe for about ten to twelve months. We continued to pillage Armenian homes every day. One evening we went to Levon Meeleedosian's house. He was one of my classmates. His father had just returned from America a few months earlier. Somehow Korr-Mamoe knew that, so he thought there must be money hidden somewhere inside the walls. We turned the house inside out, and we still didn't find anything of value. Nothing was left, as other Turks had cleaned out the house before us. Korr-Mamoe didn't give up easily. He thumped the floors and walls with his cane searching for money. No use—he found nothing. Witnessing his greed was agonizing. I felt so sorry for the Armenians who were forced to leave everything behind.

We plundered at night when there were fewer people about. We were always by ourselves. Day or night made no difference to him, of course, because he was blind. However, I felt more at ease at night. The chance of me getting caught during the day was much greater. A fear that never left me.

We brought in a variety of goods, but mostly we stole food stored in various sizes and shapes of pottery. The contents varied from butter, honey, grains, preserved sweets and an assortment of pickles to fresh fruits and vegetables. These were all stored in his large pantry.

In addition to his own gardens, we snuck into many other gardens. Korr-Mamoe was very skillful fitting each wooden key into its respective lock. Once we were inside a garden, he would demonstrate for me how to select ripened fruits and vegetables. I was always amazed how he selected tomatoes. They were never too green or too red. How did he know? He ate them with a big appetite. His favorite food was fried eggs and tomatoes with lots of butter.

He raised twenty to thirty hens in his huge stable. Every morning he gathered eggs for breakfast. He walked into the stable and never stepped on an egg. He claimed the hens laid eggs in the same place.

I, too, have developed a liking for tomatoes. To this day, I always have fresh tomatoes from my garden. Another habit I learned from Korr-Mamoe, which I have sustained, is my fondness for honey. We stole huge crocks filled with honey and butterballs the size of a peach. Armenians preserved sweet butter for months in this manner. He taught me how to pinch off a bite-size piece of butter with two fingers and bring it up to my mouth without dripping the honey.

KORR-MAMOE FORGAVE ME

When he wasn't home, I'd sneak in and eat butter and honey on my own, feeling guilty all the while. As I pinched away at a butterball, a new one surfaced in its place, making it unnoticeable that a piece was missing, so I felt he would never know.

Occasionally, Korr-Mamoe went out on a personal errand leaving me home alone. I wouldn't dare go out of the house without him for fear of being caught. I only felt safe when I was with him. Thus, I would just sit on the floor, awaiting his return. It was a very large one room house with six pillars, a large stable where he kept his chickens and his horse, a large pantry where he kept all the stolen food we brought in, and one fireplace. A few clusters of personal belongings were stacked in *chughuns* (a square muslin to wrap goods) along the walls, some of which were his own and others were brought in from Armenian homes. Thus, I would sit on the floor in complete darkness because there were no windows and he had no use for a light. In that darkness, I would be consumed with my own fears and thoughts. By now I was very confused about what was happening and taking place. I was extremely concerned about my brothers and family. As each day passed, there were fewer and fewer familiar faces on the streets—not knowing what was happening was unbearable!

On one of those nights, I was left alone, feeling very lonely and depressed. I thought he would be gone for a couple of hours, so I decided to eat a piece of butter and honey for comfort. I no sooner had pinched off a piece of butter dripping with honey when he unexpectedly returned early. He knocked on the door. With sticky fingers, I rushed to open it. The room was completely dark and without thinking, I felt my way to the door by brushing my hands against the pillars. I hesitated a moment, making sure my mouth was clean before I opened the door. My heart was pounding. I was afraid I got caught. When I finally did open the door, immediately he asked, *"Why were you so slow opening the door?"* Without answering, I just held his arm and guided him into the house. As usual, he too brushed each pillar with his free hand as he walked toward the fireplace. I'm sure he sensed my fear and trembling. Without saying anything, he sat in front of the fireplace and started to light the fire.

Once it was lit, he called me, "Rooshdee, my son, come sit next to me by the fireplace." From the tone of his voice I felt he was going to forgive me. That is exactly what he did. His first words were that I should never be afraid of him. Without saying a word about what he suspected I had done, he took the blame upon himself and added, *"You came from a good family, whom you trusted. Likewise, you should never be afraid of me. The fact that you stole was my fault. You have been with me for so long that you have learned to steal from me. Therefore, I want you to feel whatever is in this house is also yours. Everything we have once belonged to the Armenians. Eat whatever and how much that satisfies your appetite. Just eat freely— don't eat secretly. If my eyes could see, I too would not be a thief. Stealing from the abandoned Armenian homes and gardens is the only way I can survive."*

He continued to comfort me. He gave me additional general advice. "Wherever you go, always keep yourself warm because being cold is always a danger to your health." To this day, I am still taking his advice by keeping myself warm. I am extra sensitive to cold surroundings and drafts, especially now in my latter years.

"Whatever country you may go to, for the first few days, always eat a few cloves of garlic until you get used to the water. Garlic kills the microbes."

"Just do not lie, even if they are to hang you. May God always be with you, if I'm not with you. You have entered my heart. I will never abandon you. Just promise you will never abandon me. I need you as much as you need me."

To this very day, I eat honey every day. First thing for breakfast I spread honey on my toast. At night just before I go to sleep, I have a small bowl of homemade yogurt with honey. I could never forget Korr-Mamoe. He was a good man. He allowed me to relax and to believe in him. He was a big influence in the development of my character as I grew into manhood.

Although he was blind, he was very ingenious in many other ways. He had taught himself to be self-sufficient, having developed a sixth sense to compensate for his blindness. He kept a beautiful white horse in his stable along with his chickens. He liked to ride freely on the hillsides. Whenever we took the horse out to graze and it wandered away from us, Korr-Mamoe would stoop down and press his ear to the ground. From the sensation made by the horse, he was able to tell where the horse was grazing and he would get up and walk towards it. As he clapped his hands, the horse trotted towards him.

PLEASANT VISITS

The only pleasant times Korr-Mamoe and I shared was when Ehmeenehm came to visit us. She was Korr-Mamoe's brother's widow. She would visit once or twice a week. Korr-Mamoe made up love songs that he sang to her. After she left, he taught me those songs. He always wanted me to join in with them. The three of us enjoyed those visits as we sang in Turkish:

> Ehmeenehm beer guzel, yareh ben olahm
> Daghlar cheechag olah, gulou ben olahm
> Ehmeenehm beer guzel, yareh ben olahm
>
> Ehmeenehm oturmoush poonar bahshnah
> Sahchlahruh daramusk gahshun ustuneh
> Selameh gunderrmish bahshun ustuneh.

Ehmeenehm is beautiful, may I be her beloved.
May the mountains have flowers, may I be the rose.
Ehmeenehm is beautiful, may I be her beloved.

Ehmeenehm sitting by the spring,
Combing her hair across her forehead,
Welcomes him with open arms.

Upon listening to our song, she would tell me to sing on my own as she brushed her hand across my hair, teasing me, "When you grow up, I will choose you!"

KURDISH REBELLION FROM THE DERSEEM, 1916

The following spring, the Kurds, another subjugated minority under Ottoman rule, rebelled against the Turks. They were advancing towards Medzgerd from the mountains of the Derseem, looting and burning the houses as they headed towards Perri. The Turkish soldiers weren't able to stop them.

There were a number of Armenian *fedayees* fighting with the Kurds. Together they had become a strong force.

As the Kurds got closer to Perri, Turkish soldiers were sent to help the Turkish civilians escape—many of them used their *kaylahgs* (river rafts) to cross the Perri River over to Hoshay.

One morning I had gone to the Gahmarr Fountain to fetch water. Suddenly *Doodaughsooz* (cut-lipped) Khehder, Ehmeenehm's brother, approached me. He had acquired that nickname when his upper lip was cut away as punishment for a crime he had committed. The prosecuting lawyer who found him guilty was an Armenian. Thereafter, he despised all Armenians. He knew me as Korr-Mamoe's slave and was unaware that I was Armenian. He rushed up to me and told me to forget the water, to run home quickly and tell Korr-Mamoe to get on his horse and rush down to the river.

I hurried home without the water and told Korr-Mamoe the news. "The avenging Kurds have advanced as far as Bahsue. The *Gavours* (infidels) were among them. They are burning and looting everything along the way!" Alarmed and without further questioning, he grabbed his horse and we rushed towards the river.

Winters usually began in early October in Perri and lasted through the middle of March. There were always heavy, bitter snowstorms. The rivers froze three to four feet deep. Anyone traveling with a horse or donkey with a heavy load could safely walk across the river with relative ease during the peak of the coldest season.

K. Yerevanian

Hoshay viewed from the Perri River

In no time we reached the bank of the Perri River. Because it was early spring, thick blocks of ice were still breaking loose and floating in the water. The large chunks of ice made it difficult for the fleeing people to cross over to Hoshay with their small *kaylahgs*. Many were thrown off as their *kaylahgs* collided with a boulder of ice. Once thrown into the frigid water, it was very difficult for them to swim ashore or to get back on their *kaylahg*. Many people drowned in their desperate attempt to escape.

Suddenly, I saw my twin brother, Kaspar. Almost a year had passed since our last encounter. I desperately wanted to embrace him. At best, it was a relief just to know he was still alive and well. He was also escaping with his Turkish master, Meudayee Oomoomee, and his family. As they were getting on their *kaylahg*, I quickly approached Kaspar and whispered to him to ask his *Effendi* if he would take me too. I felt it would be safer going with them. At the same time, there might have been a chance we would be reunited again.

As Kaspar asked his *Effendi*, he received a strong slap across the face and was reminded he should be grateful that he was escaping and he should not ask for more. Without a further word, Kaspar got on the *kaylahg*. As he stood up, he turned towards me and yearningly bid me farewell. With his hand held high, he sadly waved goodbye. We were both fifteen years old. I am sure he felt the same pain and fears in his heart I was experiencing. The tears flowed within our souls. We didn't even have a chance to embrace. As the tears filled my eyes, I wondered if I would ever see my twin again. There was a strong bond between the two of us. *Had I lost everyone and everything?* We were deserting Perri and at the same time, we were drifting away from each other going in different directions. Would we ever see each other again? *Akh, akh...* What painful feelings this brings back...

Sounds of gunshots could be heard coming from Perri that was about fifteen minutes away from the river. Korr-Mamoe was scared. I could tell because tears were streaming down his cheeks. He was both blind and didn't have a *kaylahg* to cross the river. He was afraid of being caught by the Kurds. *"Rooshdee, now it is your turn to save me by taking me across the river. Look to see where other people are successful crossing by foot."* I noticed we

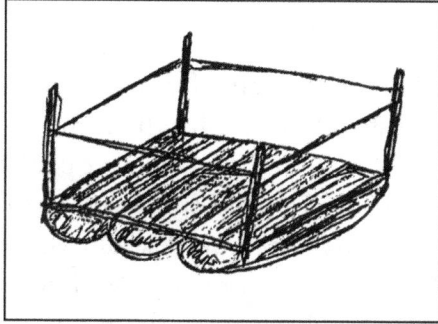

Kaylahg

were about ten to fifteen minutes from Teal, a village with which I was familiar. I told him if we walked down to that point, we would be able to cross the river more easily because the water was shallow and it would come up only to our waist. However, when we got there, we discovered the bottom of the river in that area was covered with small slippery stones.

When we got ready to cross, Korr-Mamoe told me to undress and tie all my clothing on top of my head. That way our clothes would be dry when we got to the other side. With one hand, he held onto the horse's reins and with the other he tightly held on to his clothes. I held onto him with one hand and with my other, I held onto my clothes. He advised me to walk in the shallowest area. That is what I did until we reached the middle of the river where blocks of ice were merging together, making it much harder to keep our footing. Suddenly we both slipped and fell—our clothes were drenched!

In a few minutes we were free from the ice, but now we were submerged in the water over our heads. We were lucky Korr-Mamoe had held tightly on the reins of his horse and I was still holding tightly on to him. The strength of the horse kept us from slipping away in the water's swift current. We continued to walk, clinging tightly on the slippery stones with our toes, until we finally managed to get across to the other side of the river.

However, our clothes were both wet and cold—almost frozen. Luckily we found a secluded spot along the bank where there was a bit of sunshine which somewhat thawed out our clothes. It took us about fifteen minutes to dress because the clothes were wet and stiff. We had to be careful that they didn't crack.

Once we were dressed, we proceeded to walk towards the village of Hoshay, which used to be inhabited entirely by Armenians. Kevork Yerevanian's mother was born there. Not one Armenian could be found. They had either been killed or had fled the previous year from persecution. Now the fleeing Turks had completely taken over the village. By the time we got there, we weren't allowed to stay because there wasn't enough food to share nor was there a place to sleep. Hoshay had been a very poor village.

We continued to walk. We passed the village of Demergee where there also was no food to be spared for newcomers, so we walked on until we reached the small Kurdish village of Chalkhadahn which was atop a mountain directly across the river from Perri. From there we could see Perri being completely destroyed by fire. Everything I deeply cherished, the only life I had ever known was engulfed in flames. *My dear reader,* could you understand my emotions at that moment? Words cannot convey how it feels to see your childhood home in flames. Especially when you are fleeing with the perpetrators, with all you have lost—your father, your sisters, your brothers... *Meghk!* We stayed in Chalkhadahn for five days and for all five days we watched Perri burn. Nothing was left on that hilltop—the houses, the government building, our beloved churches and schools were all gone. However, amidst my feelings of despair, I had a feeling of **vindication**. If the Armenians couldn't enjoy what was rightfully theirs, now neither could the Turks! That gave me a strange sense of satisfaction. As I saw our church vanish, I thought about all of the precious possessions we laboriously hauled in from the Armenian homes. Now they too were gone.

During that violent seizure, as the Turkish civilians were fearfully fleeing, the Turkish horsemen were on a very brutal rampage of their own. Straddled upon their horses with their swords ready to strike, they shouted, *"Kill every single living gavour. Allow not one to live!"* Any Armenian who got caught, converted or not, was brutally slaughtered in vengeance. The Turkish government had sent more than two hundred soldiers to defend Perri against the Kurds, but the soldiers failed and retreated back to Kharpert. Even while they were retreating from the Kurds, they took their wrath out on the Armenians. Hundreds of Armenians lost their lives in that seizure. At some later date, I learned my classmates, Torros Malkhasian and Avedis Maynazar, Der Boghos (the priest who converted), and Hmahyag's father (Huesnee Beg's chef) were all martyred in that rampage.

Although Chalkhadan was a small Kurdish village there were only a few Kurdish civilians who had remained. Hundreds of Turkish soldiers were sent there to establish a Turkish outpost. The soldiers had plenty of food they had confiscated from the homes of massacred Armenians, which they now shared with the fleeing Turkish civilians.

Further complicating the situation, Kurds from nearby villages drifted in and milled among the fleeing Turks. They knew the Turkish refugees fled from their homes with valuable possessions previously stolen from the wealthy Armenians. The Kurds, in turn, hoped to pillage from the fleeing Turks. The situation reminded me of one of my grandfather's anecdote in Armenian:

*Kogheh, koghen koghahtzav
Asdvadz dehsahv, yev zarmahtzav!*

*A thief stole from another thief,
God saw this and was amazed.*

As night approached, we were given a small corner in the house of a poor Kurdish peasant. They showed a gesture of hospitality towards us because Korr-Mamoe was blind. By now our clothes had dried out, but we hadn't eaten all day. Luckily, the Turkish soldiers passed out a piece of bread for each Turkish refugee; and we each got one as well.

We were both exhausted from the day's ordeal. As we began to rest, fear crept into my thoughts. I was witnessing a war within a war. I was on the run with a Turk, the *enemy*. Who was my ally in this circumstance? Who was my enemy? If the soldiers found out I were an Armenian, I would have been killed on the spot. If there was a Turk, a Kurd, or even an Armenian among all the people who had fled from the nearby villages and had now gathered here, they would be able to recognize me and turn me in for a negligible financial reward or even for a piece of food. How safe was I? How much danger was I in? Once again, I was besieged with fear.

As the days passed, we kept hearing the Kurds were advancing with Armenian *fedayees*. The Turks were still on the run. They were driven out of many villages: Perri, Medzgerd, Ismiel, Bahsue, and Vasgerd, all the way to Pertahk. They had almost reached Kharpert. If the German forces had not come and stopped the Kurds from behind, the Kurds would have gone on. At that point, had the Armenians joined with the Kurdish forces, the Turks would have been significantly weakened—maybe defeated. *Either way, the lives of thousands of Armenians would have been spared. Who knows—we might have gone back to our lands!*

A DIFFICULT DECISION
On the fourth day, unexpectedly a dear classmate and neighbor, Hampartzoum Der Garabedian, took me by surprise when he approached our room. Korr-Mamoe and I were quietly sitting on the floor. Without a word or

sound, Hampartzoum motioned for me to go outside. Korr-Mamoe did not seem to notice as I slipped away. Hampartzoum had been living in that village with his Kurdish master for some time and had learned to speak Kurdish. The Kurd was one of the farmers who had stayed to protect his small plot of land and animals when the Turkish soldiers filtered in.

Hampartzoum had spotted me when we first arrived and told his master about me, how we were close classmates and neighbors in Perri. They talked about the hazards I would face if I fled with the Turks under these circumstances. The Kurd felt I would have a hard time escaping death if I remained with Korr-Mamoe. He assured Hampartzoum he would figure out a way to remove me from this dangerous predicament.

As I went outside with Hampartzoum, we didn't dare embrace or show much emotion for fear we would draw attention to ourselves. Quickly but quietly, I went with him to his master's house. It was a small house with a small stable that was half filled with his cows, sheep, and a mule. The other half was filled with people. His master's wife had delivered their first baby a couple of days earlier. It was suggested I stay there for the night. Struggling with my fears and confusion about what was happening, I agreed to remain there to learn more about what the Kurd had to say regarding my situation.

The next day a couple of Turkish women, who had noticed I had left Korr-Mamoe and moved in with the Kurd, immediately informed Korr-Mamoe of my whereabouts.

In no time Korr-Mamoe, accompanied with two Turkish soldiers, came angrily knocking on the door. There was no place for me to hide, so the Kurd quickly hid me under the covers in his wife's bed. He was certain that the soldiers wouldn't look there. Harboring a male in a female's bed was against Moslem law. The Kurd assumed the risk and hid me under the covers! I was trembling with fear; I didn't know what to do. It was very hard for me to keep as still as possible not to be noticed. I could hear Korr-Mamoe calling my name and from his voice I knew he was angry, "I know you are in there!" When I didn't go out, he sat on the ground and called out again, "My son, Rooshdee, come out voluntarily from wherever you are hiding. If you don't, we will search the house and cut you up into small pieces."

I had no other choice; I believed what he said. I got out from under the covers and went outside. For the first time since I had known him, he yelled at me, "*Phew*, aren't you ashamed for getting next to a woman who has just given birth? Shame!" That was considered a *nahmah hahrahm* (punishable crime). We quietly returned to our quarters.

With tears running down his cheeks, once again he tried to comfort me. "You didn't do anything wrong, wanting to go there because we haven't had food for a couple of days. It is still your duty and obligation to take care of me. God is powerful and one day we will return to our house."

A few hours later, Hampartzoum quietly approached our quarters again. He silently beckoned me with his hand to go with him. Without hesitating, I told Korr-Mamoe I was going out to fetch him some water. As before, he did not suspect I might not return and said nothing as I left carrying a jug. I agreed to go with Hampartzoum, but felt very sad that I was abandoning Korr-Mamoe. He had done so much for me and treated me so very well. All the while I lived with him, he wished the best for me. Now I was leaving him when he needed my help. I felt very sorry for him. I was worried if he would be able to survive the ordeal on his own? Would he ever go back to Perri? However, we were now both in the same situation. If I stayed, he no longer was in the position to protect or save my life. If I were caught, being an Armenian, I would surely be slaughtered. The Turks knew there were Armenians mingled in with Turkish civilians and the Kurds. Under these circumstances they would never allow an Armenian to get away. My gut feeling told me I had to get away from there as soon as possible, yet there was a part of me that didn't want to abandon Korr-Mamoe when he needed me.

Within a few minutes, I had decided to take Hampartzoum's advice. I had no other alternative but to leave Korr-Mamoe. Almost a year had passed since my father left us at the Turkish school, when I first encountered Korr-Mamoe. *Now* my situation had worsened. I had no idea where my three brothers were or anything about their health or welfare. I was completely *alone* and left on my own means to survive. I was so afraid and so confused. How I wished, *if only I were a mouse searching for a hole to hide!*

I will never know if Korr-Mamoe went searching for me the second time. *I have always hoped no harm came to him and wished the best for him. He was a good man who treated me like a son. To this day, I am appreciative of his care and protection.*

Again, I have to repeat that had the Armenians united with the Kurdish forces at that time and put up a united front against the Turks, thousands of Armenian lives would have been saved!

KURDISH CARAVAN

During this siege, all of the Kurdish caravans passed through this area. On the fifth day, a new Kurdish caravan had just arrived in Chalkhadahn. Along the way they forcibly had plundered and looted all the villages. The Kurds were now in possession of all that originally had belonged to the Armenians.

Hampartzoum's master recognized the leaders of one particular caravan, and he advised me to quickly mingle in with the group and escape with them. The Kurds were on their way to a small village called Akhorr where it might be safer for Armenians.

I was once again on the run. By now, I had witnessed many heinous brutalities and knew firsthand about the many hazards I could face. **I lived with the incessant fear of being caught.** Much worse, not only was I alone, I had no one to advise me. My life depended on decisions I was making when I didn't understand what was going on or why. All I knew was the sheltered life my father provided for us with his care and protection.

Now, I was running off with Kurds. The only thing I knew about them was I wouldn't go hungry. I bid farewell to my dear friend, Hampartzoum, and his master and I mingled in with the caravan without looking back. Before I knew it, a Kurd walking by my side grabbed an expensive red *fez* off the backpack on a donkey and put it on my head to protect me from the forthcoming rain. That immediately reassured me. Red *fezzes* were worn primarily by the elite Armenian men. Now I was wearing one. That made me feel good and more secure. Even though I had been

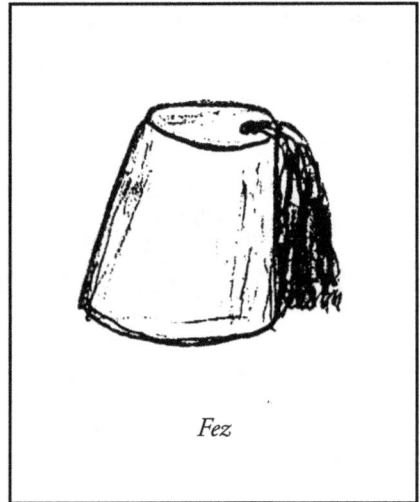

Fez

very reluctant to leave Korr-Mamoe, I finally realized I had made the right decision.

With seven to eight donkeys all loaded with an abundance of supplies and whatever else that was looted from abandoned Armenian homes and shops, we started our trek out of Chalkhadahn. The Kurds were well armed with various types of guns, knives and their notorious sticks.

It was early spring and still extremely cold and windy. The rain fell shortly after we started out and was progressively falling harder. In no time we were soaked to our skin. In some areas, fog made it more difficult to stay on the main route. We were wearing only lightweight used clothing. On our feet, we were all wearing *charroughs* (sandals) that were no more than a thin piece of leather held in place by a leather strap laced around the foot and ankle.

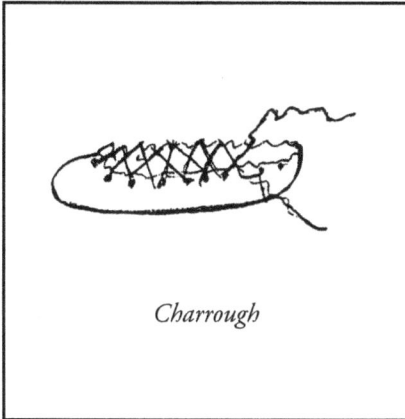

Charrough

As we walked near the Moorad River, we encountered the small *mehsheh* trees whose trunks had recently been slashed at an angle. The tops of the trees were used for firewood. The freshly cut stumps were like sharp spikes cutting through our thin-soled *charroughs*. As we forged through the rain and wind, my feet were pierced and bruised by those spikes and rocks from the hillside. Although my body felt the pain, my mind totally ignored it. I was totally preoccupied with *surviving*.

As dusk approached, we finally reached a *chaghahts* (flourmill). The Kurd in charge of the caravan ordered the owner of the mill to quickly bake bread for all of us. At first the owner of the mill, who also was a Kurd, objected, insisting the flour had to be used for villagers on the following day. But when he realized he was outnumbered by men who were well armed, he reluctantly obliged and baked *pagharch*, a flat bread baked only at the mill.

Not only were we tired and hungry, we were soaking wet. The weather had taken its toll on us. We were all much happier for the opportunity to rest and dry off than to satisfy our hunger—despite the delicious aroma that filled the room. We huddled around the warm *poorr*. After several hours our bodies were rested and dry, our hunger was well satisfied from the freshly baked bread. We continued our trek in the rain and wind until we reached the village of Akhorr.

Chaghats

20. AKHORR

MY LIFE AS A SHEPHERD

Now I had a Kurdish master. He didn't speak Turkish and I didn't speak Kurdish. I soon learned he knew only a few curse words in Turkish which he uttered frequently. In his youth he had been a slave to a Turk. At this time he was a landowner and considered himself an *Effendi*. That became evident as I later observed him strutting around the mountains on his horse.

Upon reaching the village of Akhorr, we went directly to his house. He had two wives. His first wife was a Kurd and the second wife was an Armenian. From the beginning, I was not mistreated. Within a few days, I realized the Kurdish wife was becoming somewhat hostile towards me. I felt she suspected her husband was treating his second wife and me with more respect because we were Armenian. Although, I was fed fairly well with yogurt and bread both for breakfast and for dinner, I never felt comfortable in the atmosphere of the household. I didn't feel at ease or safe.

The Kurd raised thirty to forty animals. He had cows, sheep, goats, oxen, and one *koemesh* (water buffalo). My main job was to help care for and herd the animals. This was my first experience as a shepherd. I worked with another Armenian boy, Musto, who was about twelve to thirteen years old and had previous experience herding sheep on the mountains. He had arrived several months prior to my arrival. At night we each had our individual chores, but during the day, together we took the animals to graze.

We both slept in one area of the stable that was relatively small—we felt crowded because we slept next to the animals. Since the weather was still cold, the only way we were able to warm ourselves during the night was to turn over the animal dung and pat it down firmly before we went to sleep. While we slept on the floor, the heat generated by the dung kept us warm throughout the night. That was a common practice because the weather was very cold during the winter and early spring months.

In addition to my main job, I had other responsibilities when Musto and I returned in the evening. Because there was no source of light in the stable, we worked in the dark—the moon and stars was our only source of light. I fed the animals once again and made sure they had enough water. Then I brushed the *koemesh* with a *khashahvoo* (special brush). The buffalo was a very dirty animal— brushing helped keep it cleaner. Another caretaker took it out to the river; that was not part of our job. I never knew what they did with the buffalo—I saw about eight to ten buffalos while I was in Kharpert. When all that was done, I raked up the dung that Musto and I used at night… there was no mattress or comforter. We just had the bare floor and the dung to keep us warm. We were oblivious to the stench because we felt fortunate we had a safe place to sleep. *Akh, akh* it pains me to remember how quickly we adapted to those conditions at such a tender age. We were no more than fifteen and thirteen year olds! All the while, we lived and worked under the cloak of fear—fear of what could happen next!

Early in the mornings Musto and I walked the animals up to a nearby mountain top to graze. At dusk when the sun began to set, we rounded up the herd and returned home. As we walked them into the stable, the Kurd did a head count to make sure we had not lost an animal.

NEWBORN LAMB

One day as the Kurd was counting the herd, he discovered that one sheep was missing. Immediately, he sent us both back to find and bring it back. Musto and I quickly ran back to find the missing animal. Much to our surprise and concern, the sheep was nowhere in sight. We searched everywhere, covering the whole area where we had been during the day. When it got darker, I became fearful that we might be attacked by a pack of wild dogs. As we swished through the tall grass, the noise of the thrashing blades began to haunt me. Was the devil making that sound to spook us?

We both grew tired and hungry but were too afraid to go back without the animal, so we fell to the ground in a deep sleep. As the sun rose the following morning and we were just beginning to wake up, we heard soft cries, "Bah, bah, bah." As I opened my eyes, I saw a black longhaired sheep standing nearby rhythmically licking her newborn. With a sigh of relief, I picked up the baby lamb and we quickly headed home with the mother sheep following us. The Kurd pardoned us for leaving the sheep behind, but warned us to be more careful in the future.

THE ACTIVE KID

No more than a few weeks later, we were confronted with yet another problem. As we were rounding up the herd, a two-month-old *ooleeg* (kid) couldn't maneuver its way down from its precarious perch upon the rocks on the mountain-top. Kids are not only extremely cute, they are very active; they jump and climb places where even dogs won't go. Not knowing what to do because it was getting dark and cold, I threw my *mahsoosah* at it in an attempt to scare it into coming down. The *mahsoosah* was a stick about twenty four inches long spiked with a sharp nail on the tip that I carried to ward off wild animals. Unfortunately, the stick hit the kid as it leapt down. When I went to pick it up, I noticed an eyeball was hanging out of the socket. Musto and I carried the kid to the riverbank and yanked the eye out, hoping to ease the pain even though the kid wasn't making a sound. Then we carried it home. When we arrived, the Kurd counted the animals and was satisfied that all of his animals were home. We made sure he couldn't see what had happened to the kid.

Early the next morning, while it was still dark, we walked the animals to graze. Again, we carried the injured kid with us. When we got to the mountain, Musto came up with a solution for our problem. His idea seemed very plausible to me, since he had more experience herding animals than I did.

Musto went back and told the Kurd that a young kid had eaten a particular grass that had poisoned it. Musto asked the Kurd what we should do with it. The Kurd told Musto to kill the kid before other animals got sick. Musto suggested we behead the animal since that was the easiest and least painful way to end its life, and the Kurd fortunately agreed. That is what Musto and I did. We carried the kid's headless body back with us when we returned that night. As we walked into the stable, the Kurd's Kurdish wife cast a suspicious glance towards me and ordered me to bring the head back the next day so she could determine why the kid died. I couldn't sleep that night. I thought that if I brought the head back, she would notice the eye had been gouged out. I feared she would blame me and have me punished by her husband. Therefore, I decided I would take the animals to the mountain the next day and then take off.

Musto didn't go with me the next morning. He was too afraid. While I was making my plans to leave, I considered the risks I would be taking. If I left the animals alone on the mountaintop and took off, I could easily be spotted on the roadside. If I stayed, I would be punished. Either way, I would be punished; I didn't have a choice. During the five to six months I had been with the Kurd, I never felt my situation was very secure. I decided I would be better off leaving regardless of the risk of getting caught.

As soon as the animals were grazing in their customary areas and everything seemed normal, I gradually started to walk away, down the hillside. I didn't walk too fast in fear of drawing attention to myself. My biggest fear was that the Kurd would come after me on horseback. Thus, he would have a clear view of me from the mountaintop. I wouldn't have a chance to escape and I cringed at the idea of his punishment—he always kept a whip at his side. The further I walked, I hastened my stride, but with a sense of guilt I had abandoned the animals—what if harm came to them? I have often wondered if they were safely rounded up and taken home. I was greatly affected when I accidentally injured the innocent, harmless kid. The care and concern I shared with those animals, as I took them out to graze and brought them back "home" safely, was my only source of companionship and comfort. . . those were cherished memories.

I was just beginning to reconcile with my emotions that my own life was now at the mercy of those who provided a roof over my head and substance barely enough to keep me alive. Being a shepherd was a significant turning point in my life–brief as it was, I not only was alone (no father, no family), I was going further and further away from Perri, my home and I had no idea what was happening or why.

As I walked, I remembered hearing Armenians were still safe in Itchmeh, a farming village only a three or four hour walk from Akhorr. Already I was beginning to feel I had made the right decision.

21. ITCHMEH

CAMARADERIE AMONG FRIENDS

After a long, tiring walk consumed with fear, I finally reached the bridge. Itchmeh was about a four-hour walk on the other side of the Pahloo River. To my surprise, there was a bridge keeper. I needed to pay ten *para* (coins) in order to cross over the bridge. I didn't even have one coin. Luckily, I was able to convince the keeper that once I got to Itchmeh, I would be able to earn money to pay him back on my return. He allowed me to cross over the bridge.

It was almost nightfall when I reached Itchmeh. The first thing I noticed was the fountain. Many people were milling around it—some were fetching water, others were watering their animals. I stopped and asked a man if he knew where I could find work. He directed me to a farmhouse not too far away, which belonged to Yulash Effendi.

In due time, I learned he was half-Turk, half-Kurd. His mother was a Turk, and his father was a Kurd. It was general knowledge that Yulash Effendi respected and liked Armenians very much. They were good farmers in contrast to Turks and Kurds. He spent most of his time in Kharpert where he had an official job. From time to time, he came to Itchmeh to make sure everything was running smoothly on his land.

As I approached the house, I spotted a boy about my age and size. In Turkish I asked him if they needed a worker. He led me to Anna Khahtoon, the woman in charge of Yulash Effendi's workers. She was older than the other women in the household. Again in Turkish, I asked her if she needed another helper. Her reply was that she did, if I was willing and able to work along with the other workers. There were already twenty employed, and now with me, we became twenty-one— we were all Armenians.

Hahsan, the boy with whom I had spoken to earlier, took me to the stable— the workers' quarters. Within an hour he brought dinner for all of us. I was deeply touched that my portion of food was exactly the same as all the others, even though I had just arrived and had not done any work.

Soon after dinner, Hahsan showed me the area which was to be my sleeping quarters. I immediately fell asleep because I was extremely tired after that long exhausting day. My fears had waned *and* again I felt I had made the right decision to leave Akhorr—the village where I would always remember that I was once a shepherd tending to the sheep and lambs—a nostalgic memory.

I was still using my Turkish name, Rooshdee, as were the other Armenians. In no time I was accepted as one of the group and likewise, I liked all of them immediately. *This was the first place and time that I felt the love and warmth of a family since I left my father's house.* The more I showed my appreciation, the more they were congenial towards me. Whenever I was in need, they were helpful. Finally, I was among my own people! Much to my regret, I do not remember all of their names.

Most of the work had to do with farming. The main crops were wheat and cotton. In addition, there also were oats, garbanzo, hemp, flax, sesame, and a few other crops. They also roasted and crushed sesame seeds to make a paste for ourselves. It was delicious, just as I remembered the way Aghavni and Sultahn made it. Sesame seeds were used in many foods and it was easy to grind. Therefore, they were sold in great quantity. Oats were used mainly for animal feed because they helped the cows and goats produce more milk.

Because I knew how to write in Turkish, my prime responsibility was the bookkeeping and the calculations necessary for the sale of seeds. We sold seeds for the same crops we planted. I helped farmers calculate the amount of seed they needed for the area of land in which they were going to plant a particular crop. I weighed the seeds to calculate their cost. During my free time, I helped out wherever an extra hand was needed. Mainly, I helped cultivate the soil using a hoe, making sure it was turned evenly. Occasionally, I was asked to guard a stretch of several fields to make sure everything was running smoothly. On this job, I rode on the back of a donkey so I would have a better view of all the activity taking place because there was a vast area to cover.

During the planting season, we hired additional Kurdish help to cultivate and plant the fields—we couldn't cover the area on our own within the time required.

That was how my days were spent. I enjoyed my chores and did them with pleasure. In the evenings, after we cleaned up, everyone gathered together in a large room on the second floor of the main house. We had a delicious dinner that was prepared by the older women. We ate as much as we wanted, because we grew and raised everything. No one was denied food; however, we never lost sight of how fortunate and blessed we were to have escaped the hunger most Armenians were experiencing.

After dinner, while we were still sitting on the floor, we worked on indoor chores such as cotton husking or cleaning small stones from the lentil and other grains. Anna Khahtoon recited poems and riddles as we munched on various dried fruits and assorted nuts. We spent many happy evenings together. I have never forgotten the camaraderie we all shared. We were like one big happy family. Yet, we never lost sight of the fact that we were living in an inferno.

Itchmeh was located mid-way between Kharpert and Pahloo. It was about an eight-hour walk to either city. Therefore, it had become a major station for merchants and businessmen. Lower Itchmeh was a huge farm area. The shops and businesses were not as exclusive as those in Upper Itchmeh. Upper Itchmeh had once been much nicer than Lower Itchmeh. Many Armenian families had occupied most of that area which now lay in ruins and inhabited primarily by Turks and a few Kurds. There was a very large spring about a meter wide, whose water was extremely cold. It flowed from under the Armenian Church. The name "Itchmeh" means "don't drink," a warning that the water was very cold.

The force of the gushing water was powerful enough to turn six water mills. The mills were built in a descending order, one beneath the other going all the way down to Lower Itchmeh. They were used primarily to grind wheat into flour. Itchmeh had become a center for several nearby villages to have their wheat ground. Likewise it was the source of water for nearby orchards, vineyards, mulberry trees, wheat fields and other crops grown in Lower Itchmeh.

In all, I remained in Itchmeh for a little more than seven months. There are several incidents I recall within that time period.

FIRST BLOW TO THE BACK

I experienced the first blow to my back while on watch. One day, while I was riding on the back of a donkey, guarding a vast area of workers sowing seeds, I noticed one of the Kurdish workers selling seeds to a passerby for a mere three *khooroosh*. As the worker started to pocket the money, I quickly ran over to him. Realizing I had seen the illegal transaction, he knew he would be reported. As I came up to him, the Kurd hit me hard over my back with his *mahsoosah* and ran off.

With that one blow, I fell to the ground. Luckily, I managed to grab the bag of seeds from the Kurd's hand as I was going down. I was in terrible pain and knew I had a severe wound. After lying there for a few minutes, I managed to pull myself up. Thankfully, he had not run off with my donkey. I slowly lifted myself onto its back and returned home.

I was hurt worse than I realized. I not only had a big welt on my back, but a bad gash. It took about two weeks for me to make a full recovery. I deeply appreciated the loving care and concern I received from the whole group. We never saw that Kurd again.

A CHURCH THAT ONCE WAS

I had heard so much about the spring in Upper Itchmeh. One day when I had free time, I went on my own to see the source of the water we were using in

Lower Itchmeh. The road was a winding one-hour climb. Immediately, I was taken aback by what I saw. The Armenian Church lay in total ruins. More depressing was the great number of bones. *The bones of the slaughtered Armenians who had built the mills and had laboriously toiled on the land that was now providing abundant food for the Turks.* How did God see justice in that? Thousands of Armenians met their final fate at the bottom of that spring. Their bones were strewn everywhere with no one to care for their souls. It was very devastating for me. I quickly went down and never returned to that location again.

LORD'S PRAYER REMEMBERED IN ARMENIAN

On January 6, 1980, the Day of the Epiphany for all Armenians, my dear wife Ovsanna was preparing dinner. As I watched her prepare the frozen chicken for dinner, I recalled a memory from Hell, an incident that occurred one day in Itchmeh.

Early one morning while it was still dark an Armenian woman, who also worked for Yulash Effendi but lived two houses away, awoke me. In a quiet voice she whispered, "Come with me—an Armenian boy has died. Let's go bury him."

Without asking questions, I quickly rose and went with her. The boy was no more than seventeen—just a little older than I was. He was frozen stiff. It was the first time I had ever seen such a body. He was completely naked. As the woman sobbed, she confessed she had removed his clothes earlier because she had a brother in need of clothing. Times were dire and she was desperate. She didn't do that with malice. I completely understood her situation. I felt sorry for her.

Emotionally and physically our task to bury the boy was very difficult. His arms and hands were frozen against his torso. Reluctantly and with much difficulty, we first pried his arms and hands from his body and then cautiously dragged him over the snow-covered ground, which was quite a distance away from the village. We must have gone a half-mile up a hillside. We thought that was a proper place for his burial, a place where his body would not be disturbed.

The snow was packed very deep at that time of year. I dug through it with the small shovel I had taken with me. It was so cold that my fingers ached. I must have dug about three to four feet when I came to a point where I was hitting either frozen snow or a rock and could dig no further. Together we dragged his body into the shallow hole and covered it with snow. That boy's body was the first one I had buried with my own hands. It was a most painful and emotional task. As we stood over him in the bitter cold, I recited the Lord's prayer in Armenian. We accepted his burial as a truly Christian experience. My last words to him were, "Go and tell all the martyrs we are still suffering down here!"

Only until recently, when it was pointed out to me, I realized how *amazing* it was that I was able to recite the Lord's Prayer in Armenian when I had totally forgotten my mother tongue!

During that flashback, "Happy Harry" in his weekly radio program was playing Armenian hymns. The images of the frozen chicken and of the frozen body renewed the pain in my soul. *Akh, akh* try to forget... Again, I remembered my father's home and how we prayed for God's help. What was the final fate of my parents? The renewed realization of what I had experienced, living a dog's life for six years was an excruciating reality, not a myth.

"Generations of Armenians,
Children of grief..."

SERENITY INTERRUPTED

About that same time, word began to spread that the Russians were retreating from Khughee, *meghk* (unfortunately)! With an additional few days they could have reached Kharpert. As fate would have it, the Bolsheviks had come into power and the Czar's troops began to retreat. A Turkish *Bin Bahshee* (commandant) with a thousand soldiers was charging towards the Russian soldiers in the area of Pahloo, Jahbaghchurr, and Khughee.

One day our serenity was interrupted when the *Bin Bahshee* arrived with his soldiers. He took over the largest and nicest house for himself. The other soldiers entered every house confiscating all the food they could find and ransacking the homes for whatever else of worth they could find. At the same time, some soldiers were looting the shops taking whatever supplies they needed. All twenty-one of us were busy fulfilling our daily jobs when they barged into our quarters and demanded we prepare the best meals and fresh bread for them.

The *Bin Bahshee* demanded that the prettiest virgin between twelve and thirteen years old be sent to him for that night. The Turkish women in the community were given the task of selecting the girl. They had their eye on Juvo, Hahsan's first cousin. She was his paternal uncle's daughter. He was very protective of her since they were the only two who had survived from their family. They had escaped from Haboose. Juvo was barely thirteen—she was tall, slender and very beautiful. She looked much older than her age. In no time the Turkish women ordered the Armenian women to bathe and dress Juvo nicely for the *Bin Bahshee* for that night.

As soon as the Armenian women heard those orders, they planned a scheme to rescue Juvo, completely ignoring the jeopardy in which they were putting their own lives. Those women not only were courageous, but they were sincere in helping one of their own.

The women immediately called upon Hahsan and me. First, they asked if we were willing to do something for our nation, **and** if we had the courage to assume an extremely risky assignment. They went on to inform us that we had to rescue Juvo and the only way to do so was to sneak her away.

As soon as it got dark, the three of us snuck out from behind the stable. We were told to take Juvo to Zartahrich, a village several hours away. We had a hard time deciding the best direction to follow in order to avoid being caught by the Turkish soldiers. Just as we started off, a heavy snowfall began.

Even though it is now the year 2003 and eighty-six years have passed, I can **still feel the fear** I felt that night. What would those barbaric Turkish soldiers have done to us if we were caught? The three of us were aware that this was a life threatening risk. We knew Turkish soldiers were **positioned all around us.** There we were, two sixteen-year-olds rescuing a thirteen-year-old girl who had been chosen for the sexual pleasures of a vicious *Bin Bahshee.* The fear that consumed my soul during that night has never left; it will remain with me even after I die. I will tell it to the saints, St. Margos and St. Giragos—I wonder if even they will understand the complexity of my fears.

Luckily, Hahsan knew in which direction we should go. As we trudged through the snow, Hahsan led in front, Juvo was in the middle and I was in the rear. The snow kept hitting across our faces. At times one of us stumbled, fell or sank into a patch of soft snow, but we pressed on.

Finally, we reached Zartahrich where Yulash Effendi's best friend, Osmahn Effendi, lived. It was completely dark when we arrived. We could barely see a light coming from the house. Suddenly we heard **barking dogs.** I had always been afraid of that situation. They were loose and running towards us. They could have torn us apart! At that moment we heard voices shouting to us to quickly lie down and to be still so the dogs wouldn't harm us. A couple of men ran to our assistance and took us into Osmahn Effendi's house. He became very angry upon learning of the fate facing Juvo. As we talked, we took off our wet clothing and warmed ourselves by the fireplace. By the time we had finished a delicious warm dinner, Osmahn Effendi had decided what had to be done next.

He sent Hahsan to Kharpert to inform Yulash Effendi what had happened. I was sent back to Itchmeh with a guide. Osmahn Effendi wanted me to return home before daylight because I had a better chance avoiding the soldiers while it was still dark. He instructed me to enter the stable from the back and added that, if the Turkish soldiers caught me, I was not to reveal what had taken place nor indicate that I knew anything about Juvo.

As I entered the stable, the other young man who had accompanied me home left and returned to Zartahrich. Two soldiers were inside the stable waiting. The minute they saw me, they asked about Juvo. They grabbed me by the arm and took me in front of the fireplace, and without giving me a chance to give a reply, they struck me on the back with a half-burnt stick. I dropped unconscious. Thinking they had killed me, they left.

When I awoke the next day, I was in a bed in the upstairs room where the women slept. It was daylight. I could hear Yulash Effendi outside the house yelling at the Turks and Kurds, *"How could you allow such an incident to happen?"* The Turks and Kurds were also his workers and now they had blemished his honor.

As soon as the women knew I was awake, they came in to comfort me and brought me my breakfast. It took me more than two weeks to completely recover from that ordeal. I remained confined for a couple of days. During that time, I learned that all those who had been in the house when the soldiers came to take Juvo were also assaulted and tortured. Much to everyone's dismay, the Turkish soldiers had dragged away a younger Armenian girl for the *Bin Bahshee*.

It is hard for me to relate what our pure innocent girls and women had to endure forcibly not only during the Genocide but also in the following years as well. I wonder how God allowed that to happen and why. Why does He give the Turks such strength? Forgive me when I say, "What an unconscientious God we have!"

Yulash Effendi had the power to save both Juvo and her cousin Hahsan. When I was well enough to work, I joined my co-workers again. I had missed them as they had missed me. We were all relieved that Juvo and Hahsan were safe and healthy. To this day I continue to search for anyone from that group.

In 1969, when I went to Bolis (Istanbul), I met a Haboosehtzee (a person from Haboose) who knew Hahsan. Hahsan had eventually gone to Bolis where he was the caretaker and gardener for an Armenian Church. He resumed using his Armenian name, Yervant, and had died several years before my visit. All that the man knew about Juvo was she had become Yulash Effendi's wife. So now you know the fate of our Christian Armenian girls.

About seven years ago, in Glendale, I finally met a Haboosehtzee who claimed he knew Juvo. He said that she was living in Los Angeles. He promised he would arrange an opportunity for me to meet her, but because of our poor health and for one reason or another, we have not yet been reunited. Maybe with God's will I will be able to see her yet!

ONE CHANCE IN A MILLION

It was the beginning of spring 1917, and our life had gone back to its normal schedule. One day while I was working at a routine task, Levon Gopoian walked into the stable. I immediately recognized him, and he recognized me. He was my brother Mihran's classmate, and he too was about five years older than I was. He had come from Mezreh and was on his way back to Perri. He was searching for his relatives and for other Perritzees. He wanted to inform them that there were many Armenians still living in Perri and speaking in Armenian.

His spoken words took me by surprise... "*chour*" (water), "*hatz*" (bread), "*karr*" (rock)... My whole body trembled; goose bumps ran all over my body. The moment those sounds reached my ears, it dawned on me *that there were still Armenian words after all!* Immediately, I realized I would have to learn how to speak in Armenian all over again. *What a life!* How sad it is to be forced to forget your mother tongue. Levon further surprised me by giving me hope that my sister, Zaruhy and brothers were living with my aunt. A day or two later, while he was planning to resume his trip back to Perri, I impulsively decided to go with him with the one hope there might be a *chance* of finding my family.

Parting from Itchmeh, however, was extremely difficult. The thought of leaving these friends who had been so kind and gracious with me was painful. This was a place where I knew I would never feel hunger and I would always have a job. What kind of a risk was I taking? What would my fate be?

I knew I didn't have the emotional strength to tell anyone of my intentions. I knew they wouldn't want me to leave. They were as attached to me as I was to them. The care and love I received from the older women reminded me of my own family. Then there were those precious moments of laughter when we got together in the evenings. With all of our fears and misery, we were still able to enjoy some simple moments. How could I think of leaving this situation? In my soul I knew that *I couldn't stay even if there was only one chance in a million that I would find my family again.* As it turned out, it wasn't until many years later, when I arrived in Mexico, that I experienced the love and care of a family once again.

22. RETURN TO PERRI

Early one morning, without saying a word to anyone, Levon and I headed back to Perri. We had been walking four to five hours when we reached Demergee. We were very tried and hungry so we decided to rest and buy something to eat; Levon had enough money for a loaf of bread. We were stunned to discover there was no food to be bought. The villagers told us that they were surprised we were even searching for food. The scarcity of food had worsened within the last year since the last time I had passed through during the Kurdish rebellion. The villages were in a very bleak situation.

In order to save time, we gave up our search for food and resumed walking until dusk. About eight hours after we had left Itchmeh, we finally reached the village of Hoshay. We were now directly across from Perri. Levon quickly rented a *kaylahg* and we crossed over into Perri—what had they done to our village?

A strong feeling of *nostalgia and despair* swept throughout my body from head to toe. Levon and I departed from there. He went directly to the Izigians who were friends of his family.

K. Yerevanian

Perri destroyed after the Kurdish rebellion

It was still daylight. The first thing I recognized was our church. It lay in ruins. A chill went up my spine; for a moment I recalled the scene of Perri consumed in flames for five days. *Akh, akh, meghk* what a tragedy! I hastened my pace and started to walk as fast as I could to my aunt's house. My expectations of reuniting with my sisters and brothers escalated my hope that I might even find my father.

All that came to an abrupt end. The moment my Aunt Aghavni saw me, she burst into tears. The first words she cried out were "Why did you come now? We are all starving!" Tenderly, she continued, *"Yes ahnotee, toon ahnotee* (I am hungry, you are hungry). For months, I have been surviving by eating only *buhloreeg yonchah* (a particular grass with a green, round leaf the size of a silver dollar that grew along the edge of the streams) with a meager amount of milk my cow gives." That night we both went to bed hungry. We couldn't even find *buhloreeg yonchah* to sustain us.

Much to my dismay, I not only realized how hungry everyone was, but much worse; *my aunt was all alone.* Zaruhy and my brothers were not there, and there was no news about my father. Even Aghavni's husband was gone; he was in the army at that time. The meager feelings of hope and optimism quickly lapsed into stark pessimism and despair! Were my hopes shattered forever?

The next day Aghavni sent me to see Meudayee Oomoomee, Kaspar's *Effendi*. Since he had an important government position, she thought he might be able to help us. When he fled from Perri during the Kurdish uprising, he took his family to Broussa, a seaport near Bolis (Bolis is the Armenian name for the city that once was the Greek city of Constantinople which the Turks now call Istanbul) in Western Turkey where it was much safer; he left them there with Kaspar. However, because his official duties were in Perri, he returned alone.

Kaspar's *Effendi* was now living behind the Armenian Church in the large house confiscated from the Mishmeeshians. I have never seen another house built like this. It was a unique house. It had a beautiful garden with an assortment of fruit trees planted also by the Mishmeeshians.

When I arrived at the house and knocked on the door, I noticed Kaspar's *Effendi* saw me through the window and immediately opened the door. As a sign of respect, I kissed his hand and told him I was Rooshdee, Rahsheed's twin brother.

He invited me in and asked me to sit down. He was in the process of boiling *bulghur* for himself. He offered me a small bowl with a very small piece of bread. Even he did not have butter. As I glanced at the food, he looked into my eyes and said, "You must eat all of it here in front of my eyes. You can't take it with you"— he didn't want me to share it with anyone else. His facial expression reflected the acknowledgement of despair that the dire food shortage in the area was the result of what the Turks had done to the Armenians. Consequently, they too were suffering. Even though he showed some concern, I knew that he too was *guilty* of personally making decisions that took the lives of hundreds if not thousands of Armenians—Nishan was one of them!

He left the room to get a family photograph that included Kaspar. While he was out of the room, I took the opportunity to sneak the meager piece of bread into my pocket. When he returned with Kaspar's photograph, tears filled my eyes. He empathized with my pain and also became tearful. With some sense of guilt, he suggested I go see a farmer he knew who might be able to hire me. Before I left, he advised me to tell the farmer that he, Meudayee Oomoomee, had sent me.

I quickly walked back to my aunt's house and offered her the piece of bread that was no larger than half the size of the palm of her hand. Without saying a word, she took the bread, walked towards the only opening where she could see the light from the sky, bent down on her knees and said a prayer. I don't remember if she actually chewed or just swallowed the whole piece with one gulp. It was heart wrenching to know she had been hungry for such a long time. As I observed her pathetic situation, I remembered how much her cooking once had meant for all of us—what a shame!

The next day I immediately went to see the farmer and told him Meudayee Oomoomee thought he might have a job for me. The farmer's first question was if I knew how to plow using oxen. Unfortunately, I had to admit I did not. Despite the fact he realized he couldn't use me, he was considerate enough to invite me to share dinner with him and his family that night. I was very appreciative of his generosity and that I was served the same food with the same portions as everyone else. Even though the meal was no more than diluted soup of some sort, I was still very thankful for that! The last time I had eaten a meal was in Itchmeh—and I was desperately hungry. Hunger was everywhere. There just wasn't any food.

AN EERIE MOMENT

On the way home, I ran into Levon who was looking for me. He too had not found his relatives and admitted he had been misled. Now that we both had discovered there weren't any Armenians left in Perri, Levon suggested we leave Perri as soon as possible. *Everything had been plundered and destroyed if not by the Turks, then by the fire.* We even heard the Kurds had built houses on the grounds of the Armenian cemetery utilizing the head stones of the graves of our loved ones—nothing was left sacred. *Akh,* what more can I say? Levon knew we no longer were safe there.

An eerie feeling swept throughout my soul. Perri was *still* my home and this was my immediate neighborhood, yet I was unable to see my house—the home I yearned for in my heart. My mind had blocked the love and security my family once had provided and felt the emotional pangs of a child seeking the comfort and security of his father. I didn't dare allow myself to wonder where my father could be or what had happened to him. Even though, within my heart I still clung to the hope he was alive and one day, somewhere, I would find him and once again we would all be together... was I that naive that I felt we would all resume our lives as we once knew in Perri? *Akh...* what memories I had! If there were a God, He surely would make this come true.

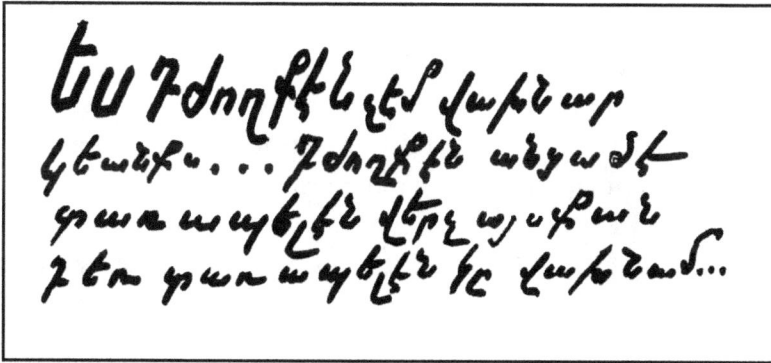

I am not afraid of the torments of Hell
I have suffered persecution, tribulation and affliction
I am afraid that I might encounter those foes again
And that is what I am afraid of!

It was now the beginning of the summer of 1917 and for two and a half years I had lived like a hunted dog, always trying to find one soul with a conscience who would dispel my fears of being unmercifully tortured and killed. The continuous melancholy howling of the dogs searching for their homes and yearning for their beloved owners haunted me even more so. They too were searching for food and fearing starvation. Their whining still wails in my ears. How could I ever forget all that I experienced?

It was like that everywhere in Turkey for all Armenians like myself whose main goal was just to survive. *Reminiscing is painful for me and the older I get, the more painful it becomes.*

TURKISH CARAVAN

Before departing, I dropped in once more to tell Aghavni we were leaving. We had spotted a small caravan with five to six Turkish *chorrehbahns* leaving Perri. Their donkeys were laden with goods they were taking to Kharpert—a distance of four days from Perri. Everyone was in the same wretched condition. From our appearance it was difficult to differentiate between Turks and Armenians—

traveling with the group was a good disguise. We quickly joined in and felt very fortunate they allowed us to go with them. It was much safer crossing over the mountains and open roads in a caravan. The caravans always had a guide who was familiar with locations of water sources and the easiest terrain to travel. There was less risk of being attacked by Turks, Kurds, or wild dogs. I was almost more afraid of the dogs than a Turk.

Along the way we had no food or money—for the first two days neither one of us had anything to eat. We were feeling pangs of hunger. When we spotted a few trees bearing *chahghahlah* (green almonds), we hoped they were edible! The hillside along the way from Perri to Pertahk was generously covered with wild almond trees. The caravan stopped, the Turks were as hungry as we were. We all picked a few and ate them as we walked on, but to our misfortune, within a few minutes we vomited it all—they were too green!

Soon we reached Pertahk, a village, which was very similar to the farm areas presently surrounding the vicinity of Fresno, California. There was one house for every twenty acres of farmland. There were a few wheat fields that were just beginning to sprout. Had the stalks been taller, we would have had something to eat. Green wheat kernels are edible just before they ripen, and they would have been a good source of nourishment; unfortunately, we were too early even for that.

Somewhere along the way we had heard my brother Kerop was in Pertahk. We were fortunate the caravan stopped here for the night. As we started to search for a familiar face that might have been able to give us information about his whereabouts, we encountered a young boy from Perri who knew him. He told us he had seen Kerop the previous year and that he was alive, feeling and looking much better. He had grown much taller, and his stomach was much smaller. Since childhood, Kerop had had a tapeworm that caused his stomach to protrude. Kerop was now herding sheep for a Turk who wasn't too violent with him. That was the good news. Unfortunately, he continued to give us the devastating news that all of the younger boys who were too young to work for a Turk were thrown into the Moorad River. What kind of a heart could commit such a horrendous crime? However, he had no specific knowledge of Nishan.

Levon nudged me as a reminder we had to rejoin the caravan that was leaving. We had been here for one day and we didn't have the means to stay any longer and search for Kerop in the nearby vicinities. We had neither food nor money in a very unsafe environment.

As we bid farewell to the young boy, we reminded him if he saw Kerop again, to tell him we were going to Kharpert and Mezreh, and if he could, he should try to go there to find us.

We resumed our trek with the caravan to Kharpert. For two more days we walked without food, but we still felt fortunate because we had plenty of water from streams and springs along the hillsides. We drank freely and therefore stayed alive. As we later discovered, even that God given gift was denied mercilessly to those unfortunate Armenians who were forced to march through the hot deserts to their death! The barbaric Turks made sure those vulnerable souls did not get one drop of water to quench their thirst before they took their last breath.

Two or three times a day, the caravan would stop to eat and rest. Levon and I would search for a tree a distance away from the other travelers to sit under and rest. We were also very tired and welcomed those breaks. Not only did we not feel the pangs of hunger because we had become accustomed to not having food for several days at a time, our feet had become accustomed to the abuse they experienced in our flimsy *charroughs* (sandals).

As we approached Kharpert, Levon took the first opportunity and bought a loaf of bread with the ten *khooroosh* he had guarded in his pocket. Upon receiving the bread without hesitation, he divided it into two equal pieces—handing me one half. How could I ever forget his sincerity?

23. DR. MIKAHIL

PARADISE FOUND

As soon as we arrived in Kharpert, we found Levon's saintly mother, Yeghsah Bahgee. The German Protestant missionaries had provided her with a small room in the Upper City. She was in charge of six Armenian orphans. Their daily allowance of food was half a loaf of bread each. Bread and water was the only food the little orphans had to sustain their bodies. Upon our arrival, she realized that we too hadn't eaten for a long time. She quickly pinched off a small piece of bread from the ration of her six charges. She gave Levon, her son, three pieces and then gave me an equal amount—a gesture that can never be forgotten.

That was the last time I saw Levon until 1939 when I visited him and his family in New Jersey. His precious mother had prepared a most scrumptious dinner for us. For desert she had baked an apple pie. Upon serving me, she said, "Tonight this *whole* pie is yours!" We all had a good laugh. Slowly the laughter was followed by tears as we all reminisced our past. May God rest her soul in peace and may she relate to the angels all that we suffered, endured and witnessed down here on earth. Levon and I kept in touch with each other with yearly Christmas cards until his passing in the 1980s.

The next morning Yeghsah Bahgee took me to see Mishmeeshentz Zaruhy with the hope she might be able to find me a job. Zaruhy was my aunt, from my father's side—she was a Mishmeeshian bride. She was the sole adult survivor of that large family. The four brothers, along with their wives were slaughtered. As much as I know only she managed to escape—she must have been in her early mid-twenties. At that particular time she was Dr. Mikahil Hagopian's washerwoman. Without hesitation my Aunt Zaruhy told me the doctor might be able to use my help. There wasn't one Armenian in Kharpert who had not heard or benefited from the doctor's generosity or medical assistance, directly or indirectly. Not only was he recognized as a benevolent man and a skilled doctor in Kharpert, but also in the neighboring vicinities. At that point I had no idea just how *prestigious* he was.

As we briskly headed towards the doctor's house, neither one of us gave a second thought of being self-conscious or concerned with my appearance. By now, almost everyone was oblivious to how he or she looked. We were only concerned with our day-to-day survival—a safe place to sleep and just enough sustenance to keep us alive. We were all suffering in a similar manner in that wretched inferno. We were always prepared to help each other. Most Armenians instinctively did whatever they were capable of doing to assist each other. There was a mutual concern just for our mutual survival… to stay alive.

Upon reaching the doctor's house, we knocked on the door and the doctor's wife came to the door within a few minutes. Without hesitation, my Aunt Zaruhy inquired if the doctor needed additional help with menial chores.

The doctor's wife **grimaced** as she looked me over. She did acknowledge that they were in need of additional help, but she could not accept me with the way I looked. There I stood barefooted, dressed in dirty tattered Kurdish clothing. My hair was long, filthy and unruly. Who knows how I smelled? I had not bathed or changed clothing since I had left Itchmeh. I had walked and slept in the same clothing. I didn't have the means to do differently. My only concern was to stay alive and not get caught. All I needed was a little food and a place to sleep. I didn't even think about the fact I was barefooted, because almost everyone went barefoot at that

Dr. Mikahil in Kharpert

time. We all looked the same. Old, young, men, women—it made no difference. We were all experiencing the same demeaning situations. I felt fortunate whenever I had a pair of *charroughs* to wear. They never lasted very long, as I trekked over the rough terrain going from one village to another. At one point, I noticed my feet had flattened out with my toes spreading apart and that they had thickened. I hadn't worn *yehmahnees* since I left Perri.

As the doctor's wife turned to close the door, she hesitated a moment and said, "Go home, clean him up, and then bring him back tomorrow." That might make a difference." I think she noticed our disparagement and didn't want to hurt Zaruhy's feelings. She was a good woman.

Early the next day Zaruhy's nearby friends and neighbors all chipped in and gave any amount of money they were able to spare for my clothes. It is heart warming to realize how willing and generous everyone was in any way they could

Doodoo remembered for her care and concern for Kerop and me

to help me, someone they didn't know, especially taking into account their own dire, wretched situation. *I couldn't help but feel I belonged to them, and in turn, every Armenian belonged to me. We had to help each other. We were alone in the world!*

First, I took the bath I sorely needed. Being clean from head to toe made me feel so much better. Then we went to the *beat-bazaree* (flea market) and bought me a complete set of used clothing. The last thing I tried on was a pair of shoes. I mentally blocked out the pinch I felt from their ill fit. Lastly, we went to the barber for a haircut.

Early the next morning dressed in my new, clean attire and sporting well-combed hair, we returned to the doctor's house. This time the doctor's wife offered me the opportunity to assist the doctor with menial chores. I was accepted and treated as a family member. **From the very first day, my life had changed from night to day and dark into light. The merciless God gave me a miracle!**

I began to live like a human being again. Every night I knew I had a safe, clean, warm place to sleep and sufficient food to ward off hunger pangs. I was with a warm, congenial Armenian family who treated me with dignity. Doodoo, the doctor's mother-in-law, was especially good to me. She was always sensitive to my well being and circumstances—she took care of my personal needs. The ominous fear of the Turk, however, still permeated all around us. Hunger, fear and despair were always with us. No one ever dared to let his guard down.

My sleeping quarters were indoors in a small storage room next to the kitchen in the main house… it was *not* the stable. I had my own mattress and comforter. The doctor had a two-story European style home. The one and only time I was allowed to go upstairs was the time the doctor contracted malaria during one of his trips to Malatya. The night of his return, I was called to his room. I put him in his tub and gave him a hot bath. I repeatedly changed the bath water, emptying out the dirty water and going out to the well for clean water that first had to be heated. After several days of this same treatment, the doctor had recovered enough so that there was no need for any more baths, and he was able to go downstairs.

In turn the doctor aided me. One morning while I picked up the basket to go shopping, I felt a sharp pain in my hand. I was bitten by a tarantula, but Doodoo, who was sitting nearby, was untouched. Luckily the doctor was home and heard me scream. He yelled from upstairs, "Hold your finger tightly until I get there!" He quickly came to me, grabbed my hand and immediately started to scrape off the tissue from my bitten finger. Next, he wrapped it tightly with gauze so the poison wouldn't go up my hand. I too healed within a few days.

I have no recollection that the doctor or his wife had social visitors during the time I lived with them. The doctor was always occupied with one task or another.

BASIC RESPONSIBILITIES AN CHORES

My basic responsibilities were not arduous. I was always grateful to have work and tackled my tasks with pride and diligence. I was kept busy for most of the day with various duties. When patients came to the doctor's house, I invited them in and showed them where to sit and told them when the doctor would be available to see them. All of the doctor's patients were Armenians. Before the doctor went on a house call, I would go to their house in advance to remind the patient of the time and day the doctor would arrive. That reminder also gave the patient's family time to clean and prepare the patient for his call. The doctor not only gave his medical care and medicine to his patients; he also gave pocket money for those who he thought were in need. When he did charge a fee it was whatever the patient was able to pay and usually it was not in monetary form.

Whenever the doctor heard that an Armenian was arrested for one reason or another, he quickly sent me to the local jail with money to bribe the guards to release the prisoner. The doctor knew the longer a prisoner remained in jail, the more he would be beaten and tortured. Many lives were saved with this one gesture.

With all these situations, I am sure the doctor gave more than he actually could afford. He offered of himself all that he could to help ease the wretched conditions of his people. Not once did I ever see the doctor turn anyone away who sought his help.

My *favorite daily chore* was to go to the doctor's garden that was directly across from the German orphanage. This was about a twenty-minute walk from the house along Pahpooryoly, the main road that went directly up to Upper Mezreh. Every kind of vegetable could be found in the garden: cucumbers, carrots, tomatoes, eggplants, squash, peppers and *toot* (mulberries). Their gardener was Asadour—he was from Kasserig. I would gather all the ripened fruits and vegetables in a basket. Then I crossed the narrow path to the German orphanage that was also completely surrounded by a brick wall about six feet high. One by one, I threw each piece of fruit or vegetable over the wall. The orphans were always standing near their wall waiting and hoping I would come. I could hear their cries of joy as they caught whatever I threw over. I knew they would be waiting for me and that made me feel very happy! I threw the food over the wall because that was the only way we were sure the children got the food and not the adults.

Occasionally when the caretakers took the orphans outside of the compound for a walk, I was able to see them. They were all cleanly dressed, but they were noticeably very thin and malnourished. Once, at a social event in Los Angeles, while I was telling that very anecdote, our well liked priest, Father Diyiar Dervishian, came to me and said he was one of the orphans who waited eagerly for my daily visits. He said he was one of those who were always yelling out for more. He remembered very well how hungry he and the other orphans were.

Another one of my daily chores was to clean out the well. That practice assured us that we always had clean water for our daily use. I, also, would go to the market place to purchase whatever was needed for the household. To keep me fully occupied, the doctor's wife, Aghavni Khanum, had me make *kooshkurr* (square bricks made from a mixture of animal dung and *herrt*, wheat chaff). The 12"x12" squares were dried in the sun. They were used in the fireplace when tree logs were not available. Adjacent to the doctor's property was a large square where Arab merchants brought their camels laden with wares to be sold. From the second floor window, Khanum had a good view when the Arabs came and left. She would quickly have me go down and start raking the dung before anyone else got to it.

The chore I *enjoyed most,* during my free time, was taking the doctor's son and daughter for a walk to their garden. The boy was about three and the girl about two. I would carry her upon my shoulders, and he would walk alongside me with his little kid. I really loved the children. I couldn't hug them enough. As I look back upon my life I now realize I hugged and kissed them more than I subsequently did with my own children. They brought so much love and joy into my life at a time when I was filled with fear and despair. They gave me the opportunity to regain a sense of solace within my soul. I often wonder if I would have survived without this brief respite while living a dog's life in hell.

Hagopig and his sister Mary remembered for their love and playfulness

Even today, eighty-five years later in the year 2003, I still hug and kiss Hagopig whenever I see him. He reminds me of his father's deeds of benevolence. I have kept an eternal bond with both, father and son.

UNEXPECTED HAPPENINGS

One day while I was with the doctor at a patient's house, we ran into the pharmacist, Mardiros Effendi, who also had his servant with him. The boy was about eighteen to nineteen years old. He was a tall and handsome boy from Baghdad. We wanted to become friends. I told him the location of the doctor's garden that was directly across from the German orphanage. On several occasions he did come while I was there. When I found out that his name also was Hampartzoum, we established an even closer friendship.

One day while we were in the garden he was eating *toot* and noticed I wasn't and asked why. I told him I had a toothache and it hurt more when I ate sweets. He quickly told me he could pull my tooth. I was very afraid to have it pulled thinking it would be very painful. He assured me he could pull it without pain.

City of Kharpert
(Upper City - Veri Kaghak)

Chaghpure Aghpure
(spring)

Scattered
Armenian bones

Yeprahd
Orphanage

Huschneeg

Vineyards &
Gardens
Affluent houses in ruins

Moreneeg

Kehsehreeg

German Consulate
Kricor and Garabed worked here

Two storey pharmacy

Poorr ★

Two storey post office

American
Hospital

Camel rest stop

Dr. Mikahil's two storey house

Dr. Mikahil's garden

German Orphanage

Dr. Mikahil's closest neighbors
(Kricor and Garabed)
a one story house

Stores and businesses

Pahpuryolee Road

Road to Malatya

Wheat sold here
Boughdah Mahlahsee

Asorie fabric shop where Hagop Hagopian
repaired shoes

Two-storey government building
where Armenian men were rounded up
to be killed

Two storey police station where gendarme frees me

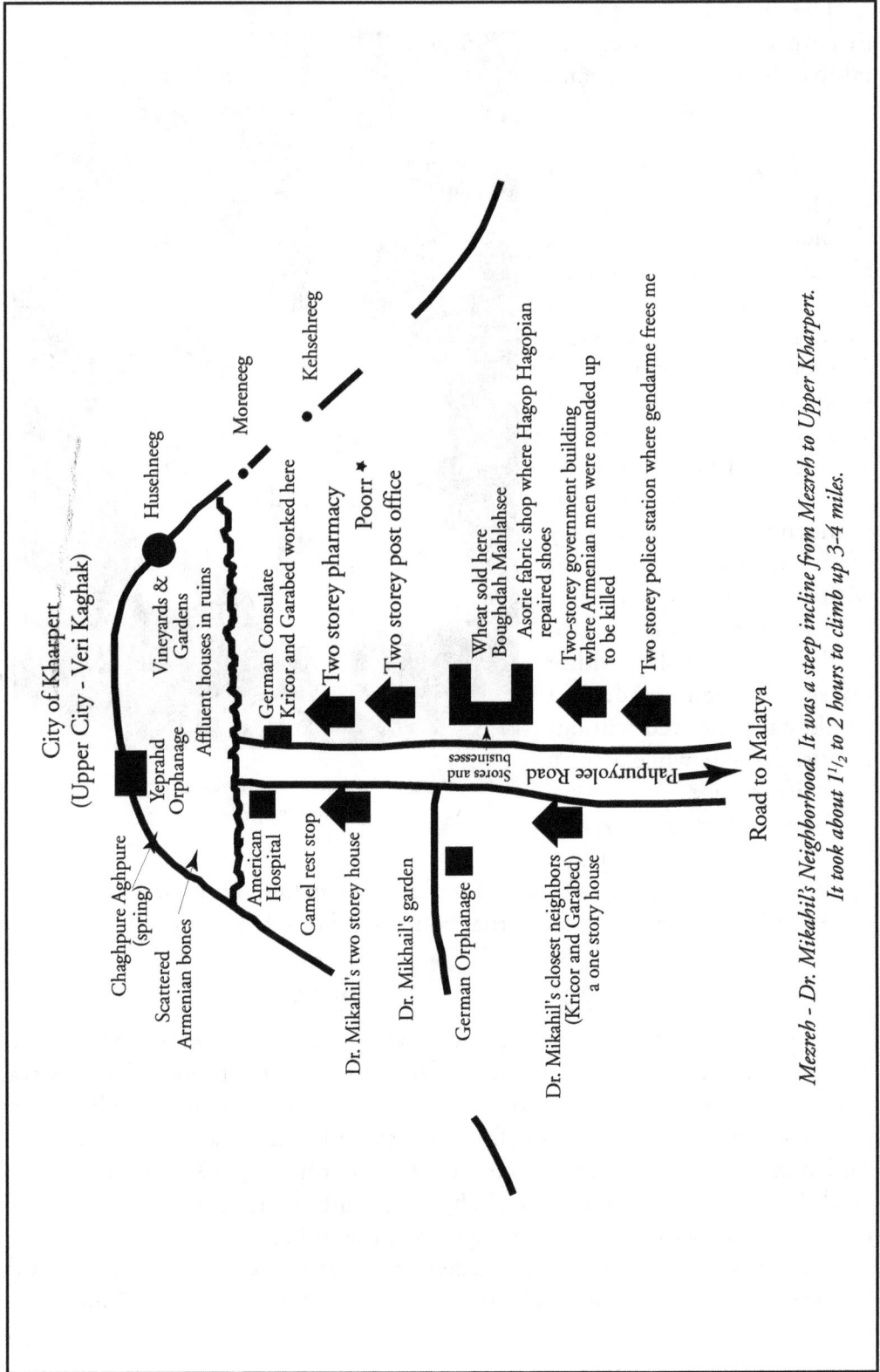

Mezreh - Dr. Mikahil's Neighborhood. It was a steep incline from Mezreh to Upper Kharpert. It took about 1½ to 2 hours to climb up 3-4 miles.

He told me to hold on to his mustache as he slipped his fingernail under the tooth and I was to pull on it when I felt pain. As we proceeded to do this, I waited for him to pull my tooth so I could pull on his moustache. Hampartzoum laughingly asked, "Why don't you pull on my moustache?" I answered, "Why don't you pull my tooth?" I was amazed when he put it in my hand. How did he do it without my feeling any pain? That was the first tooth I had pulled. I washed a little blood in my mouth using water from the creek and experienced no more discomfort.

On several other occasions I saw Mardiros Effendi on the streets of Mezreh, primarily on Pahpooryoly. He used to work at the pharmacy near the government building. A couple of times I saw his wife walking behind him. I was always taken back, half-impressed and half-confused. She had two guards on each side of her and two younger slaves holding up the tail of her skirt so it didn't drag on the streets. That was a strange site, especially during that time in Turkey. I often wondered then, as I do now, whether or not the Turks had granted them some kind of protection.

The Turks kept alive all those Armenians who had strategic skills that couldn't be replaced by Turks. Apparently, some of the Armenians were officially protected until they no longer were needed.

In the early 1950s at an Armenian picnic in Los Angeles, I encountered Mardiros Effendi while playing *tavlee* (backgammon). Thereafter, we socialized a few times before he moved to Fresno with his wife and two children. During those visits, he never revealed anything about his position in Mezreh, or if he helped or didn't help Armenians, or why he was given protection.

Turkish gendarmes stationed not far from the German orphanage were always milling around the main roads. One evening, as I was passing through while on an errand for the doctor, I encountered them drinking and celebrating as they sang in Turkish:

> *Yashasoon Hurriyet.*
> *Ahdalat, Moosehfat.*
> *Yashasoon meellat.*
>
> *Long live Liberty*
> *Ahdalat and Moosehfat (Justice and Fraternity)*
> *Long live the people.*

They were celebrating a Moslem holiday when they fasted during the day and feasted after sunset. Shivers ran up and down my spine, as I hurried away, attempting to go unnoticed. By the time I returned to the doctor's house, I realized those words were similar to what we were taught at the Turkish school when the *Mullahs* attempted to convert us—it was a heart-wrenching moment to recall.

A DREAM OR REALITY

By 1918 famine had spread throughout the interior regions of Turkey. It was almost impossible to find bread regardless of what you were willing to pay for it. Somehow, however, the doctor managed to find a way. He found a *poorr* that was located in a remote area on the way to Kehsehreeg. The baker was ordered to bake bread only for the Turkish soldiers stationed in the area. Giragos Aghpar, was an Armenian, a Kehsehreegtzee, who was willing to help the doctor for humanitarian endeavors to help the Armenians. So, in a clandestine manner he filled a *chooval* (burlap sack) with anywhere from twenty to fifty *somoon* loaves or how many he was able to smuggle out for that day. Since each loaf was fairly large (10" x 5" x 6"), my load was heavy and noticeable. All three of us were at risk if we were caught.

Early each morning, taking extreme caution, I walked quite a distance to the *poorr*, picked up the bread, and with *great anxiety* slung the bulky load over my shoulders and hustled back to the house to avoid detection. While I was fully aware of the risks I was taking, I was mindful of the importance of that task. I had great satisfaction knowing I was able to personally hand out food to those who were *famished*. As it turned out, that became the *most* rewarding chore for me. Once I got home, I would cut each loaf into four quarters, to distribute to the destitute from nearby villages. I gave one piece to each person who came to the door.

During this time, almost everyone was affected by the famine, including the Kurds and the Turks. To avoid further problems, I was obligated to give bread to anyone who came to the door. However to make certain mostly the Armenians got the bread before the day's supply ran out, I told my schoolmate from Perri, Hagop Holopigian, to inform the Armenians to come early in the morning. When bread ran out, there was nothing left to hand out for the rest of that day. Hagop was good at repairing shoes, much better than I was. He worked in front of the large fabric store in the *shoogah* (market place) owned by an Assyrian. He was doing very well for himself. Most of his customers were Armenians.

One day I heard *two loud knocks* on the door. I assumed there must be two people waiting, so I went to the door with two pieces of bread to hand out. Hagop greeted me at the door with a small poor orphan about eleven years old. I quietly reminded Hagop not to knock so loudly, because the noise bothered Khanum and she would complain.

While I was talking with Hagop, I handed a piece of bread to the orphan, but *he never lifted his head.* His head was bowed down the entire time and he *didn't accept the bread* I was offering him. He just kept looking down. So, I offered him

Dr. Mikahil's wife Aghavni, son, daughter and himself

both pieces, thinking he might have been very hungry. Still he refused. Therefore, I asked Hagop why the little orphan wasn't accepting the bread.

At that point Hagop told me to lift the boy's chin to see if I could recognize him. As I lifted the orphan's chin upward and looked into his eyes, I realized he *was my younger **brother,*** Kerop, my brother with whom I had a special bond since we shared the same bed at home. *What a moment!* I hadn't seen him for more than three years since he had walked away from me from Korr-Mamoe's garden. For three years my concern for him and Nishan incessantly plagued me. Had the conscience of my merciless God awakened? **Was this a dream or reality?** *Yeraz te Iraganoutiun.* The emotional impact was too much for me. My vision began to blur, and I felt faint. I was lucky the doctor was home. Immediately, he recognized what happened and applied medication to my eyes. Gradually I calmed down.

The whole family warmly welcomed Kerop. As soon as we all entered the house, Kerop explained what had happened to Nishan. He repeated the same account his friend in Pertahk had told us earlier. With an official order all the boys remaining at the Protestant orphanage in Perri were eventually taken to Pertahk where Turks and Kurds were allowed to claim any boy they saw fit to be a slave. That is where a Turk grabbed Kerop, leaving Nishan standing alone, crying, "Mama, Papa!" Neither was given the opportunity to say a word to the other. There was not a final farewell or any comforting words. Kerop agonized over his little brother's cries. **Where was God?** The ungodly God? We were all in tears as we realized what took place at that disastrous moment.

Those poor innocent souls were too young, too small and perhaps not capable of working as slaves. They were cruelly mocked that they were to be reunited with their parents in America and barbarically dumped into the Moorad River to die! **Do those who deny the Turkish atrocities hear or *understand* what was just said?**

That was *the final account* I heard about Nishan, my sweet baby brother. He was the most handsome of us all with his fair complexion, light hair and beautiful big dark eyes. He resembled my father. Sad and black days came and passed—they punctured our souls and left. My dear reader, have you had a joyous and sad moment of such magnitude simultaneously? Put yourself in my place and *try to endure that moment and still not find fault with your maker after experiencing so much grief.* There is no end...

How does one *reconcile* those two emotions? One younger brother was swept away in the Moorad River and the other found alive, healthy and standing right in front of my eyes. What an *inexplicable* moment! I still didn't know the fate of my father and sisters. Had God started to notice me? *Was there still hope?* Would I find them alive one day?

Our constant fearful struggle of survival was compounded with those ceaseless feelings and thoughts of hoping and searching, constantly eating away on our conscious and unconscious state. Discovering what had happened to Nishan only intensified these feelings—yet you never allowed yourself to give up hope!

I never did ask Hagop where he found Kerop. I just was grateful he had found him. Kevork Yerevanian wrote in his book, *The Story of the Armenians in Charshanjack,* that by 1918, with the presence of American soldiers, Turks and Kurds were told to take all of the young Armenian children working as slaves to a particular square in Kharpert. That is where relatives or acquaintances were allowed to claim their loved ones.

It was in that square where his nine year old brother, Khosrov, was found. Frantically, relatives were searching for lost loved ones. Orphans were crying out their family names, if they still remembered them. So many of the younger children could remember no more than "Mama, Papa." Khosrov was the last child to be claimed. As he waited alone, he was terrified his Turkish master would take him back in the event he was not claimed. He dreaded the thought because his owner used to beat him harshly. At the very last moment, he heard the sweet sound of his Armenian name, "Khosrov, Khosrov!" Still bewildered, he turned around and saw his aunt rushing to embrace him. Finally he was claimed. He wasn't going back with the brutal Turk. He was now safe. He was back with his mother, brothers and sisters. I have often thought *that must have been* the same square where Hagop Holopikian found Kerop in Kharpert.

The following few days at the doctor's house were the happiest for us. Kerop was alive and we were both together in a loving, protective home. The family, very warmly, accepted us both. We were well fed, we had a clean comfortable place to sleep and clean appropriate clothing. Our wash was taken care of along with theirs. In the beginning, my Aunt Zaruhy did the wash. At some point, she left and another women did their wash.

Now, during my free time, we both took the doctor's children for our walk. Kerop carried the daughter and I carried Hagopig. Regardless of how much I hugged and kissed him, he was still jealous of his little sister and wanted all of my attention.[*] The four of us and their little kid walked up to their garden, laughing and playing. I never wanted those moments to end.

As *fate* would have it, that miracle lasted for only a short time. A government official informed the doctor he could only have one slave. The doctor had no choice but to take Kerop to the Yeprahd College, which by now had been converted into an orphanage to house Armenian orphans run by Protestant American missionaries. It was located on the mountaintop in Kharpert, *Veri Kaghak*

A Dream or Reality?
I found Kerop (cir. 1918, Mezreh).

[*] Whenever she pleaded for me to carry her over my shoulders, he would admonish her by yelling out "pees" (bad girl) He wanted me to carry "him"!

(Upper City). From the doctor's house in Mezreh, *Vari Kaghak* (Lower City), was a one to two hour walk up a steep, winding road. Once a week, Doodoo prepared a nice dinner, with enough food to last a few days. She used a three-tier container in which hot coal was placed in the bottom tier to keep the food warm in the upper tiers. I took that food to Kerop, both for additional nourishment and to comfort him; to reassure him I was nearby.

Kerop's situation was relatively secure. However, each time I left him, he would express his dismay because he remained behind while I returned to a caring family. I am certain he also feared I would not return. One day when I took the basket of food to him, he bit my arm. When I asked him why he bit me, he replied he did so because I would be leaving again without him. *He cried each time I left.*

I went back and forth to the orphanage for a few months. Each time I left and returned to the doctor's house without him became harder and harder for me to endure. I could not reassure him that I would come back and that was very painful for me.

PARADISE RELINQUISHED

The idea of taking Kerop from the orphanage and leaving the doctor's house began to consume my thoughts, even though I felt I only had one choice. That was another *heart wrenching decision* I had to make. I knew we couldn't find any other accommodation for the both of us as good as those at the doctor's, but I couldn't tolerate our predicament any longer. I also knew we would *never* find those wonderful circumstances again. *I didn't have the heart to say farewell to my most beloved doctor.* So one day, I told only Doodoo about my decision to leave. She understood my situation and left it up to me to decide what to do.

There were many reasons why I didn't want to leave that haven. *The most painful one was separating from the doctor himself.* He was the most humanitarian person I had ever met. He was a most compassionate and generous person who genuinely engaged himself to help the few remaining Armenian survivors during the most horrific period of the Genocide.

At that point of my life I was old enough to recognize how he gave of himself with his personal means to care *for the despondent survivors of the most brutal carnage imaginable. His efforts were spread throughout Kharpert and surrounding vicinities.* My wife has mentioned about occasions he was called to Malatya to help her family, as well as others.

For house calls, when needed, he traveled on horseback provided by his patients. I don't recall if he owned a horse. His time and energy was devoted solely his people. I remember once a small child no more than five or six years old came to the door alone. The poor boy was covered with fleabites—all of his body cavities were infested with bites. It was difficult to listen to him relate what had

Dr. Mikahil Hagopian remembered for all that he did for his people during the most ominous period in their history

happened to him. One day in fear, he was trying to hide from the vicious Turks who were chasing him. Having no choice, he buried himself in a wheat stack, on the *galls* which was infested with fleas. The poor child had no other choice but to stay put until he felt safe enough to come out. It was agonizing to watch as the doctor tenderly and sympathetically cleansed and healed his wounds and gave the boy a few cents before he allowed him to leave. *Typically that was how he cared for all of his patients.*

With his own money, he had me purchase bread daily to give to the very hungry. How many survivors escaped starvation with this generosity? He gave free medication to those who had cholera. He exposed himself to malaria and other communicable diseases that were spreading out of control from thousands of slaughtered corpses strewn unburied in the rivers, ravines and canyon. The ruthless wrath of the Turks was bestial. That was the same man who opened his heart and home when I was reunited with my younger brother Kerop and tried his best to provide for both of us. **I shall never forget that kindness.** *Dr. Mikahil Hagopian did everything in his power to help his people during their most horrific days. He gave more of himself than he had to give. I have never seen anyone else as genuinely sincere and committed to his people. He served from his heart, and yet, there has been no*

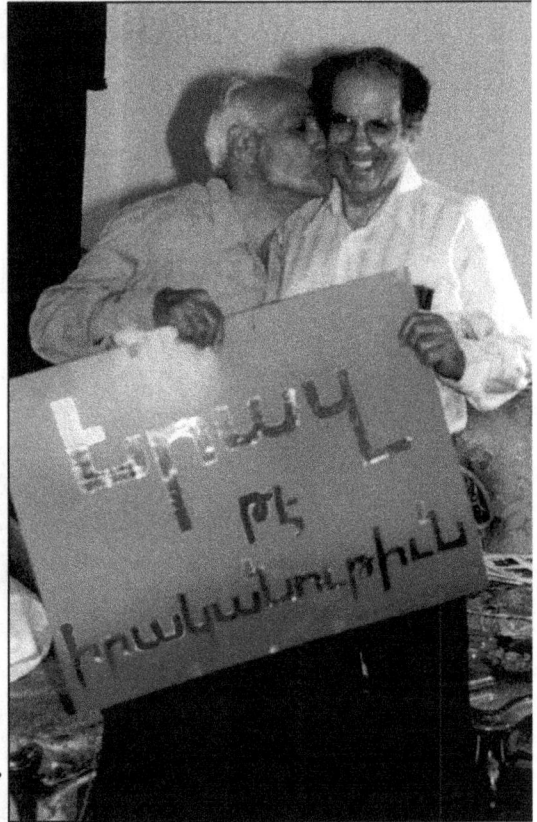

A Dream or Reality?
One kiss is for Hagopig and one for his father

public acknowledgment for all he did. I feel indebted for his kindness and sacrifices. If there is a heaven, I am sure he is there among a handful of our most revered heroes.[*] **For such a man we should show our respect with one moment of prayer.** *He comes second to God in saving Armenian survivors.*

The next and only other time I saw the doctor was in Fresno, California. By the early 1940s, I had barely established myself well enough to afford to take off one day from my grocery store in Los Angeles. When I was offered a ride to

---

[*]   May our youth aspire to follow his path.

Fresno, I took it. I didn't want to miss that one opportunity of a lifetime. We drove off with a couple of friends, one of whom who was also an acquaintance of the doctor and had his address. When we arrived at the doctor's house, even then, he was busy with a patient—which didn't surprise me. A few moments later, he and his wife came out to greet me. At first they didn't recognize me. By now I was taller and older, no longer a kid. However, as soon as Doodoo saw me, she exclaimed, "That's our Hampartzoum!" *That* was a moment in heaven for me. *What a memorable feeling!* The visit was too short, but no amount of time would have satisfied my hunger to see him once again. Realizing he was still busy caring for his patients, we bid each other goodbye. I didn't want to rob any more of his time from his patient. This time, separation was not painful, but there was a strange feeling of nostalgia. My mind was now at peace knowing that he and his whole family *had escaped* from the carnage safely.

Unfortunately, Hagopig and his sister were not at home. The next time I saw Hagopig was in the 1960s—twenty years later. We were at the showing of an Armenian film, "Where Are My People?" At the end of the film, when the producer was introduced to the audience, our dear Malatyatzee friend Aram Jamgochian alerted me that the film producer could be *my* Hagopig. Aram had heard my story many times and knew how much I raved about his father. Aram pieced the facts together more quickly than I had. When I rushed up to ask if by chance he was Dr. Mikahil's son, he answered, "Yes." What an exhilarating moment! That *was* a surprise from heaven. It had been forty-three years since I had last hugged him... Dream or Reality?

Since that day, we have seen a lot of each other. Every time I see him, I can't hug him enough in gratitude for his father's kindness towards all the other survivors and me, and for the joy he, as a child, brought me during the most terrifying years of my life. *Unwittingly, he allowed me to have the comfort of love and tenderness along with joy and playfulness.* Those few moments gave me comfort and solace during my torturous years.

Hagopig, who is now known as Dr. J. Michael Hagopian, became a prominent documentary film producer, and has spent most of his life documenting the demise of his homeland, the Armenian Genocide in 1915. *His father would have been very proud of his son's accomplishments, devotion and endeavors.*

24. WANDERING FROM VILLAGE TO VILLAGE

STRUGGLING HARD TO PROVIDE FOR KEROP

After I had expressed my predicament to Doodoo that I was no longer able to leave Kerop alone, I picked him up from the orphanage and left my most cherished haven behind. I was on the road again, aimlessly roaming through small villages around Kharpert looking for work.

The first thing we needed was a place to sleep. I soon spotted a shepherd walking his herd back home for the night. We mingled amongst the animals and walked with them until we got to their stable. There I asked the shepherd if he had a place for the both of us to sleep for the night. Of course I was given chores in exchange for that space.

Beginning the next day and thereafter for some time, I searched for additional work. Most of the time I was able to find jobs caring for animals and cleaning stables.

Much to my dismay, I soon discovered that Kerop could not tolerate the fleas and lice that infested the stables. So he stayed outside while I completed my chores: raking up animal dung, spreading fresh straw in the stable, brushing animals, fetching water from the spring, *logh*-ing rooftops and any other job I could find. With my work done, we walked back to our quarters in the stable.

For these odd jobs I was usually compensated with enough food to sustain both of us. On a few occasions I was paid with some change, ten to fifteen *para* (coins), barely enough for two loaves of bread. Occasionally, I would also receive a bag of mixed grains that I saved for Aghavni. Whenever I ran into Ago-Ebo delivering goods in Kharpert with his donkey, I gave him a bag or two to take back to Perri.

A few times during that period I allowed Kerop to go back with Ago-Ebo and stay with Aghavni for a day or two. I soon realized, however, that they were too poor and it was a hardship on them. I do remember on one of those days when I went to pick up Kerop, he was left home alone—Aghavni had gone out for a visit. Before anyone returned, I quickly took that opportunity to cook a batch of pilaf for Kerop and me with the grain I had taken for Aghavni. Immediately, I washed the pan and put it away to conceal what we had done. *I felt guilty* having eaten a meal that was intended for them.

Kerop and I stayed no longer than one or two weeks in each village. The jobs and living conditions were usually more or less the same. Much to my dismay, Kerop had difficulty adjusting to them. He couldn't endure that lifestyle of constant moves from one village to another, changing from one stable to another. Finally, I had to accept the fact that I had *no choice* but to take him back to the Yeprahd orphanage.[*]

Upon our arrival we discovered my Aunt Zaruhy was now the *Mayrig* in charge of the orphans. With that knowledge, I felt reassured Kerop would be in good hands. My fears for his safety eased. To reassure Kerop, I promised him I would try to remain in the vicinity and take him whatever food I came upon. I attempted to visit him at least once or twice a week. It was early summer and *toot* was very abundant. This was still a treat for us and at the same time, it satisfied our hunger. *Next to bread, toot was the staple that kept us alive.* Strangely enough, I still have a strong desire for that *toot*—it was sweeter than honey. I have never found *toot* to match the taste of the *toot* from Kharpert!

Some weeks later, I remembered Yeghsah Bahgee, Levon's mother, was here in Upper Mezreh. I rushed over to her house hoping she might be able to help me find a better and more stable job, once again. Tears filled her eyes when she recognized me and noticed how

From left, Zaruhy Mishmeeshian and Olga Kuludjian. At the end of 2002 we learned from Olga Kuludjian that her mother, Zaruhy Mishmeeshian, and couple of other Mishmeeshian children had survived the Armenian Genocide.

---

[*]   I refrained from going back to Dr. Mikahil's house because I knew he was under government surveillance.

distressed I was following my departure from the doctor's house. She went on to express her concern for me and that she was happy to see me again.

ALTOON BAHGEE

After listening to my request, she thought that Altoon Bahgee would be in a better situation to find work for me.

Early the next morning we went to Altoon Bahgee's house. She was related by marriage; her husband, Alexan Amo, was a distant uncle who had fled with the *fedayees* and hadn't been heard from since. Her oldest son, Setrag had gone to America to avoid the Turkish draft. Her other son, Hovannes, had died earlier from hunger. She was now living with her nine-year-old daughter, Margarite. Altoon Bahgee had been a slave for a well-to-do Turkish family. She was given a large room on the first floor of the house. Next to her room was a room where the family took their bath and she did their wash. Adjacent to that room, in the corner, was another small room for the toilet.

As soon as she realized who I was, she took me in. Without much hesitation, she quickly prepared my bath and gave me a new set of clean, used clothing. Much to my surprise, she also fed me well. All of that quickly changed my disposition. For the last several months, I really struggled to provide for Kerop and myself. I was beginning to feel despair. I didn't know how much longer we would have been able to exist in this manner.

The very next day she took me out to find a job. People were getting ready for another long, harsh winter and needed help. I found a variety of small odd jobs that took one or two days to complete.

Every day when I returned home from work, she had my hot bath water ready and a change of clean clothing awaiting me. I was not allowed to enter the living quarters for dinner until I had bathed and changed clothes. She was very particular about cleanliness. Even on those rare occasions when we went to visit neighbors, upon returning home, the three of us immediately changed into a clean set of clothing. Invariably the clothing we had just shed was infested with fleas. In general the population at large was infested with fleas at that time. That was another aggravation we learned to tolerate.

Altoon Bahgee's disposition was both pleasant and endearing. In the evenings after we had bathed, changed into clean clothes and finished dinner, she would sing, recite poems, and tell stories. The main point of the stories was to encourage me not to shirk away from hard labor and to make sure I always did my best. She advised me that a good man should accept any job to provide for his loved ones. At the same time, she assured me how much she cared for me.

She was very different from my Aunt Aghavni in Perri who had a difficult time existing on her own resources. While living in my father's house, so much was done for her. She was never allowed to leave the house alone. Now she was left completely on her own. Even her husband wasn't present. He was in the army. I felt very sorry for her state of dependency. It hurt knowing I couldn't be of more help to her.

Altoon Bahgee was different. She was very self-reliant. She was a very resourceful woman who was full of life and captured the attention of all those around her, with her enticing personality. When she had spare time, Turkish women in the neighborhood invited her to do their light housework just to listen to her sing love songs and recite poems. In exchange for her *entertainment* and light house work, she was given fruit, vegetables, leftover food, used clothing and such.

In addition, on the way to those homes, whenever she encountered a butcher carrying a skinned lamb over his shoulders, she enticed him for a little bit of fat from the *tuhmagh* (a fat pouch that hung from a lamb's rear). *Tuhmagh* is found on a special specie of lamb, *Mawkee*. I have never seen *Mawkee* sheep outside of the Middle East. With a small amount of fat, she added whatever grains and vegetables she had on hand and prepared a good meal. It was in that manner she managed to have a little more of the basic necessities than others. Hunger was still a grave problem, especially for the Armenian slaves.

One day she came home and told me she had found a more lucrative job for me. Having confidence in her advice, I agreed to accept the job even though I really didn't know the nature of the work. As it turned out, the job was to clean out the latrines of the large Turkish houses. In Upper Kharpert the houses on the hilltops had the latrines built a short distance away from the house. They were similar to a cesspool, built so they could be cleaned out with a hoe-like tool when filled with waste. I accepted the job because it offered me four *mahjeeds* (a silver coin) apiece, and that was exceptionally more than I could have received from my other jobs. Each latrine took three to four days to clean.

From the very first day, Altoon Bahgee noted how difficult the job was for me. The stench made me sick to my stomach, and I had a hard time breathing. I would vomit all that I had eaten for breakfast because of the repulsive odor. She constantly reminded me, as long as I had a job so that my family could eat, I should never feel shame when an acquaintance or stranger passed by and saw me covered from head to toe with filth.

Whereas, some men were reluctant and lazy to work, I had always worked hard to help support my family, just as my father had done. While on the job, I brought to mind what I once heard about the Turk who publicly called out alluring the starving Armenians to go to him so he could give them a loaf of bread. When the

Turkish baker was questioned about his generosity, he replied, "I want to teach Armenians how to beg!" Despite my situation, I never begged for food. With this anecdote in mind, I was more determined to cope with the filth.

Altoon Bahgee had her version of convincing me not to give up that job. One evening she related a tale:

> *There were two friends, one had a job and the other was a lazy man who didn't like to work and thus had no job.*
>
> *One day the lazy man ran into his friend, who was knee deep in filth, laboriously cleaning out latrines. It was the only job he was able to find that gave him enough money to provide sufficient food and shelter for his family.*
>
> *Ignoring his friend's circumstances, the lazy man began to beg for money from his friend. With disgust the diligent worker replied, "Don't make me sick, or I will shove you into the filth." The beggar still didn't understand, as he laughed and said, "You are up to your mouth in filth, just what do you mean?"*
>
> *The worker replied, "When I finish my job for the day, I clean up and go home with enough to provide a nice meal for my family and then we enjoy a pleasant evening. Lazy people like you are worse than the filth itself. You have come to beg from a hard worker. People like you are worthless and have no shame!"*

The tale made a big impression upon me not only then, but throughout my life. I strongly felt that it was better to clean the filth than to succumb to begging. I was making one *mahjeed* a day. Four *mahjeeds* were worth one gold piece, which was good money. I felt I would earn quite a bit from this job. None of my previous jobs had paid so well—it was very difficult to acquire money.

GOODWILL UNAPPRECIATED

One day when I was almost finished cleaning out the third latrine, I glanced upward in the midst of my work. It was around noon when I saw someone crying. At first, I didn't recognize the person, but I felt sorry for him so I rushed up to his side. I ignored the fact I was in my dirty, smelly clothes.

Suddenly I realized it was Markar, one of Dikran Amo's sons and Altoon Bahgee's nephew. There he stood in dirty tattered clothing that hung together with bush thorns. He was shivering and coughing, as he stood barefoot on that cold winter day. His face was gaunt from hunger. What a contrast from the handsome boy I remembered from the past. What a pathetic sight. This was another day that our good Lord had gifted us with!

Immediately, I dropped my hoe thinking I would finish cleaning that latrine the next day. Unaware that Altoon Bahgee had brought him and left him there because she couldn't endure his filth and stench, we headed straight towards her house. Along the way, he didn't say a word—he didn't give me a clue on what had transpired previously. She was his aunt. She surely would bathe, clean and feed Markar as she had done for me. She would accept him as a very special guest. Even though we got home earlier than usual for me, I was confused when she didn't even allow Markar to enter the house. She had nothing to do with him. In fact, she didn't want me to stand too close to him.

That was when I learned Markar had *tuberculosis*. She feared he was highly contagious and was very concerned about her health, that of her daughter's, as well as for mine. She made it very clear that Markar could not stay in her house. I was now in a dilemma. How could I turn him away, alone, especially now that I knew the seriousness of his condition? Without being concerned about my own health and safety, *I felt it was my obligation to take care of him.* Throughout the entire time, Markar was coughing and shivering. I tried to explain to Altoon Bahgee how I felt and why I had to go with him. I was leaving behind a good, clean place to sleep, where I had enough food to satisfy my hunger. More importantly, I had a good job and had earned ten *mahjeed*s so far. I knew I couldn't find that opportunity elsewhere.

When I asked Altoon Bahgee for my wages, which I had given her for safekeeping, she claimed that she only had four of my ten *mahjeeds*, and that was all she could give me if I was determined to leave at that time. Four *mahjeeds* were only worth one gold piece. Doing what my conscience knew was the right thing to do, I forfeited the other six *mahjeeds*, which were worth a great deal to me since I had earned it with great difficulty. Her deception took me by surprise—one that I still cannot justify!

She tried her best to persuade me to change my mind not to leave. She quickly reminded me of the hazardous situation in which I was putting myself into, the fact that I could also contract tuberculosis. However, she had the decency to allow me to clean up after she realized my determination to leave. She quickly heated water so I could have a bath and change into clean clothing, as I was still covered with filth. Ordinarily when I came home the water was heated. Since I had come home early, the bath water was not ready. With a bath and clean clothes and only four *mahjeeds* in my pocket, Markar and I left.

Once again, I found myself giving up a relatively secure situation and taking on the hazards of the unknown. *Had I made the right choice?* Until now I had never given a second thought to my previous departures. In the past, I had always made the right decision. This time I was not so sure. Now years later, in hindsight, I would have done *differently.*

I left with Markar because I felt I had to take care of him. I could not and would not have left him alone. I accepted the fact that I'd have to go from village to village once again, hoping to find a place to sleep and enough food for the two of us. We were caught in the midst of winter; it got dark early and we were both freezing. It was especially hard on Markar—his coughing never seemed to stop. Before dusk we found a room at a *khan* (small inn) for ten *para* for the first night. We had barely fallen asleep when we both started to itch all over. There were *ohcheels* (lice) and bed bugs all over the place. It was too cold to go outside. We were forced to stay even though that obviously was no place to sleep.

The next morning we quickly left the inn and started down from Upper Kharpert. We walked until we reached Yelboghahzee, the name of which means the *mouth of the wind.* Sure enough it was a very windy, but a clear day. We climbed up a hilltop where we felt very isolated and no one could see us. Immediately we undressed and shook out the bed bugs from each piece of clothing. There were so many bugs that it took us a long time to get rid of them all.

During that ordeal I longed for Altoon Bahgee's nice clean warm room, clothing and her cooking. As I sit here, writing these lines 85 years later, I can still feel the bed bugs all over me with the urge to scratch them.

Once we were rid of the last bed bug, we started off again. We walked a long distance before we reached Yertmeneeg. We had heard Armenians were accepted in that village. As we came upon a large house, we inquired if they needed any extra help. As before, we would ask only for enough food to sustain our bodies and a place to sleep.

We first talked to two Armenian women who obviously were slaves themselves. With some concern, they went to ask their Khanum, "Do we have work for two people?" We could hear the reply, "No, I don't need additional help. But they can stay overnight in the stable and tomorrow they can seek work in the nearby homes." So, even though we didn't get a job, we did get a nice, clean and warm place to sleep and we felt safe.

The next morning we found out that during the night, the two Armenian women had gone out seeking jobs for us. They found a rich family that needed someone to care for their oxen. All we had to do was to water and brush them down and clean the stable. They already had two boys to care for their many other horses, donkeys and sheep.

We stayed for about two months in each village. Since Markar was too weak to work, he rested in the stable while I went out to nearby areas to find additional work for food for the both of us. Each day I had to go out further and further away to find daily jobs. It got to a point where we had to leave that place and find a new place to sleep. Because of Markar's illness, we were repeatedly turned away. Our situation got worse as we now had to walk in the cold wind, rain and snow.

Our luck changed for the better when we reached Tadem. A boy from Mezreh approached us when he heard we were searching for work. He told us about a job in Mezreh. An innkeeper needed a doorman to check all those who went in and out of the *khan* and record how many pieces of luggage they came and left with. We immediately went there and Markar applied for the job. It was work Markar was able to do despite his frail health. Now we were very happy. Before he could start, however, I had to purchase a clean set of clothing for him from the *beat-bazaree* (flea market). Markar got the job. All he had to do was to sit by the door and observe who went in and out. It was a nice, clean comfortable job that he kept for a long time.

As the months passed, I wore the same clothing, dirty and tattered. It was only during the summer months when and if I had the opportunity that I could strip to wash my clothes and bath in the river. I swam until my clothes dried. Feeling refreshed, I resumed my search for a place to work and to sleep. Going barefoot was not that uncommon.

For the winter months when the rivers were frozen, I would save any little amount of money I had earned from here and there, from one job or another. With that money, I bought a change of clothes. The "flea" markets sold all of the confiscated clothing from the abandoned Armenian homes or those that were right off the backs of slaughtered Armenians. These clothes were sold very cheap (for a four para)—did I have any other choice?

Armenians like myself were all in the same situation. That was the life we led. Everyone was just grappling to stay alive. There was no way we were able to understand what was happening. We lived hoping to find our loved ones— wondering what were "their" circumstances—what was their fate?

I continued searching jobs for myself. When I couldn't find one, I decided to repair shoes. I bought a box and a few necessary tools. I really didn't know how to do such repairs. I observed others and thought I could figure out what to do. Unfortunately, most of my repairs were not successful. Many times customers came back, yelled at me and demanded I return whatever they had given me in exchange for the repairs. For weeks, I continued to work like this, repairing shoes and searching for other jobs in one village after another.

When I wandered from one village to another looking for a job and a place to sleep, I soon learned it was safer to join in with the shepherds while they were returning their herds back to the stable. In this manner, I avoided vicious dogs who were on the loose guarding their village, deterring strangers from entering. If need be, I continued on to the next village hoping to find one safe to enter before it became dark. It was extremely hazardous and difficult during the winter months walking through the deep snow. Thus, when I felt it was safe, I would mingle in with the animals undetected. Ultimately, I acquainted myself with the shepherd who usually took me to his stable to sleep for the night. Only our merciful God knew my fate for the following day. If I was lucky and was accepted by the master, I was given a job and compensated with a place to sleep and something to eat. The food could have been the scraps and leftovers from that night's dinner diluted with water—most of the time it was a piece of bread. The place to sleep was always the *akhor* (stable), among the animals whose dung kept us warm.

I was lucky I always found a place to sleep. I ignored the discomfort and was thankful that yet another weary day had passed. Being left **all alone** with no one to talk to in complete darkness, cramped next to the animals, resting on their dung to keep warm was **very difficult emotionally.** In addition, the stables were infested with fleas making it impossible for a good night's rest. **Most of the time, I was lonely and afraid.** To have only the silence of my mind, consumed me with fear— fear of what could happen next or tomorrow. It was always disturbing to see the less fortunate curled up anywhere on the ground exposed to the elements, where their bodies just gave out. Within my soul, I *fought* to maintain my dignity, to live as a human being…

During the day, I was willing to do any job that provided me with a bite to eat to maintain my body's strength. Sometimes, I had to cover two or more villages in one day looking for work—especially now when I had to make sure Kerop had enough to eat.

25. PARCHANJ

KHANUM—A KINDHEARTED TURKISH WOMAN

I continued to walk on, going further away from Mezreh, with the hope I would find a better job. Finally, I reached the village of Parchanj, which had a large Turkish community. I didn't let that deter me. I was in need of a reliable job, otherwise I would have gone hungry. With good fortune, I quickly found a kindhearted, elderly Turkish woman who was looking for a live-in workman. She lived in a large two-story house with only one daughter who was about twenty-five years old. They took me in as a slave. My chores were to care for their garden, which had many *toot* trees and a small vineyard. She also had a donkey and two cows that I took out to graze, groomed, fed and cleaned their droppings.

The stable was large and kept very clean. It had a very large *sahkoosee* (a wooden deck about three feet above the ground, built on one side of the stable). Most affluent stables had one; some were larger or better than others were. Usually a mattress of sorts was provided, which was a cotton sack stuffed with hay or other dried grasses. Part of my job was to keep the stable clean. This gave me a nice place to sleep. For my labor, I was given just enough food to satisfy my hunger. Even Khanum, like everyone else, felt the scarcity of food. Nevertheless, she was sympathetic with those who were hungry.

Markar remained in Tadem and I continued to help Kerop in the Yeprahd orphanage. From time to time, I would bring Kerop back with me to Parchanj for a day or two. When I took him back to the orphanage, he always took additional food I had put aside for him—mainly bread and *toot*. Fortunately, there was an abundance of *toot* from her trees—she had all three varieties, both the small and large white *toot* and the red *toot*.

Here too, I had to make *kooshkoorr* bricks. I brought them in and piled them in the back corner of the stable. The stacks covered an area about four feet wide by eight feet high. Khanum used the bricks in the fireplace to warm up the house, as well as to heat water for bathing and cooking. Early one morning, shortly after I started to work for her, she came down to the stable while I was stacking up newly dried bricks. She had me take down the old bricks and re-stack them so the new bricks were at the bottom with the old bricks on top. While we were in the process of setting aside the old bricks, we came upon a covered pot. I immediately looked away and stepped back. She noticed my actions and quietly continued with whatever she had to do, ignoring me for about ten to fifteen minutes. Then she called out, "My sweet dear boy—come, let's continue with our work." That *reminded* me how Korr-Mamoe used to talk with me. I appreciated her attitude towards me.

I am sure she hid her valuables there. In some areas, the Kurds, for revenge, sporadically attacked the Turks for the Turkish atrocities inflicted upon them. They too plundered Armenian and Turkish homes, taking whatever they wanted and then destroying the rest. Most likely the Kurds would not suspect a stack of *kooshkoorr* as a hiding place for valuables. Without a word, Khanum and I completed stacking the newly made bricks.

THE SHOE REPAIR BOY

A few weeks later, a young man about twenty to twenty-five years old approached me about a place to sleep. I took him in with Khanum's approval. He slept in the stable with me. He repaired shoes and had a toolbox. Khanum gave us a little more food so we could share.

One evening shortly after his arrival, Khanum was preparing to bake bread. Following custom, she shaped the dough into small balls, then placed them on large trays. Next she covered them with a clean white cloth. Then she took the trays down to the stable to a nice clean area, which was quite a distance from the animals and dung, and it was warm enough for the dough to rise.

Early the following day, her Turkish neighbor across the street smelled the sweet aroma of freshly baked bread in her home. When she asked her Armenian slave about the source of the aroma, the slave described how a young man had approached her earlier that morning and asked if she would be kind enough to bake the two pieces of dough for him. He had convinced her he had just enough money to buy the dough, but not enough money to have it baked at the bakery. Believing what he said, the Armenian slave obliged and baked the two pieces of bread for the boy.

The neighbor felt something was wrong after listening to that explanation. She knew Khanum was preparing to bake bread that day. Therefore, she went directly to Khanum to inquire if all was well. At that point Khanum was not suspicious of any wrongdoing. To dispel their doubts the women went down to the stable together to make certain. They immediately noticed two pieces of dough were missing. As they glanced all around the stable, they saw a small pile of tools, scraps of leather, needles, thread and a pair of scissors scattered on the floor. While I was tending to my morning chores in the stable, Khanum asked me if I knew what had happened. I told her I was not aware that the dough was missing. I was fortunate they didn't cast any doubt on me, and I was not suspected or punished.

The new boy was nowhere to be found. His box was missing but its contents were scattered on the floor. The neighbor then told Khanum about what had taken place early that morning at her house and that answered their questions.

A YOUNG INNOCENT SOUL

Shortly after that boy left, one evening at dusk, when I was tired and very sleepy, I heard the stable door opening. I soon saw a small boy entering. "Would you please give me a place to stay?" he asked. Homeless people would approach a house for shelter around dinnertime, hoping there would be leftovers and thus had a better chance to be fed a meager portion of food. Because he was so young, I let him in without Khanum's permission and told him to come up and sleep in my area. The *sahkoosee* was not only much cleaner than the stable floor, but it was much warmer. At first he refused, but I convinced him by telling him there was plenty of room for the both of us.

At the usual time, Khanum brought me my dinner and noticed the new boy. Without a word, she left and returned with one more piece of bread for the boy. After we both ate in silence, we immediately fell asleep. We were both very tired.

During the night, his loud snoring awakened me. As I stretched over to move his position, I was startled to notice the *boy was a girl!* She awoke, got scared and started to cry. I quickly convinced her she was not in danger and that everything would be all right. She calmed down and began to tell me a little about herself. She was barely eleven years old. In the aftermath of the genocide, she and her mother were the sole survivors of her family. Her mother was gravely ill, so now she had to find jobs to provide enough food for both of them. Being a girl, no one gave her a job. So she dressed as a boy and cut her hair like one too. In the morning after eating a little piece of bread, she thanked me for guarding her secret, kissed my hand, and left. **What an incident to remember,** how many children were left begging in the street? What had these young innocent souls done? **Where was their protector?**

THEFT IN DESPERATION

Several months later, while I was lying down in the stable trying to fall asleep one evening, my eyes focused on the second level towards the pantry where Khanum stored her food and kept her bread rack. The stable was a huge room. In one corner there was a feed bin next to the trough where the cows and donkey were fed. Right above the bin, on the floor of the second level, there was a large hole through which the feed was poured.

For weeks, I had been greatly concerned that Kerop wasn't getting enough to eat in the orphanage. I knew even though the orphans were kept clean and had a relatively safe place to sleep, *they were underfed to the point of being malnourished.* I knew I had to try to take him more food. As my concern intensified, an idea emerged in my mind. I figured out the details of how I could get up to the pantry from the stable. A plan began to unfold. One night when I felt confident my plan would work, I started to act. First, I filled a large burlap bag with chaff until it was firmly packed and I placed it in the bin right under the hole. Unfortunately, it turned out to be taller than me, so then I had to figure out another way to get up onto the bag. Working in the dark was slowing me down.

Next, I grabbed a large sheet to wrap the bread and a rope to lower the bread from the pantry. I tied them both around my waist because I had to keep my hands free. With another piece of rope, I tied the donkey to the pole so it couldn't move from that spot. With everything in place, I climbed onto the donkey's back and jumped on top of the stuffed burlap bag. From there I was able to grasp onto the side of the hole on the pantry floor and slowly pull myself up.

Without losing time, I quickly grabbed eight loaves of flat bread. I wrapped them in the sheet, tied the rope around the covered bread and carefully lowered the bundle down into the stable. Now I was ready to lower myself back down through the hole. As I dangled my feet down on top of the sack, it suddenly toppled over and I fell right into the sack. I was completely covered with the chaff. It took me a long time to brush myself off. At this point, I still didn't know how I was going to sneak the bread out of the stable and get it over to the orphanage. I was confident I would come up with a solution.

Finally, I was able to go to sleep. A big burden was lifted from my mind, a daring task had been completed, and so far I had not been caught. At no time did it occur to me to worry about the consequences of being caught. Khanum or her daughter could have walked into either the pantry or the stable. If I had been discovered, without a doubt it would have been the end of me!

Early the next morning, I had come up with a scheme to get the bread to Kerop. First, I slightly dampened the bread to prevent it from cracking and wrapped it up in the sheet. Next, I filled one sack halfway with chaff so the bread would not touch the ground. Then I placed the wrapped bread on top of it and covered it with more chaff. I filled another sack with chaff, tied a sack on both sides of the donkey, and started towards the Turkish bath where the chaff would be burned to heat water for the baths. My plan was still working...

When I arrived at the Turkish bath, I negotiated with the attendant and he agreed to buy the chaff. I quickly volunteered to empty the sacks myself. As I emptied the sack containing the hidden bread, I discreetly guarded the bread so my actions would not be noticed. The attendant paid me for the chaff and I left. So now *I* was a thief. I still had not been caught. Apparently since Khanum had recently baked bread, the missing 8 pieces went unnoticed. *I think even God liked what I did.*

Feeling enlightened with my accomplishment, I proceeded to walk towards the Yeprahd orphanage. When I got to the door, Mayrig Zaruhy welcomed me. As I handed her the bread, I advised her to give Kerop the bread gradually so it would last over a long period of time. Her response put me to shame. She pointed to the other orphans who obviously were also malnourished, and asked, *"Do you think they will not share your bread?"* She was right. I asked for her forgiveness for my oversight and reassured her I would do my best to find food for all the children.

I stayed with Khanum for almost a year. When all of my chores were completed, she allowed me to go to nearby villages *for additional work*. Sometimes I was given a few cents, but for the most part I earned extra food. In that way, I was able to provide Kerop and the other orphans with a little more nourishment.

On one of those days, I had walked as far as the village of Komk looking for a small job for the afternoon. The fields were covered with wheat, ready to be reaped. There was much work to be done, so finding a small job was not difficult. It was a very hot day. By then, I was feeling weary with an empty stomach.

The workers in the field were Kurdish, Turkish and Armenian. I was offered a task to deliver the noon meal to them. The cook in the farmhouse was an Armenian. For that particular day she had prepared *Khooretly Kufta* with *mahdzoon abour* (meatballs made with *zehzadz* in yogurt soup).

I got up on a donkey and was handed a large pot filled with the soup and meatballs. Slowly, I headed toward the field where I saw three Kurdish workers in the distance. The delicious aroma drifted up to my nostrils—I was extremely hungry and my stomach was making loud gurgling noises. I stopped the donkey, briefly, slowly and carefully brought the pot up to my lips and took a couple of sips of the soup. I was right, it was delicious! I couldn't resist, I quickly gulped down one *kufta*, followed by another—each was almost the size of a tennis ball! As I took one, another surfaced up in its place assuring me there must be many more and my theft would go unnoticed.

With my hunger somewhat satisfied, I continued nonchalantly, towards the workmen who were anxiously waiting for me. They quickly took the pot. I got down from the donkey and waited for them to return the empty pot. As soon as they had finished eating, they angrily stormed over to me shouting and raising their fists. Apparently, there were only four *kuftas* left and they had figured out that each worker was to get two. They accused me of eating the missing meatballs. I got scared and quickly confessed. The three men pounced on me, punching me in my stomach and head. After a severe beating, they finally realized that no good would come of the beating so they let me go.

This incident came to mind on November 6, 2001 when my dear neighbor Nazar Hatzigian came to visit me and brought me a bowl of yogurt soup with similar *kufta* that his wife Hermine had prepared. *Akh*, there is so much more to remember, but where do you stop?

1918-1919 PLAGUED WITH FEAR

This must have been some time around 1918-1919. **The situation was getting more hazardous for me and I was plagued with the fear of being captured** by the Parchanjtzee Turks who were extremely hostile towards Armenians. Those were the years when *ethnic cleansing* should have subsided in accord with the new government decree. Instead, it worsened. At any given time and for whatever official reason, hundreds of Armenians continued to be rounded up and executed simultaneously in one barbaric fashion or another. *Chettehs* (Turkish or Kurdish thugs) were also incited to take their personal hostilities on any innocent Armenian.

Kerop never realized the acute danger older boys like myself were experiencing. We were constantly afraid of getting caught. Throughout each and every day, the *moonehdeeks* (Turkish town criers) carried posters, chanting, "Anyone harboring an Armenian will be fined and jailed for five years with a chain around their neck!" That *incessant chanting* never seemed to stop. **The sting and threat of those chants** never left my ears or my gut! I was always on guard and terrified when I heard or saw them on the streets, especially in Parchanj.

One day during this cloud of terror, I had the fright of my life. I was returning home to Khanum's house carrying a *goozh* of water from the spring, when suddenly I noticed that a gang of *moonehdeeks* was walking straight towards me. Loudly and viciously, their words penetrated right through my gut. I was defenseless, there was no place for me to hide, and I knew I couldn't run. I did the only thing left for me to do. I grit my teeth, held my breath and prayed as I continued to walk. I don't remember how, but I reached Khanum's house untouched! **Was I walking side by side with God?**

Whenever a Turk was suspicious of any young, healthy looking Armenian man or woman who was working for other Turks, he reported the offender to officials. Within minutes the gendarmes picked up both the offender and the suspect.

I was keenly aware of how the older Armenian boys were rounded up and killed. Their disfigured bodies were strewn in one area or another. Some bodies were left to decay in the ravines and rivers. Strands of long hair belonging to young girls clung to the branches of nearby brush, sometimes still in braids, some just a cluster of dark brown or gray strands. Those strands of hair revealed the torture and fate of the victims. Those Armenians who witnessed such scenes cried for the martyrs saying the last rites for the victims as they passed by.

As the years passed, I learned that hair was the last part of the body to decompose. The sight of the bodies of older women and young children was the hardest for me to witness. *Akh*, no one was spared. My dear wife was also witness to similar incidents when the family was deported from Malatya, in 1923. The strands of hair particularly affected her because she too had long, beautiful, auburn braids, a feature that brought her numerous compliments from others—she had a difficult time dealing with what she witnessed.

That practice of slaughter terrorized all those, like myself, who had not been rounded up. Although I felt there was an almighty God,

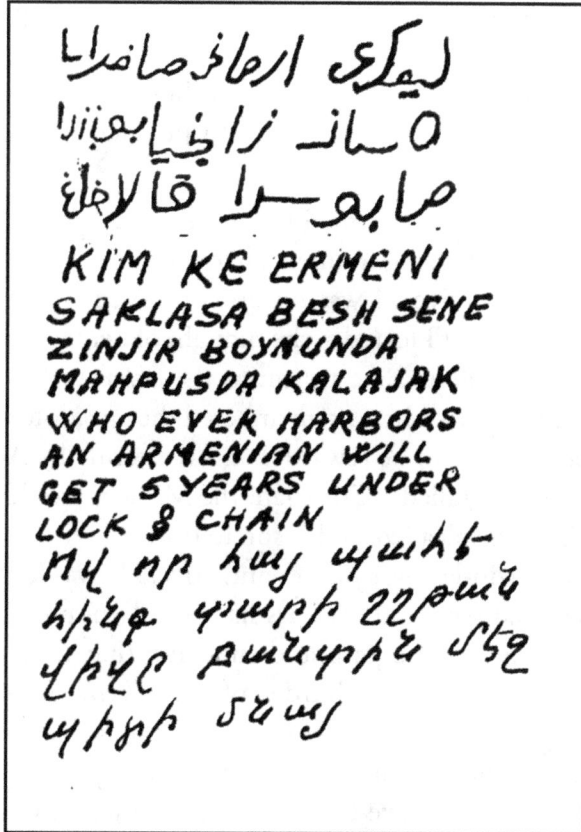

ليككي الرهاخ صاضراليا
سانخ زرخياابعزيزا
صابوصرا قالرخلأ

KIM KE ERMENI
SAKLASA BESH SENE
ZINJIR BOYNUNDA
MAHPUSDA KALAJAK
WHO EVER HARBORS
AN ARMENIAN WILL
GET 5 YEARS UNDER
LOCK & CHAIN

*A chant from hell **

where was He then? How could He bear witness to such atrocities inflicted on those who had staunch faith in Him? Any *lahgode* (Turkish punk) who had the least bit of suspicion would stop a suspect and force them to curse upon the cross.

Khanum's brother-in-law, who was in his sixties, was very hostile toward Armenians. He lived a few houses away from Khanum and frequently dropped in

---

*   This chant pierced through my bones as I charaded as a Turk for six excrutiating years. To this day, the flesh on my bones still trembles with fear when I recall those words.

unexpectedly to visit with her. Khanum immediately would warn me to hide in the haystack, because if he caught sight of me, she knew he would report me.

Ironically, he was married to a young, beautiful Armenian. They had two lovely daughters about two and three years old. He was very devoted to those girls, but he was always quarreling with his wife. Their neighbors could hear their voices. I often heard older children taunt the girls by chanting, "Your father is *using* an Armenian woman!"

I couldn't believe my eyes and ears one day when I saw Khanum, in front of her brother-in-law, swearing on her marriage certificate that she had no Armenians in her house. For all those months that I worked for her, she not only prevented my capture, she also put her own life and that of her daughter's in jeopardy.

As for myself, while I hid in the haystack, my whole body trembled relentlessly with fear. During moments like that, I felt it was much easier being a martyr than being a survivor. I was *always* consumed with the terror of being caught. Dying was not what I feared—the thought of being tortured plagued me more. Each time Khanum alerted me to run to the *akhor* to hide because her brother-in-law was coming to visit her; I remembered the anecdote about the old blind Turk's request for a chance to be rewarded in his afterlife by Allah. He held the belief whenever a Moslem killed a Christian, the Moslem would go to Paradise. As his health was failing, he pleaded for his son to bring him an Armenian to kill. I knew Khanum's brother-in-law was just as vindictive. He was looking for such an opportunity. My eyes had seen and my ears had heard enough to torment anyone. Survivors not only endure the pain and suffering that they personally experienced, but also endure the pain and burden of the *collective suffering and losses* they witness. What person could digest and cope with the human indignities and annihilation of his people and still maintain a normal existence? I knew very well that the martyr's demise could have been my fate at any given moment. For the rest of my life, I bore the torment I felt while hiding in the haystack in Khanum's stable. For six years I suffered in that manner wherever I went. *I always wished for the grace of God, that I were a mouse searching for a hole in which to hide and not be caught.*

To make matters worse, Khanum's Turkish neighbor who lived across the street had a son whose name was Abdullah Effendi. He was a gendarme. In the mornings he went off to work in Mezreh sharply dressed in his uniform. As he walked, it seemed to me, he purposely clicked the heels of his boots to ring the "shuck, shuck, shuck" sound of the ornaments on them.[*] He also detested Armenians and whenever I heard him coming, my fears intensified.

---

[*] That same sound, "shuck, shuck, shuck," made by gendarmes' boots was frightening to my wife in Malatya.

He too was married to an Armenian. Her Turkish name was Fahtmah Khanum—her Armenian name was Anna. They had two beautiful sons, two and three years old. Fahtmah Khanum had a five-year-old daughter by her Armenian husband who had fled to America to avoid the Turkish draft.

Fahtmah Khanum was very hostile towards other Armenians and me. Whenever our paths crossed, she called me *Gavour Boghee* (Armenian filth). That name pierced my soul each time I heard it. Apparently she was trying to impress her husband, mother-in-law and others that she no longer identified as an Armenian. Although she took good care of all three of her children, she was extra protective of her Armenian daughter. On the few occasions when I brought Kerop to spend a day or two with me, Fahtmah Khanum and her daughter would come to visit with my Khanum, but she never brought her two

Seated. Anna Kaprielian (Fatmah Khanum) with her daughter Yeranuhi on her left (Haleb, 1922)

sons. While I prepared sitting places on the rooftop, Fahtmah Khanum warned her daughter to stay away from the *Gavour Boghee*. I was forced to send him into the stable. His crying sobs pierced my ears, even though I knew he didn't understand the situation at the time.

Surprisingly, the two Armenian Turkish wives, Fahtmah Khanum and my Khanum's brother-in-law's wife, used to taunt each other. Shouting loudly from their rooftops from one house to the other, they attempted to frighten each other, "I have two daughters, my husband won't leave me. He won't be able to find anyone to take care of two girls." The other would shout back, "I have two sons, my husband won't leave me." They argued back and forth. Were the women worried that one day they would be turned out? Then what would happen to them?

With that realization, it was easier for me to understand Fahtmah's attitude toward Kerop and me. I really could not blame her. She had to do whatever was necessary to protect herself and her daughter. Her attitude was very similar to what I endured on many occasions when I was suspected of being an Armenian and had to prove otherwise. A Turkish punk, suspecting me, would order me to draw a cross on the ground and defecate upon it and at the same time to recite in Turkish:

Khach, khach gurban khach.
Bashen gahldur gozun ach.
Osmahnlee duhrr, zhorlee duhrr
Topouzlahry ghalun duhrr
Vourdee bahnah suchdeem sahnah.

Cross, cross beloved cross.
Lift your head and open your eyes
He is Ottoman, he is strong.
He has a strong fist.
He strikes me and he makes me defecate upon you.

It shames me now to even repeat those foul words and it is not worth repeating them in Armenian. However, if I hadn't submitted at the time, I wouldn't be here today. I was forced to comply with this act many times. *Don't bother your heart nor blame Fahtmah Khanum.* She had no choice but to protect herself and her child. That was God's will. As my father always said, "Without God's will, the leaves on the trees do not move!" *"Getzeh Asdvatz!"* ("Bravo, God!") The forgiving God willed that for all Armenians. Then how do we know? After all, it was God's will why I am still here.

On several occasions when I was stopped by a Turk and did not show respect by saying, *"Behlah Effendi"* ("Yes, sir!"), all he had to say was, *"Deeneemeh Sogdee!"* ("He cursed my religion!") and I would have been jailed or killed by any means they pleased.

While writing these memoirs, I have relived so many emotions a million times. It seems they tell me the world should be damned and cursed. Man should not have been born, nor have had a life like that. **It has been a dog's life!**

Unfortunately, Khanum's reassurance didn't rid me of the reality of what I was hearing and experiencing daily in the streets of Parchanj! I was plagued with fear of getting caught, tortured and killed on any given day. At times I still relive the chill of fear those chants instilled within my soul. My mind was affected with intense fear!

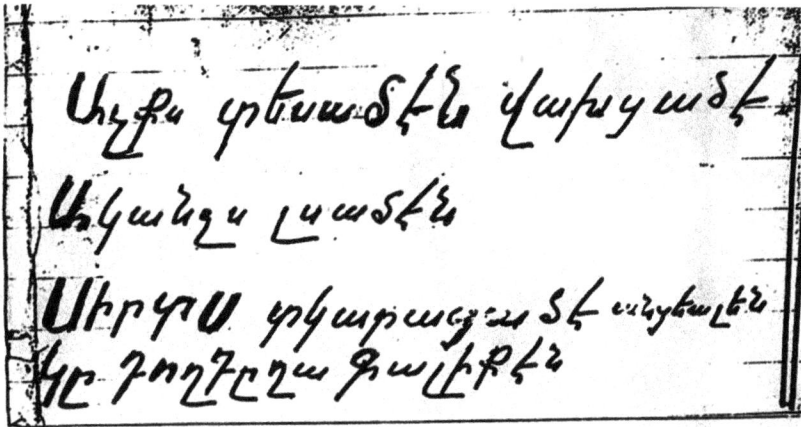

My eyes are frightened with what they have seen
My ears from what they have heard.
My heart has weakened from the past and
trembles from what is yet to come.

OVERCOME BY A HUGE WHITE GHOST

As my fears got worse, one day another small boy who was left all alone approached me for a place to sleep for a couple of nights. This time with Khanum's approval, I took him in until he was able to find a place for himself. Again, we shared the *sahkoosee*. On that particular night, during my sleep, I awoke abruptly and *saw* a huge white ghost coming towards me. *"Juzz, juzz, juzz,"* the stable door was swinging slowly back and forth. Suddenly, the ghost yelled at me in a low, loud voice, *"Should I come and get you?"* The moment I heard his voice, I yelled out in fear. Khanum immediately rushed to my side. She gently awakened me and began to comfort me. "You were frightened in your sleep. There is no danger. There are no ghosts nor devils." Realizing I was still trembling with horror, she took me upstairs and continued to reassure me that everything would be alright. "As long as I am here by your side, you are safe. The feelings that are frightening you are caused by men who have no feelings or conscience." Throughout all the commotion the small boy didn't awake, he didn't see what I saw.

For the next several nights, I continued to see and hear the ghost who was trying to open the door. Each night, I kept hearing the door opening and closing—*juzz, juzz, juzz* and the ghost "Should I come and get you?" Each night, Khanum tried her best to console me and to reassure me that everything would be all right. I kept on awakening, yelling and breaking out in a cold sweat. Feeling helpless, my Khanum reluctantly advised me to find a close relative. Perhaps then I could get rid of the nightmares.

Confused and scared, somehow I agreed that that might be a solution. Again with mixed emotions, I left that wonderful kindhearted woman. Not really knowing in which direction to head for, instinctively I found myself heading back towards Mezreh. The thought of getting away from Parchanj was beginning to feel better and better. The *further* away I got, the better I felt. It was only then that I realized how terrified I was by the gendarme living right across from Khanum's house, when her brother-in-law dropping in unexpectedly made me run in panic to hide in the haystack, or the non-stop chanting of the warning of repercussions for hidden Armenians. All of those fears grated on my nerves until they overpowered my appreciation for the warm, clean quarters, the sparse but certain amount of daily food, and most of all, the caring protective disposition Khanum had for me. Gradually, I realized I had stopped hearing the incessant cries of the lynch mobs—and the ghost never reappeared.

Without too much difficulty, I found myself a place to sleep. Within a few days, I found an odd job with a crew of men who were building a couple of houses. I was paid barely enough to buy food. My job was to carry heavy red tiles up a ladder to the roof. I was able to do that only for a few days. I had not recovered from my previous ordeal and didn't have the physical strength or endurance. The Armenian woman housing me had heard that the German orphanage in Mezreh was housing Armenian boys from the ages four to eighteen years. The atmosphere in the villages showed signs of renewing calm. People in general were feeling more at ease. I accepted the woman's suggestion to go there with the hope of finding a safer place and a more suitable job nearby.

As I look back, was it the hostile Turks in Parchanj, or was the situation for Armenians continuing to worsen? *Maybe both...*

26. THE GERMAN PROTESTANT ORPHANAGE

JOB AT THE POORR

In 1918, Mr. Johannes Ehmann was the missionary in charge of the German orphanage caring for Protestant Armenian orphans. However, there were also about thirty-nine *Loosavorchagan* (Orthodox National church) Armenian boys, ages seven to seventeen, who lived in the stable behind the impressive building of the orphanage, which housed the younger boys.

Within a few days after I moved in, I decided it would be much safer and easier if I brought Kerop and Markar to live with me on this orphanage compound. When I went to pick up Kerop, I discovered my cousin Hmahyag and Markar's six-year-old cousin, Gegham, were also living at the Yeprahd orphanage. I took all three with me, and went to pick up Markar who was still working at the inn in Tadem. Within a couple of days of his arrival, he was given a similar job at the orphanage registering the names of all of the orphans spending a night or two in our new compound. Each day he gave his report to Mihran Effendi Derderian for his approval of the day's activities.

Along with the other older boys, I was given only a place to sleep. I still had to provide for my own food. Fortunately, I found a relatively good job at the Turkish *poorr* (bakery) which wasn't too far from the orphanage. For my compensation, I was allowed to eat as much bread as I wanted while I was on the premises. The *somoon* loaves were baked primarily for the Turkish soldiers. Only a small number was sold outside in front of the *poorr* for the local civilians.

My job was to fetch water from the spring. I carried two five-gallon tin containers using a makeshift yoke, which I made, over my shoulders. Each day I made about six trips—the spring was a good distance from the bakery, so by the end of the day I was quite tired.

There were about eight other Armenian boys, three Kurdish boys and three Turkish boys all working on various tasks such as kneading the dough, baking and caring for the fire and one boy sold bread in front of the

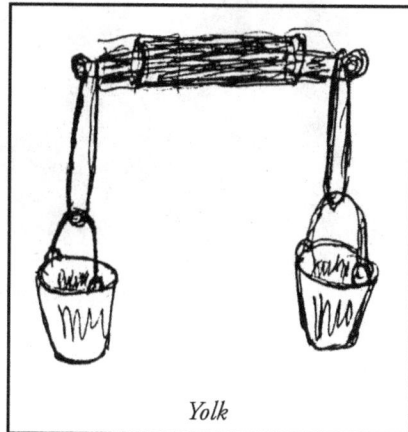

Yolk

Gegham, Kerop, and Hampartzoum. Mezreh, (cir. 1918)

bakery. In addition, there were two official guards in charge of all the workers, making sure our work was done correctly.

It didn't take long before I noticed when the loaves were taken out of the *poorr* there were scraps of bread that were dropped in a nearby bin. With the guards' permission, I took them. I knew the younger boys at the orphanage would appreciate *the scraps.* At the end of each day, I gave that bread to *Mayrig* to disperse among the younger boys.

One night when I returned to the orphanage, a four to five year old orphan ran up to me and yanked on my arm. In a soft, gentle voice, he said, "I've been waiting for my mother, but she isn't coming. My mother loves me a lot. One day she is going to come after me, *I am so hungry now.* Next time could you bring a little more bread so I could feel completely full?" I will never forget his facial expression and his hungry *plea for more food. Mayrig's* eyes and mine filled with tears. Two little older boys took notice and one asked the other, "Why are they crying?" What had those innocent babies done to deserve such punishment? **Where was their God? Where was their protector?** That was the only life he knew, but his stomach was asking for more food. His plea convinced me to find additional ways to bring more bread for the orphans.

I wasted no time. That evening, I came up with a new scheme. I knew, however, I would need the help of a younger nine-year-old boy whom I always saw at the spring where I filled my tins with water. We would both be taking a *dangerous risk,* but there was no other solution. The younger orphans were starving.

The next morning when I entered the *poorr,* cautiously and nonchalantly, I picked up the two empty tins as usual. When I found the opportune moment, I dropped a *somoon* loaf in each tin and hurried towards the spring. From the distance, I saw my accomplice waiting for me.

When I gave him the bread, he ran up to the orphanage and gave the two loaves to Mayrig. Then he came back to the spring and waited until I returned again with two more loaves for him to take up to Mayrig. This routine was repeated six times throughout the day. Meanwhile, I continued taking home the daily scraps of bread as before. Altogether, the boys enjoyed more than twelve loaves each day.

My cousin, Hmahyag, has been the only person whom I helped that has acknowledged and thanked me for the effort and risks I took. In 1969 I saw him again when I made a visit to Soviet Armenia. He called me, "That boy who had the courage to steal from the Turkish *poorr* to help the boys in the orphanage. No one else would take *that* risk." His acknowledgement meant so much to me. I then knew the risks I took for others *were appreciated!*

TWO THIEVES

As the days passed, my little helper and I continued our secret mission, until one day when one of the Kurdish boys noticed I was sneaking bread from the *poorr*. He quietly approached me and began to insist I share one piece with him. If I didn't, he warned me he would turn me in. As I contemplated his *threat*, I noticed he too was sneaking out wheat in his pant legs. In those days Kurdish boys wore *shalvars* (baggy pants) gathered at their mid-calf, tied with a string. Before I did anything, I waited a few days to be absolutely sure he repeated his theft in the same daily manner.

When my conviction was confirmed, I decided to snitch on him before he snitched on me. I knew if my allegation proved to be false, the guard would turn on me with vengeance. I knew I couldn't make a mistake. Therefore, when I was absolutely convinced he was a thief just like myself, I confided my plan with another one of the Armenian boys for moral support. So the two of us waited until the Kurd filled his trousers with wheat and started to walk out of the door. Each pant leg was full of wheat. He walked towards the door, unnoticed by the guard. We waited a bit more, until he stepped out of the door, and then we called the guard. We told him the Kurd snuck out of the *poorr* with wheat hidden in his pants.

Immediately the guard angrily raised his club at us, his growl was very intimidating, "Are you absolutely sure of what you said? If your accusations are false, you have taken the risk of being executed yourself!" He went on to inform us that, under Islamic law, that was *nahmat* (sinful) because wheat was considered a stuff of life. Thus, the act would be very offensive to Moslems—the Kurd had committed two sins!

The guard pushed the Kurd aside, and with his sword, he made one swift strike right above the knee. Wheat poured out like a stream of water. Without hesitating, he beat the Kurd to a pulp with his club and within seconds, the Kurd fell to the ground, wounded so viciously that he could not speak. We just heard his wails, whimpering cries and groans. I couldn't tell if he lived or died. We cringed in our shoes with our own fears. We did not wish that fate for the Kurd. However, he brought that upon himself. Had he not threatened me with his intentions that would not have happened. He left me with only one choice. If it hadn't been him, it would have been me lying on the ground whimpering. Despite the brutality, no doubt the Turk was more lenient with the Kurdish boy than he would have been with me, an Armenian.

While that incident enhanced my awareness of the risks I was taking, I was still compelled to sneak extra loaves of bread in my tins. **The orphans were still hungry**—they needed to eat.

SOLACE AT THE SOORSOOREE VANK

Markar's illness continued to worsen. Whenever I had free time, after doing my chores, I took him to the hot springs in Soorsooree, a nearby village. I would invite a few other boys to go along with us. In silence, we walked all around the ruins of the Soorsooree Vank, an ancient Armenian monastery. As we stepped around the sacred stones of the past, *we all prayed for a way out of our misery.*

Trying to remember and repeat his grandfather's prayers, Markar would pray much like a priest. He felt the spirit of the setting was more conducive to having his prayers answered as a cure for his illness. The time we spent there gave him renewed hope, as nothing else was helping him to get well.

I took him as often as I was able to get away. I still shudder in my shoes when I think of *the precarious risks* I took for a distant relative. All of us were revealing our identity just being at the site. It seemed to be God's will that I acquiesce and like so much of God's *will* that I never have understood.

I'm sure Markar must have known the sacrifices I made for him. Undoubtedly, he must have told his parents and brothers about all of the risks—the chance of being caught—*I took for him.*

ARMENIAN CHILDREN, CHILDREN OF GRIEF

One day when I had just returned from work, an Armenian man about twenty-five years old who was blind in one eye, had just walked in looking for a place to sleep. Markar went to record his name on the ledger. Suddenly one of our little boys about six years old started to foam at the mouth and trembled uncontrollably. Within seconds, he quietly crumbled unconsciously to the floor. Mayrig and I sat down on the floor and cradled him in our arms. For about an hour, Markar read aloud from his Bible, hoping that might relieve the boy. We really didn't know what else to do.

Gradually he started to regain consciousness. He opened his eyes and asked, "Is he still here?" We didn't know to whom he was referring. After we tried to soothe him, we reassured him that he was in safe hands.

Slowly and softly he began to relate his terrifying experience:

> *A Turk took my mother and me to live with him. He treated me well only in the presence of my mother. When my mother was not around, the Turk treated me cruelly. That went on for quite a while until one day the Turk told me to leave the house with him. Without a choice or suspicion, I went out as he instructed. We walked towards a hole that had previously been dug. As soon as we got to it, he hit me hard over my head with his shovel, and then he shoved me in. He quickly covered me up*

with dirt. Thinking I was dead, he walked away. Gradually I tried to climb out on my own. My head was hurting and I was too weak to crawl out. As I was throwing dirt out of the hole, a woman passing by noticed me. She quickly helped me out of the hole and brought me here.

When he finished his story, we asked if he knew who frightened him in the orphanage. Still a little agitated, he said the Turk who buried him was blind in the same eye as the Armenian man who had just come in looking for a place to sleep for the night. He mistook that Armenian for the Turk.

Whenever I remember that incident, I also recall the song Hmahyag learned in the Protestant orphanage.

> *Generations of Armenians, children of grief*
> *Wounds we have which could never heal*
> *Beaten, bludgeoned, maimed, tortured*
> *Deportation, deprivation, exiled*
> *They filled our lives with eternal pain*
> *Orphans we became, poor and alone*
> *Wandering aimlessly from door to door*
> *Abandoned, wretched, despairing*
> *Be sympathetic, my friend... be kind*
> *Rescue us from these painful wounds. . .*

Our eyes had been frightened by what they had seen and our ears had been frightened by what they had heard. We were not afraid of Hell, as our lives had passed through Hell.

SIXTEEN AMERICAN BUSES

In 1918, when the war ended, the Germans retreated from Turkey. The American Consul was already there and soon the American soldiers arrived. On one clear dark evening, sixteen American buses drove slowly into Kharpert, down the main road, Pahpooryoly, which was a dirt road not meant to accommodate motorized vehicles. The caravan of buses rolled in two lanes, one bus after the other, all were equally spaced from each other. The bus lights formed an impressive stream of lights in the clear evening sky, a novel sight thrilling for us to witness. Simultaneously the shrill of the sirens—jeeve, jeeve, jeeve—blasted into the cool air. What a spectacle! Suddenly the buses all stopped together in a strategic location. The whole city lit up!

All the older Armenian boys and I positioned ourselves on the dilapidated rooftop of the stable to get a good view of that unique event—we were lucky it didn't give way with our weight. None of us dared to go any closer. It would have been suicide if an Armenian approached any nearer to the parked buses—their identity as Armenians would have become obvious. *Had the Americans really come in defense of the Armenians?*

I can still clearly envision the bright lights that lit up the dark skies and hear the sound of the sirens that broke the silence of the suspense—*jeeve, jeeve, jeeve.* For a moment, even I felt someone had come to rescue us. Could it be that there really was a God who protected *all* of his living creatures?

The fact that the Americans had come in defense of the Armenians horrified the Turks. They, too, abandoned the streets leaving them desolate! What a feeling this created, incongruous to the precarious existence of the Armenians.

While I realized that was a moment to remember, deep in my heart I couldn't rejoice. The Turks were not that easy to yield or to surrender. The disappointment from the Kurdish rebellion in the Derseem still lingered in my bones. If the Germans had not stopped the Kurds, history might have been different. *What an act of betrayal to all of humanity that was.* **Perhaps that very area of the world would be in peace today** *if the furry of the Kurds had not been deterred. When will the world powers respect all people of the world and guarantee their right to live on their homelands, land that they had occupied for thousands of years… and not act only for their self-interest?* **The one day I so wanted to see…** *Meghk!*

First the English came to help us, then the Germans, now the Americans had come with much fanfare, but we were still in great jeopardy.

The next morning when I got ready to go to work, there still was a carryover of the commotion from the events of the previous night. With mixed emotions, that uncertainty kept me even more on guard as I walked down to the *poorr.* I wasn't too surprised to find the shop was closed with no one inside. As it turned out, all of the shops and businesses, even the government building, were closed. Not one gendarme was in sight. Usually they were crawling around like ants, making sure the spurs on their boots clattered poignantly to heighten the intimidation of all those they pursued. From the minarets, instead of the usual threatening cries for anyone harboring Armenians, now they were crying out, "The Americans are our friends, as they are of the Armenians!" Don't be afraid—open your shops and businesses, go about your usual daily activities!"

Still, all establishments remained closed for the next four days. Now, I experienced one of the greatest moments of joy in my lifetime—**I saw Turks display fear!** This fear was reflected in so many ways. Now, the Turks were running to the German orphanage for refuge, pleading so they would not be hurt. The orphanages were already overcrowded with hundreds of Armenian orphans.

They were pleading to Armenians to have mercy on *them* and to help protect them from the Americans—a most bewildering moment! Even a Turk came up to me, "*Effendi*, please rescue me!" Although I took great delight in seeing him squirm and hearing his fearful pleas, *I was still well aware of my own doubts and fears. I knew it was not safe to reveal I was an Armenian.* What would happen tomorrow was not at all clear? Therefore, I simply responded in a congenial manner. Instinctively, I *felt* that the Americans, like the other European powers, would betray the Armenians and take sides with the Turks. Much to my dismay and bitter disappointment, my instincts were right. *Why? Why?*

A MESSAGE WRITTEN IN BLOOD

An American soldier had started rounding up a few older Armenian boys to take him to find the large Armenian houses. The Americans were looking for houses that were suitable to convert into orphanages for the increasing number of Armenian orphans.

As I turned around to go back to the German orphanage, the soldier also approached me. Not having anything better to do since the *poorr* was closed, I volunteered to help and joined the group.

The first village we went to was Buzzmehshen. Most of the previous owners of those homes had been farmers—even the largest farmhouse was too small for the American's purpose.

By now there were about ten to fifteen local boys who took the soldier to Vartahtell, which used to be an Armenian village. We found a large house that had a spring within the structure. When we knocked on the door, no one answered, but we heard voices from within. Suspecting Turks were inside, we called out in Turkish that the Americans were demanding the use of that house. When they still didn't open the door, the soldier gave one strong kick on the door, and it swung open. The Turks started to plead that they not be killed and they would leave immediately. So they did, leaving everything behind.

It was a two-story house. The soldier told us to throw all of the contents out of the windows. As we started to throw out everything, the soldier was inspecting the other rooms. In a few moments he stopped us, because he had found an official seal that claimed the house and its contents belonged to the Turkish government—all the items had to be accounted for. At the same moment, a shriek from one of the boys led us to the large subterranean pantry. *The whole room was splattered with blood;* one wall was covered with Armenian writing written in blood. As we began to read what was written, the soldier was overcome with distress, *"They brought us here. They beat us to a pulp. Now, they are taking us to the bottom of the valley to be killed!"* There were from fifty to seventy five names listed next to the message on the wall.

By the time we left the room and departed from the house, we were **all emotionally distraught.** What we had done there was emotionally incomprehensible. We had totally ransacked the precious belongings of innocent people who had been tortured and then slaughtered by the Turks.

Within three to four days several large houses from both Kharpert and Mezreh were found and converted into orphanages. Soon they were *filled* with orphans gathered from the nearby vicinities. I only worked with the group for one day. I did not have the emotional stamina to disturb someone's belongings. I also had to work to provide food for the five of us.

The American missionary, Mr. Henry Riggs, had now replaced Mr. Ehmann, the German missionary. From what I heard, not only was Mr. Riggs in charge of the Protestant orphanage, he also had converted the Yeprahd College into an orphanage. He became headmaster of all of the Protestant Armenian orphanages subsequently established in that area of Kharpert and nearby villages, such as Husenig, Morenig, Soorsooree and Khoylee. Within a short period of time, he had more than two thousand five hundred Armenian orphans gathered from the area. Mr. Riggs was both well respected and liked by the Armenians, and he spoke Armenian fluently.

A SACK OF ARMENIAN BONES SOLD FOR ONE AMERICAN DOLLAR

During that same time, other American soldiers were hiring Turkish boys to canvas the area to collect Armenian bones that were strewn throughout the vicinity. Some bones were still in the exact spot, where the Armenians saw their fate. Other bones were stacked in mounds several feet high.

For each gunnysack that *Turkish rogues* gleefully filled with Armenian bones, they were *paid one American dollar.* Another insult! The Turks even profited from the bones of the Armenians they had slaughtered. Did the Americans have *no conscience* at all? *Akh, akh* what more can be said?

Chaghpiur was a very large waterfall at the edge of the cliff next to Yeprahd College. The ice cold, swift flowing water from the fall spilled over the cliff, about forty feet. Below was the *gohl* (base of the waterfall) where the water gathered. This fall was the source of water the local Armenians had used for their gardens and crops. It was one of the *main areas where the Turks had killed* and dumped thousands of Armenian bodies, old and young. They had been forced to leap down onto rocks in the *gohl.* The force of the water was so swift and powerful that many people died before hitting the bottom. Those who hesitated to leap were prodded with the Turks' swords. Depending on the crazed mental stage of Turks, some were first tortured, their bodies mutilated before they were pushed over.

Many Turks financially profited by collecting the Armenian bones at the foot of that one waterfall. *Did God see the justice in this?*

Today, Armenians want to know the whereabouts of the bones that American soldiers witnessed and had collected by the Turks under official American orders, with American taxpayers' money. Mounds of Armenian bones were spotted throughout Turkey wherever there were predominantly Armenian towns and villages. Many foreign officials and missionaries saw these mounds. However, what is a million times worse is having official denials of these facts by some of the strongest countries in the world today. *Humanitarian values have been, and are today, rapidly warped by monetary greed and political deception. How does that correlate with human rights policies, with religious doctrines, with Christian values? Write that on my back!*

These were the same scenes I witnessed and which I have never been able to forget nor forgive. How could **they?** How could **God!**

27. THE AMERICAN OFFER TO ARMENIANS

KUDE ARCHBISHOP MEKHITARIAN

News was spreading that the Americans were offering to take Armenian survivors from all of the nearby areas in and around Kharpert to Bolis. The sixteen empty buses were to be used for that purpose. The bus fare from Kharpert to Bolis was fifty dollars per person. To be eligible for the offer Armenians had to provide proof they had relatives in America who were willing to send additional passage money to sail from Bolis. As soon as a bus was filled with passengers, it left. Altogether buses remained in Kharpert for more than two months. Once the Armenians reached Bolis, they were somewhat safer and allowed to depart to their chosen destinations.

That offer was very encouraging news, especially for me. I was losing faith that we would be spared if we remained in Turkey. We were all getting older and larger, thus becoming a more vulnerable target for the Turks. With this renewed hope, I gathered Kerop, Hmahyag, Markar and Gegham. We walked briskly towards the American missionary office to see Mr. Riggs and to register our names. We qualified. We all had relatives in America and felt certain they would send us money once they knew we were alive—and they would do everything in their power to help us to escape from those atrocities.

We listed all of our names along with the request of fifty dollars apiece for the ticket. This notice was printed in the *"Djagadamard"* which was an Armenian newspaper published in Bolis and circulated in various cities both in Turkey and around the world wherever there was a significant Armenian community. With the use of this paper, many relatives and friends were reunited with lost loved ones and acquaintances. Fortunately, this paper circulated in Chicago where my brothers lived at the time.

About this same time, Kude Archbishop Mekhitarian had come to Kharpert to establish a headquarters within the Loosavorchagan compound. He attempted to renovate part of the church structure that was in ruins. In the back of the church were the partial remains of the old stable. It was a much smaller structure and more severely destroyed by the Turks than the stable on the German compound.

Loosavorchagan orphans, ages four to eighteen, were housed in this structure. Here too, the older boys were provided with only a place to sleep. They had to find food by their own means. Kude Archbishop Mekhitarian's main purpose in Kharpert was to enforce Mustafa Kemal's newly declared government decree to free Armenian slaves who still might have been in the vicinity from bondage and release them to relatives or to the local Armenian orphanages.

When I first heard about this new orphanage, I began to think it would be safer for all of us to move there. Even though the stable at the Protestant orphanage was more comfortable, it was more of a risk for those of us who were not Protestants. From my past experiences, I knew when situations were at their worst the missionaries had orders to turn out anyone who was not a Protestant—whenever they barely had enough resources to protect their own. I also felt safer to separate from those pathetic Armenians who snitched on anyone vulnerable for selfish reasons. That is the Armenians' Achilles Heel, snitching on one of his own! Therefore, I decided that living in the Loosavorchagan compound would indeed be in our best interest. Shortly after I moved in, I brought Kerop, Markar and Gegham to join me. We felt safer living together all in one place. I started to repair old shoes *(peenehchee)* and accepted any job I could find to provide food for all of us.

ENFORCING THE NEWLY DECLARED TURKISH DECREE

Shortly after we moved in, Baron Baghdazar, a lawyer from Kharpert, was brought to the compound under the Archbishop's care. The Turks had beaten him so severely that he was mentally crazed. When left on his own, he wandered around the streets. The Turks took further pleasure by taunting him, chanting, "*Vooroun,* Baron Baghdazarah *vooroun!*" ("Beat him again, beat Baghdazar again!")

Immediately, when he heard the chants, he thrashed his body against the nearest wall. At the same time, he desperately searched for a place to hide. Then, he searched for a fire in order to inhale the smoke. The smoke somehow soothed his emotions and calmed him down.

The Archbishop had given him a place to sleep in the church. His mattress was filled with straw. Whenever he was in one of his crazed moments, he pulled out a piece of straw, lit it, and inhaled the smoke. Subsequently he quietly fell asleep.

That incident alerted me that the situation was steadily getting worse for the Armenians, especially for me. The older and larger I became, **the more precarious** my situation became.

Kude Archbishop Mekhitarian wasted no time. He started to gather Armenian slaves kept by the Kurds or Turks and helped them to reunite with their parents, relatives or friends. One day a Kurd brought in two little boys about five to six years old. The boys no longer spoke or understood Armenian. They incessantly cried and yelled out in Kurdish, they did not want to stay there and they did not want to eat bread provided by a *Fuhlah,* (the Kurds called Armenians *Fuhlah*). The boys wanted to go back with the Kurds, since they had been raised to fear and dislike Armenians.

Not willing to give in, the Archbishop gave the Kurd money in exchange for the boys and bid the Kurd farewell. The boys were soon turned over to their relatives.

Armenian offspring, children of grief... God's most reverent Child, Jesus Christ, was crucified within a few days, nailed to the cross. In one day He found His peace. The Armenian survivors suffered mercilessly during the atrocities and forever more during their lifetime! Their suffering was much worse than that of God's reverent Child!

One afternoon in the mid-1990s, I visited Mary Najarian's father in the Ararat Armenian Convalescent Hospital in Mission Hills, California. He was born in Vasgerd, but for many years after the "chart" he had lived with Kurds in Kharpert. He too had forgotten his Armenian and spoke only in Kurdish.

I became aware that he was more capable reminiscing about our horrid past in Kurdish than in Armenian. Since I never really learned how to speak in Kurdish, I began to sing to him a Kurdish song that I vaguely remembered. Within seconds he joined in with me and we both had a delightful moment reminiscing about our past!

> *Derico, Hoy, Hoy Derico, Jan*
> *Aghcheeg eh fuhlan, tahseegeh sehlan*
> *Derico, Hoy, Hoy Derico, Jan*
>
> *Derico, Hoy, Hoy Derico, Jan*
> *Nahveh Nazlee, Khacheegeh pinzee*
> *Derico, Hoy, Hoy Derico, Jan*
>
> *Derico, Hoy, Hoy Derico, my love*
> *An Armenian girl has a shining cup*
> *Derico, Hoy, Hoy Derico, my love*
>
> *Derico Hoy, Hoy Derico, my love*
> *Nazlee her name has a golden cross*
> *Derico, Hoy, Hoy Derico, my love*
>
> *Derico, Hoy, Hoy Derico, my love*
> *Her stature is short, complexion fair*
> *Derico, Hoy, Hoy Derico, my love*

I only remember the third verse in Armenian; there were two more verses, but I have forgotten them completely. I could tell from his eyes and his voice that he was slowly remembering the past. After sharing a few memories, we said our good-byes with tears in our eyes. This was an emotional experience mutually understood among all Armenian survivors. We all share the same brutal pains and injustices executed by the Turks.

As I bring those incidents to mind, I appreciate now more than ever how Kude Archbishop Mekhitarian was completely self sacrificing in all of his endeavors to help his people in their bleakest days. Most of the clergy I have encountered since have been inept—as they say in Kharpert, "Throw them into the river going downstream and search for them going upstream!"

> *Yehrehsen boobook, meechen choorook.*
> *They look good on the outside, but are deceitful on the inside.*

The clergy mainly extend their hands for a handout. Moreover, their priorities do not reflect a sincere concern with a helping hand for the dire needs of their parishioners. I recall a story that explains how I feel towards the clergy:

> *Once a priest was swimming in a pool, suddenly he got a stomach cramp. His host noticed the problem and rushed over to his side and offered his hand to help him out "Der Hayr (Father)* **give** *me your hand, I could pull you out." The priest did not respond, and at the same time he was splashing his arms more helplessly.*
>
> *The host again called out, this time even louder, "Der Hayr,* **give** *me your hand!" Again there was no response. Now, the host was concerned and couldn't understand why the priest was not responding.*
>
> *The host stopped and changed his strategy . . . "Der Hayr,* **take** *my hand and hold on tightly." Finally he saw the priest grasp for his hand and the priest was rescued from the pool! . . .*

A QUESTION LEFT UNANSWERED

Several weeks later all five of us eagerly walked back to Mr. Riggs' office to check if anyone had discovered our notice in the Armenian newspapers.

A list of names of those whose relatives that had responded to the published notices was tacked on a wall. Markar's father had responded! He was living in Chicago. That is where my two brothers also lived. Markar's father was the eldest family member, though far removed. He was known to be well educated and a devout Dashnag. He proudly announced, "I am from Ismiel, Der Nerses Kahanaheen *vorteen* Dikran." He was the son of a priest and we knew him as Dikran Amo. He went to America with my eldest brother, Bedros, to avoid the Turkish draft in 1909. He left behind his wife and three sons.

Dikran Amo's response **raised our hopes** as the rest of us eagerly scanned the list hoping to find our names. After several minutes and repeated scanning, we felt a sharp pang of disappointment. We only found **one name**. Markar was the only name listed. We did not believe that could be true. We quickly continued to read *once more,* frantically searching for our names. However, Markar's name still was the only one we found. How could that be? All five of us had registered together. Surely my brother would have responded with the money needed for our rescue from Kharpert now that he knew we were alive!

The person claiming Markar was his father, the son of a priest! How could such a person have the conscience to leave his blood relatives in the claws of the Turkish vultures especially during the most dangerous time when we were getting older and larger and could have been captured more easily? The price of salvation was only fifty American dollars! Markar's father was coming all the way from America to save only his one son!

Twenty years later, in 1939, I went to visit Dikran Amo and his brother, Manoog, who still lived in Chicago. It was a real disappointment when I learned Markar had died within a few months after he arrived in America. When I went to his grave site, I talked to him in my mind:

> *Even for one glass of water, gratitude should be acknowledged. Please give me an answer. Why didn't your father or brother inform me that you had told them how much I risked my life to take care of you? No one has uttered a word to me. They have all been silent!*
>
> *If there were a telephone line from Earth to the Hereafter, I could verify all that I have said. I risked my life and my health taking care of you when I knew you were infected with tuberculosis. I did everything in my power to make your life more bearable. For four years I endured so many risks and hardships because you were with me. You were with me—you knew the hazards and discomforts we suffered together.*
>
> *What perplexes me most is when your father came to pick you up from Bolis, didn't you tell him the danger the rest of us were in and insist that he rescue the three of us in gratitude for all I had done for you? You knew our danger was escalating each day. Even my brother, Kaspar, was in Bolis the same time you and your father were there. Yet nothing was said!*

It seems God, likewise, wanted Kerop and me to suffer a little longer, "to be ravaged by hunger and fear." *Without the will of God, the leaves of the tree do not move.* My father's words were still embedded in my mind. The worst was yet to come...

We were *devastated* because only Markar was to be rescued. Still in a stupor, we slowly walked back to the orphanage. The other boys tried to console me. They encouraged me by saying my turn would come next, surely my brothers would respond! We would soon go to America.

A few days later, after we put Markar on the bus to go to Bolis, we became even more distraught. We felt like crumbled bulghur pilaf! However, to what avail? Years later, after reading my brother's old letters it was even harder to learn that my brothers had paid Dikran Amo 300 dollars passage money for Kerop, Kaspar and me.

OVSANNA WAS OUR ANGELIC NURSE

A few weeks later in our weakened physical state, five of us contracted typhoid fever. Kerop, three other boys and I got very sick. We were taken to the American hospital from the orphanage. Hmahyag and Gegham* were left untouched. A nurse from Kehsehreeg cared for us until we all got well. Her name was Ovsanna and she had one glass eye. She was an excellent nurse. What I would have given to be able to see and thank her one more time in subsequent years. I have never met another nurse to match her compassion and skills. She nursed us for more than two months. That was the first time I had ever slept in a real bed. Previously, I always slept on a floor mattress, the stable floor, or when I was lucky, the stable deck, *akhorreen sahkooseen*.

We were alarmed when she tied both our hands and feet to the bedposts without any explanation. That frightened us because we had seen so much, and we did not know why it was done. Sensing our concern, she immediately calmed us down and continued to reassure us this was for our own safety since we were trembling and thrashing about so much.

Next, she shaved all of our body hair and then gave us a bed bath. For a whole month we had nothing to eat. All we were given was water and medicine. While lying in bed, we saw many patients die. Their bodies were immediately removed from the hospital and taken to a remote area to be burned to avoid the chance of spreading further diseases.

As tired as she was, Ovsanna kept reassuring us that we were doing well. She told us it was her duty to see that we recovered, and it was our duty to serve and protect our nation when we were released from the hospital.

One day, we were startled when a new patient, Giragos, was brought into the hospital. He was a man from the village of Khoolah and for several years he was a slave for various Turks. He had been tied to a post with his face strapped upward

---

*   After we left the hospital, we never saw Gegham again.

facing the blazing sun. Night and day he had been exposed to the elements without a drop of water to drink. The scorching sun had blinded him. After four days his whole body was completely drained and he was dropped off at the hospital. The more I witnessed these barbaric means of torture, **the more despondent I became.**

The hospital was congested with so many patients that there was not a bed available for him. He was placed on a mattress on the floor next to my bed. They also tied his hands and feet. A couple of days later, they noticed he no longer was moving at all. To determine whether he had died, they stuck a long needle in the sole of his foot. When there was no response, he was pronounced dead and his body was removed.

The poor soul never had a chance with those barbarians. Their mind only worked as a machine creating the most hideous ways of torturing and killing.

Why had God created such minds? For what purpose? Even worse, why did He also create those who **blatantly deny** what they did, and in turn allow the Turks *to continue* with fiendish barbaric schemes into the new millennium? Whose God is responsible?

Exactly thirty days after we were admitted to the hospital, Ovsanna brought each of us a small piece of bread. After putting a small bit of bread in our mouths, we were horrified to discover we couldn't chew. Our teeth had no sensation! We all started to cry.

Had they extracted all of our teeth? We didn't know what to think except to worry about what else they might have done to us? We had seen so much mutilation. Our eyes had been frightened by all that they had seen. Our ears had been frightened by all they had heard. We had become suspicious of **everyone.** Especially now that we were tied down.

Again, Ovsanna quickly tried to reassure us. "Don't be afraid," she repeated several times, "Touch your teeth. They are still there in your mouth. You haven't lost even one tooth." She continued to console us. "Because you have not eaten for a month, your teeth feel soft. Little by little you will soon feel better. Tomorrow I will give you a larger piece of bread. Within a few days, you will feel your teeth and discover they are just fine."

Within two weeks, we were indeed feeling better, and we each were getting half a loaf of bread each day. Ovsanna continued to bathe, reassure and console us daily and we no longer needed medication.

A week later, an Armenian speaking Danish nurse, Tanta Katarine, who was in charge of the hospital, came to see us. After examining us, she told us we were well enough to be discharged from the hospital. She told us we had to leave so she could make room for new patients.

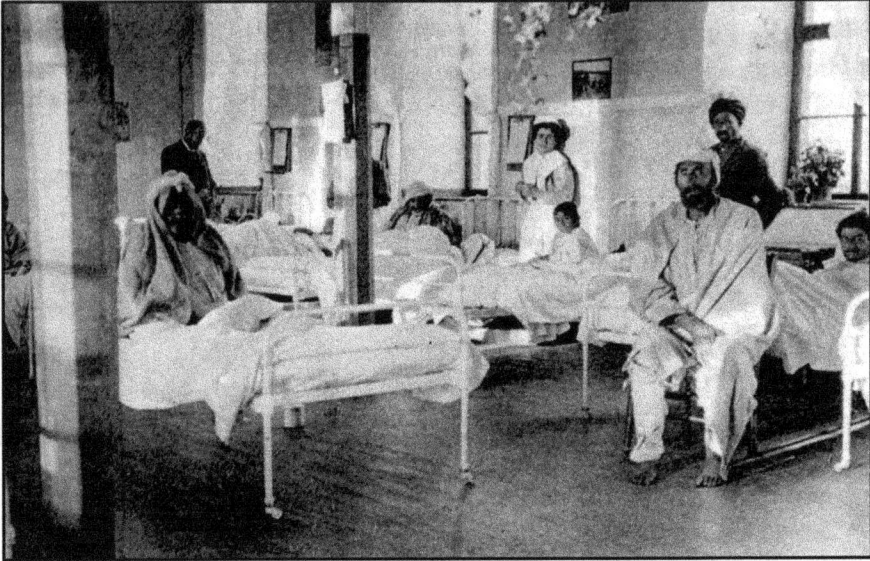

Inside of the Hospital

We were still physically weak and we knew we had no place to go. There was no one to care for us until we were strong enough to fend for ourselves. We were still hungry and in need of nourishment. **For the first time**, I felt too weak to work for food and a place to sleep for all of us. Tears welled up in my eyes—the other boys felt the same. Crying didn't phase Tanta Katarine. She was the nurse in charge and she needed the space. "Do you want the boys outside to die?" Once again, Ovsanna recognized our dilemma and **volunteered** to care for us a bit longer until we felt strong enough to fend for ourselves. She did so, even though she too was overworked with her other patients and duties. A few days later, when we felt a bit stronger, we realized how much our space was needed for those in more life threatening situations. We thanked Ovsanna for all her care and concern and left. I have **never forgotten** her sincerity and devotion for her patients. How I have wished to have had the opportunity to thank her once again in subsequent years.

My wife, Ovsanna, likewise spoke highly about the Danish nurses in Malatya. Ovsanna became familiar with them when they went to the seamstress to have their dresses sewn. From the age of nine Ovsanna worked for a seamstress as an apprentice. She always spoke about one nurse in particular, Miss Jacobsen. In addition to remembering how kind and beautiful she was, she remembered her for adopting an Armenian girl. The girl was a cute blond girl from the Dingilian family. Her mother gave up her daughter for her daughter's safety. She deeply feared what the Turks would do to such a beautiful girl.

Outside of the Hospital

In the 1950s, Mrs. Dingilian used to visit us frequently in Los Angeles. I remember well how she talked about the circumstances why she made the sacrifice. She always carried a picture of her daughter and the nurse. She never regretted her sacrifice because she always knew her daughter was alive, safe and loved, and getting excellent care. Her nephew R. Bonapart practices law in Los Angeles.

I was also appreciative of the Danish nurses for their compassionate care of the Armenian patients and very impressed with how fluently they spoke Armenian.

BILKED IN THE EXCHANGE: TEN TURKISH BANK NOTES FOR TWENTY-FIVE AMERICAN DOLLARS

The American missionary's office was the first place we decided to go once we left the hospital. We hoped by now my brothers had responded to our notice. There was no doubt they would have sent our passage money to go to Bolis. We still had a chance. This was a unique opportunity provided by the American government. But to our misfortune, again our names were not listed on the board.

At some point during the time that we were in the hospital, Dikran Amo had sent an additional twenty-five dollars to his friend Avedis Tassjian, who had a job at Bank Ottoman as well as in Mr. Riggs' office. Dikran Amo instructed Tassjian to give the money to Marker for *pocket money* that he might need on his way to Bolis, not knowing Markar had already left Kharpert.

When we arrived in Mr. Riggs' office and inquired about a response from my brothers, Tassjian immediately *realized* our situation. Without my knowledge, he quickly got my first and last name from Kerop and wired Dikran Amo that he was going to give us the *twenty-five dollars* because Markar was no longer there.

A few minutes later, sympathizing with our situation, Mr. Riggs handed us *ten* Turkish bank notes. Immediately, we thought Markar's conscience had awakened, and he finally sent us a *token* of gratitude for all that I had done and risked for him. By this time more than two to three months had passed since we had sent him off to Bolis.

The ten Turkish bank notes were barely enough to buy a meager amount of food for two weeks and considerably much less than twenty-five American dollars! Again God felt we had not suffered enough. Our fate was asking for more. It was *devastating* to realize how quickly some people will take advantage of a situation to bilk another if they could get away with it—*even at a time like this*. (This transaction of money was made known subsequently from Dickran Amo's letters written to my brothers.)

KUDE ARCHBISHOP MEKHITARIAN TOOK US BACK

Having no other place to go, we headed directly back to the Loosavorchagan orphanage. At first, to our dismay, Kude Archbishop Mekhitarian felt he couldn't take us back because by now his orphanage was filled beyond its capacity. All of his burdens were more than he could handle. When he became aware of our weakened condition, he not only took us back, but he also reassured us he would try his best to help us regain our health. In turn, we promised him we would look for another place as soon as we were physically able. Armenians are an industrious people and given the opportunity, they will not go hungry.

Slowly, as I was recovering, I started to work at a variety of odd jobs from working in the fields, herding animals, and repairing old shoes. By now I had learned many skills. I went back to the same spot Hagop Holopigian repaired shoes. By then he had started to write letters for those Armenians who did not know how to read or write. With the American presence in Turkey, Armenians had resumed writing letters within the country and abroad. At some point during this time, I was **re-connected** with my brothers in Chicago and we resumed our correspondence.

One of the first letters was dated November 8, 1919 when I informed my brothers in America that Kerop, Hmahyag and I were still alive, that Kerop and I were living in the Loosavorchagan orphanage, and Hmahyag was at the Protestant orphanage.

Hampartzoum, Kerop, Hmahyag. Mezreh, (cir. 1918)

*M. Aziz**

1919 November 8

To Bedros and Mihran Chitjian

What happened in 1915, the mind cannot comprehend nor the pen explain. Akh, Akh where are my father, mother, brothers, sisters, relatives and friends? They are not here. No one is here. When I open my eyes and look around, I experience blaspheme. Infidels using their swords and minaret. Cursing upon the cross, forcing Islam upon us.

—Don't slight me with a quick glance.

—Don't destroy me with fire. You are the only branch I could cling to.

—Don't leave me dangling alone...

There are mountains between us. We have lost all means to survive. You are the master of the Earth and the heavens.

Our hopes are solely dependent upon you. Brother if you send me snow or send me the ice on top of Mahrahmah—to what avail. The route is too far. The snow won't reach us.

Send me compassion. Your yearning for us. Send us hope.

M. Aziz

1920 January 8

This part of my letter is intended for Dikran Amo, Markar's father.

With great concern, I come to inform you that one and a half months ago your dear son departed to join you, and since we have not received a word or news of his whereabouts. I hope we did not lose a three year friendship we had established. Every night in our dreams and during the day, he doesn't leave our thoughts. We worry that some harm could have come to him en route because of his severely weakened condition throughout his treacherous ordeal. We fear his condition might have worsened or he might have had a mishap with an automobile. Please inform us about his welfare.

In ending my letter, I send my regards to you with love. Give my regards to Markar and tell him not to forget us nor the miserable times we suffered together and let him write a couple of lines to appease our hearts...

---

*   Mamuret-ul-Aziz: Turkish name of town and province.

DISFIGURED WITH TATTOOS

One day while I was walking along a street in Mezreh, searching for work, I recognized Anna Rahanian, our principal's wife from Perri. She was our beautiful, kind teacher who taught in the girls' school. She was loved and respected by the girls and boys. Immediately, I remembered my feelings when I used to collect flowers on the way to school to make perfume just for her. Now, I could not believe my eyes. I was horrified when I realized what they had done to her beautiful face. Her whole face was *mutilated* with tattoos. How they must have tortured her!

As I approached her, she recognized me. Tears came to her eyes. She quietly told me how she and her husband were *brutally tortured* and soon after he was killed. After a short and very painful visit, *I left, but that memory still haunts me.*

GEE DEHK, SHE SAID

While I was still living at the Armenian orphanage, we began to feel less intimidated because the Americans were still there—**a false sense** of calm prevailed. Both the American missionaries and soldiers encouraged Armenian boys to assist Kude Archbishop Mekhitarian to carry out his mission to rescue Armenians still held in bondage by Turks and Kurds.

Many Armenian women who had been forced to become Turkish and Kurdish wives left their children fathered by Turks or Kurds and fled to the Armenian Protestant orphanage. Others refused to give up their children and made the choice to remain, just as my Aunt Aghavni refused to give up her children and remained in Perri. I tried to convince her many times but to no avail. While I realized what a difficult decision that must have been, I greatly admired the women **who left their children** and fled when they found the opportunity.

With this opportunity in mind, I remembered the slave who worked in the gendarme's house in Parchanj. She always treated me well, while her Khanum, Fahtmah, always taunted me by calling me *Gavour Boghee*. One day when I had the opportunity, I decided to go to Parchanj and rescue the slave. I knew I was risking my life if the gendarme caught me. Nevertheless, I went. First, I dropped by to say hello to Khanum, the kind, elderly woman who had always treated me well. It felt good to know she was very happy to see me. She inquired about my problem with the ghosts. After a short pleasant visit, I told her I had come just to see her. Then I left.

I quickly went across the street and went up to the second level of their three-story house where the slave had her living quarters, above the stable. The Armenian slave came out as soon as she saw me. Quickly and quietly, I told her why I had come. I was surprised by her response. Apparently, she and Khanum had anticipated my intentions when they saw me in the area and had made their own arrangements. The slave assured me that she could escape whenever she saw fit, and that it would be better for me to take Fahtmah Khanum herself. For some time, she was preparing to escape. Khanum had previously sent her daughter away to safety. Now, she was waiting for the opportunity to escape herself and was willing to part from her sons. So now she was relying on me to take her away—*that* day!

I was struck by the sudden realization that the person who had been so cruel and hostile towards me, shouting *Gavour Boghee* at me every chance she had, now wanted me to risk my life to help her escape from her Turkish gendarme husband who terrified everyone just with his barbaric presence.

I knew the gendarme or his mother could enter that room at any moment. So, we had to escape immediately. Without giving her suggestion a second thought, I agreed and quietly followed the Armenian slave up to the third floor. Fahtmah Khanum was ready and waiting for me to take her away. Silently, without a word, she motioned for us to go down the back stairs. She was dressed in her white *charshaff* (sheet). Her body and face were concealed. I had never seen her face before, nor did I see it then. Only her eyes were visible.

"*Gee dehk*" she said in Turkish. "*Let's go!*" Bidding us farewell, the slave whispered, "*Be careful—don't get caught!*"

When we got downstairs, I peered from behind the house to make sure no one was in sight. The coast was clear, so we fled, walking as fast as we could, making sure we did not attract anyone's attention. Fahtmah Khanum walked briskly by my side and never uttered a word.

The walk from Parchanj to Kharpert was about two hours. After walking for some time on the road through Kehsereeg, I decided it would be safer to change our route, even though it would be much longer. By taking the new route, I avoided passing by the police station that usually had at least sixty policemen milling around.

I was greatly relieved when we finally arrived in Mezreh. I took Fahtmah Khanum directly to the Armenian Protestant orphanage. Without a word, I quickly left. All the Armenian women and girls were housed there. Reverend Yeghoyan had converted his *zhoghovahran*, meeting hall, into an orphanage.

TERRIFIED BY HIS SINISTER LOOK

For a while, I continued going from village to village looking for work. I was willing to do almost anything. One day while I had walked more than an hour, and was half way to the Upper City of Kharpert (Veri Kaghak) from Mezreh to see Kerop, I took heed of a large Kurd walking straight towards me. He had a large staff in his hand and a large dagger at his side. He looked mean and stern. Walking alongside him was his donkey with a woman sitting on its back. As we got closer, I hastened my pace so I would pass him by as quickly as I could. There was something *sinister* about his look that sparked fear within me. I did not know why, but my heart began to beat fiercely in my chest—**I feared for my life! Was this my last day?**

Sometimes it was getting harder for me to recognize the difference between an obvious threat and a more generalized fear that was incessantly plaguing me. The fear that any Armenian boy my size and age could be picked up for interrogation for any alleged offense, or could be brutalized by some crazed rogue encouraged by the **leniency** of the Turkish officials, penetrated my soul.

Just as we were about to pass each other, the Kurd suddenly started to walk directly towards me. By now I was really afraid, and my mind was racing to find a way to escape! When we were an arm's distance from each other, I thought for sure he was going to kill me. *Just thinking about that exact moment, I am still overwhelmed with the same fear.* The trembling stopped, and I just stood still. Frozen! With a sharp disconcerting voice he said, "The Khanum wants to speak with you." Instantly, without even looking up towards the woman on the donkey, I replied, "I don't know the Khanum." With a determined voice, he insisted, "She wants to speak to you!" At the same time, he was *shaking his staff right up to my face*. Simultaneously, I heard the soft but inquisitive woman's voice, "Do you recognize me?" She was still sitting on the donkey. I looked up at her for the first time. Still consumed with fear, my tongue was tied. I still had not recognized her.

Maybe she became aware of my fear. Anyway, she started to get down from the donkey. For the first time, I noticed she was cradling a baby in her arms. As her feet touched the ground, she handed the baby to the Kurd who had come to help her.

She came closer to me and embraced me with one gentle hug—then she let go. Stepping back and looking straight at my face, she said, **"The world is like this. What can you do?"**

I remained *frozen* with fear. At the same time, everything within me turned upside down. My head was *spinning*—was she someone from my past? I detected she must be married to a Kurdish *Agha* (the title for a rich Kurd). The baby was hers, and the Kurd accompanying her must be her slave.

Gradually I began to recall, and finally I recognized her. She *was* Vartouhi, the daughter of our neighbor, Giragos, Varteeg Bahgee's brother. We were good neighbors in Perri during our childhood, when we led a relatively normal life. Now there was a *gulf* of difference in our current lives.

Somewhat more relaxed, I had a flashback of the night when she and her parents had come to visit my parents. As we customarily sat in front of the fireplace, the adults and children visited with each other. At some point parents and grandparents exchanged stories for all to enjoy.

It was one of those nights. I was probably no more than six or seven years old. I was sitting behind her. She must have been about five. When I noticed one of her braids had come undone, I started to redo it. Both sets of parents took note of my action, and they all broke out in a merry laughter. Immediately both mothers began to say, "Oh, look—how nice! They are just right for each other. These two shall be betrothed. When they get older, they shall marry!" *Behsheek Kastmah* was our custom where parents matched children at a very early age for marriage. The laughter and merriment continued to the end of the evening's visit. That was the life we once had with our families, mother, father, siblings, grandparents, neighbors and friends. At that moment, it was difficult for me to realize that **I ever really had that life!** Now I understand very well what my childhood neighbor meant when she said, "The world is like this! What can you do?"

After calming down and relaxing, we exchanged our acknowledgments with some feeling of solace. **We were now in different worlds, both yearning for the past.** Knowing we could not go back, we bid farewell and continued our interrupted course. As I approached Upper Kharpert, I gave a big sigh of relief. Another day had passed, and I was not caught. *I was still alive!* That was one of my most life threatening incidents. Unconsciously, I was so terrorized by the Kurd's stance. Was the *real* threat (of being caught) my obvious size and age?

28. SAKO MAHLAHSEE

A NEW JOB, WRITING LETTERS

By now it was the early part of 1920, and I must have been about nineteen years old. Gradually, as I began to regain strength from my bout with typhoid, I started to look for another place to sleep to honor my promise to the Archbishop that I wouldn't stay in the orphanage once I was strong enough to find a new place.

One day, as I was returning to the orphanage, I ran into my sister Zaruhy's godmother, Juharr, who lived in a one room house in Sako Mahlahsee which was about a one hour walk from the orphanage. She said we could move in with her. I had never been to her house. However, whenever my father used to go to Kharpert, he stayed overnight at her house. On a few occasions, he took Zaruhy to visit with her, for a few days. Once when he returned home, he told us about the unusual way Juharr served dinner. "What a strange custom, she served dinner on small individual plates. *I came home hungry!*"

Upon my arrival at her house, I was immediately devastated by what my eyes witnessed. Juharr had not warned me about what I would confront. I am sure she was *numbed* to the deplorable sight, and it did not occur to her to warn us. *The quantity of bones* strewn about the area was extremely unnerving. Sako Mahlahsee was about a half-hour walk from Kehsereeg. That same sight extended north throughout the vast area from Moreneeg to Hueseneeg and continued on to Upper Kharpert—what had taken place was incomprehensible!

The ruins of the Armenian houses were just as depressing as the bones of the inhabitants that lay scattered along the hillsides—forgotten and abandoned.

Soon after Kerop and I moved in, without a word, Juharr left and never returned. I never saw her again. We thought perhaps she had gone to live with her married daughter. However, before she left she told me a rumor she had heard a couple of years earlier. A Kurdish woman had told her my father's *keervah* (Kurdish friend who greatly respected him), had hid him for a period of time. After the Kurdish rebellion, she never saw or heard about him again... *Akh,* I will never know what happened to my father. To think about what could have happened to him is much too painful to bring to mind...

Juharr's house was one of six Armenian homes in the area that was habitable. The house was on the road to Kehsereeg. The small French Catholic Church was on one side of the road and on the other was a Turkish police station. Now there were only six Armenian homes at the opposite end. Hovannes Dekmejian lived there with his mother's sister. After his escape from Turkey, he lived in Los Angeles with his family for many years before moving to Washington, D.C. to be closer to his daughter. The Dervishians (Garabed, Kaspar and their sister, Sultahn) also lived there. After their escape, they settled in Fresno. Their cousin, Diyiar Dervishian, who lived in the German orphanage, settled in Los Angeles where he became a priest. Those families were originally all from Ismiel. There were three other families in the area, but the only other name I remember is Kezerian.

Soon after Juharr's departure, I brought Altoon Bahgee and her daughter to live with us. It did not take long before she found work there too. As before, she cleaned houses and did the wash for wealthy Turkish women. A member in one of those families was a lawyer. With Altoon Bahgee's suggestion, I went to him to improve my Turkish script. Hagop was still writing letters in Mezreh. That job was more lucrative than repairing shoes, and emotionally more rewarding. There were many grammatical rules that I did not know, since I had taught myself to read and write in Turkish. With a few lessons, the lawyer taught me the format of formal letters using the proper heading, closing, date and address.

Excerpts from letters I wrote to my brothers show critical information was written in allegorical form to avoid suspicion by the censor to pass censorship.

> M. Aziz
> 1920 March 13[*]
> This part of my letter is for my brothers Bedros and Mihran.
>
> I would like to have us consider together my situation. I want to see what you would do if you were in my place. I am going to give you a concise, brief description of my situation:
>
> a) Should I cry and complain that I was hospitalized for more than a month with typhoid?
>
> b) Should I cry and bemoan about my homeland, that it is completely barren, destroyed, and lost?
>
> c) Should I wail in despair and grieve with a bleeding heart for the time of day whenever I bring my parents to mind, my sweet parents..?
>
> d) My tearful eyes do not open so they won't bring to mind Kerop's fearful pleas that I won't abandon him—a plea he has the right to make... For Aghavni's plea, begging help from me for food; she still

[*] Hampartzoum could not understand why they were not rescued along with Markar.

remains in Perri with an Armenian husband who has converted. Only a man of steel with a heart of stone could endure all of this!

e) Is what happened to our father written in the wind? He planted six trees anticipating to harvest their fruit. The trees blossomed, sprouted their leaves and bore fruit. They encountered a tragedy, the lion's roar, scattering the trees on the mountain tops of different hills and whisked him up to the clouds in heaven.

Think dearly upon what I have written but do not sadden yourselves, what is lost will not return. Remain happy and together. Let us pray to God that He will see fit to have us re-united, Amen...!

M. Aziz
1920 March 14
To Bedros and Mihran Chitjian
...Once there was a gardener who had planted a field of trees with much care and devotion so they would blossom, grow and bare fruit for him.

His neighbor who was at odds with the gardener coveted what he saw in the garden. One day, as he approached the garden which wasn't gated, he noticed the garden was unprotected on all four sides. In the dark of night, he entered the garden and yanked out the newly sprouting roots, completely destroying each plant bit by bit. This was done with such malice that you couldn't detect there ever were flourishing trees on the land.

Upon reading this letter don't censure me why you previously haven't been receiving letters from me. Don't think I am not capable of realizing and understanding what has transpired. I have a fairly good grasp of what has taken place.

We don't dwell about it, because everything is kept in the dark. We can't do anything about what has already happened. . .

When I finally decided to write and read letters for other Armenians who needed help contacting loved ones in various countries, but mainly America and France, I began to search for an appropriate site. I needed a suitable place to sit and write with adequate space so my clients would be able to gather around me.

Next to our house among the scattered ruins of an Armenian house I found a location that met my needs. One day, as I began to clear the rubble away with my hands for my work area, I suddenly found myself *cradling a baby's skull* in the palm of my hand. The realization of what had happened to that infant overwhelmed and debilitated me. I couldn't go on working until the next day, and even then, I was in a very somber mood. Subsequently, I made a mound from the rubble with a slight incline allowing me to sit slightly above my clients.

Next, I rented a mailbox at the local post office. I recorded my name as Mahammed Oghlee Rooshdee. All replies to the letters I wrote for my clients would be addressed to my attention at my post office address.

I was only able to afford the minimum quantity of supplies needed for my work. I saved money by using turkey quills as my writing utensil. Wild turkeys were plentiful on the hillsides and when I whistled at them, they ran away, invariably dropping a few feathers. I would pick up a suitable one, whittle the tip to a fine point, and make a small split.

I planned to charge two *khooroosh*, a nominal amount, for each letter I wrote and two *khooroosh* for each reply I read. That price included the expense for paper, envelopes, ink and postage. I planned to go to the post office once a week to mail the letters I had written for the week and pick up replies to letters previously sent.

I notified a few people of my intentions and the location of my work area. One morning, I went up to the mound with my supplies in hand. Sure enough, one or two women approached me and from then on I was kept busy.

For the first few days, I only had a few clients. By the following week, I wrote eight to ten letters a day. As my clientele gathered around me, one by one they came up to the mound and sat next to me. My writing area on the mound was safe—I was not afraid of the Turks harassing us.

As my clients proceeded to dictate everything they wanted me to write in their letters, I was very cautious about what was included in the letters. I primarily wrote about their daily family events, their health and well being and their yearning for those abroad. Critical information was deliberately left out, because we were afraid of the censor.

Each week, I personally handed the letters to Mehmed Zahkee Bey, the official censor. I immediately made a point to befriend him. Thus, by personally handling my letters, he made sure they were all sent and without delay. At the same time, I picked up the incoming mail directly from him. That contact made me feel safer.

Most of my clients had the complete addresses where their letters were to be sent. Some were only able, however, to give me the name of the country or perhaps just the name of a city. To my amazement, many of those letters somehow made their way to their intended recipient.

As the number of my clientele grew, it became increasingly difficult to accommodate everyone. Therefore, I drafted a form letter covering general basic information. In the evenings, I prepared many copies during my free time. Because, I spent less time with each client, I was able to help more people and at the same time I made more money. I concluded each letter with their personal information.

As one person came up and sat next to me, the others kept their distance from us. That arrangement instilled a feeling of confidence that their information would be kept private. They were all very considerate of one another.

They eagerly anticipated my weekly trip to the post office to pick up the incoming mail. On those days, I normally had a much larger group awaiting me. Receiving replies meant far more to my clients than the letters they sent out, so I always read those before I wrote any new letters. After I read a reply, invariably the recipient pleaded for me to re-read the letter again, sometimes several times. The recipient's resulting tears and joy affected everyone present. When they were finally satisfied, my clients were ready to reply with a new letter either that day or soon thereafter. In their letters, they mainly sought money from abroad, searched for the whereabouts of loved ones, and anxiously inquired about those who survived the atrocities inflicted on all Armenians in their homeland.

I also sent many of their letters with incomplete addresses to my brothers in Chicago with the hope they might be able to find a way to deliver them. They in turn searched for relatives and/or friends who knew my clients. In that way many more letters were delivered, but still some never reached their destination—some of those were returned.

The saddest part of my job was to hear the cries from those who never received a reply to their letter. I can still hear their piercing pleas, "*Chaghas*, my dear child, call out my name too! Please! Why didn't you call my name?" It was gut wrenching for me not to be able to respond positively. Not receiving a reply was a heartbreaking experience. It was almost better to receive a reply with sad news than not to receive a reply at all. **When you are barely surviving in an inferno, knowing that the flames will consume you sooner or later, your charred body desperately seeks help from someone, from some place, from anyone, from anywhere! It just wants help!**

RAHAN—EMOTIONALLY SCARRED

One day, family friends brought us a relative for whom we had to provide care and shelter. She was my grandfather's first cousin's daughter, Rahan. She was about fifteen years old and had been severely abused by the Turks.* That traumatic experience left her with deep psychological scars.

Several times a day she found a private place where she sat in a transient state and went through the motions of nursing a baby. She caressed her arms against

---

* They not only slaughtered her family, but her baby as well.

her chest as though she were clutching an infant, took out her breast and continued to soothe the imaginary infant by stroking its back. After a few minutes, she would regain her conscious state and resumed her household tasks. She reenacted this routine several times a day.

In a desperate effort to help her, on several occasions I took her to the ruins of an Armenian Church with the hope the *saints* would rid her of her torment. Unfortunately, she did not find much relief there. It was suggested I take her to the Asorie (Assyrian) Church, which was in Upper Kharpert and was the largest church in Kharpert and in better condition. At one time it must have been a beautiful church. As soon as we got there she went into prayer and within an hour fell into a deep sleep. I was reluctant to wake her up so we stayed there overnight. During the night she got up but still in a deep sleep she walked for three to four hours along the *dahjar* (railing) where candles once had been placed. I don't know how, but she kept her balance on the railing, even though there was no light and it was completely dark! I was afraid to awaken her for fear of startling her and causing her to fall. Near morning she finally awoke on her own and came down from the railing. She sat down on the floor next to me and fell into yet another deep sleep.

When she finally woke up for the second time, she asked me to take her home. Halfway home, as we were coming down the hillside, she abruptly stopped and opened her tightly clasped hand. In the middle of her palm was a red mark the size of a silver dollar. I thought it looked like a mark caused by the pressure from her fingernails digging into her skin, but she exclaimed loudly with great despair, "I shouldn't have opened my hand before we got home!" No more was said, as we continued to walk home. She was so concerned something bad was going to happen to her now.

As the days passed she continued the ritual of nursing the "baby" several times a day and then in a normal manner proceeded with her household chores. When we sat down to eat, she made sure to cover most of her face with her headscarf, as if she was a new bride. During that time she related to us without showing any signs of a mental problem. Sometime later, the relatives who brought Rahan to us returned and took her back home with them. They left without a word in the same manner they had brought her to us.

WHO WAS THE CULPRIT?

A few days after her departure, we all witnessed what the Turks had done to a boy from Kehsereeg whose body was thrown over a donkey's back. The boy's legs dangled on one side and on the other side, his head. They had slashed his neck. As the donkey walked along, the poor boy's head was swinging side to side,

Margarite, Rahan, Altoon Bahghee, Kerop and me (Sako Mahlahsee, 1920)

slapping against the donkey's back. With the draped body over its back, the donkey was paraded through the village square as a warning to all Armenians that punishment awaited them for any alleged offense. A sign written in Turkish strapped on the donkey's back explained the boy's offense. The boy had killed several Armenian girls who had been rescued from their Turkish masters and taken to the Armenian Protestant orphanage. Probably because the girls couldn't tolerate the hunger and bleak conditions there, they snuck back to their Turkish husbands who might have offered them a little more comfort. The boy hid out in the hills. When he found the opportune time, he snatched the girls one by one, killed them and dumped their bodies into a well.

It took a long time for the Turks to find him. He was quite clever, deceiving his pursuers as he carried out his mission. Unfortunately, the Turks spotted his sister taking food to him while he was in hiding. At that moment, he was caught and killed. Fear towards Turks intensified as Armenians watched the boy's body paraded through the streets.

Even though the four of us were getting by with my job writing letters, the circumstances for our personal safety were gradually getting more precarious. It seemed each day made us more aware of the dangerous conditions in which we were living, *especially for me.*

AGHAVNI AND THE DUNDESS

On another day, on my way to the post office, I encountered Vaskertzee Mardiros' daughter, Aghavni, one of my former schoolmates from Perri. Every morning I used to get our yogurt from her father. With pain, anguish and despair, she revealed to me about her father's tragic demise. When word began to spread that the Turks were rounding up the Armenian men, a Kurdish *keervah* who was very close to her father immediately convinced her father he could help him. The Kurd knew that Mardiros was well to do and advised him to deposit his money in the bank in Kharpert for safekeeping. Up until then, the Kurd was a trustworthy friend so Mardiros agreed, and the two left for Kharpert. When they were some distance away from Perri, the *keervah* struck Mardiros on the head, killed him and ran off with his money.

Immediately afterwards, another Kurd abducted Aghavni and her mother. After torturing both of them, he let Aghavni go and kept her mother. Aghavni had nowhere to go and was alone, hungry and distraught. With luck she ran into the school's custodian, Vartan, who also was left alone. He too was the sole survivor in his family so the two shared living quarters for a while. At some point I heard, however, they had gone separate ways. Eventually Vartan found his way to

America and worked for my brother in Los Angeles for a short time. I never heard what became of Aghavni.

A NEW WAVE OF SLAUGHTER

Shortly after that, I found out what the Turks had done to Arteen Agha on the road to Kehsehreeg. He was tied to a tree and beaten mercilessly with a whip in an attempt to make him reveal where the Armenians allegedly had hidden guns and to reveal the names of those who owned guns. Despite the fact that they continued to incessantly beat him to a pulp, Arteen Agha revealed nothing. Frustrated, the Turks brought his wife and began to assault and brutalize her in front of him until she fell to the ground. Arteen Agha still didn't say a word. Then they brought his little daughter and proceeded to brutalize her as they had with her mother. Again, Arteen Agha did not say a word. At that point nothing was going to stop the Turks' savagery. **They continued beating even though they had no evidence of hidden guns. They proceeded to torture him as an example of how they would use any excuse to terrorize the surviving Armenians.**

When all else failed, they brought Arteen Agha's son who was three or four years old. One by one they began to pound long nails into the poor child's soles. With the blood gushing out, the boy yelled out with excruciating pain, *"Hayrig, Hayrig"*... "Father, Father." With his last words, the boy passed out. Arteen Agha couldn't take any more. He began to curse Mohammed and called the perpetrators vicious animals. At that moment one of the Turks pulled out a gun and shot Arteen Agha. The poor soul was finally free of his misery. **Most likely there were no guns, especially at that time.** All Armenians who passed the site of that horrendous incident placed a stone to create a grave marker for Arteen Agha.

Another common form of torture by the Turkish street rogues was *pahlahkhan*. Armenians were thrown to the ground and a board was slipped under their knees so their feet faced upward. Then with a long tender tree twig, a Turk whipped the soles of the victims' feet until they bled profusely and the victims passed out. They were left unconscious, lying in the street until it was safe for nearby Armenians to rescue them. With a makeshift stretcher, the victims were carried to the Armenian orphanage. Kude Archbishop Mekhitarian found women to care for them until they were well enough to sneak out of the area.

Terrorizing the few Armenians who had managed to survive continued to intensify. It got to the point when a Turk spotted an Armenian, he was easily arrested without cause. When no grounds could be found to support false accusations against an Armenian, the most common and easiest accusation was to proclaim, *"Deeneemah Soghdee"*... "He cursed my religion!" That was a sufficient cause to arrest, torture, jail or kill any innocent Armenian.

As I got older, I grew taller and larger. I knew Armenian boys especially my age and size were in great jeopardy at all times for retaliation. Whenever an Armenian caused some harm to one Turk, it was not unusual for Turkish police to round up a couple of hundred older Armenian boys at a time and they would never be seen again.

I always wondered why Armenians, who were fighting for our cause, did not communicate with one another before they acted. They surely would not have proceeded with their plans if they knew the price other Armenian would pay for their actions. Surely they realized one Turk, or even ten Turks, was not worth the life of one innocent Armenian, much less the lives of several hundred.

FEARS COME TRUE

Soon enough, one day the police apprehended me. I was walking alone towards the market place to purchase a few items for the house. My guard must have been down. I ordinarily mingled in with a crowd to be less conspicuous and thereby felt safer. I was, therefore, caught by surprise when a policeman, *a fear that had been haunting me for six years,* grabbed me!

Everything happened so quickly. Before I knew it, I was in the police station being accused of bringing supplies from the Derseem to sell in Sako Mahlahsee. As they began to interrogate me, I was shoved down on a swivel chair. I tried to defend myself by replying I had never been in the Derseem. The officer, not believing me, gave a swift kick to the chair causing it to spin around so fast that I started to lose consciousness. As I started to slump over, I was given a strong blow to the head. Instead of collapsing completely to the floor, I fell on my knees and was able to hoist myself up. I was stunned when the officer then dismissed me, shouting, "Go... skat!"

Greatly shaken up, I forgot my pain, regained my balance and composure, and walked out of the police station. "He doesn't have any fuzz on his face," were the last words I heard as I left the building. When I got a good distance away, I began to ponder about what I had just experienced. I knew *I was lucky,* because I was in one piece and was not hurt or mutilated.

Was I really lucky? For the moment I was. However, I also now realized how easy it would be for me to be picked up again. I worried about what they would do to me the next time I was apprehended and whether or not I would be able to endure their heinous atrocities. *The brain cannot stop when it's in that mode; the persistent fear destroys one's psyche.* I was now convinced if I were to survive, I had to get out of Sako Mahlahsee. Although letter writing was a good source of income, within my soul I knew the time had come for me to *leave* Kharpert. My homeland, the home of my father and mother, the land of my ancestors who had lived here for more than three thousand years—*that was the hardest decision I finally had to make!*

My dear reader, does anyone *really* understand what that means? The person living a dog's life for six excruciating years was me, Hampartzoum! I lived the dream that everyone would eventually come back and we would all return to Perri, **why else did I survive???**

I endured both the suffering I personally experienced, as well as the suffering I witnessed all around me only because I was hoping I would not have to experience this last agony, to give up my homeland, my *Yergeer! Akh, akh...* I knew at that moment I would never be free of the acute pain caused by the forced exodus from my homeland.

I am now one hundred and two years old and God is my witness, my body, soul and mind have never been at rest or at peace. They yearn for my *Yergeer* and the pain continues to pierce my heart and soul. It will follow me to the grave and beyond...

Much worse at this age, eighty-eight years later, *I still cannot understand* how a blatantly crazed and vicious government was allowed to get away with such crimes when there were several so-called civilized super powers of the world involved. They *witnessed* the hideous crimes, yet allowed the Turks to go untried for their acts. Where were the Christian nations? *Where are they today? Where are those who proclaim human rights? Where is the truth? Lies, lies and more lies! Everything is a lie!*

Succumbing to my fears, I knew I had to leave. However, how? My feet were the only means I had to rely on. I had no money to plan for a safer way out. The safest and closest place for me to escape was Yerevan. I had no other choice.

By now I was almost nineteen years old. I was quite tall. It was 1920, the war was winding down, but the Turkish army was still grabbing Armenian boys my size and age. They were being forced into hard labor, working on the roads and railways. Eventually, when they no longer had the physical strength to work, they were brutally tortured and slaughtered. Their bodies were dumped into *Misak's Spring*. I was personally aware of hundreds of boys who disappeared and were never seen again. At times we had the misfortune of spotting a familiar face among the bodies strewn amidst the hills and valleys.

Although for a few days I continued to work writing letters, nothing was the same for me. I was still sending Kerop to school[*] at the Loosavorchagan cathedral during the day. I did not know how long we would be able to continue.

> *I am not afraid of hell.*
> *My life has passed through hell.*

---

[*]   At the age of sixteen, Lucia Jafferian was one of the teachers.

After suffering for so long,
I am only afraid of what is yet to come.

WAS I SET UP FOR A KILLING?

Shortly after, again, on my way to buy some household items, I had no choice but to go towards the *boughdah mailah* (market place) where wheat was primarily sold. I knew very well the jail was nearby and I had to be very alert. I was gripped with fear.

As soon as I left the house, a neighbor from Haboose joined me. Without talking, we walked on. As we passed the *veri mailah* (uptown shopping area) by the jail, the police grabbed us both. We were told the government wanted us, *"Huekuemeht sehnee eestehrr,"* and they took us to the jailhouse. As we were going through the door, they shoved the other boy out and told him to go home. Although he was much smaller than I was, he was not younger.

I was pushed into a small room crowded with forty to fifty other Armenian boys about the same size and age. There were many familiar faces, even though we did not know one another.

The Haboosehtzee boy ran home and told Altoon Bahgee what had happened to me. She quickly came down to the jail with Kerop. Suddenly my name was called out, "Chitjee Oghlee, go to the window." From the window I saw her holding on to Kerop. When he saw me, he started to cry out in Armenian, *"Agha'par* (older brother!)—come out, let's go home!" Altoon Bahgee quickly covered his mouth with her hand. In Turkish I quickly replied, "Go home. I'll be coming home soon." What else could I say?

I was taken back to the packed room. We were standing shoulder to shoulder. We had no room to move. Some time later a sack of bread and a jug of water were placed on the floor in a corner. No one touched it. We all felt certain we were going to be killed and were numb. We remained standing shoulder to shoulder all that day and through the night. The room was completely dark.

The next morning they started to separate the boys from each other, preparing to take some to **Misak's Spring** where they would be killed. We were all agonizing with our situation. Suddenly I noticed Fahtmah Khanum's husband staring straight at me. The very gendarme whose mere presence had terrified me, even when times were quieter! Now what was he going to do to me? Had he found out it was I who had helped his wife escape? Those thoughts and fears were *bombarding* in my head, while my heart was pounding even more strongly. Was this to be my last day? I was struggling with those emotions when suddenly over the heads of the crowd of boys he beckoned *to me* to go to him. *My worst fears came true!* As I walked towards him, I was numb—what was he going to do with me? Then, we silently walked out of the door.

As soon as we got outside, he told me his wife had left him and their two sons. She had gone to the Armenian orphanage. He wanted me to go there and convince her to go back home to care for her two sons. He could no longer endure their incessant cries for their mother. He said I was the only person whom she would respect and who would be able to convince her to return. She would listen to me more than anyone else. If she went back, he would accept her as his wife as before. If she refused to go back, he thought she should take her two sons with her as he felt they could not survive without her.

I was stunned and confused when he handed me two one-gallon water jugs. He instructed me to go up the hillside and when I got to the spring, I was to drop the jugs and run out of the area as fast as I could. He would fire five shots behind me, but I was not to be afraid because he would not hurt me. Once I was free and felt safe, I was to go to the orphanage and take his wife back to Parchanj. He warned me not to get captured because, if they found out he had allowed an Armenian to escape, he too would be killed.

No more was said. With his hand he motioned for me to start. I did not know what else to do but to race up the hillside to the spring as he had instructed. When I heard gunshots—pot, pot, pot—*I was terrified.* For a moment I could not tell whether or not I had been struck by one of the bullets. *Was I set up for a killing?* I turned back to see what he was doing. Much to my surprise, he was motioning with his hand for me to take off and run.

With disbelief, I dropped the jugs and darted out of the area. I soon spotted the ruins of some Armenian houses. I could hear several policemen chasing after me. Feeling like a hunted animal, I quickly dropped down and nailed myself against a wall of one of the houses, thus concealing my presence. I held my breath as the police were right above me. I could see their boots and I dared not make a sound or move. Luckily, they did not spot me. After a long and frightful time, they finally left. I waited a while longer to make sure they were nowhere in sight, but in truth I was so scared at that moment I probably couldn't have moved even if I wanted to. Finally, I started ever so quietly to sneak out.

Within minutes I spotted Huesnee Beg's house which was not too far from our house. He too had moved to that area after the Derseem Kurds had burned Perri down.

After the *charrt*, Mardiros Mooradian, Hmahyag's father, worked for Huesnee Beg as his chef. He was both liked and respected by Huesnee Beg's family. They lived next door to Korr-Mamoe in Perri. Whenever my uncle saw Korr-Mamoe leave the house without me, he would call me over to Huesnee Beg's house and gave me the burnt crispy portion under the pilaf that was drenched in butter (a treat coveted by everyone). Likewise, on special occasions, when he baked *komah*, he would save a generous piece for me. *Komah* was baked in a pan thirty-six inches wide and ten to twelve inches deep filled with alternate layer of filo dough and a layer of *"Khahvoormah,"* shredded lamb cooked well in its own fat. This was baked until the top layer of filo was nice and golden. These two foods were very special treats for me, especially at that time. Unfortunately, after the Kurdish rebellion Hmahyag's father was never seen again.

As I came running towards the house, still eluding the Turkish police, I suddenly realized I was at the side of the house called the *nameh hahrem,* an entrance only for women. It was a punishable sin for a male to enter through that area. With the police so close behind me, there was no way I could have changed my course of direction. I knew the risk I was taking. I felt trapped. I was running from one fire into another. However, I knew that if I was to avoid being captured by the police, I had no other choice but to take that risk and use that entrance.

Immediately, a woman appeared. I quickly told her I was Hmahyag's cousin. My luck saved me again, apparently Hmahyag had previocely told her about me and that I was still alive. Since she had respect for my uncle, she accepted me and allowed me to hide there for over an hour.

When we thought it was safe, I cautiously snuck out and ran back to my house in Sako Mahlahsee. Once I got there, I was too scared to go outside for several days. Kerop and I went out only at night to gather wood for the fireplace.

My situation got worse when I heard that only a few boys survived out of the forty to fifty boys who were held in jail with me. The rest were all killed and their bodies were thrown into Misak's Spring.

My mind would not let go of the fear of what would happen if the gendarme found out it was me who took his wife to the Protestant orphanage. Surely he would pursue me relentlessly—he would have torn me apart with his bare hands if he ever caught me. *Ironically,* it is *because of him* that I am still alive in 2003. It was only after I took my first breath in Iran when I finally began to let go of that fear. *How could anyone forget being minutes away from a barbaric death?* I was left to wonder yet again if it was the Islamic God or my God that saved me.

On one of the days, I was too terrified to go out of the house during the day. I was glancing out of the window. Suddenly I saw two gendarmes coming straight towards our house. I realized again that I did not have a chance to run out and escape. At the same time, I did not have much of a choice for a hiding place in the small, one room house. The only thing I could do at that moment was to hide under the pile of firewood and pray.

Quickly Kerop and I moved the pile of wood to the center of the room. I got in the corner and knelt down. Then Kerop boxed me in with the wood and piled it on me until I was completely covered.

When the gendarmes burst into the house, they interrogated Kerop. They demanded to know who else lived in the house. As best as he could, Kerop stammered that only his Aunt Altoon Bahgee and her daughter resided there. They then turned and left when they realized he was too frightened to say anything more. The next day we learned the gendarmes were hunting for Dekmejian.

Within days, an ominous feeling of fear blanketed the area. I went out only when it was absolutely necessary and then with the full realization of the risk I was taking. It got to the point where I could not handle the horror and danger any more. I could no longer work. *I had to give in. We could not go on like that.* I had to get out as quickly as possible!

Now my problem was to find a way to escape. I could not come up with a plan that seemed like it would work, no matter how much I thought about it. I decided that I could not take Kerop with me. I would find a way to rescue him once I had found my own freedom.

If an Armenian were reading this, he too would wish he were a mouse looking for a hole to hide in.

Perri

KHARPERT

1

2

3

3

4
5
6
7
8
9
10
11

12
13
14
15
16
17
18
19

20
21
22
23
24
25
26
27
28
29
30
31
32

ruined houses

bones

ruined houses and fields

bones

MEZREH

Pabpouryolee - main dirt road

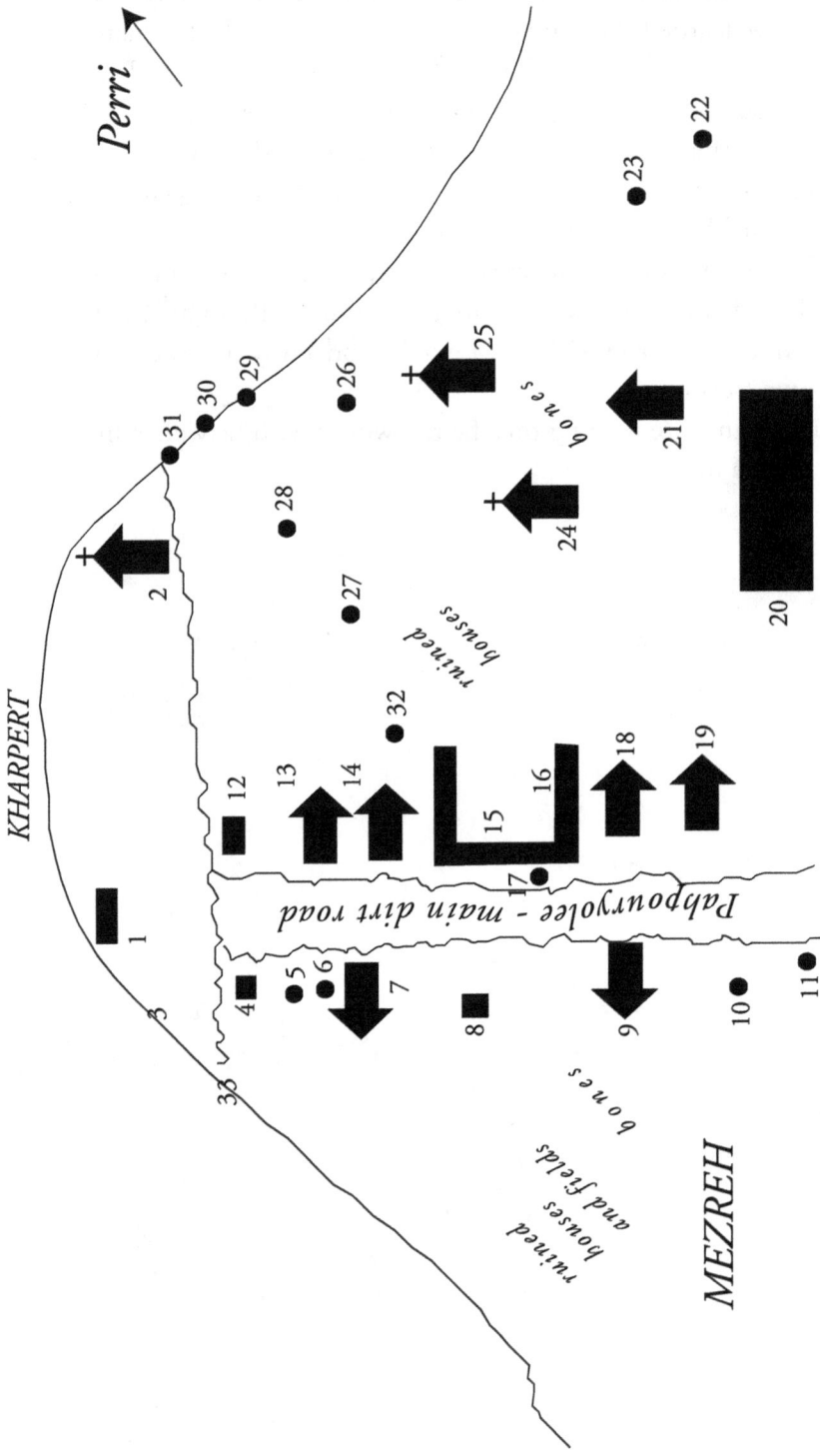

Locations and distances are relatively indicated due to the hilly and mountainous topography

Key to Map on Facing Page

I. City of Kharpert—Veri Kaghak (Upper City). Large and more affluent
   houses, gardens, vineyards, orchards, stores and businesses all in ruins.
1. Yeprahd College/Orphanage.
2. Asorie (Assyrian) Church.
3. Chaghpure Aghpure (spring). Cliff, a very steep slope, and a long drop.
   Thousands of slaughtered Armenians were dumped here.
   American soldiers paid Turkish thugs one dollar for a sack of Armenian bones.
II. Mezreh—Vari Kaghak (Lower City).
4. American Hospital.
5. Camel rest stop - dung.
6. Well.
7. Dr. Mikahil's two-storey house.
8. Dr. Mikahil's garden, German compound.
9. Dr. Mikahil's closest neighbors (Krikor and Garabed). One story house.
10. *Poorr* where I stole bread.
11. Road to Malatya. "Pahpouryolee" name of main road.
12. German Consulate, Mr. Eymond; American missionary, Mr. Riggs;
    Krikor and Garabed worked here.
13. Two-storey pharmacy - Mardiros Effendi, pharmacist.
14. Two-storey post office.
15. Boughdah Mahlahsee - wheat sold here.
16. Shops and businesses.
17. Asorie fabric shop where Hagop Holipigian repaired shoes.
18. Two-storey government building.
19. Two-storey police station where gendarme frees me.
20. Five two-storey houses along the roadside: each brother had 5
    bedrooms. Each gave gold in body-weight to be spared;
    killed anyway.
21. Mardiros Effendi's house.
22. Spring where I dropped pails and fled from gendarme.
23. Jail where I was pushed onto a swivel chair.
24. French church in ruins.
25. Armenian National Cathedral destroyed twice. Kude
    Archbishop Mekhitarian's compound.
26. Sako Mahlahsee. Ruined Armenian houses.
    Armenian scattered bones.
    Wrote letters.
27. Poorr where I got somoon bread for Dr. Mikahil.
28. Yeghekee where I brought prater book.
29. Kehsehreeg.
30. Moreneeg.
31. Husehneeg.
32. Soldiers' Headquarters (Armenians to be killed were detained here).
33. Yelboghahzee.

29. EXODUS FROM KHARPERT
MAY 18, 1921

ESCAPE TOWARDS YEREVAN

A short time later I found the opportunity to leave with Kurds going towards Yerevan. By now it was 1921. The White Russians had retreated, and there was a critical food shortage throughout the country. Word was spreading the Turkish government was offering the Kurds both money for food and expenses to repopulate Bayazid, Erzeroum, Van, and Bitlis to plant and replenish sorely needed wheat crops. *There were no Armenians left* in those villages to replant the crops.

Altoon Bahgee had been helping a very poor Kurdish neighbor by sharing food with him. He was always very appreciative of our help. The Kurd knew how hazardous it was for me to remain in that area because of my age and size. One day he confided in me that he and his family had decided to accept the Turkish incentive to relocate and that they would join the Kurdish caravan, which was leaving the next day.

He asked if I wanted to go along with them. The caravan was going towards the border of Armenia. He swore on his Koran that he would protect me all the way to the border. I would have to give him ten gold pieces, to bribe the Kurdish leader of the caravan to allow me to travel with him and to provide me with protection along the way.

Before giving the Kurd my answer, I talked to several Armenians who knew about others who had previously traveled with the caravan and had reached their destination safely. Giragos Mirakian's mother advised me to leave with the Kurds. *With that reassurance* I decided to go. Nonetheless, I still knew I couldn't let my guard down because *this* Kurd knew I was an Armenian. I had no other choice— I felt I had to take the risk.

I quickly made arrangements to leave Kerop in safe hands. The decision to leave Kerop tore me apart internally. I knew how dependent he was upon me. This news would devastate him, but I also knew *I had no other choice*—if I were killed he would have been left alone anyway. With this decision I would still have a *chance to rescue* him once I had found my freedom. I decided to leave him in the care of the priest's widow. Her husband had been a priest in Medzgerd, a village next to Perri. He had been killed, along with all of the other priests, at the onset of the Genocide. She had three daughters living with her. She wanted me to marry her eldest daughter Aghavni when I settled down in a safe place. I felt more secure leaving Kerop under her care when I was no longer there for him. I feared Altoon Bahgee might take undue advantage of Kerop financially, as she had done with me in the past. I gave the woman eight gold pieces. That was all I had left after I had paid the Kurd the ten gold pieces.

In the late 1980s, one of her younger daughters visited a relative in Northridge, California and made a special effort to see me. I was surprised to learn that her older sister had become a nun for a short period of time, but subsequently had married.

Early the very next day, on May 18, 1921, I joined the caravan. Within a few hours we reached the village of Gomk. The Kurds stopped there to buy wheat. I remained standing and waiting along with the others. Suddenly a woman approached me. As she got closer, she opened her head scarf just enough for me to recognize her. It was Rahan. Without wasting time, she told me that ever since I had taken her to the Asorie Church, she was cured of her affliction. Now, however, she felt that the devils were chasing me. She said if I allowed her to pluck two strands of hair from my head that would stop the devils from harming me and thereby my life would be spared. That is what she did. Will I ever know if that is why I survived?

The caravan began to move on. Saying goodbye, with two strands of my hair in her hand, Rahan departed as quickly as she approached me. I never saw her again, nor ever heard what happened to her.

About eight hours later, we arrived in the village of Itchmeh. We stopped there for the night. The caravan had more than 150 men, women and children.

ENCOUNTER AVEDIS AND NAZARET

More than four years earlier, I had been in Itchmeh for several months. As the memories rushed back into my mind a warm nostalgic feeling swept through my whole body as I remembered the sincere love and camaraderie we shared with each other and the night we saved Juvo from the clutches of the *bin bahshee*.

I didn't dare allow myself to even think of trying to find them or to even wonder if they were still there or learn how they were doing. That was an *extremely* difficult decision for me to make. I just couldn't take the risk of being discovered by the Kurds that I was an Armenian.

I did allow myself, however, to go up to the spring for one more drink of their cold water. Just as I was getting up from the water's edge, I saw a boy standing next to me. After saying hello to me in Turkish, in a very soft voice he asked if I was an

Armenian. As I looked into his eyes, he went on to say his name was Avedis and introduced his cousin, Nazaret, who was standing nearby. Nazaret was the son of Reverend Yeghoyan's brother. They were both from the village of Khoylee. I soon found out that they had paid the Kurds eight gold pieces each to travel with the caravan to Yerevan.

The next day was much like the first. We continued to walk until we reached Pahloo. That night the three of us came together again. We were happy that we had found one another. The more we were together, the more secure we felt. However, we knew we still had to be extremely careful.

The following day we walked until we reached the village of Jahbaghchoor. Along the way, Kurds from other villages joined our caravan. That night we stopped under a big *Puhreench* tree, a tree that has small, red fruit similar to a cherry, but smaller and much sweeter with a larger pit. To not draw attention to ourselves, we did not pick the fruit even though the tree was laden with *Puhreenches.* We were very hungry.

Nonetheless, seemingly without provocation, a couple of Kurds from one of the groups that had just joined the caravan called us over. We got scared. They started to interrogate us about where we were going and how much gold we had each paid for our expenses. Because they were speaking in Kurdish, we couldn't really understand what they were saying about us. We assumed they didn't believe us and were thinking of sending us back to Kharpert. They could have gotten one *mahjeed* (a silver coin) for each one of us if they turned us in. They must have realized that we were three husky boys who could be of much help for them. That is what happened. We tended the livestock and helped set up camp for the night.

Several hours later, we saw about ten or twelve girls sitting away from the others in one area of the camp. Soon one of the Kurds in charge, Hahgee Ahlee, began to call out to the Kurdish men to come and take any girl they wanted to use for their own pleasures for the night. The defenseless girls all began to scream and cry in Armenian, *"Yeghpayr, yeghpayr* (Brother, brother) please help us!" They probably suspected there were Armenian boys in the caravan. However, what could we have done? We were outnumbered and there was no place to run!

Only God knows what happened to those girls. Again, I must repeat myself, I curse all those who made matters worse for us by their division of action and caused other innocent Armenians to suffer. I have never forgotten those pathetic screams. . .

Generation of Armenians, children of grief...

The next evening the three of us again were ordered to care for the livestock. Again we felt they suspected that we were Armenians. They kept us under close surveillance. We ate what they ate, mainly *sahgee hatz* (bread cooked over a fire on a flat pan).

Three days after we left Khughee, we reached the village of Aintab-Doodough. A snow capped mountain appeared before us. We asked the Kurds the name of the mountain. They told us the Armenians call it Ararat. At that point we realized that we were not too far from Yerevan.

Avedis was one of the few Armenian soldiers who had survived after serving in the Turkish army. While he was in the service, other Turkish soldiers had taken his wife. During that time she had contracted syphilis. Consequently, when Avedis returned to her, the disease was transmitted to him. Dr. Mikahil Hagopian tried to cure him, but to no avail. He was advised not to eat any kind of fish. He was also told to drink tea made from cornhusk when possible.

That night the three of us discussed our perilous situation with the Kurds. None of us were comfortable around them, especially after we witnessed what happened to the girls. We felt sooner or later we would either be discovered and turned over to the Turks in Kharpert for ransom or, for whatever reason, killed. Therefore, we decided to look for the first opportunity to escape from the caravan.

THREE MONTHS OF RAW FISH AND GRASS

One night we found the opportune time to escape! After we left, all three of us immediately felt relieved that we were finally free from those beasts. We felt confident Mount Ararat would serve as a good landmark for us to follow, and we eagerly started to walk towards that direction.

Although we walked only when it was dark, day or night, we were always on guard. Whenever we saw smoke from chimneys and light from fireplaces, we were cautious to keep a distance from the houses. We also had to be extremely careful of watchdogs roaming around the area. Barking dogs alerted homeowners that someone was out there. If the dogs were not tied or fenced in, they could have torn us apart. *Being attacked by a dog was no different than being attacked by a Turk. I was always afraid of dogs.* On several occasions, I had seen how vicious they could be, especially the rabid dogs that had fed on the corpses of slaughtered Armenians that covered the hillsides and ravines.

We didn't walk more than one to two miles a night for fear of being caught. We had not eaten for several days since we had left the caravan and we knew we couldn't go on much longer without food. So we started to identify grasses we thought were edible. We had no problem finding drinking water. There were plenty of small streams, rivers and springs. Most of that water came from the melting snow of Mount Ararat. It was clean and cold.

My most reverent prayer book

Along the way we came across many Armenian villages that lay in ruins. They were first trashed by the Turks and then ravaged by the Russians. We were deeply saddened by those scenes. We kept thinking about the former inhabitants of the homes and what became of them. Those scenes exacerbated our own misery; reluctantly we were also sneaking away from our homeland, our *Yergeer.*

In one area we saw abandoned military equipment and a lot of rusty barbed wire. In one spot we saw a stack of small boats rotting away and thought Lake Van *might* be nearby.

The lettering on that equipment was neither Armenian nor Turkish. I prayed to God if only their owners would deliver us to their country—anywhere, just somewhere where I could feel free and safe. That was all I wanted in life.

My small prayer book was my only source of comfort and strength. I had bought it from a little Turkish boy. One day while I was walking towards the village of Yeghekee, he was walking towards me. He was flipping the pages and immediately I recognized what he had in his hands. After making sure there was no one else around, I quickly offered the boy enough money for one piece of bread in exchange for the book. Both of us then happily continued on towards our destinations. Ever since that day, I have kept that book with me. *I still cherish it* with the same faith when I carried it with me throughout those treacherous years.

During the day, once we found a good hiding place to stay, I read the prayer book cover to cover, over and over again. I was hoping to receive an explanation of what we were going through. *Why were we going through such horrendous experiences? What had we done?*

The first opportunity I had, I wrote on the inside cover, "May this Book never reach the hands of an unworthy person or an unworthy priest. This Book has brought me much comfort during the bleakest days of my life. I have much faith in this Book. *Many times I have felt if I didn't have my faith in God, I would not be here today."*

FEAR AND HUNGER BECAME OUR ADVERSARIES

As the days went on, *we ate nothing but different grasses and the raw fish* that we caught with relative ease because we had become skillful fishermen in our youth. We knew which fish, like the different grasses, were more edible than others. *It didn't take long, however, before eating raw fish became repulsive; and we became quite ill.*

With that ghastly diet, our appearance completely changed. Our lips became swollen, and the color of our faces became sallow. Our hair, our bodies and our clothes were filthy. The raw fish we caught from the Pahloo River distorted our eyes and mouths. One time we thought perhaps we could cook the fish by setting it in the hot burning sun for a period of time. However, that was a stupid mistake. The fish turned to slime and the smell made us ill.

We had no other choice but to make the best use of whatever we found. Avedis was in the worst shape. His body was completely covered with sores that not only looked awful, but also were extremely painful for him. I really felt sorry for him.

We got increasingly *desperate for food.* As the days passed, our hunger grew, we knew we had to change our original plan. We knew we had to take some risks to find *real* food just to stay alive. We decided the next time we saw someone alone, we would have to take a chance and approach him for help. Shortly after we made that decision, we saw a Kurd coming down from the hillside. I'm sure, however, that he didn't see us.

We assumed he was on his way from his village quite a distance away to plow his fields and he was driving his oxen to help him. We were most fortunate that he didn't have a dog at his side. If our assumption was correct, he would have had his lunch with him or at the very least, some bread. It didn't take long for us to think of a scheme to get that bread without getting caught or draw attention to our presence.

Avedis was still wearing his military uniform. So our plan was that Nazaret and I would go down and approach the Kurd, tell him we were Turkish soldiers and ask him for food. If necessary, we would scare him by saying Avedis was our *bin bahshee.* Sure enough that is what happened. When we asked him for food, he quickly refused us. He went on to explain he had just enough food to last until he finished plowing his fields. At first he didn't cooperate, so we began to threaten him. As we pointed towards Avedis who was standing in an imposing stance, we told him the *bin bahshee* would get angry if he refused and it was only then when the Kurd reluctantly handed us his much coveted two pieces of a crude bread made with coarse grain.

Before parting, we asked him how close we were to Mount Ararat and the Persian border. He said if we walked eight hours a day, we should get there in five to six days. As we left him, we warned him not to leave the area or attempt to notify anyone as the *bin bahshee* was nearby with his gun.

We hurriedly walked away. Only when we were a good distance from the Kurd did we feel it was safe to eat *our* bread, the first piece of 'real' food we had in fifty to sixty days. It wasn't much for any one of us, but it sure felt good in our stomachs if only for a short time. This incident reminded me of the tiny piece of bread I had once secretly taken to Aghavni from Kaspar's Effendi's house.

We continued our trek, again without food for another fifteen or more days. Still, our pace was one to two miles a day. Walking up the hillsides demanded more energy from our weary, hunger ravaged bodies. We were still afraid of being caught. Gradually without being aware, we were losing all hope of getting out alive.

One day, while I was looking at Avedis' face, *I began to cry*. His face was completely distorted. He asked why I was so sad. When I told him, he laughed and added, "If we had a mirror, you would be able to see *your* face!" Thus, *hunger, fear, and the lack of sleep had destroyed us all.*

Although we didn't travel in daylight, we were almost always awake. Being on guard, making sure we were not caught, we were fearful all of the time and therefore too afraid to fall asleep.

Again, at some point we decided we had to come down from the hilltops and travel along the main road. We could no longer survive without food. We were now hoping that we would run into someone, *anyone!* We also had to find out just where we were going. *We had completely lost track of where we were.* The three of us were beginning to lose all hope. For the first time we were consumed by the gnawing question as to whether or not we were ultimately going to survive... *to get out alive.*

We hoped we were near Yerevan or perhaps Iran. At this point it didn't matter where we were, just as long as we found food.

RESCUED BY KURDS

Much to our wishes, one day we noticed a Kurd walking towards us. He was riding on a donkey. As we got close to him, judging by our appearance, he thought that we were runaway Turkish soldiers. Avedis' uniform helped us again! He went on to say he could help us in several ways, and at the same time he would help us regain our health.

Together we started to walk towards his house. The fields on both sides of the road were covered with tall grass about six feet tall. The fields of grass stretched out as far as the eye could see. He said he could find us a job cutting the grass and taking them to sell in Bayazid.

By the time we reached his house, it was dark. Since it was only the beginning of spring, the days were still shorter. Luckily for us, it was dinnertime. He knew from our appearance that we hadn't eaten for many weeks, and that we were **literally starving.** He gave us a meager portion of food, explaining that if he gave us more, we would get sick. I knew he was right because of my experience in the hospital with Ovsanna, the angelic nurse. He assured us he would increase our portion gradually as our health improved. We appreciated his concern for us. Sure enough, as we slowly regained our strength and health, he increased our portions of food.

The next day he told his Kurdish helper to take us to bathe at a fountain that was quite a distance from his house. Along the way, we passed many fountains, some large and some small. The fountain he wanted us to go to was unusual in that there was both hot and cold water right next to each other. That is where the Kurds did their wash and bathed.

We quickly took our baths. Finally we were clean from our hair to our toes for the first time in months. That felt so good. The Kurdish helper then gave us a new change of clothing. **From the way the clothing was sewn**, we knew they were taken from Armenians.

After three to four days, with the gradual increase of food and a daily bath, we regained much of our strength and peace of mind. The feeling of optimism was gradually coming back… **we still had a chance to find freedom.**

Despite Avedis' limited knowledge of Kurdish, we were able to learn we were very close to Bayazid. Thus, we were very close to Iran. *In one direction was Iran and in the other was Eastern Armenia.* He continued to explain that the Arax River ran nearby. One side of the river was covered with Turkish soldiers and on the other side Armenian soldiers.

I TOOK OFF ALONE

After giving much thought to what the Kurd told us, I felt going through Iran would be easier and safer. Getting past the troops near either bank of the Arax River without being caught by soldiers during the day would be very difficult, because of the loud thrashing sound we'd make passing through the tall grasses. We surely would attract attention.

At night, the guards patrolling the borders would not be stationed as close to one another and most likely would be paired only in a few strategic spots. This made it easier to find an unguarded spot to sneak in, and we also wouldn't have to pay a custom fee to enter the country.

That night I revealed my plan to Avedis. I explained to him that this was an exceptionally good opportunity to escape out of Turkey. Once and for all we would be free! After that, our lives could only get better. Life just couldn't get any worse than what we had endured the last six years. If we left at midnight, the guards most likely would be asleep or not very alert. We had been there for more than four days and had regained some of our physical and emotional strength. Now was not the time to stop our momentum. If we lingered around, we would increase our chances of being caught. We were so close to freedom. We had to go now!

Since Avedis' sores had gotten exceptionally worse, he didn't think he would be able to keep up with me. However, he agreed that **my plan was a good one**, and he felt the odds were in my favor of finding freedom. He advised me to set out on my own. He said he and Nazaret would cover for me by making up some story that a Kurd had come and taken me away. He promised they wouldn't reveal to anyone where I was heading.

Terrified and extremely anxious, I took off. That was the first time I had attempted to escape completely on my own and all alone. The fact that I was in a complete strange terrain also made my efforts all the more risky and difficult.

Walking through the tall grasses immediately became a *problem*. They were more than six feet tall, towering over my head, impeding my sense of direction. I knew that if I lost complete sight of my intended course and couldn't tell the general direction I should keep, I would be in trouble. On the other hand, I knew they were providing me with cover, by making it much more difficult for someone to spot me. I was also aware I had not heard the paralyzing sound of barking dogs and that was a big relief. All I heard was, **"shuck, shuck, shuck"** the sound of the blade-like leaves rustling in the wind. The more I walked, the more the blades thrashed against my body and face. The sting on my face was slowing me down, while the deafening noise **"shuck, shuck, shuck"** became unbearable. At some point, *it seemed the devil was making that haunting sound. As if he were chasing after me.* It was getting harder for me to forge through the tall blades. For the first time I suddenly realized I was alone and I had no idea where I was. I was completely engulfed by the grass. A new fear crept in my mind. I was lost and I didn't know what to do! I was more fearful than ever. Gradually, as night fell and it got dark, I was totally devastated with fear. I must have passed out and fallen down.

The next morning when I awoke a Kurd was prodding me with a stick. He said something in Kurdish, but he realized that I could not understand him. In broken Turkish he asked if I was a runaway Turkish soldier. Not knowing where I was or how far I had walked the night before, I said yes.

He took me to his house. As it turned out, his wife was Armenian. They started to question me in Kurdish, wanting to know where I was from. Not feeling secure about their intentions, I told them I was from Konia. In the event they should send me back now, Konia was much safer than Kharpert for Armenians. Eventually, I realized they were trying to find out what skills I possessed, and if I had a trade. I told them I was a shoemaker. Although I had repaired shoes, I had never made them. My relatives, the Mishmeeshians, who made new shoes, came to mind along with the few occasions I had watched them work with their tools, so now I felt I could fake it.

My answer made the Kurd happy. He quickly brought out two big stacks of leather. The faces of the shoes had been sewn already. The only thing left to do was to sew the top piece to the sole. I thought the Kurd was probably so stupid he couldn't figure how to do it himself.

The wife, suspecting I was an Armenian, wanted to be more hospitable with me. She offered me a piece of bread with melted butter, a favorite treat among Armenians. That's all I remember. I must have felt sick and fainted.

The next morning the Kurd told me a blacksmith could forge the tools necessary to sew the shoes. He was an Armenian in the village of Kehleeseh Kand, Iran. That sounded great to me. *Had I finally found a way to escape from Turkey?* That would be **a miracle.** I began to feel better, even though I was still a little weak and dizzy from the butter I had eaten the previous night.

THE SUN, THE LIGHT, AND THE HOPE

The next day I felt strong enough to travel. Early in the morning the two of us started off towards Kehleeseh Kand. At the Turkish-Iranian border two soldiers stopped us. The Kurd quickly offered a pair of shoes for each member of their respective families if they would allow us to cross over the border into Iran to have our tools made. They accepted the bribe, and miraculously, we walked across the border.

We were now in Iran! I will never forget that moment! I rushed to a nearby fountain and drank *their* water. I took a handful of mud and rubbed it across my forehead. I felt I was wiping away the fear of the barbaric Turk out of my soul!

The sun beating down on me no longer belonged to Turkey. This is when and where I realized I was really free! **This was not the Turkish sun, this was not the Turkish soil, and this was not the Turkish air!** I was now free from the barbaric Turkish claws. This is where **I prayed to thank God.** To this day I can still remember the sun, the light, and the hope. What a feeling, what emotions! I still tremble just remembering that moment. I was finally safe. This was truly an incomprehensible moment... one that I have never forgotten!

As great as that feeling was, it was a bittersweet victory. What price had I paid for this freedom? I had lost my father, my mother, my sisters and my baby brother. However, more painful, I had lost my homeland, my *yergeer*. Who was my God? From the memories of my experiences and the depth of my soul, I feel...[*]

> In the name of Our Father: the earth is God
> The Child, a saint: water is God.
> The Soul, a saint: air is God.

Without lingering any longer we continued our trip until we reached the village of Kehleeseh Kand. We went directly to the Armenian blacksmith. Even though he mainly made shoes for horses and donkeys, he also made tools to make wine from raisins or almost any other tool that was requested.

While we were asking the workers if we could speak to the owner, I noticed several of them were Armenians. At the same time, I overheard them mention the owner was greatly respected by the governor who was also the tax collector, Sahlahree Hmahyoun.

Immediately, I realized a cordial friendship with such an influential person as the owner could protect me and that realization further enhanced my hope for freedom. Abruptly, however, at the same time I felt the sense of fear again. What would happen to me if the Kurd found out I was an Armenian?

One of the workers told us the owner had gone to the cemetery and showed us how to get there. When we got there, I knew it was an Armenian cemetery because the name of the village, Kehleeseh Kand, meant *"the village of a church."* The cemetery must have been built when a larger number of Armenians lived there. I never did find out what became of them. The Armenians were now very few in number. We soon saw the owner, the *angelic man.* He was brushing debris off a tombstone, reading the written script to a young child who was playing at his side.

Within myself, I was bursting with happiness. *Finally,* I had found an Armenian who was a *free man* and one who possibly could help me find *my* freedom. Unfortunately, however, I couldn't share those feelings of joy and relief with anyone. Suddenly, I felt fear again. What if he couldn't help me? So far I had been talking in Turkish. He probably didn't even realize I was an Armenian. From the *instant* I saw him my instincts told me he was an *angelic* man. He was about sixty-five years old, and his bearing reflected he, too, must have experienced a lot himself.

Without wasting time, the Kurd asked him if he could make the tools we needed. Likewise, without hesitating, the Armenian said he could and that it would cost about twenty *khran* (Persian currency).

---

[*]   Ever since, in my heart I have carried a soft spot for Iran. That is where I found my freedom and safety!

The Kurd looked at me with a questioning glance as to whether that was a fair price. I knew he really didn't have that much money on him. I quickly convinced the Kurd in Turkish to go out and get a bite to eat, and I would stay and try to convince the owner to lower his price. The Kurd agreed. He told us he would go to the teashop and instructed me to go after him when our tools were ready.

As soon as the Kurd left, I looked at the Armenian who obviously was angry with me. He didn't want to talk to me about lowering the price. Not wasting a moment, I took the only chance I had and got a little closer to him, and I inquired quietly, **"Father, I am an Armenian! Could you rescue me from this Kurd?"** This time I spoke to him in Armenian.

ANGELIC MARGOS

The God-loving man turned his back towards me, knelt down and rigorously scratched the ground with a stick in his hand. He still didn't utter a word to me. A little louder and with more urgency, I repeated my plea. As soon as I said, *"Hayrig* (father), please, listen to me!" He immediately replied, *"Arri, kuhnank"* ("Come, let's go"). I had read the word *arri* in books, but now for the first time I was hearing someone saying it. It was an Eastern Armenian expression. I sensed he too was crying from within because he had found an Armenian—a survivor. This time with more conviction he repeated again, *"Arri,"* ("Come, let's go"). I followed him home. Neither one of us spoke a word as we walked side by side with each other.

When we arrived, he knocked on the door. It was a subterranean house. His wife opened it and stood at the bottom of the stairs. He quickly told her, "I have found your son."

The wife previously had a husband and son in Turkey. They had both been killed. She somehow escaped to Iran and married this Persian Armenian. Looking up at me, she uttered, "He doesn't look like my son."

As we went down the stairs into the house, she quickly embraced me and called me Krikor, her son's name. I told her my name was Hampartzoum and I had come from Kharpert. I had come a long distance. The wife reassured me that it was all right that I really wasn't her son. She would accept me for myself.

With tears and laughter we mingled with each other. *What paradise!* What a happy day that was! I couldn't remember the last time I had really laughed, or felt real joy. For six years I had totally forgotten emotions of happiness. This *angelic* man's name was Margos and his wife's name was Nevart. He told his wife to bring dinner for me for surely I must be hungry. Within minutes, she placed a big bowl of Persian *kufta* (meatballs) with rice soup on the table right in front of me. There was flat bread beside the bowl. When they noticed I wasn't attempting to begin, they both insisted I start eating. Margos soon realized the problem and told his wife to bring him a bowl too. His wife reminded him he had just eaten a short while earlier as she set a bowl in front of him. Margos immediately pinched off a piece of *kufta* with a small piece of bread, dipped it into the rice soup and put the whole piece in his mouth. Not a drop of soup ran down his arm.

As I watched, I wasn't sure I would be able to do the same. It seemed, however, that I had no choice but to try, as there were no utensils. Trying to imitate exactly what Margos had done, I took a piece of flat bread, pinched a piece of *kufta* with the bread and dipped it into the rice soup. Then I attempted to bring it up into my mouth. Immediately the soup ran down my arm. I made a mess. We all had another good laugh. Margos told his wife to bring me a spoon that they had for people like myself.

While eating I asked him again, *"Can you help me? Can you keep me safe?"* He had not answered me at the cemetery. This time Margos pointed to each wall on which hung a loaded gun. "If the time comes that we cannot protect ourselves, we will shoot ourselves rather than surrender to the enemy."

At that moment, there was a loud knock on the door—the Kurd had come after me. He said it was late and we had to hurry if we were to return home before nightfall. "Tell 'the soldier' to come out," he called out again.

In a stern response, Margos answered back, "He is going to stay here with me. *He is an Armenian.* He appreciates that you brought him here." The Kurd sarcastically responded, "Oh, so now you are converting a Moslem into an Armenian!" and he stormed off.

I stayed with Margos for about three to four months. He reassured me that his friend Sahlahree Hmahyoun would give me a good job. Because I knew how to read and write in Turkish, my job was to inspect and record all the goods the Arab merchants brought to that stop point. At the end of each week, I turned the list over to Sahlahree Hmahyoun.

A LETTER WRITTEN WITH ONION JUICE

One day an older Arab merchant, with two donkeys loaded down with goods, spotted me. As he came closer, I felt he had something he wanted to tell me. He jingled his money pouch in front of my face and said that if I didn't unload and check his goods to be taxed, he would give me a good tip. The pouch filled with coins would be mine. Without hesitating, I quickly asked him where he was going. He answered that he was going to Bolis. I told him, "Because of your age, you must have good experience. I don't want any money from you. However, I have a letter I want delivered to Bolis. If you deliver it and return with a signed letter of receipt, I will cooperate with you. If you don't return with a receipt, it would be in your best interest never to return here again." He promised and reassured me he would deliver my letter and return with an answer and a signed receipt.

That evening when I returned home, I squeezed the juice out of some onions. I used the juice to write a message in Armenian on the back of my letter. In school I had learned how to write with onion juice. When the juice dries on paper, the writing is no longer visible. As soon as the paper is held up to a light source, the writing becomes apparent in a dark brown color. This lesson became useful to me on that day.

On the front side of the letter, I wrote with regular ink in Turkish. Since the letter was to be delivered to Bolis, it would be censored. In Turkish I identified myself as Mohamed Oghlee Rooshdee and gave my regards and a few general non-incriminating details.

On the back I wrote in Armenian with the onion juice and identified myself as Hampartzoum Mardiros Chitjian, my father's name. I included my current address in Iran where I could be reached. Finally, on the face of the letter on the Turkish side, in tiny script on the bottom corner of the letter, I wrote in Armenian, "Hold this letter up to a candle."

The next morning the Arab, pleased with our secret arrangement, agreed to all of my conditions. Again, I reminded him that I wanted a receipt signed by Hrant Mooradian. Mooradian was Kaspar's friend in Zonguldak, who was a well-known merchant who used the address of his partner's well known brother, Dr. Hagop Yeghyaian who lived in Bolis. Luckily, I had remembered his address despite all of the intervening tribulations I had suffered. (I had written many letters to Kaspar from that address from Sako Mahlahsee)

The Arab left reassuring me that as long as he was alive, my letter would be delivered to Mooradian. He expected to return within a few weeks.

Months later, when I resumed corresponding with my brothers did I find out what ultimately happened to the Arab and my letter. For reasons unknown, the Arab was put in jail in Bolis. *Even so, he honored his word.* He found a messenger to go to Mooradian's house to tell him he had a letter from Iran held by an Arab in jail. He should go down to the jail to pick it up.

Coincidentally, during that time my brother Bedros had returned to Bolis in search of an Armenian bride for himself. Fortunately on that very day, when the messenger delivered the Arab's request, Bedros was visiting with Mooradian at his house. When Mooradian heard about the message from the Arab, he became suspicious and fearful because he didn't know anyone in Iran. Bedros realized his concern and offered to go in his place. He reasoned that the Turks wouldn't harass him because he was now an American citizen. That is what they did. They went to the jail and asked the Arab for the letter. Bedros signed the receipt with Mooradian's name.

When they returned home and read the letter at first, it made no sense to Mooradian because I had only written about general daily life and signed the letter "Mohamed Oghlee Rooshdee." I had not identified myself in Turkish.

The letter was passed from one person to another several times with the hope that by reading and re-reading it, one of them would realize who had sent it and what it really meant.

Finally, one of them noticed my Armenian script while passing it from one to the other. "Read the backside of this letter in front of a candle." They quickly held the back of the letter up to the candlelight and discovered in brown colored letters what I had written in Armenian.

Bedros was overjoyed to learn I was still alive and of my whereabouts. He immediately notified Kerop who was still in Kharpert and greatly worried about my well being, he also sent my letter to Mihran and to Kaspar who by now was in Chicago.

From the time I fled from Sako Mahlahsee, Kerop and Kaspar were frantically searching for me. Kerop kept writing to my brothers in America, pleading with them to tell him where I might be. He was so concerned that he feared something had happened to me and they were not telling him. In the same manner he also wrote to Kaspar in Zonguldak. You could imagine how frightened Kerop must have felt when he was left alone and abandoned in the clutches of the vicious Turk.

While Kaspar was in Zonguldak and later on in Bolis, he was doing the same. He not only wrote dozens of letters to America to Mihran and Bedros, but also wrote dozens of letters to the American Consulate in Kharpert. No one knew where I was.

SECOND THOUGHTS

I am glad now that I took the risk to write that letter and had it delivered by the Arab. Even though, right after I made the deal with the Arab and gave him my letter to deliver, once again I was struck with panic. What if the Arab was caught and forced to tell on me?

Immediately I had second thoughts as to whether I had done the right thing. Had I placed myself in jeopardy? What if the Arab snitched on me?

As the weeks went by and he did not return with a response. My fears intensified—especially as I became increasingly aware how criminals were punished in Iran.

One day, I had witnessed how an offender was punished for petty theft. He was brought to court by two mullahs on the street where the theft occurred. He was interrogated and convicted right on the spot of his offense. After hearing the verdict, two male family members were instructed to carry out the punishment of several strong lashes across the offender's back.

After witnessing other similar incidents, I began to really worry about what they would do to me if I were caught.

> *I am not afraid of hell*
> *My life has been through hell*
> *But after so much suffering*
> *I am afraid of being tortured.*

Dear reader, read on if you are not tired.

REUNITED WITH AVEDIS

A few months passed when one day, while I was checking the goods on another Arab merchant's caravan and listing what he had brought, I noticed one of Margos' workers running toward me. Struggling to catch his breath, he excitedly exclaimed, *"I have your brother here with me! He has been searching for you!"* With guarded hope and with doubt, I wondered how Kerop could have gotten there on his own.

When I walked up to them, I realized it was Avedis. He was alone—his body was still covered with sores. Despite his condition, I immediately hugged him. All the workers shouted out to me, "Don't touch him. You too will catch his disease!" I was so happy to see him that I did not care. He was my friend. I was really surprised that Avedis found me. I thought that no one knew where I was any more.

Some months earlier, I had told my co-workers about my escape from Kharpert with two other boys. They knew about my relationship with Avedis and therefore, without hesitation, befriended him too. They all had a glass of wine to welcome him and made a toast to his good health. Within a few minutes, a couple of boys took Avedis to bathe with hot water and gave him a change of clean clothing.

That evening Avedis told me about what happened to them after I snuck away. He began by telling me that the Kurd who brought me into Iran was furious when I didn't go back with him to finish the work on the shoes. He was equally furious that I had fooled him by telling him I was a Turkish soldier when, in reality, *I was an Armenian.*

He expressed his anger among the other Kurds in the village about how he had been fooled by an Armenian. At some point, the Kurd still helping Avedis and Nazaret heard that story and realized that he too had been fooled. He had cause to be even angrier for he took us home and nursed us back to health when we were literally starving to death. He was so angry that he wanted revenge.

At some point, he realized that Avedis and Nazaret must also be Armenians. So one night when they were softly talking to each other in the stable, the Kurd quietly snuck up close enough to listen to their conversation. Sure enough, he caught them speaking in Armenian. He was able to detect the language because at one time he had been a slave for an Armenian.

The next day he reported the two boys to the local Turkish officials. The boys were immediately arrested and taken to jail. The Kurd received one *mahjeet* for the capture of each boy.

While in jail, Avedis' condition got much worse again. He was now under a lot of stress and feared for his life, both from the officials and the other inmates who were wild and vicious because not only were they poorly fed but because they detested his sores. They did not want to be near him. Avedis knew his life was in great danger from those beasts.

One night he noticed that the guard, who was supposed to be on watch, was fast asleep. He felt that moment might have been his only chance to escape. However, because Nazaret was fast asleep, he was afraid to awaken him for fear he would make noise, thus, arousing the guard and thereby losing his only chance to escape. Fearing for his life because his sores were now becoming unbearable, he decided to escape alone.

He had also heard from the Kurds that I had escaped and was free in Kehleeseh Kand, Iran. Therefore, he decided to go there to find me. Since he was unfamiliar with the terrain, he wandered about the hills for weeks until he found a way to sneak across the border into Iran and slowly made his way to Kehleeseh Kand.

He too found his freedom in Iran. Now my dear friend and I were together again. Margos and his wife also befriended Avedis. I will never forget the kindness of angelic Margos. He protected me when I was in desperate need of help finding my freedom. He had two daughters, a little child and a fourteen-year-old with whom he wanted me to wed. There weren't many Armenians left in Kehleeseh Kand, and he feared she might end up marrying a Persian. However, in my heart I longed only for my brothers. The political environment was also very precarious—no Armenian knew what his fate might be.

I shared my longing for my brothers with Margos; he was sympathetic and understanding. He did not pressure me; he accepted my decision.

The situation remained like this for some time. One day, when Sahlahree Hmahyoun was making preparations for a regular trip to Tabriz to turn in the collected taxes from this area, Margos arranged for him to take Avedis and me with him so we would be able to continue with our plans to go abroad.

I later found out that Bedros had written a letter to me, in care of Sahlahree Hmahyoun's address in Kehleeseh Kand. Since that letter arrived after I had left for Tabriz, Sahlahree Hmahyoun forwarded the letter to me in Tabriz in care of the Archbishop. For whatever reason, I never received that letter either.

30. ARRIVING IN TABRIZ

TWENTY-THOUSAND STARVING SOLDIERS

Sahlahree Hmahyoun had a large beautiful four horse-drawn carriage. I felt privileged, like a king, as I sat up front with him when we drove off. Besides the two of us, he had four or five Persian passengers. There were also several armed guards to protect the large sum of money he was transporting with us.

Our first major stop from Kehleeseh Kand was Khoy. From Khoy we went to Mahgoo. At each stop he sacrificed a lamb for the local people in the vicinity. That event created a feeling of goodwill among the villagers, which, in turn, diminished our chances of being robbed. At each stop, we too enjoyed a lavish barbeque feast.

Finally, after traveling for a week, we reached Tabriz. We went directly to the Khalahtah Church office. Avedis and I felt confident we had arrived in a safe place. We were told there were many Armenians there.

Sahlahree Hmahyoun knew Archbishop Nerses Melik Tankian quite well. After talking with each other for a time, Sahlahree Hmahyoun told the Archbishop he had delivered two survivors from the *bear's mouth,* meaning we had escaped from the vicious Turks. Sahlahree Hmahyoun felt we were now among friends and out of harm's way, so he bid us a cordial farewell and continued on to his destination. Being entrusted to Archbishop Melik Tankian's care was reassuring to us. We both felt the Armenians in Tabriz would welcome us with open arms to console our souls for the unconscionable torment we had endured for six years. Little did we know what was in store for us.

Immediately Archbishop Nerses Melik Tankian told his aid, Dikran, to give us each five *tumahns* (Persian currency) for pocket money and to alert us about conditions facing local Armenians.

This was the first and last time I ever received help from an Armenian organization. I have always been able to find a way to work to provide for my basic survival. I did, however, appreciate the gift of the five *tumahns.*

Just as David and I stepped out of the doorway of the church, we were taken back by the soldiers' pleading cries, *"Mayrig, Mayrig, here is my military certificate given to me by Antranig. Please give me just one bite to eat!"* Some twenty thousand starving soldiers had been ousted from Eastern Armenia when the Bolsheviks took over. Their relentless, poignant cries burn in my ears to this day. I couldn't understand it then and it's impossible to comprehend today. For six years I was gripped with a fear of the Turkish sword and had barely made it to Tabriz alive. *I was surrounded by twenty thousand Armenian soldiers ravished with hunger.* It was overwhelming—too difficult to comprehend. I was not prepared for what was taking place. *Was there no place where Armenians were allowed to live in peace?* We had only one enemy. A million and a half Armenians perished at the hands of the barbaric Turks and driven off their homelands of the past three thousand years.

Just knowing there were Armenian soldiers during those six years of terror had given me strength and hope. *At this point and time to see thousands of Armenian soldiers starving and begging for a bite to eat was much too painful for me to witness.* In their weakened conditions the soldiers were too afraid to collapse to the ground, and yet too weak to stand. They had no place to rest. Anyone found lying listlessly on the ground was taken for dead, quickly picked up, and driven away to be burned to avoid a possible epidemic of one disease or another. That would have compounded the existing misery!

The cries went on, *"Mayrig, Mayrig, here is my military certificate given to me by Antranig. Please give me just one bite to eat!"* What a devastating plea!

Although the circumstances were different, *Armenians were still suffering, and dying from starvation.* Of all the places I personally witnessed starvation, *this* was the worst. There were just too many people crammed into one area at a time where food was in desperately short supply.

Archbishop Melik Tankian tried his best to work within the Armenian political schism. He made every effort to feed and console his pathetic flock. He is the *only clergyman* I have personally encountered who sincerely and compassionately pursued peace among his people. I have often wondered why clergymen who have taken the *same* oath to serve their people have not shown that same compassion and commitment.

Before we left the church, we were warned of the dire situation we would encounter outside its doors. We were also *warned* to make our money last as long as possible. Initially we didn't understand the real impact of that warning. We could not have conceived the severity of the situation in Tabriz in the fall of 1921.

MUHRRDAHL

As we walked a short distance from the church, the first thing we noticed was a street vendor selling watermelons. Even though we were not yet hungry, we contemplated whether to buy one. Avedis and I stopped to look them over. The vendor startled us by yelling at us. Nearby Armenians realized our predicament and rushed over to help us. They explained that Persian law forbids Moslems to touch or possess anything owned or touched by Christians. Christians were considered *muhrrdahl* (untouchables).

Merchants had a small special plate they used to receive or give change to avoid physical contact with a Christian. That practice seemed to be unique to Iran. I have never seen or heard of it being practiced elsewhere. An explanation for this practice suggested that years earlier when the shah had used Armenians as slave labor, he issued a decree-forbidding harm to his subjects. Thus, he prevented Moslem Persians from attacking or touching the Christian Armenians.

Therefore, because Avedis and I each had touched a different watermelon, we were obligated to buy both. We shared it with our newly found Armenian acquaintances. Within a day or two we realized the heedless folly when we squandered *our precious five tumahns* on watermelon we did not need.

That Moslem law presented other grave problems for us. It kept us from finding a job, and without a job we had no means for food. Finding a place to sleep was not a problem. There always was some place where we were allowed to sleep for the night. Finding food became a grave matter. Our five *tumahns* did not last long, even though we both tried to stretch it. It was hard to believe hunger was more severe in Tabriz, than in Kharpert.

ENLISTED WITH THE DASHNAGS

Within a few days, we became aware of the political conflict among the Armenians. The Bolsheviks and Dashnags were at odds with each other. The conflict was somehow related to the super powers that were fighting each other in the area.

On the main streets, groups of men were shouting the doctrine of their respective party. Each party tried to influence the men on the streets. Because Avedis had relatives in Armenia, he was determined to go there. He joined the Bolshevik Party, and I joined the Dashnag Party because of what I was taught in school and all of the nationalistic songs that were embedded in my soul and meant so much to me. Both parties gave its members one *tumahn* a week, enough to buy bread to appease their hunger.

During the day we went to our respective areas. At night we returned to our room as good friends and compared notes about what we heard and saw. We were each given a small book explaining the doctrine of our party which we read to each other and discussed the similarities and differences. I thought the Bolsheviks had some good ideas, especially where it stated all people should be treated equally. However, I remained with the Dashnag Party. I had to get to America to be with my brothers.

One night Avedis never came back. I never saw him on the streets. I never found out what happened to him. I hope he found his way to Yerevan.

As for his cousin, Nazaret, years later when I settled in Mexico and I was relating my experiences to Kerop about how I escaped out of Turkey via Iran, I was surprised to hear what he in turn told me. When the Kurds captured Nazaret in Bayazid, he was sent back to a jail in Kharpert. While in jail, he somehow got a message to Kerop, telling him to go to the jail to see him. When Kerop got there, Nazaret told him I had escaped to Iran and was alive and free. That is all I know about Nazaret's fate.

About two weeks later, two Dashnags in their twenties approached me on the street. They had an assignment for me. Initially that made me feel good. Finally, I would have a job to pay for my keep. I felt that no job would be too hard or undesirable for me. I was stunned when they quietly began to tell me that an Armenian by the name of Levon had to be assassinated. They gave me no explanation. That was to be my first assignment. It didn't take a split second for me to reply, *"I could never kill an Armenian! I cannot kill anyone!* I have seen so many hideous acts of killings, innocent Armenians slaughtered." Without listening to what I said, they continued to describe how I was to carry out the mission. First, I was to hit Levon over the head with a club, then stab him in the chest with a knife. They showed me a picture of the man—he was about twenty-five years old. They went on to tell me I was to hide between the buildings and wait for him to show up. When he came close enough, I was to strike immediately.

I couldn't believe my ears! After all of the Armenians I had seen tortured and slaughtered by the vicious, godless Turks, now they wanted *me* to do the same to kill another Armenian. Since the *charrt,* I have *never* waived from my belief that any Armenian was mine and I belonged to him. Differences of opinion could be resolved and we should never forget the *charrt.* We should join hands and multiply. If we don't, God help the Armenians!

I recalled how proudly I sang the nationalistic songs* my Dashnag teachers had taught me and the sermon when our principal had stressed that we had to fight for our freedom. However, this didn't make sense to me. I just couldn't see one Armenian killing another. Surely those men had *not* seen what I had seen! They continued to try to convince me to carry out that heinous act. Being unsuccessful in persuading me, they decided we should draw straws to decide who would carry out the act, I agreed. On the first draw, I was chosen. The second time, I was chosen. The third time, I was chosen! At that point I repeated, "I cannot kill an

---

*   *Farmers, ranchers, husbandmen*
    Brothers, come, let us unite and go forward
    To protect our labor and our Cause

    Hand-in-hand, let's support our Dashnagtsoutiun
    United Dashnags, let's go to our Sasoon
    Our fathers and brothers are waiting for us!

Armenian. Give me any other job, and I will do it! I have never killed a chicken, so how could I kill a man and an Armenian at that!"

I had *miraculously* escaped from Kharpert. I had reached *this* point with the help of Armenians and by helping Armenians, not by killing them! I still couldn't believe I was being asked to assassinate an Armenian just because he believed in another doctrine! With this as my final decision, they kicked me out from the Dashnag Party.

Even the Turks didn't make a distinction as to what political doctrine or church Armenians belonged. They slaughtered all of us equally. Any one who had personally seen the ravines and valleys filled with the bodies and bones of slaughtered Armenians would never have thought of taking so much as a strand of hair from another Armenian. He would find a solution to resolve the differences between the two parties and then work together to accomplish that, which was most advantageous for the Armenian cause. Only a meager few Armenians had survived the Turkish inferno. **How could they destroy each other? How could they emulate the Turk!**

ABANDONED AND ALONE

Now, I was left alone, completely on my own. Iran was very different from Turkey. With no job nor money, I had no means to buy food. There was a nearby restaurant owned by two Kharpertzee brothers. I went there with the confidence that I could get a job. They turned me away, because I was dropped from the Dashnag Party. I offered to wash the dishes for free. I thought while cleaning off the dishes, I could eat the scraps and lick off the plates before I washed them. They turned me down again.

Within a few days I was so hungry that I walked aimlessly near other restaurants to see where they dumped out their dishwater. I thought I might be able to retrieve some of the greasy water to get *some* nourishment. However, when I tried that at several different places, I discovered the dishwater was too soapy— and I just could not digest that!

With all the threats and perils in Turkey, I was still able to find work that provided me with enough food to survive. The situation was different in Iran. I knew if I didn't find a solution soon, I could starve to death. Every day I saw bodies of dead soldiers picked up, dumped into a truck, and driven away to be burned. In addition, I was greatly troubled that I had not heard from my brothers. I had been writing to them every day, sometimes twice, yet I still was not receiving any replies. Were they getting my letters? Were they aware of my situation? Surely they wouldn't abandon me now!

As time passed, I felt increasingly desperate. I no longer was able to think of a means to find enough food to stay alive.

A TRUE FRIEND

One day as I was standing under a wall, I fought to keep myself from falling down. I was extremely terrified that I would be dumped in the back of a truck among the corpses if I crumbled to the ground. My nose started to bleed. A tall and handsome boy approached me. His name was David—he was a Buzmehshentzee, as I later found out. He saw what was happening to me and said, "Come with me, let's go home!"

There were eight other boys in that room. They were Kharpertzees, Chemeeshgahtzahtzees and Buzmehshentzees. Two of the Kharpertzees were from Soorsooree Village, Yeghia Zadourian and Minas Keyahian, whose brothers were in Fresno, California. Just like me, all they had were the clothes on their backs. Now, we became nine friends who looked out for each other. For the most part, we were on our own during the day. I don't know where they went when they left the house.

The very next day David took off his undershirt and pants, and washed them well. When they were dry, he told me to accompany him. As soon as we got outside, he started to shout out that he had an undershirt and a pair of pants for sale. Within a few minutes he had a buyer. He sold his garments for one *khron*, (worth a quarter). With that coin in hand we walked straight to the *fahroon* (bread bakery). There was a restless crowd—many people had their hand stretched out trying to buy bread. David did the same. As he handed the cashier his one *khron* and brought his hand down, he had a piece of bread and the coin was still in his palm! He quickly slipped the coin to me. I, in turn, stretched out my hand and gave the coin to the clerk who gave me a piece of bread too. David and I quickly walked away with the *two* pieces of bread, trembling with fear we might be caught. Had we played a trick or was it pure luck? *Was God watching?* Did He finally feel sorry and decided to give us a helping hand? Who knows?

We went straight home. Much to our delight, no one else was there, so we didn't have to feel guilty about not sharing the bread with the other boys. David was aware how hungry I had been and was really concerned about my survival.

After eating the whole piece, I felt I hadn't eaten a thing. I was still so terribly hungry and severely malnourished. *How much longer could I go on? I wondered which was worse*—the fear of torture and brutal death by the Turks if I had been caught, or the hunger and starvation I was now experiencing in Tabriz!

To make matters worse, Armenians were restricted to two main areas in Tabriz where there were only two main streets. One area was Khalahtah *Tagh* (district) the other area was Keeleeseh *Tagh*. Armenians were forbidden to go elsewhere in the city, seemingly an extension of the *muhrrdahl* decree that prevented all nine of us from going out to look for work in other areas.

The situation became intolerable for me. I felt trapped and thought that I really had no chance to survive, even though I had come so far by managing to find a way to survive out of the inferno. Because of my inability to find a means to get food, I was weakening, both physically and emotionally. I was in a foreign land, completely cut off from my brothers and not allowed to work. While I never stopped writing to them, I still couldn't understand why I hadn't received at least one letter from them. I knew no one, I was completely **alone!** *I was losing all hope... No one knew where I was, or if I had died, where and how I died...*[*]

Out of sheer desperation I sat down and wrote a note on a small piece of paper. I wrote about myself, who I was, and where I had come from; and about my unbearable situation and fear of starving to death. I took the note, went to an affluent Armenian home, and knocked on the door. A young girl answered and I handed the note to her. I remained on the doorstep. Within a few minutes, she returned with five *tumahns.* That was charity!... *I needed a job!*

During all of my wretched experiences in Turkey, I had never begged. I had always found work, and that provided me with enough food to get by. I was in Iran, starving and couldn't find a job—I was absolutely desperate. *That was the first and last time I would ever ask for money.* The five *tumahns* lasted for five days for the nine of us. After that was gone our hunger returned. I never did find out where the other boys got their money.

BROTHERS CONTACTED

One day when I had gone to the post office to mail one of my letters, I learned that it cost three *tumahns* to send a telegram. I thought perhaps I should try to contact my brothers with a telegram since my letters had gone unanswered. On some days I wrote three or four letters. I never found out why I never received a response to any one of these letters. Asadour Asadourian, a tailor, lived with his mother, Yeghsah, in the room next to ours. Both of them became our friends. One day I noticed he had saved more than three *tumahns* from his work. I asked him if he would loan me three *tumahns.* I offered to pay him back three times the amount in exchange for such a favor. The next day I quickly went back to the post office and wired the telegram. The following day I was notified it had not gone through because its cost exceeded the three *tumahns.*

David went to the post office with me to see how much more money I needed. Since we didn't have the difference, this time David took off his very expensive *bookhahrah,* a gray Persian hat made of baby lamb fur worn by men. He laid it down on the counter and asked the clerk if he would accept the hat as collateral until we received the reply to our telegram. The clerk accepted the offer and sent off my telegram for the second time.

Two weeks later we received notice that a response had come from my brothers, and there was a big sum of money for me to pick up. When we went to pick it up,

[*]   One of my first letters from Tabriz was dated November 1, 1921

I was asked to give my brother's name. I replied that his name was Bedros. The clerk said that was not the name on the telegram and therefore he refused to give me the money. He said I would have to furnish him with more specific evidence of my identity.

Having no other proof of identification, I was obliged to go to the church office to see if they could help me. The first question I was asked was if I had another brother at that address. I realized then that Mihran or Kaspar must have sent the money. I received a written statement listing all of my brothers names from the clergy. Upon returning to the post office, I approached the same clerk and gave him the names of my other brothers, Mihran and Kaspar. We found out the money had been sent under Mihran's name.

The postal clerk handed me twenty-five *tumahns*. Sometime later I found out Mihran had wired an extra dollar so that I should have been given *twenty-five American dollars* and not the equivalent in Persian *tumahns* whose value was worth much less. We were deceived yet again.

After we retrieved David's hat, we went directly to a restaurant and ordered a nice meal. I remember it well—we each had ordered two earthenware bowls of *gouvach* (an onion soup with garlic and lamb). We ate until our stomachs felt full. For the first time we were both very happy. However, when we returned to our room, all nine of us were still hungry. We sent out for enough food to satisfy everyone.

They first brought in some drinks, and the boys insisted I, too, drink a toast to our good health. Since I never had the habit of drinking, one drink knocked me out. Immediately, I fell asleep without having a bite to eat. David put me in my bed. When I awoke the next morning, I was panic stricken. My first words were "Where is my money?" David quickly replied, "Don't be afraid—your money is all here." He nodded with his head, indicating where he had hidden the money in the wall.

The first thing I did that morning was to pay Asadour the nine *tumahns* I had promised him for his loan. In return to show his appreciation, he took my measurements and made me a nice suit for my pending journey. He and his mother had always been nice to me. They too had relatives in America, but didn't have the address. In my letters to my brothers, I asked them to search for Asadour's relatives. Asadour and his mother were from Upper Mezreh. Her brother's name was Khazar and he was from Hueseneeg. His father, Mugerdich Sehrahbian was in Boston.

Later on that day, David went with me to apply for my passport. I had no legal papers verifying my place of birth, or date of birth. A short time later when I received my passport, it indicated that I was born in Salmast, Iran on August 15, 1901. I didn't object and thought it might be safer to omit Turkey as my birthplace. I have kept that as my 'official' birthplace and date of birth. I knew for certain that I was born in 1901.

We both decided the shortest route to America for me would be to go to Baku, then to Bolis, and on to the seaport of the Black Sea where I would then board a ship sailing to America. I notified my brothers of my chosen route from Tabriz to America and began to prepare my journey to reunite with them!

As fate would have it, I saw David again one more time in Los Angeles, California, about forty years ago. He had come to Los Angeles to visit his sister, Ovsanna Emerzian. Sadly, he had changed. He was no longer that very handsome man I remembered. He bore the scars of additional tragic experiences. The change was very difficult for me to observe. I had wished only the very best for him. He was a very gentle, trustworthy, helpful and intelligent friend. He was helpful to all of us, not just to me.[*]

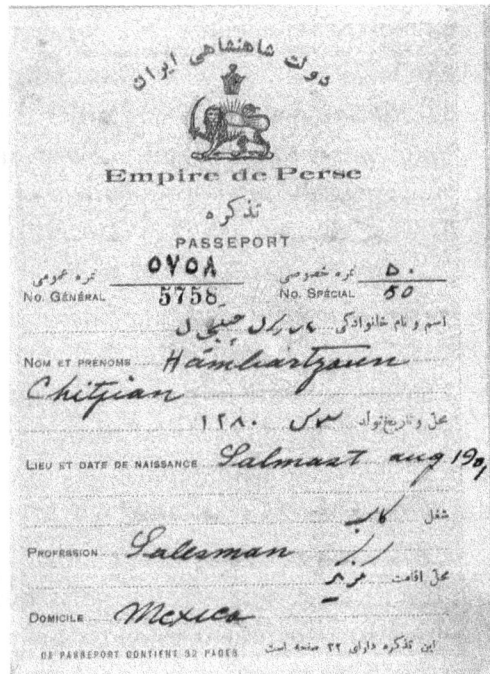

My Persian passport, 1922

---

[*]   David Djolakian died in Paris, 1969.

31. THE ROUTE TO AMERICA

KHAZBEEN, HAHMAHDAN, KERMANSHAW, BAGHDAD

While I was making final arrangements in the bus station for my departure from Tabriz, I encountered Khachadour Amerian among a small group of Armenians who were exchanging travel plans and information. From them I discovered the route I planned to take via Baku would be very dangerous. The Bolsheviks and the Dashnags were fiercely fighting each other in that region.

Without my knowledge, my passport had been stamped with an official Dashnag seal. Apparently, when I was removed from the party, the records were not updated. Because I didn't want to delay my departure, I didn't have the time to have the seal removed from my passport. Since Baku was Bolshevik territory, anyone going through that area with a Dashnag Party official seal on his passport would be in great jeopardy. I knew I had no choice but to change my route.

Fortunately, I overheard Khachadour say he was going to Bahsrah which was the next nearest seaport. I felt that would be a safer route for me and I changed my route accordingly. Even though his final destination was Egypt and mine was America, we decided to accompany each other up to Bahsrah. On April 14, 1922 I left Tabriz and started my journey with Khachadour, leaving behind eleven months of unbearable hunger.

We started our journey on a bus that carried primarily Arab and Persian passengers. In Iran, from Tabriz, we drove through Khazbeen, Hahmahdahn, Kermahnshaw until we arrived to Karatoot at the Iraqi border. Baghdad was to be our first major stop in Iraq. Whenever the bus stopped at restaurants, Khachadour was not allowed to enter. He was well shaven, with no beard or moustache. The Persian innkeepers took him for a Christian and thus considered him *muhrrdahl*. By now I had a moustache, and I was not suspected. So, I would go in and purchase tea and a bite to eat for the both of us. I held my purchase with a handkerchief and made sure I never touched Khachadour as I handed his portion to him. If I had touched him, onlookers would have suspected we were both Christians. For the entire journey through Iran, I had to pretend I was either Arab or Persian. If we stayed overnight in a hotel, he had to sleep on the bus. There too, I took him his dinner.

In about twenty-five days, we reached Kermahnshaw. We saw beautiful peacocks that were strutting all over the streets. This was the first time I had seen a live peacock. Although they were very beautiful, they made a horrible noise and were extremely messy.

As we boarded the bus to leave again, we were asked to show our passports. Khachadour got on first and was passed on. As I got on, I showed my passport as I had at every stop, but this time I was stopped. It jolted me when I was told to step off the bus. I was taken aside and asked all sorts of questions. The only part of the interrogation I understood was when they asked me where I was going, and I answered "America." Not knowing what to do because I was afraid the bus would leave without me, I just answered "yes" to the additional questions. Finally, I was allowed to board the bus again. I later discovered that because I was dressed in a relatively nice suit, they thought I was going to Kalbahlah, a Moslem pilgrimage. My passport was now stamped "America" on one side and "Kalbahlah" on the other.

From Kermahnshaw the bus rolled on to the Iraqi border city of Karatoot. At this stop we were transferred from the bus to a train. As we boarded the train, we had to show our passports. Once again I was singled out and instructed to step aside. This time I was taken inside a tent and told to wait a while. For some reason, I thought I was going to be treated well—maybe because I now knew my passport was stamped with a Kalbahlah seal.

However, what I didn't know was that the news was out that an Armenian priest had been killed in Tabriz. Since I was coming from Tabriz, I was considered a suspect. To make matters worse, the suspect was a Dashnag and my passport bore the official Dashnag seal!

When a considerable amount of time passed and no one came back into the tent, I got scared. I didn't know why I was being held. Suddenly, I felt an ominous feeling and began to cry. I couldn't figure out a way to protect myself. I could hear the engine of the train preparing to depart. Yet no one had returned to the tent to tell me why I was being detained.

Finally two *Asorie* (Assyrian) men came to interrogate me. Noticing that a man in his twenties was crying, they sympathized with me. After asking me a few questions, I heard one man tell the other, "He doesn't seem to know anything." They let me go.

I rushed to catch the train when I suddenly remembered the warning I had heard in Kharpert, "If you could hear a train's engine, stay far away, or the train's wheels could sweep you up!" Never having been near a train before, I became afraid. Luckily, it was barely moving and I was able to jump on. I was relieved to see Khachadour and knew we were still together after all.

It was May 11, 1922. It took us more than a week to reach Baghdad from Karatoot. We were taken to a beautiful hotel with a nice patio where people were sitting around tables drinking tea and talking. Everyone seemed happy. The patio was lined with palm trees with bunches of dates hanging from the branches. In one corner of the patio, there was a rushing stream that created a cool, refreshing breeze. This was a pleasant sight to see and to feel in the hot desert.

When we sat down at one of the tables in the patio, we were handed a menu written in Armenian, Arabic, Turkish, Persian, English and French. Since then, I have never seen a menu written in so many languages. My eyes quickly spotted *mahdzoon, leban,* yogurt. I decided that was exactly what I wanted—nothing quenched your thirst like yogurt, especially in the hot desert air. Simultaneously, I was yearning for the fresh yogurt we purchased every morning from Khazanchee Mardiros in Perri.

In less than a half-hour after eating the yogurt, my stomach was in great pain. I became very ill and was taken to my room. The hotel's doctor came to examine me. Meanwhile, Khachadour had contacted relatives who came after him and took him to their house. I was sick and left all alone in the hotel room.

I was detained for more than two months before I was strong enough to continue my journey to America. By then, I had spent most of my money. Twenty-five cents was all that I had left and I used that to telegram my brothers asking for more funds. Several days passed by without a reply. It occurred to me that my brothers could have been confused about getting a telegram from Baghdad when I had previously informed them I was going to America via Baku. Additionally, I had just signed my message with Hampartzoum. Ignoring the fact that anyone else could have used my name in an attempt to bilk money from them, I had failed to give them personal information identifying myself.

I quickly sent off another telegram, signed with all of my family's names—Torros, Mardiros Tervanda, Bedros and Mihran. My hunch that they had been suspicious of my first telegram was verified when I was reunited with my brothers in Los Angeles.

While recuperating, I was confined to my room. Next to the hotel was "Cinema El Iraqi." It was similar to a drive-in theater. I wished I could have gone in to watch the movies. Not only was I laid up in bed because I was too ill to leave my room, but I had run out of money and I couldn't afford to go anywhere. Nonetheless, I was able to hear the movie—I just could not see it. There was a wall between the hotel and the cinema obstructing my view.

One day the Arab chefs were cooking eggplant with oil in a large kettle at the foot of my bedroom wall. The delicious aroma rose up and taunted me. I longed for a piece of *lavash* bread that I could attach at the end of a rope, dip it into the kettle and let it soak up the savory smelling juices. Then I would quickly reel the rope back up. While I was sure that would have been delicious, I also knew I was not well enough to indulge myself. I was still feeling very sick.

A few days later, in the evening, the hotel suddenly began to shake. Then there was a big jolt. I was in bed so I held on tightly to its sides. I heard noises and commotion coming from other rooms. *I was really scared.* I didn't know what was happening. Before I could get up, someone rushed into my room, told me not to worry, and informed me we were experiencing an earthquake. I had heard about earthquakes before, but had never been in one.

Soon the shaking subsided, and much to my surprise, I noticed the wall between the hotel and the cinema had collapsed. My first thought was how lucky I was that the wall fell away from the hotel. Had it crashed into the wall of my room, I could have been killed—*nobody would have ever known where I was or what had happened to me.* While those unnerving thoughts were running through my mind, I made a wonderful discovery. With the wall gone, finally I was able to see the movie screen!

That was my first exposure to motion pictures. I was very impressed with such an invention. I still remember one of the first scenes of a movie was the ocean. I felt as if the water was coming straight towards me. That too was my first exposure to the ocean and a memorable experience for me.

From my window I was also able to see the beautiful, colorful streetlights adorning the whole city of Baghdad. That was a very impressive sight, as well as an emotional experience. What elegance! Tabriz was nice, but nothing like this.

The first time I had ever seen an electric light was in Mezreh on Papureyohly, right across from the government building. A man had set up a little booth and for five cents he allowed people to go in to see the bulb glow for a few minutes. I still remember standing there in awe. It seemed as if the light from the stars and moon had been *encased in the bulb* for all to admire. I must have been seventeen to eighteen years old at that time. You could imagine how impressive these lights were.

I started writing letters to my brothers once again. I was feeling very lonely and alone. All this time I had guarded the pencil Kerop had given me when I left him. Just holding onto the pencil gave me emotional comfort and strength. Before going to sleep, I would kiss his pencil *to console my yearning for him.* When I started to feel better and was still waiting to receive money from my brothers, I got a part-time job setting tables for an Englishman in one of the dining rooms in the Daejlah Hotel where I was staying. My job was to set the tables three times a day—at 8 a.m., noon and again at 8 p.m. After setting the dishes and utensils, I served the order for each table. I received five *rupees* (Iraqi money) a day in wages. The bill for my hotel room was eight *rupees* a day. My wages didn't cover my expenses; thus I went into debt.

Because of my illness and no money, I wasn't able to see much in Baghdad. One day when I had free time and felt well enough, I went out of the hotel and walked along the two main roads leading to the hotel. Although they were narrow, they were still very impressive. On another day, I was taken to an old Armenian Church. I didn't find anyone there to socialize with, so I never found out the name of the church or when it was built. The local people were also poor. This is all I remember about Baghdad.

I finally received a response from my brothers. They sent me one-hundred and fifty dollars. I prepared to resume my trip to America now that I had the money to cover my expenses. Since I had not completely recovered from my illness, I was warned that my chosen route through the Indian Ocean would be hazardous for me because of the hot weather. I agreed and took the advice *and changed my route again for the third time.*

It was suggested that the safest route for me was to go to Haleb (Aleppo), then to Beirut, and from there on to America. Unbeknownst to me at that time, my fate was improving. Was my merciless God beginning to notice me? Did He feel I had suffered enough? Why was I running into obstacles that kept changing the course of my route to America?

During my recovery, Khachadour had visited several times and inquired about my health and recovery. When he learned about my new plans, he too liked the idea of going to Haleb because there were a good number of Vanetzees there. He was a nice, shy, handsome boy, but he didn't like to work. He sat all day in the hotel, looking in the mirror and squandered the hard earned money his father sent from Egypt.

When I was well enough, I helped him make the changes on his passport so we could continue to travel together. When all our arrangements were taken care of, we met at the bus station. To my surprise, he had brought his cousin, David, with him.

FROM BAGHDAD TO MOSUL TO HALEB

We boarded the bus at noon and arrived in Mosul in two days. It was noon when we stopped at a hotel for the night. Before we got off, the bus driver advised the passengers to give him their valuables for safekeeping in the morning before we resumed our journey. He warned us that there were many bandits in the area, and the bus might be held up. He wanted to take all precautions to protect our belongings and us.

When the three of us got into our room, we discussed the situation. We all agreed the best thing for us to do, other than comply with the bus driver's advice, was to sew our money in our clothing. That is what we did. As David knew how to speak Arabic quite well, he was able to get three needles and thread from the hotel's desk clerk. I still had nineteen Turkish gold coins from Baghdad worth

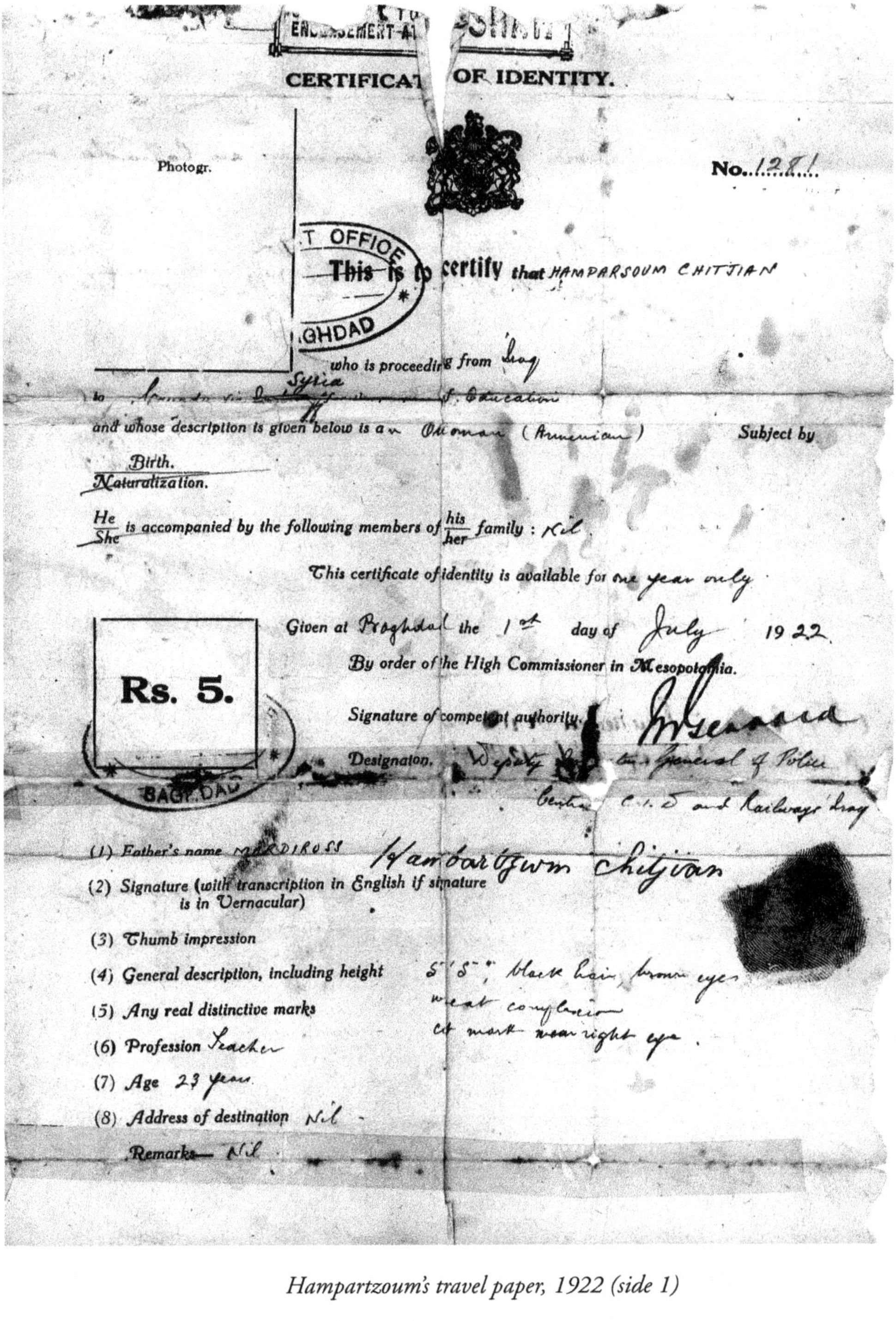

CERTIFICATE OF IDENTITY.

Photogr.

No. 1281

This is to certify that HAMPARSOUM CHITJIAN

who is proceeding from Iraq

to Syria

and whose description is given below is an Ottoman (Armenian) Subject by

Birth.

Naturalization.

He/She is accompanied by the following members of his/her family : Nil

This certificate of identity is available for one year only

Given at Baghdad the 1st day of July 1922.

By order of the High Commissioner in Mesopotamia.

Rs. 5.

Signature of competent authority.

Designation. Deputy ... General of Police

(1) Father's name MARDIROSS

(2) Signature (with transcription in English if signature is in Vernacular)

(3) Thumb impression

(4) General description, including height 5' 5"; black hair, brown eyes

(5) Any real distinctive marks wheat complexion

(6) Profession Teacher

(7) Age 23 years

(8) Address of destination Nil

Remarks — Nil

Hampartzoum's travel paper, 1922 (side 1)

Hampartzoum's travel paper, 1922 (side 2)

more than one hundred dollars, enough to get me to America. I decided to sew the coins on the inside of the front straps of my suspenders. My suspenders were fastened to the waistband of my pants with buttons. The other two boys sewed their money in their jacket collars, sleeve cuffs, or pant cuffs. We did not confide to one another the exact place where we each put our money, but we all kept a little change in our pant pockets for food.

The next morning we got on the bus and sat in the back seats again. About an hour later the bus stopped to have the tanks filled with gas and water. The passengers all got out to buy something to eat. Before boarding back on the bus, the bus driver announced to all of the passengers that we should buy something extra for the midday meal so that he wouldn't have to make an extra stop and thereby we would save time. The aroma of the barbecued chicken was very inviting, and we decided to buy one. We tightly wrapped it and placed it in our tote bag where we already had bread, fruit and other personal items. We thought the chicken would keep warm until it was time to eat.

The bus drove on. About two hours later we got hungry and eagerly looked forward to eating our chicken. Since we were sitting on the very back seat of the bus, we thought we would not offend the other passengers.

As we started to unwrap the chicken, we were sickened to discover the whole bag was filled with squirming white worms. We had no choice but to throw the whole bag out of the bus window. Our hunger and appetite went out with the chicken!

Shortly after that misfortune, we heard gunshots coming from behind the bus. The bus came to an abrupt stop. Bandits got on board and ordered the first five rows of passengers to get off. Judging from their attire, those people seemed to be quite wealthy. The minute they got off of the bus, they were ordered to take off their outer clothing. The bandits quickly started to slit the collars, cuffs and trouser flies, searching for valuables.

Watching all this from the bus, I thought about slipping off my suspenders and leaving them on the bus when we were ordered off. Then I decided it would be too risky to separate myself from them. So I unbuttoned them from my pants and left them hanging loosely over my shoulders. When we were ordered off the bus, the three of us lined up with a couple of other passengers. Luckily for me, I was at the end of the line. As the bandits were searching the others and taking whatever they considered of value, I quickly dropped my suspenders, covered them with sand and stood right on top of them. When they finally came to me and searched my body, they found only a few coins in my pant pocket. When we were told to re-board the bus, I stooped down to pick up my trousers, grabbed my suspenders and then got dressed. We all took our same seats again and the bus took off. I was feeling very fortunate that no one had seen my scheme. I was not caught!

Everyone on the bus was shaken up by our frightening ordeal. A tense feeling permeated throughout the bus as the bus driver drove on. We had gone some distance in the desert when we were startled to see a mirage, something I had never experienced before. From a distance it appeared we were approaching a beautiful garden of greenery and flowers. As we got nearer, the images disappeared. Then we saw another one and that too disappeared. Each new mirage was different from the other. The mirages were strange, yet pleasant. The mood in the bus began to lighten up again.

During that time, David had noticed that I still had my suspenders intact and surprised me when he nudged me to let him wear them, trying to assure me when we got to Haleb, he would give them back. When I refused, he got a little angry.

A few hours later, the bus stopped again to fill up with gasoline and water. The passengers got off once again to get a drink or a bite to eat. The minute we got off, David pushed me aside saying this was a good time for me to hand over the suspenders. This time he warned me if I didn't do so, he would tell the bus driver and if the other passengers found out the bandits did not get my money, they would accost me since they were all stripped of their valuables. Reluctantly, I handed the suspenders to him to avoid alerting others that I was carrying nineteen gold pieces.

We boarded the bus and headed towards the Der Zor Desert. After several hours we stopped at our hotel for the night. Because the bus passengers had no money, the hotel management did not charge us for room and board.

The three of us were given one room. As soon as we settled in, I told Khachadour to go out and get us some drinking water. Then I immediately bolted the door and jumped on David, demanding he give the suspenders back to me. We got into a fistfight, banging against the walls and floors. The Arab management heard the commotion and knew something was going on. They pounded on the door, trying to get in. However, the door was bolted and we didn't respond to their demands. We continued fighting. Thus, a couple of Arabs crawled in through a window and got into the room.

At that time the area was under the English mandate, but the officials who came in spoke Turkish, even though they were Arabs. They stopped our fight and ordered us to follow them. They took us to a makeshift courtroom. The person presiding as the judge interrogated us about the gold coins.

One of his first questions he asked was which one of us knew the numbers on each coin. Neither one of us knew the numbers. He continued with a couple of other questions that did not solve our problem. At that point I asked for, and was granted, his permission to say something.

I told the judge to look at the buttonholes on our trousers and compare them to the size of the buttons on the suspenders. The buttons were an exact fit for the holes on my trousers. The buttons on David's trousers were much smaller. The imprint of the buttons on our respective trousers also proved who was the rightful owner of the suspenders. The judge was very impressed with my point. He was one hundred percent convinced I was the owner. He told us to become friends, and instructed David to give the suspenders back to me.

Knowing we were Armenians, he told us he had something he wanted to show us that he thought would help us to reconcile our differences. He drove us quite a distance away from the hotel. As we approached our destination, he stopped the car. In front of us we saw two huge mounds of human bones, each the size of a room. He didn't say much, only that they were Armenian bones. *"Who knows whose bones these are. They could be those of your family and friends. Isn't it better to be friends and helpful to each other, rather than fighting with one another?"* We were emotionally overcome by the shock of seeing the bones in such huge quantities; they were the bones and skulls of Armenians of all ages.

It was most gratifying to meet someone other than an Armenian who sincerely empathized with the unfathomable plight of my people, someone who showed real concern about the Armenian bones in the Der Zor Desert.

The compassionate Arab continued by instructing us that life was more precious than money. I promised him I would help my two companions as much as I could. Indeed that is what I did.

> *Der Zor cholarheendeh gunash parlyor,*
> *Osmahnly askehree goorshoon yaghleeor,*
> *Ermehnee moohageeree yahmahn aghleeor,*
> *Deenee beerr oghroonah geeden Ermehnee! (Turkish)*

> *In the hot desert of Der Zor, the sun shines fiercely,*
> *The Turkish soldier oils his bombarding guns savagely,*
> *The Armenian refugees weeping profusely,*
> *While tenaciously clinging on to his Armenian Christian faith!*

My mind raced to the bones I had seen in Perri… bones in the abyss of the valley Khazahn Dahrah, close to the village of Hoshay, and all of the neighboring villages of Perri—bodies in the Perri River, hair along the river banks, strewn and hanging on the willow tree branches lined along the river, the long locks of hair and braids of innocent women and girls… huge piles of small bones of babies and young children under the bridge on the banks of the river in Khooshee… the body of my favorite classmate, Krikor Noroian, strewn amongst bodies of many other Perritzees on the river bank of Mahlaheen Tsor, his one eye staring up at me… the three headless men tied together at their ankles dangling from a tree that I witnessed on the day I walked with Korr-Mamoe to his friend's house, the abandoned, scattered bones throughout the hillsides going from Kehsereeg, Moreneeg to Hueseneeg.

Where are those bones today? Whose bones were they? Whose mother, father, baby sister, brother, aunt, uncle, grandmother, grandfather was slaughtered and callously cast aside? In 1969, at the Antelias Armenian Monastery in Beirut, I was shown a *few* bones and skulls from Der Zor. What happened to the *sacks* filled with bones by the American soldiers for their government? Why did the US government have the bones collected? Why did the government compensate the Turkish rogues one dollar for each sack they turned over? Why? *Do you want me to remember more? Or, are you tired of listening to me?*

In a solemn but congenial mood, the Arab drove us back to the hotel. A short time later we boarded the bus and again were on our way to Haleb. David was still unhappy about returning the suspenders to me, their rightful owner; however, with great reluctance, he finally did so.

32. WITH GOD'S WILL I WENT TO HALEB

SEARCHING FOR KEROP

On July 17, 1922 we finally arrived in Haleb. For the first few days, we shared a room with eight other boys from Kharpert in the Vazeer Khan Hotel. Within a day or two, the two cousins wired their respective families—one in Lyon, France and the other in Alexandria, Egypt. When they received money from their families, they both repaid me what I had spent on them after the robbery. They arranged for their passports and left within a month. I still cherish the photograph taken of us before I saw them off.

Left to right. Yerzngatzee Haigaz (an aquaintance in Haleb), Vanehtzee David, Vanehtzee Khachadour and sitting in the middle is me. (Haleb, 1922).

Refugees from all over Turkey were being brought into Haleb by train. I went to the train station every day hoping to find a familiar face. From a couple of people I encountered, I was reassured Kerop and Hmahyag were still alive!

My first task was to find a way to rescue Kerop out of Turkey. As soon as I encountered a Kurd who had established a reliable reputation rescuing Armenians out of Turkey, I promised him ten dollars in advance and another ten dollars when he actually brought Kerop to me in Haleb. I gave the Kurd a letter to give to Kerop, which assured him to trust the Kurd.

Some time later, again from newly arriving refugees, I learned that the Kurd and Kerop had come halfway to Haleb when they were caught and sent back to Kharpert. In order to save their lives, the Kurd bribed the Turk with the ten dollars.

Shortly after hearing that news, I found Krikor, a *khajakhgee* (a man who secretly rescued refugees). He was from Beyhezneh and had become a Moslem. I chose him because he knew my cousin Hmahyag. Earlier he had promised to bring Hmahyag with him the next time he went to Haleb. I learned Hmahyag was in a very bad situation because he tried to help a Jew escape and was caught and severely beaten as a consequence. *Since conditions were continuing to worsen throughout Turkey and becoming more dangerous* the *khajakhgee* wanted to help Hmahyag escape. When I told him Hmahyag was my cousin, he was eager to help me too. I promised him twenty dollars for each if he brought Kerop and Hmahyag out of Turkey together. He reassured me he would rescue both boys and then left on his mission. I felt more at ease if they were to come out together because Hmahyag would be more protective of Kerop if they ran into danger. He would make sure Kerop would not go hungry.

Rescuing Armenian orphans out of Turkey was *also* becoming increasingly more difficult and dangerous. We had heard about a caravan from Dikranagerd with five hundred orphans, gathered in and around the vicinities of Kharpert, that was repeatedly and *viciously attacked along the way until they reached Trahbluz.* From that point on to Haleb, they traveled on buses or the train.

The news that completely *devastated* the Armenians in Haleb was the fate of the orphans who were to be rescued by the American Red Cross. The American Red Cross directors from Kharpert—Mr. Krite, Mr. Hekimian[*] and Mahmed Effendi—were sent to Sooroodge to wait for the arrival of a caravan of orphans to accompany them to Haleb.

However, when the orphans arrived, the mayor of Sooroodge would not turn over the orphans to Mr. Krite because he had direct *orders from Mustafa Kemal* to send them back. The orders stopped the orphans from leaving the country. Mr. Krite, Mr. Kekimian and Mahmed Effendi returned to Haleb empty-handed. All hope of rescuing those orphans was lost.

The reason given for that order was that Turkey had declared war on Greece, and so the orphans were sent to Urfa, not back to Kharpert. *The news of the orphans' fate completely drained everyone emotionally who was waiting for loved ones in Haleb. We all felt so helpless.*

We also heard that Mr. MacKay, another Red Cross employee, had gone to Beirut to talk with Turkish government officials in pursuit of a way to get the orphans released. They wanted direct permission from Mustafa Kemal to allow the orphans to go to Haleb as originally promised.

---

[*] Names discovered in letters sent to brothers in Chicago.

With all of that news coming directly into Haleb, I was able to learn what was transpiring from those going and coming. I didn't dare change my location or make arrangements to go to America. I had promised myself *I would not leave the area until I had rescued Kerop, regardless of how long it took to do so.*

This dismal situation continued through 1923 when the Turkish government, under the rule of Mustafa Kemal, gave Armenians a *grace period* to leave Turkey. Turkish soldiers and citizens were ordered *supposedly* to stop their heinous acts of torture and murder of Armenians.

The same barbaric acts of violence were, however, committed by the *chettehs,* mentally crazed and vicious criminals, who were *intentionally* released from jail to terrorize the fleeing, weary deportees—*a deceptive ploy to appease the super powers!* I later learned that Kude Archbishop Mekhitarian was one of those who experienced the horrors inflicted by those *chettehs* as he led his caravan out. He had made his last attempt to round up all of the remaining Armenian orphans in Kharpert, a group composed mainly of women and children. The older boys and men had either escaped by then or been slaughtered. Only when he thought he

The Turk who protected the Sarkis Piloyan family, in Malatya, 1915-1923.

had rounded up all of the remaining Armenians did the Archbishop lead his caravan towards Haleb.

That was also the year when my beloved wife, Ovsanna and her family, were driven out of Malatya. The Turkish *Effendi* who had saved her family in 1915 *no longer felt he would be able to protect them.* Finally at that last stage when all Armenians were in imminent danger under Mustafa Kemal's command, he was powerless to protect them from harm. He advised her father to take that opportunity to leave Turkey. He promised them personal protection with two of his most reliable guards to ride on horseback alongside the family in a caravan of deportees towards Syria. With no other alternative, Sarkis Piloyan, Ovsanna's father, agreed and joined a caravan of deportees walking towards Syria.

Together with his wife, two daughters, Maritza and Nevart, and son, Hagop, they departed from their ancestral homeland. *They left behind all of their possessions, house, and most precious, their homeland of Malatya—their souls never left Malatya…*

When they were halfway to the Syrian border the caravan was attacked by *chettehs*. One of the *Effendi's* guards swiftly rode back to Malatya and informed the *Effendi* what was taking place. He immediately ordered one hundred armed horsemen *(tsiavor)*, to meet up with the caravan, to assure the safety of the Piloyan family, to the Syrian border. From there, the train took the refugees to Haleb.

ZARUHY'S LAST WORDS…

During the day I spent most of my time walking around the train station and the *Hokey Doon*. The *Hokey Doon* was the hub or center for all Armenian activities—only a few boarded there. People went there primarily to find information about loved ones and friends, or to find out the latest news pertinent to the plight of the Armenian refugees.

One day while I was walking alone towards the *Hokey Doon,* a woman recognized me. Waving her hand, she called out my name, "Hampartzoum! Hampartzoum!" A warm feeling went up and down my spine. It was a nostalgic sound to hear my Armenian name called out by a familiar voice from Perri. As she got closer, I recognized her. It was a pleasant surprise and realization to know there were **other survivors from Perri!**

After a few words, her mood changed and her eyes filled up with tears. She proceeded to tell me she had seen my sister, Zaruhy, in the *Hokey Doon* on one occasion several years earlier and hadn't seen her since. Nor had she heard what happened to her. That encounter took place when Zaruhy reached Haleb. She was very exhausted and weak when she began to tell the woman what had happened to her father and family. As Zaruhy began to relate her story to the woman, it was obvious she was unable to endure the agony of recalling the painful ordeal before completing her story. Zaruhy felt faint and collapsed to the ground. Medical attendants from the *Hokey Doon* rushed to her assistance and carried her away. Thus, the woman was able to tell me only what little Zaruhy managed to convey to her and no more:

> *After returning home from the Turkish orphanage where my father had taken my three brothers and me, he went home to pick up my stepmother, his sister Marinos, and my three sisters Zaruhy, Sultahn and Yeranuhi. They joined the other neighbors from Perri who were being forcibly deported, leaving behind their personal belongings and their*

homes. They were not given time to make preparations for the ordeals of deportation. As soon as they reached the banks of the Perri River, my father advised my sister Sultahn, who was only sixteen at the time, to throw herself into the river for a more peaceful death. Because of her crippled arm, he felt the Turks would only abuse and torture her, then inevitably they would kill her. Even though she was a pretty girl, no one would take her as a wife. Aware of what they had already done to my father, as evidenced by the dry bloodstains on his coat, Sultahn promptly threw herself into the rushing waters of the Perri River.

After a mournful prayer, the family resumed walking with the others. As they drew nearer Hoshay, a Turk attempted to grab my stepmother. At that point, my father tried to stop him, but the Turk reacted swiftly by slicing off my father's ears...

As much as we know, those were Zaruhy's last words, and with tears streaming down her face, she collapsed. Apparently her exhausted body and devastated soul couldn't endure any more. We will never know how she managed to escape from the demise of the others or how she managed to trudge across the horrible Der Zor Desert on her own. Was there a God? Nor will we ever know why the clergy or others at the *Hokey Doon* didn't help her when she first arrived in Haleb. She had two brothers and a husband in America. Months before the Genocide my father tried unsuccessfully to find a trustworthy person with whom he felt secure to escort Zaruhy to America to be united with her husband.

During my East Coast visit in 1939, I saw her husband, Boghos Khatounahian. He too said he had not heard from Zaruhy. He had since married a Greek. *Those were the final words about my precious father. There has not been any other witness to tell me more about him.* I wished at that moment I were not alive to have heard her account. I wondered if there was a God. Was there the Son of God with the name of Jesus? *For seventeen hundred years Armenians have been crushed. It is a pity for those who believe in Him!*

My blessed father prayed the *Havadov Khostovaneem* each and every day. It did not help him or the million and a half other Armenians who were slaughtered. He would end the prayer by reciting, **"This much hardship, this much grief our children should not forget..."**

The wind took my father's dreams away. Much worse however and unforgivable, his children and grandchildren were scattered in different directions and were oblivious to his words. This was much worse than the bloody Genocide! This was, and is today, the "White Genocide," assimilation into foreign lands, cultures and religions. Meghk...

My sister Zaruhy. Photo taken in Perri at the request from her husband in America. He sent $10 to cover the cost. The in-laws kept the money.

A NOVEL DIVERSION

During the time I was anxiously waiting for Kerop's arrival, I was intrigued by the boys riding bicycles. I had never seen a bicycle before. It seemed like an easy way to get around. When I found out bicycles were not too expensive, I decided to buy one. At that time I felt somewhat financially secure because I still had most of my nineteen gold pieces.

The shopkeeper taught me how to ride the bicycle before the sale was finalized. Once he was satisfied with the way I handled it, he gave me the bike. I spent many enjoyable days riding around the city.

One day while I was riding around the train station, I heard a woman's voice call out, "There goes our Hampartzoum!" I was stunned to see Aghsah Bahgee Marabian, who lived right behind our house in Perri, sitting on the ground not far from the train tracks. Her two daughters, between the ages of ten and twelve years old, were at her side. They were bewildered and distraught; they didn't know what to do. Dressed only in their underclothing, they were overcome with shame and abandonment. Aghsah Bahgee told me they had been robbed of their meager possessions and stripped of their outer clothing by the Turkish *chettehs*. I quickly reassured her I would help them. I told her to wait for me, that I would return shortly with clothing for her and her daughters.

I rode my bike to the closest shop that sold women's clothing found three dresses that I thought would fit each one. I left my bike with the shopkeeper because I didn't know how to ride it while carrying a package. I walked back as fast as I could and gave them the clothes. After they got dressed, we walked back to my hotel room. By now the other boys had left, so I had the room to myself and was able to accommodate them. The next day we sent a letter to her husband in America. Within a month or so she got a response from him, and all three departed for America.

In 1939 while, I was visiting in New York City, we called Aghsah Bahgee from the home of my wife's sister, Nevart. Aghsah Bahgee quickly notified the other Perritzees living in the vicinity of our visit. They all got together, rented a small banquet hall, and gave a party in my honor. I have never forgotten the love, camaraderie and joy we all shared that evening. When Aghsah Bahgee first saw me, her embrace even surprised her husband!

The next day she phoned Hampartzoum Der Garabedian who had married her older daughter. They were living in Philadelphia at that time. Therefore, that was our next destination. The four of us, my wife and two children, boarded a train to visit my dear classmate who used to help me harvest my father's mulberries, and who helped me escape out of Chalkhadahn during the Kurdish rebellion by encouraging me to leave Korr-Mamoe in order to save my life.

What a memorable and cherished week we shared, we covered a gamut of emotions! *We shed tears of great sorrow and pain, and a few tears of joy, joy that we had all survived in one piece.* Hampartzoum had just had his first born, a beautiful little girl. I had my wife and two children with me. That evening was so memorable for me. We kept in touch with our yearly Christmas cards until his early death in the 1970's.

The novelty of my bike not only gave me a sense of strength and joy, but it mainly was a diversion from my concern about Kerop's safety. I really enjoyed riding it about the center of town. Soon I felt I wanted to venture out, away from the hub of the city. One day I decided to go in the direction where the trains began to emerge into view. The road was not level; there was a moderate incline up a hill.

It was quite difficult pedalling up that hill. Because the ground was so sandy I had a hard time breathing as I pedalled with all my strength. I finally made it. Once I got to the top of the hill, I turned around to start back down. As I began coasting, the bike accelerated, and I could not control it. I knew it was not safe and I was really afraid as I neared the bottom of the hill. I managed, however, to get down without any problems.

After that experience, I knew I had to teach myself how to navigate slopes better so, one day, when I felt a little more confident, I rode up the same hill again. This time, the bike just sped faster and faster down the hillside until I completely lost control. I didn't know how to slow down. Before I knew what happened, I felt a jolt and flew into a pile of sand. I was completely engulfed with sand—sand was in my nose, mouth, ears and clothes. When I got up, however, I felt lucky I was in one piece with no broken bones or scratches. Now, I was too afraid to get back on the bike, so I picked it up, walked to the shop, and returned it to the shopkeeper.

PATIENCE REWARDED

During that time of grave uncertainty for the safety of the last deportees out of Kharpert, I still had not heard from the Armenian *khajakhgee* whom I had paid to rescue Kerop. By then, I was *distraught with fear* that I may not be able to save Kerop. So when I learned the American Red Cross was going back to Kharpert again to try to rescue remaining orphans, I *offered to pay* them if they brought my brother back to me. They gave me encouragement and told me to write a letter to Kerop explaining he was to cooperate with them. Even though it meant paying a third time for Kerop's rescue, this time I thought he would be safer traveling with the American Red Cross than with the *khajakhgee*.

Little by little, I was informed by the arriving orphans that Kerop was on his way and that he would be arriving soon. With that hope, I went to the train station every day, hoping he would be there to greet me. As the days passed and he didn't show up, my fears and despair intensified. Departure out of Turkey was becoming even more difficult—I feared the worst. *What if they closed the borders?* The daily news of the increasing dangers was crushing my soul. My eyes had been frightened so much from what they had seen, my ears from what they heard. My heart had grown weary from my past and now my whole body was trembling again with fears of what the future might bring. *Would I ever see my brother again?* Were we going to meet each other again while my eyes were still open? I was even beginning to wonder if I ever had parents. What did it mean to have had parents? Having had parents had become a distant illusion in my mind and soul. Had I completely forgotten them?

Kerop and Hampartzoum (Mezreh, cir 1920)

I continued to mingle amidst the new arrivals, searching and hoping I would find Kerop or encounter someone who might have seen him. I ran to the station each time I heard the train coming

One day, with the grace of God, I saw Kerop step off the train. I hadn't seen him for over two and a half years. He had grown much taller. As I waved to him, he rushed towards me. What a happy moment! Finally, all my fears were laid to rest!

It was God's design that I changed my route twice to come to Haleb. I shudder to think what would have happened if I had not come here. Where

Kerop, me, Altoon Bahgee and Margarite (Haleb, 1922)

would I have found Kerop? Where would I have heard Zaruhy's last words? How would I have learned about my father's fate?

Moments later I saw Altoon Bahgee and her daughter walking towards us. Kerop quickly explained that he was not happy living with the Reverend's wife, that she had not taken good care of him even though I had given her eight gold pieces which was a lot of money. So, he had gone to live with Altoon Bahgee and they left Kharpert together.

It took some time for Kerop and me to regain our composure. *Was there a God after all?* We were alive, together, and finally free. We no longer were in the clutches of the Turks! Was He looking down at us? Six years of hell were behind us at last!

We knew at that very moment our next destination would be America and that we would eventually be reunited with our three brothers. *With tears in our eyes we acknowledged all that we had lost: our precious father, sisters, Nishan, Sultahn, Yeranuhi, our stepmother... everybody. We had left behind our Yergeer. Akh, akh, what a painful realization—the tears within our souls will never stop!*

Some moments later we realized Altoon Bahgee no longer was at our side. Without asking, she had gone to rent a room for all of us. So, I moved in with them.

There wasn't any reason for us to delay our departure. The next day, Kerop and I went to apply for his passport. Like me, Kerop didn't have any legal documents, so my passport was used to verify his identity. Thus, his passport stated that *he too was born in Salmast, Iran.*

While we were waiting for Kerop's passport one day, I was walking in front of the hotel Vazeer Khan and unexpectedly I ran into Dikranouhi, the daughter of one of my most respected teachers, Baron Abraham Eoksuzian. We had both changed and bore the scars of all that we had suffered. Somehow she recognized me. She resembled her father who was a handsome man. Although he was a strict disciplinarian, he was a very conscientious teacher. He was very concerned that we learn as he sternly lectured, "You have come here to learn, not to waste time!" Whenever a culprit was reprimanded, he muttered, "May your roots be cursed!" and then he would slam down his rod on the poor soul's knuckles. However, we learned! For that I have always been grateful!

While talking with her, I remembered when he invited all of his students to his house for a Sunday afternoon dinner. He treated us to rice pilaf. That was the first time any of us had ever eaten rice. To the best of my knowledge, we didn't have rice in Perri. The next time I saw rice was in Kharpert when I saw an American soldier exchange two bags of rice for one bag of bulghur. When Dikranouhi told us she was the sole survivor of her family and that she was left all alone, I invited her to join us with Altoon Bahgee. It took several weeks for Kerop's passport to arrive. Some time after our departure, Altoon Bahgee left Haleb with her daughter to join her son, Setrag, in Chicago.

The exhilaration of that moment was tainted by the real significance of our journey to Haleb. *What had happened from 1915-1923? Why were we here?* Why were we going to America? What business did we have in America? Those were my thoughts from the time that my father left four of his sons in front of the Turkish school, and without a word, walked away still wearing his bloodstained coat, a broken man. His destination, *America,* was the ravine on the hillsides of Perri. **May God curse and punish the culprits who destroyed an entire innocent nation on their God-given ancestral homelands! If there is a God, may that country be damned forever!**

33. FACING NEW CHALLENGES

MARSEILLES, FRANCE

Soon after we had received Kerop's passport, we went to Beirut, which was the nearest seaport. We were delayed several weeks for the preparation of the ship's departure to France.* Beirut was a small underdeveloped town infested with mosquitoes. We slept with a canopy over our beds so that the mosquitoes would not bother us.

Coincidentally, we heard that Kude Archbishop Mekhitarian was also there waiting for a ship going to France. Our initial departure date was postponed for yet another week, because the first ship was over-booked. At the last minute space was needed for Kude Archbishop Mekhitarian and the group of orphans traveling with him.

Kerop, I, and several other boys like us were asked to wait for the next ship so the Archbishop would not be separated from his group. We were *honored* to serve a man who had earned and deserved much respect. As we were promised, a week later we boarded ship. It took about five days to reach our first destination of Marseilles, France. This was our first experience on the ocean. It was just as I had expected from what I remembered from the motion picture I saw in Baghdad. *This was a new beginning in our lives.* We literally were facing a whole new world. Until now, the forces of anxiety, sorrow and anguish had taken turns consuming our hearts, our souls, and our minds. All we had lost—parents, sisters, brothers, friends and our precious *Yergeer*—was much too painful for us to keep in the forefront of our minds. We still had to feel our way, one day at a time, and to face new challenges.

I felt our future could only improve. Nothing could be worse than what I had experienced for eight years. Fortunately, I had learned that I was able to handle almost any experience God threw in my face as long as *I didn't expect too much.* That knowledge has stayed with me throughout my life.

Much to our pleasure, at mid-day on the fifth day at sea, our ship docked at the port of Marseilles. We were now in France. Turkey was starting to seem farther and farther away.

We were taken to a hotel. While settling in, I learned Kude Archbishop Mekhitarian was also staying *there.* In reality it was only a couple of years since I last had seen him, but it now seemed ages ago. This, however, gave me hope I

---

* We left Beirut either August or September 1923.

would find an opportunity to personally thank him one more time for all the care and attention he gave me and the other orphans, and how hard he worked to find and rescue thousands of Armenian orphans still held by Turks and Kurds. How fortunate we all felt when he opened the Loosavorchagan orphanage in Kharpert providing shelter and comfort for us when we were facing such precarious circumstances. I shall never forget his concern for the other boys and me.

At our first opportunity, all the boys who had given up their space on the first ship got together and went directly to visit the Archbishop in his room. Upon entering, we saw a very young, clean shaven, handsome man dressed in a European suit. We asked if he knew when the Archbishop would return. He quickly replied, "I am the Archbishop!" When he saw our confused expressions, he explained that he had disguised himself as a priest so he would be free to carry out his mission to find and rescue as many Armenians as possible without causing suspicion. *Little did I know when I was in Kharpert that he would be one of the very few people I would encounter in my lifetime who I thought **should be honored as one of our national heroes.*** Unfortunately I have not heard any more about him since that day, other than he was headed for Argentina.[*]

Shortly after that pleasant experience, within the hallways of the hotel, we were confronted with *a pathetic situation* on several occasions. A middle-aged Armenian woman, totally worn down, with dazed but desperately searching eyes and panic in her voice, would cry out whenever she saw a young man, "Don't worry, my son! Don't worry—I am coming, I am coming!" Exhausted, she would then collapse to the floor. Each time we picked her up and carried her back to her room. That continued during the five days we stayed in Marseilles. *We could only imagine what the heinous Turks had done to her son as she was forced to helplessly witness his demise.*

That was a poignant reminder that we were still fleeing from our misery of the past six years. We were not just on a voyage going to visit our brothers. *We still couldn't come to grips with man's inhumanity to man while the whole world stood by and just watched. What a pathetic commentary on mankind! Meghk!*

About the third day we were engaged in a conversation with the hotel's concierges, the two Olouhojian brothers from Malatya. They informed us that it would be wiser if we first went to Mexico and then on to America because at that particular time, immigration into the United States was closed. They added, it would be easy to go to California from Mexico by land.

That was a difficult decision for me to make because I didn't know anything about Mexico or its people. The Olouhojian brothers were more informed and assured us Mexicans respected foreigners and led simple lives. The Mexican men in the motion pictures wore large hats and had big moustaches. Later that day they

---

[*]   Kude Archbishop Mekhitarian settled in Sao Paulo, Brazil, and married Lucia Jafarian in 1924. (Boghos Jafarian (Leon Mangasarian, ed.), *Farewell Kharpert*, Claire N. Mangasarian Publisher, 1989.

took us to a local cinema and we saw a Mexican film. This gave me some idea of what to expect once we got there and I began to feel more at ease about having to change the course of our destination.

DESTINATION MEXICO

The ticket to Mexico cost thirty-one dollars—the voyage would take exactly thirty-one days. That was one dollar a day per person! However, for that price we had to sleep in the cargo level. I booked passage for Mexico and in a couple of days we boarded ship and sailed towards Spain, our first stop. Upon our arrival, we transferred on to another ship.

Since our sleeping quarters were in the cargo level, we had to accept the horrible stench. The stench became more bearable only when we thought about being reunited with our brothers. However, we were very fortunate during the day when we were allowed to go to the upper deck to get fresh air. It was the beginning of summer, and the ocean was relatively calm. The food served to us was not bad, especially for those of us who had experienced hunger.

Once we found a place to sit on the upper deck, I noticed a group of Armenians and a girl standing alone against a nearby wall. I felt too shy to approach them, so I told Kerop to walk a short distance away from me and call back to me, *"Agha Par."* Two of the men approached us when they heard me talking to Kerop in Armenian. They introduced themselves. One man was Levon Bodosian and the other was Khachadour Nazarian. Both men were from Sepastia. We soon developed a very good friendship with everyone in the group—all together there were eight people.

When we docked in a port in Spain, our new friends asked if our eyes had been checked for a contagious disease. Without that test, they told us we might not be allowed to get off the ship. Kerop and I went to a cabin where our eyes were checked. A technician dropped a solution into each eye and said, *"Bono,* your eyes are healthy." Along with the other passengers, we changed ships, and our passports and visas were checked again. Eventually, we were reunited with our friends.

At this point, I felt more confident and decided to befriend the girl who had kept to herself. I walked up and introduced myself to her. I learned that her name was Anna Gabriellian, and she was a mail order bride. She had exchanged letters with her intended husband. She took out a picture from her purse and showed me a photo of the young man waiting for her in Los Angeles. She was to marry him as soon as she arrived. When I told her I also had brothers in Los Angeles, she showed me an envelope with his address. *I couldn't believe my eyes,* the address on the envelope was the same as my brother's market! Thus, we became good friends and she joined our group. She, too, was much happier to be in a group.

From Spain we sailed directly to Cuba where we docked for only half a day. Just before we came to port, the man sleeping on the bunk above me got sick and vomited all over me. That made me ill, and I didn't feel like going up on the deck. I was busy cleaning myself off.

However, Kerop went up and noticed people eating a strange fruit. He came down and told me about it. He described the fruit as large, with skin that had to be sliced off and it had a yellow, fleshy interior. I gave him one dollar—he came back with five of them. We later found out the fruit was called *pineapple*. All five were still green. We didn't like them and we threw them overboard.

From Cuba we sailed to Vera Cruz, Mexico. Many Arabs were working around the port. They had been in Mexico many years. They greeted all new arrivals hospitably, which we really appreciated because we did not know the language or customs of Mexico.

Luckily for us, Anna had lived in Baghdad for a few years. She had escaped from Malatya after her whole family was killed. She had learned Arabic on her own and spoke it quite well. Anna was able to converse with the Arabs and had them tend to all our needs. After registering in a hotel, we had a bite to eat and went to sleep. We felt content. Our sea voyage was over, and we had only one more country to go through to reach America.

The next day the Arabs put us on a train headed for Mexico City, where we had a couple of difficult days on our own before we met some Arabs again. This time Anna asked them if they knew of any Armenians living in Mexico City. To our delight, they knew of *one* and took us to the man's store. It was obvious he was well established and well to do.

THE FIRST ARMENIAN IN MEXICO CITY

We waited outside while the Arabs went in to inform the proprietor about us. We could see them through the window, talking with a gray haired man. We also noted he had one wooden leg from the knee down (he had had a corn infection on one toe). Soon fifteen bottles of alcohol were placed on a nearby table. The Arabs shook their heads in a gesture of disapproval. Then a barrel was placed on the floor next to the table—that too was not accepted. This was followed by yet another barrel at which point the offer was accepted. The Arabs then came out and invited us to go inside. They introduced us to the owner, Gabriel Babayan, a humble and very nice man. One of our traveling companions, Levon Bodosian, said, *"Parev hairehnahgtzee"*... "Hello, our countryman." Babayan took a deep breath and began to stutter, *"Puh, puh parev."* For twenty-nine years he had not seen an Armenian or had spoken his native language. As much as I know, he was the first Armenian to immigrate to Mexico City.

He was obviously overwhelmed by our presence. He was very moved and seemingly consumed with his past feelings, as he looked upon us one by one. He made a few attempts to speak to us in Armenia. He was as happy to have found us as we were to have found him.

He took us to his back room where he had his private office. He offered us chairs and made sure we were comfortable. He promptly called his wife and told her to prepare a lavish dinner for his special guests.

As he was recalling Armenian words, which he once knew and greatly yearned, he told us why he had immigrated to Mexico City. He was born in Dikranagerd. *He was a young man during the massacres in 1894-1895. While defending his parents, he killed a Turk.* Fearing for his life, he fled and ultimately ended up in Mexico. He married a Mexican woman, had two daughters and one son, and slowly became a successful businessman.

Before leaving the store, he called Hotel Capuchinas and reserved rooms for all of us. Then he took us to his house that was a short distance from his store on Avenida de Capuchinas.

His wife had prepared a lavish Mexican and Arabic dinner for us, and surprised us with Arabic *pakhlava*. As I ate it, I recalled the circumstances of my first piece— the piece that Kaspar cautiously offered me on the streets in Perri. How could I ever forget that moment! *We were both still alive!*

We all had a wonderful evening. Everyone was in a happy mood. There was music and singing. Noticing that Anna had a good voice, Babayan beckoned her to sit on his lap, gave her a little kiss on the forehead and asked her to sing an Armenian song. While Anna sang a few songs, tears ran down his face. He had not heard Armenian songs for twenty-nine years. *He was very nostalgic and obviously yearned for the life he once had in his homeland with his family and friends. At the same time, he felt resentment for the reasons that forced him to flee.*

It was well past midnight when Babayan's son-in-law, Arturo, drove us back to our hotel. He had paid for our room and board for a whole week.

The next day I sent a telegram to my brothers in Los Angeles and gave them Babayan's address. In a week we received a response. My brothers sent two hundred dollars to cover expenses for us to go to Los Angeles via Tijuana.

BORDER CROSSING IN TIJUANA

Immediately we purchased train tickets to Colima, a seaport in northern Mexico. From there we went to Ensenada. In Ensenada, we hired a car with a driver to take us to Tijuana. Here too Anna was of great help to us, as she also knew some English and knew how to use a telephone. Once in Tijuana we called my brothers to tell them we had arrived at the border.

They advised us that, as soon as they found a driver, they would come down to get us. We checked into Hotel Tijuana and waited for their arrival which took three days. While we were waiting, several times a day, the three of us walked back and forth through the border crossing station onto the American side. We were never stopped, nor did anyone say anything to us. On the third day it was quite hot by mid-morning. The three of us were sitting and talking on the hotel's balcony. Kerop had gone in to wet his handkerchief, when I saw two young men walking towards us. As they got closer, I recognized my brother, Bedros, whom I had last seen fifteen years earlier when I was only eight years old. I shouted to Anna, *"That's my brother!"* In Armenian I started to talk to him, but Bedros didn't recognize me. He inquired in English, "I've come to pick up my brother, Hampartzoum. Have you seen him?" *"I'm Hampartzoum!"* I shouted back in Armenian and immediately embraced him. *After a good cry,* he asked about Kerop. I reassured him that Kerop would join us in a few minutes. The person accompanying Bedros was an American. They had come down in his car. He was the driver.

I just had one large suitcase with me. In Iran, I had purchased a beautiful, expensive wall carpet and with seven dollars I bought 17,000 Armenian rubles from the Republic of Armenia of 1918-1920. In Haleb, I bought a large woolen comforter—all as gifts for my brothers.

When we were ready, the five of us drove down to the crossing station. Bedros and his friend went in to talk with the officials. When he came out, I asked Bedros what happened and was stunned when he replied, "We got caught." The officials came out and escorted Anna, Kerop and me to separate rooms. We were all interrogated. When they were convinced we were not involved with any illegal activities, they let us go back to our hotel. They told Bedros to return to Los Angeles and obtain the proper papers for our entrance into the United States. The three of us would have to remain.

The next morning I divulged a scheme I had come up with the night before. First, the American driver would drive out a short distance away from the border station—far enough where he couldn't be seen. He would wait for Bedros, Kerop and Anna who would go to the border as we had previously done many times in the last few days. The guards were accustomed to seeing the three of us walk back and forth and never said anything. If all four of us, however, went down, that might alert the guards that something had changed. To avoid detection, I would sneak out over the hillside on to the road leading away from the border.

Once the three of them crossed over to the American side, casually they would walk to the waiting car. The driver would drive away slowly until he spotted me on the hillside to pick me up.

Once they all agreed to this plan, I gave Bedros *ninety-five dollars* that was left of *two hundred dollars* he had sent me. *I kept five* in my pocket. If by chance, I were caught, I didn't want to lose all the money. Finally, I put the suitcase in the trunk of the car and told the driver to drive off alone. About fifteen minutes later, Bedros, Kerop and Anna walked towards the crossing gate. It was well past noon when I took off on foot towards the hillside.

I walked quite a distance along the hillside, constantly looking back for the car. After two hours, however, I still had not seen it. So I decided to go down to the road and continued to walk alongside the curb. I soon noticed a sign that said, "Border 4 miles."

After walking an additional distance, I saw another sign, "San Diego 17 miles." By then I was getting very tired. I really thought I wouldn't be able to walk much further. I was literally walking through the hillside where there were no establishments or people. Occasionally a car passed by, but none stopped. I had all but given up hope that Bedros would ever come by to pick me up. I could only surmise that one of us was lost. I heard another car coming from behind—it wasn't Bedros, but I noticed the driver slowed down. I quickly put one hand on my face faking a toothache and pain. The driver stopped the car and said something I didn't understand. When he opened the door and motioned for me to get in, I got in. Again he said something that I didn't understand. As he drove on, he continued to talk and when I heard the words "San Diego," I said, "Yes!" I was still holding on to my face, faking my toothache. He drove quite a distance until we saw a large sign, "San Diego City Limits." He pointed to it, and again I said, "Yes!"

By now I was quite proud of myself for effectively using my limited knowledge of English to communicate with him.

Who would ever have thought that the English lessons I once had as a young boy in Perri would be so helpful years later in a country foreign to me! We had learned the English alphabet; and we were reading and writing primary phrases. I have never forgotten one of the first phrases I read aloud in English, *"Run mouse run, the cat is going to catch you!"* We always chuckled after repeating that phrase. However, I used to feel very proud when I added such phrases as, *"How are you? Are you hungry? Are you thirsty? Are you tired?"* at the end of the letters my father wrote to Bedros. Now, this knowledge was very helpful.

The sun was setting as we entered San Diego, and the kind stranger drove about another hour before dropping me off in front of a drugstore. I went inside and looked around. I quickly saw the picture of a glass of root beer and was able to read enough of the wording next to it to know one glass cost one cent. I ordered three glasses. I liked the taste, even though I didn't know what it was.

*By the age of 11, I knew more English than Turkish. An excerpt
from a letter written from Perri in 1914.*

Looking out of the window I noticed people getting on and off buses. It occurred to me that the store must also serve as a mini bus stop. On one wall I noticed a sign with names and prices, including "Los Angeles $3.50." Since I had given most of my money to Bedros for safekeeping, I had just five dollars. I bought the ticket, leaving me with only one dollar and fifty cents in my pocket.

The bus left at seven thirty that evening. After going several miles, it stopped. An inspector got on and moved the beam of his flashlight from the face of one passenger to the other. Apprehending no one, he allowed the bus to go on. Luckily, I was dressed well, so I was not suspected. When he said, "Good, go on," I felt relieved. I was safe!

Some time later, the bus stopped again. Thinking we had arrived in Los Angeles, I got off with the other passengers. I soon noticed, however, that the same people were all coming back to the bus after getting a drink or something to eat. I too boarded the bus again.

Much later the bus stopped yet again, this time at a larger station. I read a sign that said "Greyhound." As before at other stops, everyone got off and I did likewise. This time the passengers went in different directions, however, and did not return to the bus. *I assumed this must be Los Angeles.*

By now the sky was completely dark, but the beautiful, colorful streetlights and signs lit up the city. I started to walk up and down the streets. As I looked on both sides, I was hoping to find a sign that read, "Chitjian Brothers Market." *I had a feeling of calm knowing I had come to the end of my treacherous journey from Kharpert and I would soon be reunited with all of my brothers.* From within, I was happy and was now getting a thrill walking *freely* on these streets all lit up with colorful lights. Of course, I didn't see their market—I was in a different part of the city. I had no idea where I was or how late it was, but the root beer was the last thing I had to drink or eat all day. When I came to a restaurant, I entered and sat down at a table. A Greek waiter brought me a menu. Not being able to read it, I simply pointed on an item when he took my order. He returned shortly with a plate with a huge steak, potatoes and a piece of bread. I was also given a cup of coffee. When I saw all that food, I became concerned that I didn't have enough money to pay for it. Before the waiter went away, I gave him the only dollar bill I had left and kept the remaining fifty cents to telephone my brothers.

When he took the money, I wondered what he was going to do. He turned around and walked away. When he returned within minutes, I attempted to tell him that I had not touched the food, and he could take it back. The waiter slowly put seventy-five cents on the table and left. Need I tell you how happy I was! I began to eat a very tasty meal of generous proportions that cost only *twenty-five cents!*

REUNITED IN LOS ANGELES

After that wonderful dinner, I began to wonder how I was going to phone my brothers. I had never used a telephone. When I said, "Telephone," to the waiter, he pointed to one located on the back wall. I walked towards it and beckoned the waiter to come help me. I gave him a piece of paper on which my brother's telephone number had been written. He kindly dialed the number, and when Kaspar answered, he handed the phone to me. It was after midnight, and they had all gone to sleep. Kaspar was still sleepy when he said, "Hello." I told Kaspar that I was in Los Angeles. He asked me where I was in Los Angeles, but I didn't know. He told me to go outside and read the name of the restaurant, but when I

Kaspar and Hampartzoum finally reunited in Los Angeles, 1923

couldn't read it the Greek waiter helped me once again and gave the directions to Kaspar.

Kaspar responded that he would come to the restaurant in fifteen minutes. As it turned out, I was close to the Greyhound Bus Station, near East Los Angeles where my brothers lived. Half an hour later Kaspar arrived. *I jumped up to hug him,* as the last time I had seen him was when we were both running away from Perri. I was with Korr-Mamoe, and he was with his *Effendi.* How could I ever forget that moment! *How did we both survive those nightmarish six years and find ourselves in America?* I was startled when Kaspar held back and bluntly told me, "Wait until we get outside." *What* were we afraid of now? We were in *America!* Ever since I first stepped into Iran, I felt I was free from the Turks. What could my brother possibly be so concerned about now? When we got outside, out of the view of others, we hugged and cried. We always had a special bond—we were twins!

He tried to explain because I didn't have a visa to enter America that I was in the country illegally. He wasn't too sure what the consequences would be if I were caught. So *now,* I was an illegal alien! Kerop and I had to be careful. For some reason I didn't let that bother me too much. *I was reunited with my family. Besides, no one could be as brutal as the Turks* if we were apprehended.

We walked towards his car. Standing at the side of the car, by an open door, I noticed a short, young man. I asked Kaspar if he was his chauffeur. I was shocked by Kaspar's reply, "That's Mihran, your brother!" I couldn't believe him! I expected Mihran to be tall and husky. He should have been much taller than me. Mihran was the boy his classmates nicknamed *"Yehgav."* He always scared away the bullies. Now I was much taller than he was! We embraced. *Not one word* was said all the way home. We were all crying. Although we didn't verbally communicate *our tears revealed our emotions!*

It was well into the morning hours when *we reached 598 South Indiana Street,* the very address to which I had written hundreds of letters, each with the wish that I could have traveled inside the envelope. *Finally I was there. Never again would I have to send letters to that address.* On occasions I have driven past that house. I always get the chills as I recall that precious moment. Eighty-five years later the building has been remodeled but the memories remain!

Bedros' wife, Maritza, was waiting up for us. She was the woman he had chosen to be his bride while he was in Bolis. We no sooner got home when the phone rang. It was Bedros calling from San Diego. He

Bedros, Kerop (standing), Hampartzoum holding Alice and Azad in Los Angeles, 1923

told Kaspar that he had Kerop and Anna with him, but that he had lost Hampartzoum. Kaspar laughed and informed Bedros that Hampartzoum was standing at his side. Bedros couldn't believe it, until Kaspar gave the phone to me so Bedros could hear my voice. He still couldn't understand how I was able to get to Kaspar's house in Los Angeles without knowing how to speak or write in English and with only five dollars in my pocket!

I slept long and well that night. When I finally got up, it was already noon. Next to my bed was Mihran's first born son, Azad (which means *to be free* in Armenian), sleeping in his crib. His wife, Verkeen, was in the hospital with his newly born second son, Nishan, named after our youngest brother who had been mercilessly thrown into the Perri River. Two years later they had a daughter, Arax (Roxie), named after the large river in Armenia.

While I ate breakfast, I became acquainted with Maritza. I played with Azad who was about two years old. I love playing with children. The rest of the day passed quickly. Bedros finally arrived home from San Diego with Kerop and Anna. Throughout the day we celebrated our reunion. Later on in the evening, Kaspar, Mihran and Anna's fiancé joined us when they came home from the market.

During the day Anna had come to our house while her fiancé was at work. She was wearing a new pair of red shoes. When I remarked how nice they looked, she gave me a quick glance indicating she was not too pleased with her fiancé's taste in fashions and she had no alternative but to wear them. We kept in touch while I worked with my brothers. At some point, after they got married, they moved to San Francisco—and we lost contact.

WORKING AT MY BROTHER'S MARKET

Two days later I decided to go to the market on my own. My three brothers had left much earlier that morning. With the address in hand and the vague directions Maritza had given me, I set out alone. I walked until I finally found the market.

As I looked in, they were all busily working. When they saw me, they were surprised I was able to find the market on my own. They had no idea about all the walking I did from village to village for six years.

It was almost noon, and my brothers were hungry. I volunteered to fix lunch for them. They gave me a dozen eggs and a cube of butter. I was surprised that Mihran and Bedros were able to eat all of the eggs, as well as a large loaf of French bread, by themselves! What a difference! *Did my brothers ever understand when we wrote to them that we were "lucky if we had a piece of bread with yogurt after a long hard day of work"? Did they ever understand Aghavni's situation? Did they understand when I mentioned I saved extra food to take to Kerop whenever I had a chance? Did they know how it felt to go without food for days at a time? Many a night I went to bed hungry. Did they understand my situation in Tabriz—as I watched them eat with their big appetites? I could only feel happiness. Happiness that they were spared and were able to eat to their hearts' content. I felt now Kerop and I would finally be able to satisfy our appetites!* Although I was taken back when my brothers didn't offer me to join them, I thought perhaps they assumed I had eaten before I came to the market I didn't want to upset them—being hungry was something I was used to!

Starting from the following day, I went to the market with my brothers. I gradually learned how to do several jobs, the first of which was to mark the price on each item and to stock the shelves.

A few months later Bedros opened a new market in a building he had built himself. It was a two-story building with six apartments on the second floor about two blocks away from the old market. The first floor had two stores—one was the market and the other was a pharmacy. I helped Bedros with his new market. He also had an experienced American employee. I not only learned how to speak a few words of English while working side-by-side with him, but I also learned how to run a market. To attract more customers, Bedros priced most of his stock almost at cost. In a short time he developed a good business. We were very busy which made us all very happy.

About a year later a Syrian showed interest in buying the market. Bedros and the Syrian became good friends. They shared personal and family stories with one another. In one of the stories, Bedros revealed to the Syrian how Kerop and I entered the United States and thought nothing of it.

After the market was sold, I continued to work for the Syrian until he found a replacement for me. In a few weeks, the Syrian realized that he had a lot of customers, but was making very little profit. He felt cheated when he realized why that was happening so he confronted Bedros. My brother felt he had not deceived the Syrian and explained that it was better to develop a large clientele with a small profit and gradually raise prices once a reliable relationship had been established with his customers. The Syrian was not satisfied with the answer and subsequently reported Kerop and me to the police because we did not have visas.

When Bedros learned about that, he promptly drove Kerop and me to a hotel where we were to hide in the event the police came looking for us at the market. Indeed, as it turned out, an officer did come after us. We were very fortunate we were not at Bedros' house or market!

That night Bedros drove Kerop and me back to Tijuana and gave us two hundred dollars, enough money to get us to Mexico City. He felt we would be able to obtain a visa there and return to Los Angeles within a few months. Kerop and I agreed with his plan. We took the same route back to Mexico City that we had taken to get to Los Angeles about 2 years earlier.

PART 3

The Rest of My
Bittersweet Life...

*I "escaped" from the Genocide
but never survived from
the scars afflicted by the
Turkish atrocities and
their attempt to annihilate
a nation.*

34. THE TEN HAPPIEST YEARS OF MY LIFE

RETURN TO MEXICO CITY

Although Kerop and I were on the run again, returning to Mexico was uniquely different from my previous flights. We were now among civilized people and out of harm's way—no longer fearing for our lives. I had peace of mind knowing that all my brothers were safe, making a fair living, and at the same time establishing their own families.

We were men now, and not the frightened boys we were when we separated from our father amidst the carnal inferno. Now I was confronted with the challenge of making a normal life for myself. For the first time in my life, I was having a glimpse of optimism.

God must have decided I had earned *this opportunity*. Again, I remembered my father's words, "Without the will of God, the leaves of the tree do not move". The next ten years in Mexico City were the happiest years of my life subsequent to my life in Perri—which was different. *Nonetheless, for the rest of my life whatever happiness I had was **bittersweet**. I knew there could never be a true sense of happiness as long as I was living outside of my homeland. Akh, my Yergeer.* Just saying the word *Yergeer* brings back the memories that make my whole body tremble with a deep feeling of sorrow and loss. *Meghk...*

As soon as we arrived in Mexico City, we went directly to our dear friend Gabriel Babayan. He was very happy, although surprised to see us again. No one else had ever returned to Mexico after emigrating to America.

We explained to him the reason we returned and that we were afraid of being caught without visas. We had come this far with great hardship and did not want to jeopardize our opportunity to eventually settle in America. After a warm reception, we had a lengthy discussion about all that had transpired in Mexico City during the past two years. I was most surprised to learn that a large number of Armenian survivors had immigrated to Mexico.

A CONGENIAL GROUP OF ARMENIANS

Babayan advised me that the first thing we should do was to find an apartment in the vicinity where the Armenians had congregated. We went to the Zocalo near the center of the city where all the government buildings were located. The Armenians had integrated with the Mexicans primarily on two

Armenian picnic. Mexico city, 1926. Hagop Piloyan, front row, middle,
wearing a striped necktie.

streets. On one street, the apartments were cleaner and a little more expensive. With Babayan's recommendation, I rented an apartment on the nicer of the two streets.

While I was looking around for an apartment, I encountered a man somewhat older than me. He asked if I would be interested going into business with him, buying and selling used clothing. That offer didn't appeal to me at all. I just could not believe buying and selling used clothing could be a profitable business. In a few years, he proved me wrong by becoming one of the first Armenians to amass a fortune in Mexico.

As I continued to walk around, I was impressed by how much the Armenian community had grown in just two years. In 1923, Babayan was the only Armenian in Mexico and our group had eleven members. In 1925, there were several hundred and new survivors were still arriving. Subsequently, the number rose to one thousand five hundred while I was in Mexico.

We were a congenial group. We all had a common experience tainted by painful personal memories we shared amongst ourselves. In one way or another, each of our lives was devastated by the vicious Turk's wrath to annihilate all Armenians in the most heinous manner possible. We knew we were among the very few who managed somehow to survive. We listened attentively to one another's revelations, hoping against all odds for a glimmer of information on the whereabouts of our loved ones; we were still clinging onto hope. A few were lucky—most were not.

We all led a bittersweet existence exiled from our homeland. We now felt fortunate to be among our own people, and able to perpetuate our traditions, customs and values, to speak in our *mother tongue* without fear.

Instinctively we all knew those traditions would become adulterated, if not forgotten, as we integrated into different cultures. There was no escape from the *djermahg charrt,* or 'White Genocide'—assimilation.

As much as we could, we helped one another, both in business and with personal matters. On festive occasions we made a point to invite everyone from the Armenian community. We either rented a hall or had outdoor picnics in the beautiful parks of Mexico City. Those were potluck affairs where each family brought a cooked dish from their respective villages. Food was plentiful and shared among all those who attended. Savoring our favorite dishes was a great treat for everyone. The women sat together and socialized. The men sat among themselves—some engaged in sports or other games. Towards the end of the day, both men and women joined in with music, singing and dance activities in both Armenian and Spanish. We rejoiced and gave thanks for all we had. The friendships established during that time have been treasured dearly in our hearts.

I have always been appreciative of the Mexican government and the people. There was no discrimination. The Mexicans were very impressed by our desire to learn their language and to establish businesses; they helped us to achieve our goals. Everyday, I was taught a new word by my Mexican neighbors. In my opinion, second to Armenian, Spanish is the most beautiful language. The Mexicans are a fun loving people. Their spirit of happiness prevailed everywhere and helped me adjust more readily to a normal lifestyle once again. For this I have always been most grateful to the people and government of Mexico.

However, I was taken aback by the degree of poverty in that country. The land was good for farming and rich with natural resources and minerals. The climate was good all year round for farming. It was disturbing to see so many people living in poverty. I knew firsthand what it was like to live in poverty. What kept Mexicans from providing a better life for themselves in their own country, when it was so easy for immigrants to establish businesses and prosper there? I soon realized that they did not have the educational opportunities we had in our *Yergeer.* Again, I was thankful for the good education I received in Perri and felt a deeper appreciation how hard my father worked to make sure all of his sons had a good foundation. I also realized that the Mexicans were in the tight grip of their Christian religion. There was a church on almost every block in the city. I often wondered what effect their blind faith in Jesus had on their plight, as it had on that of the Armenians.

Armenian picnic. Mexico City, 1926. From left, two women wearing a gold-bead necklaces, Nevart, Ovsanna, Hripsimeh.

In 1925, many Armenian immigrants were still not well established in a business. Those of us who had menial jobs made no more than fifty *centavos* (Mexican currency)[*] a day. Thus, we had ample time during the day to gather together and stroll around the city along Correo Mayor, the main street. We were all neighbors living within blocks of each other.

On one of those days while I was walking with a group of men and women and we were all sharing the horrific moments in our struggle to survive, I recounted the time when I lived in Parchanj and how terrified I was by the sheer presence of the gendarme who lived across the street from the kind Turkish woman for whom I was working. As I was speaking about his Armenian wife who always taunted me by calling me *Gavour Boghee* and how much that tormented me, suddenly someone tapped me on my back. As I turned around, I heard a woman call out, *"Gavour Boghee!"* At first, I didn't recognize her, but as she sternly repeated, *"Gavour Boghee!"* I recognized the voice immediately.

Those were the same words with the same piercing tone that used to terrorize me when I was distraught with the fear of being caught by the vicious Turks around me: her own husband, the gendarme... Khanum's brother-in-law who hated all Armenians and the punks who used to chant, "Anyone harboring an Armenian will be jailed with a chain around his neck for five years!" Those were the days when I was besieged by ghosts.

---

[*]   100 centaros equals one peso. In 1925-35, 2 pesos equalled one American dollar.

How could I forget? I had never seen her face! Even on the day I helped her escape to the Protestant orphanage, her face was covered with a *charshahf.* However, when she finally mentioned her Armenian name, Anna, I recognized her. We all broke out in laughter... it was Fatmah Khanum from Parchanj.

Soon after our encounter in Mexico, her husband arranged the necessary papers for her and their daughter to immigrate to the US and eventually move to California. As fate would have it, her daughter Yeranouhi married Kerop in 1937 in Fresno. Even though Fahtmah Khanum daunted me unmercifully in Parchanj, I still hold her and all the other women in great esteem for having the courage and the will to desert their Turkish or Kurdish "husbands" and children and escape from Turkey in order to lead an Armenian existence in a new found country—to remain Armenian and to bear Armenian children.

Fahtmah Khanum was unlike my aunt. On several occasions I tried to entice my aunt, Aghavni, to accept a way to escape. I ignored her husband's threats that if I didn't leave her alone, he would kill me. Aghavni chose to remain. I never was able to accept her decision, even though Ago-Ebo was an Armenian and his son was an Armenian—their children must have been *compelled* to assimilate. I could only look ahead now with a glimmer of hope that those who remained "work" within the Turkish system to bring justice to the Armenian Cause! **That would be a true act of God and a reason for the wretched life they chose to live...** *Only with the will of God, do the leaves on the trees move.* For their sake and ours, I hope this possibility becomes a reality! *Akh, akh...* what a life!

PALATERIA SAN JUAN DE LETRAN

Once Kerop and I were situated in our apartment, I began to think about a job suitable for me in this country. It was a difficult decision to make because I did not speak Spanish and was not knowledgeable of the job opportunities. I had heard that Babayan had given several men sound advice about work and subsequently they had done well financially.

Once again, I went to see my dear friend and explained the purpose of my visit. He too took into consideration that I did not know the language and did not have a particular skill or capital to invest. He concluded that the easiest and cheapest way for me to start earning money was to make and sell fruit juice, as he had done. His advise sounded reasonable to me and one that I felt I could do.

First I had a wooden table made for my juice stand and purchased three large five-gallon glass containers. Then, I bought twelve beautiful crystal serving glasses. The glasses were expensive—they cost **one** *peso* apiece!

Next, I selected a spot on the street for my stand. I picked a corner where I thought there would be a lot of foot traffic. That spot was on the corner of Correo

Mayor and San Juan de Letran where there was a large building. The first shop on the corner was a German pastry and candy store. Its display window faced Correo Mayor, while the lobby entrance for the shop was on San Juan de Letran. On one side of that entrance was a small space which I rented to store my table and other equipment at the end of each day when the pastry shop closed. Adjacent to that shop on San Juan de Letran was a cinema that was not in use at the time.

Before opening my business, I decided I needed a new suit. All this time I was still wearing the same suit my dear friend, Khachadour, had made for me in Tabriz. There was a tailor shop in the *khan*, a mini mall with several shops under one roof. It had a coffee shop where Armenians congregated to exchange news, play *tavlee* (backgammon) and dominoes, and several other shops that offered an assortment of necessary items needed by the Armenian community. In the middle of the *khan* was the tailor shop, the tailor was from Bolis.

The *khan* was close to our apartments. I used to go there for various reasons. When the Armenians found out that I had lived in America for almost two years, they assumed I had a fair knowledge of English. I was frequently asked to accompany them, as their interpreter, to the Zocalo to help them with their personal and official matters. Since I did not have a job at that time, I accepted the offers and charged each person five *pesos* for my services.

When I went to the tailor shop to have a suit made for me, the tailor pointed out an elderly man sitting at one of the tables in the coffee shop. He told me the man was spreading rumors about me because he felt I was charging too much for my services as an interpreter. At the tailor's suggestion, I went over to find out what bothered him. As I started to say hello, he shooed me away, shouting, *"Gor, Gor, Gorsuveer!"*. . . "Get Lost!" He was really angry with me. Because of his age, I did not want to retort. Without saying anything, I walked back to the tailor and he called a seamstress to take my measurements. "Ovsanna, come and take this man's measurements—he wants a complete suit." A beautiful young girl wearing a pink jacket approached me and took my measurements. I wondered if her parents were alive because I could not understand why such a beautiful girl was working in such a place. There were all kinds of young men who came to the *khan* for coffee or to play *tavloo*. . . this was not a **proper** place for a nice girl.

Within a week I had a new 3 piece suit, pants, jacket and vest. I now felt prepared to open my business. I felt I was really going to enjoy this job. It was an easy and clean job, but the fact that I would be interacting with the public was most appealing to me. From the beginning, I liked the Mexicans because they were always happy and carefree. Most important, there was no fear of harm. For the first time in my life, I felt happy and free to do whatever I pleased. It did not bother me that I could not speak or understand Spanish. I knew I would learn the language quickly.

Early one morning I purchased oranges and lemons. I set up my table, brought out the three containers, filled them with orange juice and lemonade, and arranged them along with my beautiful crystal glasses on the table. I started to call out, *"Cinco centavos, cinco centavos."* People slowly approached my table. They seemed impressed with my glassware that was more elegant than the clay bowls and cups they normally used. The juice cost me one centavo a glass and I charged five centavos for each serving. Some people bought one glass, others bought two or more.

Now I was in business. On the first day my net profit was three *pesos*. I was pleased! Within a week my three large juice containers were continuously refilled throughout the day. I was having fun, laughing and joking with my customers. Each day I was learning new words in Spanish.

Within days, I had a wide variety of flavors which were all new to me, mostly from tropical fruits I found in the local market including pineapple, banana, strawberry, guava, mango, tamarindo, papaya, watermelon and *pulkeh* which was made with spoiled papaya and had an alcoholic punch.

During this time I was still sending Kerop to a school Levon Bodosian had started for the Armenian children. He was only able to help me at the end of each day for a couple of hours. As my business was flourishing, I hired someone to help me full time. Felipe Ruiz, a young boy not much older than Kerop, about eighteen years old, had approached me for a job. He assured me he had experience. I hired him and agreed to pay him fifty *centavos* a day, a generous wage for that position. I also invited him to sleep in our room at night. That arrangement made him happy, and in turn, we were happy.

As my business continued to flourish, I bought an electric popcorn machine. Made in Germany, it was beautifully crafted with colorful lights. Inside the enclosed glass case was a model of a man from the waist up holding a pot where the popcorn was made. When all of the kernels popped, the figure tilted the pot forward and the popcorn spilled out. It was an attractive novelty. Intrigued with the beautiful colored lights, large crowds of people gathered around my stand just to see the corn popping and pouring out. Now they bought popcorn, as well as a drink.

Once again Babayan advised me to expand my business. He suggested I start selling drinks with carbonated soda. This time, I charged ten *centavos* for a soda, making a fifty-percent profit on each one I sold.

One day, upon returning from shopping for fruit, I saw Felipe crying in a corner. Apparently he had broken a glass while washing it. Kerop had fired him, thinking I would get mad because the glass cost one *peso* and Felipe was not earning enough to compensate for the loss. After reassuring both boys I was not angry, I not only did not fire Felipe, but increased his wages to one *peso* a day. My business was doing very well, and he was of great help to me.

For the next two to three years, my business continued to grow. I had accumulated more than three thousand *pesos* that Babayan kept for me. At that time two *peso* was the equivalent of one American dollar.

My luck continued to improve as the cinema in our building was bought and renovated by a new owner. The interior capacity of the cinemas in Mexico City were twice the size, or larger, than those in the United States with two to three levels of seating. There was an old ice cream parlor at one end of the foyer of the cinema. It was partitioned off from the main foyer by a glass wall.

I felt that was a good time for me to expand my business, so I bought the *palateria* (ice cream parlor) for three thousand *pesos*. I ordered all new equipment and machines from America to make ice cream.

I also changed our residence. I rented a nicer apartment on the second floor right across the *palateria*. We found a separate room for Felipe behind our *palateria*.

As the renovation neared completion, I brought my three thousand *pesos* home from Babayan's office in three separate bags, each filled with silver *peso* coins. The next day I took the bags to the office of the owner of the cinema for the final sale transaction. To my disappointment he was on vacation and would not be available until later the next week. Instead of returning the bags to Babayan's office, I decided to keep them with me. I took them with me to the *palateria* when I went to check on the workmen's progress. I stored the bags underneath the cash register where they were not in sight—only Kerop and I knew about the bags.

One night during that week, while Kerop and I were getting ready to go to bed, I suddenly realized I had not brought the bags of money home with me. Anxiously, I asked Kerop if he had brought them home. The instant he said no, I looked out of the window across the street at the *palateria*. With the shadow of the night-lights it appeared as if the security bars had been lifted open. In a panic I dashed out still dressed in my pajamas and pleaded with the doorman to open the door of our apartment—I did not have the ten *centavos* to tip him! When I got to the concession, I was relieved to find the bars were not open after all. Then I realized Felipe was inside the building and if he had noticed the moneybags, he could have easily run off with them through the back door. He was a young, poor boy who never knew his father, and I am sure he had never seen three thousand *pesos* before. I felt any boy under such circumstances would be tempted to run off with the money, knowing he probably would never be caught.

I unlocked the door and rushed inside. I found Felipe sleeping next to the counter. He promptly awoke and I asked him why he was sleeping there and not in his room. Very meekly and still sleepy he replied, "Patron, you forgot your money here. I thought I should sleep here to make sure it was safe." What a relief! My faith in humanity surged in my soul. It would have been so easy for that boy to run off with the three thousand *pesos* in coin. Who could have caught him?

Now I felt I needed Felipe more than he needed me. David of Tabriz came to my mind. I have always been grateful with both boys for their honesty and concern.

Within a few weeks the renovations were completed. I had the *palateria* decorated nicely. Everything was brand new. I bought seven round ice cream parlor tables and chairs from America. I named my shop "Palateria de San Juan de Letran."

While I still sold juices and sodas, I had to give up my popcorn machine. I replaced that machine with a very attractive soda fountain that was also German made, decorated with beautiful colored lights and mirrors.

Shortly after that I bought the concession within the cinema. I had workers walk up and down the aisles selling Popsicles, juices and sodas. After school Kerop supervised them, making sure they didn't sit down on the job to watch the movies.

For two years my business continued to do very well. By now, I was paying Felipe three *pesos* a day and he was very happy. Kerop was still in school for most of the day.

THE WORLD WAS NOW MINE

I was able to pay off my business debts. However, more important to me was the fact that I had saved enough money to repay each of my brothers in Los Angeles. I wanted to thank them and show my appreciation for their financial help when I was in dire need. Without their help, I would have lost my hope of surviving. I sent $3,000, $1,000 for each brother. Although that was more than what they had sent me, I wanted them to know how much their help had meant to me.

Unfortunately, as fate would have it, the Great Depression in America had hurt my brothers' businesses. Bedros lost the new building he had built! Now it was God's will that I was able to help "them" when they were in need!

For the first time I felt the world was mine. I felt like a king and that I could achieve whatever I tackled. Nothing could go wrong. **I felt a glimmer of hope and happiness.**

It was still hard to reconcile the wrenching emotional pain of my personal losses and the six years of hell with those new emotions of optimism and success. *It all felt surreal. Survive I did, but I couldn't let go of my losses, of my father and my homeland, my Yergeer. It was a bittersweet victory, because the culprit of all of my devastation had not been reproached.*

At this point of my life I knew it was the right time for me to get married and establish my own family. My two older brothers were married, and now it was my turn. Based on our ages, I was to be next, then Kaspar, and finally Kerop.

I was twenty-eight years old and I had a good successful business with 1,500 *pesos* in safekeeping with Babayan. Therefore, I went to my dear friend to seek his advice about my ambitions of getting married. The first thing he asked, "What do you have in mind?" I replied, "I want to establish a family and a home. My intentions are to go to France in search of a wife."

He immediately asked, "Why go to France? There are many nice Armenian girls here. There is a *Malatyatzee Deh-Deh* with three daughters. The eldest just got married in 1927 and has gone to live in New Jersey. The other two daughters are of eligible age for marriage and the older

Hampartzoum (Mexico City, 1929)

one could be a good match for you. He also has a son, Hagop Piloyan, you might know him."

I knew Hagop. On occasion, he came to my shop to visit with Mihran Gopoian, my only Armenian employee. I had hired Mihran because he too was a Perritzee. In addition, he too had had a devastating life.

When we were both little boys in Perri, Mihran's father was a champion checker player. A prominent local Turkish Bey insisted on challenging his father in a match. His father reluctantly accepted the offer knowing he couldn't refuse. In the first round, the Turk lost his money. In the rematch that the Turk insisted they have, the Turk lost his horse. Poor Mihran's father didn't suspect the Bey would come after him for revenge. After all, the Bey himself insisted on having the match with Mihran's father. Unfortunately one day while he was riding the horse he had won, two Turks approached him, killed him on the spot, and took the horse! The Turks used any excuse to kill Armenians! As I listened to the tragic fate of Mihran's father, I recalled a fable my grandfather used to tell:

> Wolf: (With a frightening growl) "Khoozee, khoozee little lamb, little lamb, why did you insult my mother last year?"
> Lamb: "But I wasn't born last year." Responded the puzzled lamb.
> Wolf: If it wasn't you then it was your brother.
> Lamb: "But Mr. Wolf, I don't have a brother," responded the defenseless lamb.
> Wolf: "It matters not, then it was someone of your faith!" impatiently retorted the wolf, and suddenly grabbed the defenseless lamb in the grip of his sharp teeth and ran into the forest to enjoy his feast!
>
> Moral of the fable: When a heartless tyrant is in power, the meek are always abused.

The next day, I asked Mihran about Hagop and his sisters. He too felt they were a good family. In fact, their apartment was directly below his. He invited me to his apartment with the chance we might be able to see the girls because they usually worked on their balcony right below his.

In midday we went to Mihran's apartment. From his balcony I looked down. All I could see were the hands of a woman going forward and backward on a sewing machine. However, I liked what I saw and immediately I felt she was the right woman for me! With her capable hands, I felt she would be able to establish a good household and be supportive of my endeavors.

I told Mihran to tell Hagop to bring his sister to the *palateria*. Mihran didn't think Hagop would do that without his father's permission. He added I would have to see her father first. When I confided with Babayan, he also agreed that I should see her father first.

One day as I passed by their building, her father was sitting on the porch steps. In passing I stopped and said, *"Parev Hayreeg,"* "Hello, Father." In return he answered without hesitating, *"Puh, puh parev yev gorsuveer!"*—"Hello and get lost!"

Instantly, I realized he was the same elderly man who angrily shoed me away in the *khan*.

Feeling rejected, I went to see Babayan hoping he would have a solution for my dilemma. Babayan first expressed his disappointment that I had confronted an elderly man in the first place. However, he went on to say, "Don't worry." He would bring him to my shop. From there it would be my responsibility to prove to him I was worthy of his daughter. It was well known in the community that *Deh-Deh* Piloyan had refused many suitors for his daughters before me. He wanted to wait until the whole family had gone to America before his children married so that they wouldn't be scattered in different countries. Unfortunately his wishes didn't materialize. Part of his family settled on the East Coast, some on the West Coast, and some remained in Mexico and France.

A few days later, Babayan informed me when he and his son-in-law, Arturo, a Mexican general, would bring *Deh-Deh* Piloyan to my *palateria* to give me time to prepare for my special guests. I had the shop spruced up and instructed all of my employees to present a happy atmosphere throughout the shop. I picked my two favorite waitresses and told them to dress in their best white uniforms with white headpieces. I prepared the best assortment of ice cream to serve.

As soon as *Deh-Deh* Piloyan was seated, he was very impressed with the ambiance of the *palateria*. Babayan made sure everything at their table went according to our plan. They were all laughing and having a good time. When *Deh-Deh* Piloyan commented how tasty the ice cream was, Babayan proudly informed him the owner was an Armenian. Piloyan felt happier that an Armenian had established himself so well. While his spirits were high, Babayan pointed towards me where I was standing behind the counter in front of the cash register.

It took but a minute for *Deh-Deh* to recognize me. Irately, he stood up, threw his hat down and shouted, "Phew! You fooled me!" He got up to leave. Babayan's son-in-law rushed over to calm him down. He made sure he sat down to relax. Half an hour later, they left without saying goodbye to me.

A couple of days later Babayan called to tell me he had good news for me. When he took *Deh-Deh* home, they sat and discussed the matter with her mother and brother, Hagop.

Hagop agreed with Babayan. By comparing me with other men who hung around the *khan*, they both pointed out that I was a good man. I didn't have the vices of smoking, drinking, or gambling! In addition, I had established a good business and I was doing very well financially. Thus, I had made a good name for myself here in Mexico City. Within a couple of days Hagop and his mother finally convinced *Deh-Deh* to finally give in!

Babayan chose a day for me to go to their house and introduce myself. Up until now I hadn't *seen* the girl. I really didn't know what she looked like. All that I had seen were her hands. On the day of my visit, prior to my arrival, I sent her family a nice assortment of flavors of my ice cream. That evening, I went to meet my intended wife with a beautiful box of chocolates that I purchased from the German candy store.

As soon as I sat down in their living room, I realized she was *the same seamstress* who a few years earlier had taken my measurements for my new suit. I immediately remembered my first impression of her, **"she is a nice girl."** However, I couldn't remember how she reacted towards me, or if at all! None the less, it was settled that we were to be engaged.

Babayan wasted no time and arranged a nice dinner at the best restaurant in Mexico City. It was a cliff-side restaurant. He also suggested I should purchase a nice gift for her on that occasion. He suggested a beautiful necklace *(pontanteef)* and earrings made in France. We had a very enjoyable evening with the whole family. Babayan said the services for our engagement.

Within a few days I gave Ovsanna five hundred *pesos* to buy her wedding dress. We planned to marry in four to five months. That gave us time to set up our own apartment and make arrangements for the wedding. As it turned out, she not only sewed her wedding dress, she also sewed my suit. I decided to move to a larger and better apartment above the cinema. Adjacent to our apartment was a small room for Kerop.

During the wedding preparations, one day while I was leaving the YMCA (where I frequently went to swim and shower because I didn't like the tub we had in our apartment), I suddenly felt a pain on my face and I couldn't speak. When I looked in the mirror, I was terrified. My face was completely distorted. The right side of my face was drooping. I didn't know what had happened, and I didn't know what to do. Instinctively, I ran over to Babayan's office. Again, he comforted me. He told me not to worry. He knew of a doctor who knew what to do because the same thing had happened to the doctor himself. When we got to the doctor's office, the doctor felt confident he would be able to help me. He said he could give me a shot with a long needle and I would recover in one day, but if I took medicine orally, it would take several months for me to recover. I chose the latter—the needle scared me.

At first, I refused to go to my fiancé's house, but Babayan urged me to go. He reassured me they would understand. Although that is what I did, I'm sure they were all concerned and even had second thoughts in the event I didn't recover. During our courtship, Ovsanna and I went out alone on only one occasion when we went to the cinema and saw an Al Jolson film. On all other occasions, the whole family or her mother accompanied us wherever we went. On Sunday afternoons, I usually hired a taxi that drove us to the most scenic areas in the city. This was an activity we all enjoyed and it made a big impression with her parents.

Without delay we continued with the preparations for our wedding despite my illness (bells palsy). For the next few months, I sent beautiful boxes of chocolates and pastries from the German shop. Chico, who was one of my youngest

Nevart, Hripsimeh, Ovsanna, and me (Xochimilco, Mexico City, 1929)

employees, made the deliveries. He was a very cute and cheerful boy with a beautiful smile. I hoped this made my gifts even more pleasant to receive. In the evenings, I took an assortment of my best ice cream for the whole family.

Babayan was my *gunkahayr* (best man) for our wedding. He made all of the arrangements and suggested we have our invitations printed in Chicago. We did and they were very impressive, printed with gold ink. Since we didn't have an Armenian clergyman to perform our service, we hired an American Reverend. Ovsanna's father was a devout Protestant. Like myself her mother was a Loosavorchagan.

The date was August 31, 1929. He rented a very large beautiful banquet room. Food was lavish and abundant. One of the main courses, I remember, was *Moleh Poblano.* There was Armenian music and dance as well as Spanish music. All of our acquaintances were present; we had more than three hundred attend to help us celebrate. It was a night to remember! Both my beloved wife, Ovsanna, and I had cherished memories of that day for *sixty-eight years.*

Marriage definitely brightened and enhanced my life. Once again, I had a family, in-laws and all. I belonged! Equally important, together we established the lifestyle I cherished in my childhood. I was fortunate my beloved wife felt the same way. She was from Malatya and I was from Perri. Even though we were from different areas, which had distinct regional customs, the basic values of our *Yergeer* was one and the same.

Our engagement (Mexico City, 1929)

Our wedding (Mexico City, August 31, 1929)

With all the changes of time and place, our traditional values fostered a happy, healthy life. Our traditions were tried traditions that had evolved over the centuries. At the same time, technological innovations were incorporated to enhance our prevailing lifestyle without changing our basic morals and values. That provided *stability* within the family structure and allowed us to be a productive people regardless where we lived—*we kept our Armenian identity*. I feel the structure of our traditional lifestyle should be studied and upheld in Armenia and in the Armenian diaspora. I feel more strongly that Ovsanna and I made the right decision!

Moreover, my business flourished and I was doing very well. I soon thought of opening an ice cream concession in the YMCA. The YMCA was on the main street near the Zocalo on the way to Chapultepec, a renowned historical park in Mexico City and probably the most beautiful park in Mexico.

The YMCA building had fifteen hundred rooms. Many Americans lodged there when they came to Mexico because English was spoken. It had a huge Olympic size swimming pool. I made a point of going there several times a week. Since I still loved to swim, this was one of the few pleasures I continued from my childhood. I was very impressed when the American Consul in Mexico asked me to teach him my backstroke. He was about thirty-five years old and like Babayan he also had one wooden leg. At that time, I had no idea he would be instrumental in speeding up the process for us to receive our visas to immigrate to America to show me his appreciation for teaching him the backstroke.

Financially I did the best with my YMCA concession. I brought ice cream, Popsicles, juices, and soda drinks from the *palateria* and I started to sell candy and *Chicklets* (gum) as well. For five years I was very prosperous. I furnished our apartment with beautiful European furniture. A couple years later we moved to another apartment at 143 Calle de Uruguay to be closer to Ovsanna's parents. Every night we were either at their apartment or they were at ours.

Right about this time in 1930 Kaspar made a surprise visit with his bride, Ashghen. This too enhanced my happiness! Now I was able to share my happiness and success with my twin. Everything was going well and I intended to enjoy this moment to the fullest.

I made a business deal with Felipe whom I trusted. I offered him a deal where he would manage the YMCA concession and I would take only twenty *pesos* a day, leaving him the remaining profit and that was much more than what I took. He liked the offer and accepted it.

For the next four to five months, I took it easy, running only the *palateria* and enjoyed my life with family and friends. Mexico City was a beautiful city with many interesting places to see. I felt as though I was living on top of the world!

Kaspar and me (Mexico City, 1930)

Upon Kaspar's departure, my precious son, Mardiros, was born. He was a beautiful baby with golden hair. He was loved by all. I named him after my dear father. From the moment I lost sight of my father while standing in front of the Turkish school, I made a solemn *vow* to myself. Not only I, but my children would fulfill his *dreams and aspirations. Now,* I was able to *bestow* these dreams upon my son, his grandson. At this point the world was mine. I had a beautiful wife, a precious son, and financial security. I couldn't have asked for more!

I was ready to go back to my business full time. Much to my surprise when I entered the YMCA concession, I was served with legal papers. Felipe was demanding 3,500 *pesos* for back pay. I was accused of underpaying him throughout his employment with me. This took me by surprise because I had always treated my employees and customers with much respect and especially with Felipe. The next day my concession at the YMCA was closed with a padlock. However, my *palateria* remained open.

Needless to say, I hired an attorney recommended by Babayan. During the legal procedure I found out while I was away an attorney had convinced Felipe to make the charges. Leon Trotsky had fled to Mexico with the intentions of spreading the Bolshevik doctrine. At the time there were a million and a half people in the city. Men like Felipe were targeted to further their cause. Once again

My son, Mardiros, making a pledge to support his nation...
fulfilling his grandfather's aspiration

ARF	1935	Armenians do not fear imprisonment
Comrade	Feb. 20	Armenians do not fear death
Mardiros	4 years old	Vengeance will be sought towards the
Chitjian		evil Turk

I was caught in a political strife caused by the Bolsheviks. Fortunately, this time it was not life threatening.

One evening while I was going home on the bus, a man sitting next to me noticed I was in a dejected mood. He inquired why I was so sad. When I told him about my problem, he immediately told me not to worry. He knew a lawyer who could solve my problem. He told me exactly what to do. He gave me his own name and then the name of the lawyer. Then he told me to go to a particular restaurant where I would be introduced to the lawyer.

Since my attorney was not able to help me after a month had passed and my shop was still closed, I decided to follow through with the stranger's advise.

I went to the restaurant as instructed and asked to be introduced to the lawyer whose name I was given. I walked over to him, said hello, and gave him the name of the stranger who advised me to see him. When, I extended my hand to shake his hand, I slipped a twenty *peso* gold coin in his hand as I was instructed to do by the stranger.

The lawyer immediately asked me the names of my employee and that of his attorney. After giving him both names, I told him my shop had been officially closed with a padlock.

He quickly replied, "That's okay. You are now free to open your shop." Again I repeated, "But it is officially sealed and locked. How could I open it?" A little annoyed he repeated, "Didn't I just tell you, you have my permission to open your shop? If anyone questions your actions, just tell them that I gave you permission to open your shop!" With that I left. This stranger must have been a goverment official who opposed the Bolshevik intervention.

The next day I opened my shop. In less than an hour two policemen and Felipe came in with the intention of having me arrested. When I gave them the name of the lawyer who gave me permission to open my shop, they nodded their heads with disappointment and left my shop. I never heard from them again.

For several months my business was as good as usual. But soon I realized the clientele at the YMCA was changing. This was in the 1930s and the number of Americans had markedly decreased. In addition, there were many vendors now selling Popsicles in the streets. Gradually my business was not thriving as before. Before I knew it, I was getting a little restless. I found myself thinking maybe I could do even better in another line of business. After all, I was now responsible for a wife and son.

One day while I was sharing those feelings with a few Mexican friends, one of them suggested we try going into business together. For a few years he had worked in a glass-blowing factory and he had acquired the skills necessary to make the glassware. He felt confident that we could make and sell the crystals together in a

Samples of crystals we produced

joint venture. After discussing this prospect with my wife, I decided to sell both of my shops and go into a partnership with this new friend.

He and I went out, bought the necessary equipment and supplies, and rented a small workshop. Within a few days he made a few beautiful vases, each with a different shape and size. We took them as samples to the department store where similar vases were sold. We wanted to determine the net profit we would make if we continued with our endeavor. To our disappointment we concluded we couldn't produce the volume necessary to compete for a successful profit for the both of us. So I sold the equipment and searched for another line of work.

It didn't take long when I decided to open a shoe store for men and women. This was much more successful and gradually my business began to grow again. I was happy I had made the change.

Shortly after I had established my shoe store a new ordinance stipulated no business transactions could be carried out between the hours of 12 noon to 3 PM. This gave the laborers a siesta, time for lunch and rest. The businesses opened again at 4 PM to 7 PM. This too must have been influenced by the Bolsheviks.

One day just as I was closing the door of the shoe store, a customer slipped in and pleaded with me to sell him a pair of shoes. Since I barely had closed the door, I didn't think much of it and sold him a pair of shoes. Before he left, two police officers rushed in and presented me with a citation. Fortunately, I was able to have the citation waived by an understanding judge. He sympathized with my case and pardoned me since the ordinance had been in effect for a short period of time.

About a year later, I was surprised once more when a policeman again entered my shoe store to arrest me along with more than thirty-five other Armenians. We were suspected for the murder of an Armenian priest on the East Coast of the US. None of us even had knowledge of the alleged crime. Another Armenian (a member of another political party visiting his sister in Mexico) had falsely accused all of us. From that day on *our congenial group was splintered into factions. Meghk!* My passport still bore the Dashnag seal. Once again, I was caught as a possible suspect for a similar offense! We were all detained for several hours, until Babayan came to our rescue and had us released from jail.

By now I had a new baby, a daughter whom I named after my eldest sister, Zaruhy. My life was full and happy. I loved children and now had two of my own.

DEH DEH'S LAST FAREWELL

Unfortunately two months after Zaruhy's birth, we lost our beloved *Deh-Deh*. By this time he had made me feel he liked and trusted me more than his own son and I had great respect and love for him. We could never forget the day he died.

It was the morning of December 31, 1933 and the women were busy preparing for the festivities of New Year's Eve. My mother-in-law, who was renowned for her *pakhlava*, was busy baking. We were planning for a festive holiday. She told *Deh-Deh* to go to my shop to get walnuts.

As usual, whenever he went out for a walk, he took my son who was almost three years old. *Deh-Deh* left the house clutching Mardig tightly against his chest. He ventured to walk to my shoe store, which was a relatively long distance. However, on this particular day, along the way as he passed by his friends, he bid each one a **final farewell**. He was a devout Protestant. He had the *premonition* this was to be his last day. When he came to my shop, I was delighted to see the bond between grandson and grandfather. This reminded me of my nostalgic feelings towards *my* grandfather. When he bid me

Deh-Deh and Mardiros

farewell with a tone of *finality* I didn't understand what he meant by what he actually said. I did not suspect his real intent. I gave him the bag of walnuts. However, I noticed he looked tired, so I hired a cab and sent them home. . . *that was our final farewell!*

Upon returning home, he climbed the three flights of stairs to our apartment still clutching Mardig to his bosom. Without saying a word, he quickly handed my son to Ovsanna and took off his money belt, which he always wore. He still had sixty Turkish gold coins. He handed the money belt to his wife and laid down on his bed to rest.

Realizing he was ill, they quickly contacted Hagop to call a doctor. By the time the doctor arrived *Deh-Deh* was gone. We buried him that same afternoon. On his gravestone I wrote in *Armenian* his name, birthplace, age, and the date he died. I also included the names of his wife, sons and daughters. Sarkis Piloyan was eighty-four years old on the day he died. In Mexico, he was known as the *Malatytzee Deh-Deh*.

Deh-Deh was like a father to me (Mexico City, 1934)

SARKIS PILOYAN'S FAMILY

In 1849, Sarkis Piloyan was born and raised in Chunkoosh. At a very early age, he was left an orphan and was rescued by his cousin, Khachadour Piloyan's family. Khachadour and he were very close in age and grew up as brothers. In 1886, they left for Chicago hoping to make more money for their families. They were both married and had children.

Sarkis worked in a textile factory in Chicago where beautiful silk threads were used to make a variety of articles from baskets to handkerchiefs. Even though he

Ashken, Kaspar (sitting), Kerop, Hagop, Deb-Deh, Nevart, Hripsimeh, Ovsanna, Hampartzoum. (Mexico City 1930).

had been in American for ten years *"tomorrow morning, 7:30 come back"* were the only English words he understood. After the 1895 massacres he was notified his wife had been killed. He immediately returned to Chunkoosh to take care of his three children Khachadour, Manoog, and Margarite. Shortly after his return he learned about a suitable widow in Malatya which was a two to three hour walk from Chunkoosh. He went to Malatya and married Hripsimeh Hovnanian, who was twenty years younger.

Hripsimeh had two brothers, Aharon and Hagop Hovnanian. Their mother had given birth to eighteen sons. While only two boys survived, Hripsimeh was their only girl. After marriage the two sons and their respective families remained in their parental house. The three families lived together as one big family. The two brothers were very protective of their sister Hripsimeh.

*Both brothers had the reputation as renowned builders in Malatya. In 1915 they were in the midst of working on the hospital which was commissioned by the Germans. They were both given "official assurance" they and their families would be spared—no harm would come to any of their family members. **As soon as the hospital was completed all eighteen members of the Hovnanian family were slaughtered along with the other martyrs of Malatya—not one member between the two families was spared, small children and all. That hospital, however, was eventually converted into a Protestant orphanage as the number of Armenian orphans began to escalate.***

Although she never knew her grandmother, [*] *melancholically, Ovsanna remembers playing with Aharon and Hagop's children. Her most memorable moments were spent at their house. Whenever there were pleasurable festivities, they were found there. "Mahmentz doonuh katzee. Mahmentz doonuh dehsa." ("I went to my grandmother's house. I saw it at my grandmother's house.") Those were Ovsanna's cherished memories at the age of six.*

When Ovsanna lost Aharon and Hagop, her two kehrees (maternal uncles), and their families, eighteen members in all, the life she once cherished was gone. The Piloyan family never got over the fact that the Turkish government had fooled and tricked the two brothers. . . another cruel hoax.

Sarkis and his three children settled in Malatya with his new wife. In due time he became a successful tanner, a trade which required very difficult, demanding skills. He provided raw hide both for civilians and the military. A Turk known only as "Effendi" was one of his clients who manufactured military apparel. At the same time, Khachadour (Sarkis' first son) worked for the Turk and was the foreman overseeing the Armenian seamstresses.

One day a situation arose when the Turkish Effendi was in "immediate" dire need of eight gold pieces to pay the bribe to be exempted from military duty. Fortunately, Sarkis was in the position to give him a "quick" loan. **That** favor established a fruitful friendship forever binding.

---

[*]   Her grandfather, Kevork Hovnanian was killed along with his sons.

Subsequently, Sarkis and Hripsimeh had five children: Setrag, Maritza, Hagop, Ovsanna, and Nevart. Within a few years, he sent his son, Manoog, to Chicago. Manoog in time moved to Fresno, California and married an American born Armenian, Sadie, and had four children: Florence, Albert, Alice, and Gladys.

At the onset of the *charrt* the Turkish *Effendi* felt indebted to Sarkis for helping him when he was in need. *For more than six months during the bloodiest period of 1915 the Piloyan family remained **hidden** in his house. He put himself and his own family in danger for harboring Armenians.*[*]

One day during this perilous period Khachadour heard his best friend had been captured. Completely demoralized and without giving a second thought, he rushed out of the house in defense of his friend. Khachadour didn't have a chance; he, too, was captured and killed. The family was devastated. At the age of 25, he not only was the most relied upon, the most handsome, member of the whole family; he left behind three "Loosavorchagan" orphans, all under the age of five.

Shortly after Sarkis and the family (still under the Effendi's protection) returned to their own home, the Armenians in the community were rounded up in the "zhoghovahran". The Protestants were quickly separated from the Loosahvorchagans who were designated to be taken away and slaughtered.

Even though she herself was a Loosahvorchagan, Hripsimeh quickly grabbed and tucked the three orphans under her skirt—an act which spared their lives. Sarkis being a strong, devout Protestant, strongly admonished her "dishonest" act fearing . . . **God would surely punish the others.**[†] Although Hripsimeh tried her best to raise Khachadour's children along with hers, for some unknown reason, they all died within a year. . . Most likely yearning for their parents. *Meghk*. . .

A couple of years after the bloodiest period of the *charrt*, Setrag, the third son, was sent out of Turkey to escape the draft. He snuck out with his bride Mariam who was a kindergarten teacher in the Protestant school. During their escape they were viciously attacked by *chettehs*. Setrag and Mariam *never recovered from that attack. Emotionally and physically, they were scarred for life.* For a few years, they remained in New York but eventually, they too moved to Fresno and had three children. Setrag had a fatal heart attack in the mid-1950s in Fresno during a lecture given by a visiting Turk. When Setrag got up to raise an objection to what he had heard, he collapsed. *Meghk*, that was a tragic irony. His wife Mariam passed away in the late 1970s. Her death was followed by that of their eldest son Sarkis and daughter Lilly—only Harry remains from their family.

---

[*] He continued to be protective of the family for the next eight years—until the family safely arrived in Haleb.

[†] At this time, the Protestant Armenians were somewhat shielded with the "presence" of the missionaries.

Ovsanna (standing far right) and her varbed, master teacher (Malatya, 1916)

Likewise, Sarkis' eldest daughter, Margarite, fled to France with her two sons, Avedis and Sarkis, together with the surviving members of her in-laws. Her husband was also killed.

During this period, at the age of eight, Ovsanna was first an apprentice for a carpet weaver. However, after several months, her mother reasoned that particular skill would not be beneficial for her daughter in the long run. So by the age of nine Ovsanna became an apprentice for a seamstress and learned a skill that she mastered and utilized for a lifetime.[*] In 1917, while all of her wages were turned over to her parents, some of her wages were spent on the gold-bead necklaces for herself and her two sisters. Ovsanna saw her *varbed,* master teacher, one more time during a visit in Boston in 1965.

---

[*]   During this period, Ovsanna remembers there was a huge, festive wedding (in Malatya) for a Mustafa Kemal's sister. She particularly remembers the colorfully decorated "pytone" horse-driven carriage with colorful flowers and ribbons accompanied with an entourage of musicians. There was much excitement and merriment in the streets for days.

In 1923, when the situation got worse for the Armenians and their Effendi no longer felt he could assure their safety, he advised Piloyan to leave Turkey. Once again he provided armed horsemen for protection during their trek to Haleb. They remained in Haleb until 1925 when the family immigrated to Mexico with the intentions of eventually immigrating to the US to reunite with the rest of the family. . . Entry into the US was still closed.

After their arrival in Mexico, but some years prior to our marriage, *Deh-Deh* had expressed his last wish to go to America to visit Khachadour, his "brother," and his two sons, Manoog and Setrag, for one last time before he died. His two sons immediately obtained the necessary papers and visas for his visit. Independently from each other's knowledge, Manoog from Fresno sent him a visa and Setrag who was in New York sent another.

Without carefully reading or understanding those papers, the family put Sarkis on a train in Mexico City and sent him off to Fresno, California. When he arrived in Juarez, the Mexican-US border, with *both* visas, he was denied entry. One son had requested a visa for a *temporary* visit and the other son had requested entry for permanent status. Sarkis was unable to understand the confusion or the denial of entry. He didn't understand English or Spanish. He was greatly disappointed because he knew that was probably the last opportunity he would ever have to see his sons and "brother" for one more time.

To exacerbate that unfortunate situation, Mexican bandits attacked the train. The train ran out of control for some distance until it was derailed and came to an abrupt halt upon having a severe collision. The poor man was so terrified he was left with *a noticeable stutter,* which he never completely overcame.

What had that God fearing man done to deserve such a fate? He was an extremely devout Protestant. He didn't deserve this—he never did see his sons or Khachadour again.

After Ovsanna and I were married, with time *Deh-Deh* and I developed a very close bond, perhaps stronger than he had with his other children. He never learned how to write, not even his name. He always put an "X" wherever his signature was required. He relied on me to write his letters to his sons and to Khachadour who by now had also moved to Fresno. *I felt so proud and appreciative to have established his confidence. Once again, I myself had a father and son relationship.*

FINALLY WE WERE GOING TO AMERICA

A year later my friend at the YMCA, the American Consul, expedited my papers to enter the United States. Again, he reminded me how appreciative he was when I taught him the backstroke in the YMCA pool and now he was reciprocating the favor. Finally, we got our visas.

Because my shoe store was successful, I sold the business within a couple of months. By the **summer of 1935**, we were ready to leave Mexico. It had been exactly ten years since I had returned from Los Angeles. Leaving Mexico was a bittersweet experience. I was departing from many dear friends and relationships.

I was leaving a country where I became financially confident and successful and whose people had warmly accepted me and had treated me well!

With mixed emotions, happy and sad, we finally boarded a train and were on our way to America—like most refugees seeking freedom and justice.

My passport with family members

Our immigration visa to the United States (El Paso, Texas, 19 June 1935)

35. RETURN TO LOS ANGELES

MEXICAN-US BORDER

In a few days we reached Juarez, the Mexican-US border. El Paso was on the other side. I had 1,500 Mexican *pesos*—in gold coin. Ovsanna had guarded them in her purse. Unfortunately, the border guard informed us gold coins were no longer legal tender in the US and they had to be exchanged with paper bills. Reluctantly I turned them in—much to Ovsanna's objections. The value of the paper bills was much less than the gold coins. I was later informed that I had the right to have kept the coins as *gold pieces.*

From El Paso we took the Greyhound Bus and came to the same bus station in Los Angeles, where I had come the first time. Once again Kaspar came to pick us up. Since Kaspar had told us not to bring much, we had only brought our basic necessities.

We stayed with Kaspar for one week. Then we rented the house right behind his house for fifteen dollars a month. While we were looking for a house to rent, I was taken aback when I learned we were turned away several times because we had two children—it would have been much easier if I had said we had a cat and a dog. It took more than twenty-five years before I was able to replace the furnishings we left behind in Mexico.

MY FIRST MARKET

Shortly after we settled in our house, I found a lot 180'x100' ten blocks from our house (that had an old shabby structure) to rent for twenty-five dollars a month. Within two months, I remolded the structure and built a decent market. I hired construction workers and used some old lumber Mihran had in his yard and purchased whatever else that was necessary.

I hired a Mexican, Manuel, to rent the meat department and an Armenian to rent the produce stand. Together they paid me seventy dollars a month. I ran the grocery department. I had enough confidence from my previous experience working in my brother's market. I hired a local nine year old Armenian boy, Buddy Moomjian, to help me with light jobs and my English.

The market was located on the corner of Whittier Boulevard and Bonnie Beach Place in East Los Angeles, and I called it "Bonnie Beach Market." My customers were mainly Americans, Armenians and just a few Mexicans. The Armenians were predominantly *Roosah-Hyes* (Russian-Armenians) who had emigrated to the US during the Bolshevik Revolution.

Within a year I was able to buy a nice house half a block away from the market on Bonnie Beach Place for $1,500. It was no more than a couple minutes from the store. Both Ovsanna and I felt more secure. In case of an emergency we would be relatively close by for each other. For the first time we both felt uneasy living alone among strangers in our immediate neighborhood. Not knowing how to speak English concerned us the most. There were no more than five Armenian families who lived near-by with whom we could socialize.

Within four years, from 1935-1939, my business thrived to the extent that I was able to expand the structure and make major improvements. I invested most of my profits into the structure and merchandise.

In those days, maybe because of the Depression, groceries in many markets were sold with credit. I had a credit book in which I recorded the daily or weekly purchases of my customers. Whenever they received their paychecks, they paid off their debt and started again. Most of my customers were reliable.

As my business grew, a Kharpertzee who had been in the United States for many years—and had a relatively good grasp of the English language—sold me a fire insurance policy to cover ninety percent of the contents of my market. I felt very appreciative with that security.

In 1939, Ovsanna and I began to plan a trip to the East Coast to visit her sisters and our friends from the *Yergeer.* I stocked my market with enough merchandise to last for the few months we planned to be on vacation. I invested over two thousand dollars.

A few days before our departure date my Italian landlord and his son came to the store. He was very impressed with my business and how I had improved the structure. He noticed how much I had stocked my market and inquired if I had purchased insurance. I assured him that I had coverage. When he left, I felt good because he had shown interest in my business.

That very evening we had guests visiting and we were happily talking about our pending trip. Suddenly we heard my son, Mardiros, who was eight years old, cry out from his sleep *"the store is burning, the store is burning!"* Ovsanna ran into the bedroom to console him. She thought a nightmare had woken him up.

At the same moment, there was a loud knock on our front door. It was the pharmacist who owed the drugstore directly across from my market. He was shouting, *"Your store is on fire!"*

By the time I dashed down to the market, the firemen were already hosing down the flames that were consuming the building. My first impulse was to rush in and retrieve my credit book. Nothing else could be saved. Before the firemen could stop me, I dashed in and grabbed it. Needless to say, the firemen were not too happy with me. When I looked back at the fire, I realized I had done a dangerous thing. It was extremely painful to watch my hard-earned work go up in flames!

Luckily only a corner of my credit book was scorched. In due time, all my American and Mexican customers slowly paid off their debts. The majority of the Armenians, however, had one excuse after another why they couldn't pay their debts. The loss of money didn't hurt me as much as the reality my own countrymen would take advantage of me under such circumstances!

I got next to nothing from the insurance company. There had been a misunderstanding about the type of insurance policy I had. Either my agent didn't really understand what he sold me, or with my broken English, I didn't understand what I bought. Possibly both were a factor. As it turned out, I was compensated for only ten percent of my total loss and not the ninety percent I thought was forthcoming.

During the next few weeks feeling discouraged and in disbelief, I hired a couple of women to help me salvage whatever was possible from the charred remains. I had a fire sale, where the scorched canned goods sold for five to ten cents. It was very difficult for me to experience that loss because it was much harder to make a decent living in the United States and now I had a family to support.

The economic situation in America was still in the grips of the Great Depression. Foreigners were not accepted here as warmly as in Mexico, and it was *not easy* to learn the English language. We were all discouraged from speaking openly in Armenian or Spanish when we were in public. People were telling us, "Speak in English, please." How were we to learn English if the *odars* (non-Armenians) were not willing to make an effort to converse with us? I had to work to earn a living. I had no time to go to school. Ovsanna immediately tried to attend English language classes in the neighborhood. A couple of the other Armenian women in the class were annoyed with her because she took our three-year-old with her to class. Therefore, she dropped out because she didn't want to *inconvenience* the others. My American customers were more understanding with me and were helpful as I slowly acquired a "broken English." It didn't improve much thereafter.

OUR TRAVEL PLANS GO ON

Emotionally it was extremely difficult to see all of my hard labor and money go up in smoke. But I was young; I still had my family. We were all safe and out of reach of the claws of the vicious Turk. I knew I would succeed once again.

Therefore, both my wife and I decided to go ahead with our plans to travel, even though we knew we couldn't stay away as long as we first hoped. We wanted to have an opportunity to decide if we wanted to resettle in the East Coast or remain in Los Angeles.

Our train made its first stop in San Francisco. We stayed long enough to visit an exhibit, which displayed a new invention called the television. When we got to the exhibition hall, all we saw was a cabinet. We were told it would take two years to make it work. Even though that was a let down it didn't affect our trip.

From there we went straight to New York. Our first stop was to visit with Ovsanna's two sisters. Nevart and her family lived in New York City. Maritza and her family lived in New Jersey. During the family reunion we were taken to some very impressive sites. The most elaborate and most enjoyable was the "World's Fair of 1939." That experience was breath taking.

We were also taken to Ellis Island where we saw the Statue of Liberty. Mardig (short for my son's name, Mardiros) and I climbed up the winding stairs up to the torch of the statue. My daughter, Zaroog (short for her name, Zaruhy) was too young so Ovsanna remained below until we came down. Maybe that was for the best because it wasn't an easy climb. We also went to the Empire State Building where we all went up to the top floor in an elevator. On another day we were particularly overwhelmed with Niagara Falls—they brought back so many memories—some good, some painful!

With Nevart's help, we visited several of our childhood friends from Perri and Malatya. *These visits were of course the highlight of out trip and the most memorable! To this day I feel very fortunate we made that trip.*

From New York, we went straight to Philadelphia to visit Hampartzoum Der Garabedian who had married Yeghsah Bahgee's daughter. They took us to see the Liberty Bell. I was impressed because it represented the achivement of independence for America. From Philadelphia we went to Cleveland, Ohio where we visited the priest's wife from Medzgerd in whose care I had left Kerop when I fled from Sako Mahlahsee.

Last we went to Chicago to visit Markar's family. As I've already mentioned, I only visited his gravesite for he had died shortly after arriving in America.

Our trip took over a month. That trip was the best thing we could have done for ourselves. We had memorable experiences visiting with family and our childhood friends. . . memories that I cherish to this day. Traveling cross-country by train with two very young children with my limited English language skills was an adventure in itself. Ovsanna and I became quite skillful getting on and off the trains with our two kids and one large suitcase!

THRIFTY FOOD MARKET

Upon returning to Los Angeles, I was invigorated emotionally. My Italian landlord wanted me to rebuild on his lot again. However, when he raised the rent to ninety dollars a month, I began to suspect he might have caused the fire himself. I decided to relocate. I soon found another building just four blocks west from my old market on the same street, Whittier Boulevard. It had two stores on the ground floor and two apartments on the second floor. The building had been foreclosed. I bought it for four thousand dollars. I was barely able to come up with one thousand dollars. Thus I had to assume a three thousand dollar loan. *That was a big risk for me.* I had no idea how successful this location would be. I was greatly concerned about my monthly payments of forty dollars. I converted the two stores into one large market. We moved into one of the apartments and rented out the other.

I named my new market "Thrifty Food Market." I brought Manuel, my former butcher to run the meat department. A Japanese couple rented the produce department. During the first two years, our business grew slowly to the point where I was making a fair profit.

To my disadvantage, however, two similar markets opened directly on the opposite side of the boulevard, one on each corner. Around this time, the United States had entered into World War II. Within a few months there was a severe shortage of basic food products. Those products were rationed, hindering what and how much each family could purchase. Markets were monitored for compliance. There were heavy fines and penalties for those grocers who broke the law.

By 1942, I was barely breaking even financially. Many a night I sweated out the night worrying whether or not I could make my monthly loan payments or if I had enough quarters for the next day to keep my refrigerated cases operating.

Our business began to slow down and I couldn't figure out a solution to turn it around. As it was, I opened the market seven days a week, from 7:30 a.m. to 10:30 p.m. July the Fourth was the only day of the year I closed the market. That was to *show my respect for the freedom and safety I enjoyed in this country.* I fully understood and respected the reasons this country fought for its independence.

While I was absorbed with my financial situation, you can understand my *bewilderment* one day when my produce tenant came to me in tears and told me all Japanese citizens in California were going to be sent to concentration camps in some undisclosed area. They were given one week to dispose of all their personal belongings and properties.

That shook *me* up as much as it did my tenant. How could such a grave action like this *happen in America?* These people were born in America—they were American citizens. The only explanation they were given was that this had to be done for *their protection* since Japan had declared war against the United States. Yet they had to sell or give away all of their real property. There was no mention

Thrifty Food Market "Grand Opening." Ovsanna and me, 1940.

about the circumstances of their return. After the war, however, the Japanese were given the right to go back and resettle wherever they chose. Since then they have been reinstated all of their American citizenship rights and privileges. Fifty years later, *the American government finally admitted* the wrong it committed against its own innocent citizens and offered restitution to the surviving families, even though it was a token of the real losses that the Japanese endured.

Today Turkey has tried to justify their atrocities as an attempt to "relocate" Armenians for their safety during the war. Turkey has never allowed Armenians the right to return and rebuild. To *this* day the Armenians who remained in Turkey do not have the same rights and privileges as other citizens of Turkey. *Eighty-eight years later Turkey is still in denial. . .* it has not changed!

After restoring justice to its Japanese citizens, I cannot understand how this powerful country still refuses to recognize and address the wrongs the Turks committed against the Armenians. The Turks objective was to make sure not one Armenian survived on their historical ancestral homelands—there is a myriad of documentary evidence!

Before my tenants left for camp, they asked if I would be willing to store two large wooden boxes about six feet by six feet filled with their personal belongings. I agreed and for several months the boxes remained in my storeroom. Some of my customers became concerned and were angry with me for helping the Japanese, fearing there might be explosives in the boxes. Several months after my tenants settled in their camp, they sent for their boxes. In addition, they requested items they didn't have. I remember that I sent several items; in particular I remember sending soap.

Most of our customers who shopped for meat also wanted produce. Within a few weeks, when we no longer had produce, Manuel felt the sharp decline in the number of our customers. Along with everything else, soon there was a meat shortage. He too wasn't able to stock his meat cases as before. I not only lost my produce tenant, but Manuel left reluctantly.

The burden of handling *all three* departments was now left up to me. Even with hired help, I knew I would not be able to handle such a workload for a long period of time, especially with the competition from the other two markets directly across the street. I felt I had to take a chance and try to establish myself in a new location.

In the meantime I had joined the Armenian Revolutionary Federation (Dashnags) in 1935. Once again, I considered this a cherished saintly privilege for me. *I wanted to find some way to contribute towards the Armenian Cause.* During those most difficult years when I tried to establish myself, when I didn't have a *quarter* for my refrigerator cases, I proudly paid my monthly dues. In addition, I contributed a dollar a week for a Saturday school sponsored by the ARF for the children of the members who were old enough to attend. Unfortunately, mine were still too young. I was looking forward to that opportunity.

In 1943, when Dashnags split the church and schools into two different political camps, and **created a catastrophic and destructive schism in the community,** I reluctantly withdrew from the party. . . and will remain so until they unite—what a tragedy for all Armenians! *Meghk!*

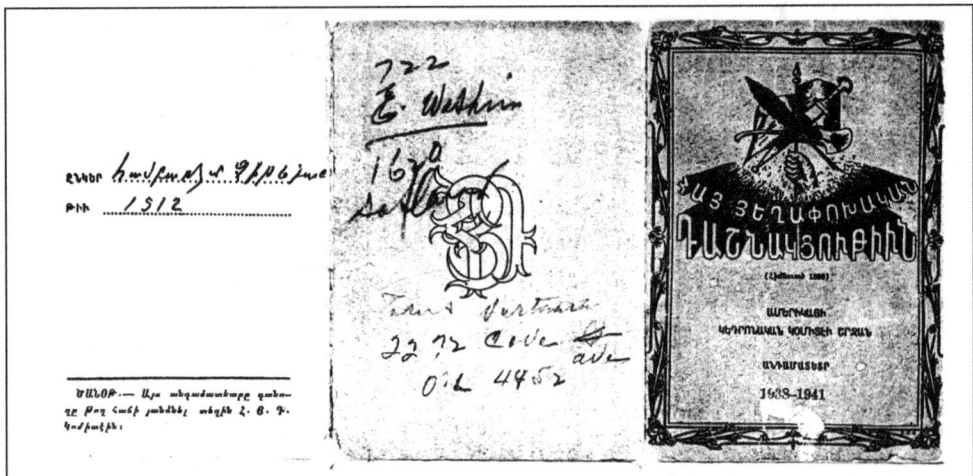

Membership card in ARF (cir. 1935-1941)

IN SEARCH OF A NEW LOCATION

I began my search for a good site to relocate my market. This time I decided I wanted a predominantly Mexican clientele. I found such a store in Boyle Heights on First Street and Cummings, directly across from the police station. Again there was a movie theater right next door to the market. One afternoon before I contacted the owner, I went into the theater to see who was attending and I was delighted to find mostly Mexicans.

During my first meeting with the landlord, I was able to negotiate the rent for ninety dollars a month until I was able to establish a profitable business. Then I would begin to give her the asking price of three hundred dollars a month.

When I selected that location, inadvertently I didn't consider how far it was from my house and family. Since I still didn't have a car, I had to transfer onto three different buses each way. If I made the right connections, I got home in an hour. If I missed a connection, it took much longer. At first I felt it wasn't a problem and that I could endure the hardship.

Without too much difficulty, I was fortunate to find both a produce tenant and a meat tenant. The new butcher literally helped me stay afloat with the grocery department. While he refused my asking price of fifty dollars a month for rent, he offered to pay me five percent of his weekly profits. Since there was no one else, I felt I had no choice but to accept his offer. Much to my surprise, the first week he gave me eighty dollars and that's the way it remained, *to my advantage!*

I really enjoyed being primarily among Mexican customers. Again, they showed me great respect because as a non-Mexican, I spoke fluent Spanish. Many felt I spoke Spanish better than they did.

Ironically, I had a very difficult time establishing a lucrative business. The United States was still at the tail end of the war. It was the height of the shortage of most food products. All basic items were still being rationed. Each household was given a specific number of chips (or coupons), depending on the number of people in the household. Collecting the little blue and red plastic chips from the customers was a laborious task. Supervisors were still coming to confirm whether or not we were in compliance. Ovsanna once was caught selling a small can of baby food without collecting a half-point. I was ordered to close the grocery department for one month—the judge was an Armenian.

There was a quota for almost all the basic products. Since my business was relatively new, the beginning base was very limited. At times the shortage was so severe I only had a few loaves of bread on my shelves to sell. I even remember having to sell butter by the gram!

Thus, I reserved the basic items for my regular and reliable customers who not only came to the market for groceries but also for meat and produce. That situation made it very difficult to expand and develop a profitable business. The large chain stores were selling the same basic items at a lower price than what I bought wholesale. How could I compete and make a profit? I literally was spared financial disaster by the rent I collected from the butcher. I never found out how or from where he was able to obtain the meat. His meat cases were full all of the time. I had the fortitude to hang on to my business and continued to enjoy the relationship with my Mexican customers.

One day an elderly Jewish woman came in and asked for a quarter pound of butter. I refused her request because I didn't even have enough butter for my regular customers. That was the first time I remember seeing her in my store. When she continued to plead with me, I realized how disappointed she was and finally gave in to her pleas because I really felt sorry for her. She was so frail and elderly. **I just couldn't refuse her.**

The woman quickly thanked me for my consideration and added, "You are a good person. Tomorrow morning my son-in-law will come here and he will be able to help you. Be sure to trust him—you can depend on him."

The very next day her son-in-law came to the market and introduced himself. He asked if he could look around to see which merchandise I could use. A couple of days later he returned with a huge truck filled with boxed groceries. I was able to purchase seventeen hundred dollars worth of crucial merchandise. My shelves were filled for the first time. He continued to return each week and kept my shelves well stocked.

Once again my business began to thrive. Again I was able to pay off my debts. As promised, I increased my rent payments to my landlord.

A few years later, as the war came to an end, merchandise gradually became more plentiful and all rations were lifted. I was making a good profit and I really enjoyed my customers who were still mainly Mexicans. Business was so good I even had full-time help.

By now it was 1946, my children were getting older, I realized **I hardly ever saw them.** I really missed that opportunity. When I left the house in the morning they were asleep, and when I returned home in the evening they were asleep.

I still rode the bus and streetcar back and forth to the market. As I got older the pouring rains and pounding winds on my tired body began to take their toll. In the beginning, I didn't mind. I always remembered past experiences when I had to walk for miles in rain, snow, wind or the blazing hot sun. With great fear and gnawing hunger I had walked from village to village looking for a safe place to sleep to avoid being caught by the claws of the vicious Turk. So now I felt I couldn't complain about this inconvenience.

However, *my desire to have more time to spend with my wife and children* convinced me to make a change. Even though by now I closed the market on Sundays and I had learned to drive and had purchased a used 1941 Plymouth, *that still didn't give me enough time to enjoy my family.* I gradually started to think of another type of work that would satisfy my needs.

When I discussed my feelings with Ovsanna, at first she didn't agree. I had just begun to make a good profit and she had apprehensions of **lean times once again.** While I understood her fears, my feelings for a change became stronger. I was tied to my job and I didn't like that lifestyle. My family came first. Selling my business before establishing a new one wasn't an easy decision to make. I now had a growing family, a thriving business, and I liked my customers. I knew finding another line of income with my limited knowledge of English and the obstacles I faced starting a new business were the reasons for me not to change. The more I procrastinated, the more determined I was to change. By now my wife saw how unhappy I was and left the decision to me.

So in the summer of 1947, I terminated my lease with the landlord and sold my business to a Syrian. Since I had a little money in the bank, I took time off to consider various options suitable for me. I definitely enjoyed my free time, to go and come as I pleased. *I wasn't tied down* in one place and could spend time with my family and friends. This was very important for me. Now I had to find a job that afforded me that freedom.

A NEW JOB TO MY LIKING

After rejecting several options, one day I walked into a realtor's office. Merle Allen was the broker. With my broken English I had a hard time explaining my intentions to him. Since he needed additional help and noticed I conversed in Spanish with his salesman, he invited me to spend a few hours a day with him in his office, which was relatively close to my house.

Whenever I felt like it, I dropped into his office. When a Mexican client entered the office looking for a particular type of house, I noticed Allen's salesmen were not translating correctly even though they themselves were Mexicans. On several occasions I teased and corrected them in a friendly way. Allen was taking note that I had good knowledge of Spanish and a good disposition dealing with the Mexican clients.

One day when a Mexican client came in, Allen asked me to go with him to show a house to the potential buyers. Because he didn't speak Spanish, he allowed me to do all the talking. The client liked the house and purchased it without delay. He paid three thousand dollars for it and paid Allen two hundred dollars commission. Allen was impressed with the speed and ease of this transaction. When all the papers were signed, he handed me one hundred dollars as he said, *"Good job, you earned that!"*

Well, *that was the easiest one hundred dollars I had ever made!* There was no effort at all. I enjoyed what I did, there was no capital outlay, and I had no language barrier. Immediately I knew *this* was the job I was looking for.

Thereafter, I went to Allen's office a few hours a day and I kept busy helping him sell houses. On a few sales, I even volunteered to make loans using money I had in the bank. The bank's interest to me was less than three percent; the interest from the loans was six percent. Now I was making money from the commission and from the interest on the loans of each house that I sold.

Soon I was doing better in sales than Allen's salesmen. One day I saw a billboard advertising a Real Estate broker's school. I called the number listed and talked with the instructor, Mr. Brown. I told him my English was not good. He encouraged me to go to class to see if I could handle the course. No one in Allen's office thought I could succeed with my limited knowledge of English. Even his salesmen who were born and raised in the United States couldn't pass the tests.

Determined to succeed, I enrolled and went to class every night, keeping my day hours at the office. When the instructor saw the difficulty I was having understanding the language, he recommended that I bring someone with me to translate. Therefore, I took my son, Mardig, who was a great help for me. At the time he was sixteen years old. After a couple of sessions, he too thought I wouldn't be able to pass the test. However, when the instructor felt I was ready to take the test, he told me to try it. Using my limited knowledge of English and Spanish, I took the test. I scored 52% and didn't pass. Mr. Brown continued to encourage me to try. I worked harder at learning the English terminology. Once again when Mr. Brown felt I was ready, I took the test. Each time there was a sixty-dollar fee—an incentive for me to try even harder. This time I scored 70%. I passed and in a few weeks *I received my broker's license!* I have always been appreciative of Mr. Brown's encouragement and confidence. He was a good teacher.

The first thing I did the next day was to go to Allen's office to show him my certificate. Everyone was very impressed and happy for me. They couldn't believe I passed the test with my limited knowledge of English. By now, **I was forty-seven years old.**

With my own license I began to buy and sell houses on my own. One day I purchased a house for three thousand dollars, did some repairs and renovations, and turned around and sold it for fifty nine hundred dollars within a few weeks. At this point I knew then that I had made the right decision. From that time on I became successful buying and selling houses in East Los Angeles. Once again, my clientele was primarily Mexican.

Ovsanna and I had created a lifestyle ideal for the both of us. Within the confines of our community with relatives and friends, we maintained our parental values, customs and traditions—*our lifestyle was very similar to what we enjoyed in our*

Yergeer prior to 1914. Ovsanna cooked and baked our traditional dishes, sewed most of the family clothing, did beautiful needlework, and visited with her friends during the day. I earned a living with my hard labor. We obeyed the laws of the land. Eventually, I sent both of my children to UCLA. In fact, we moved to the West Side of Los Angeles so they would be closer to the university.

DEVASTATED BY THE WHITE CHARRT

As life has demonstrated to me, real happiness is only transitory. Just when I thought the world was really mine, in the prime of my life when I was in my fifties, I was confronted with **the one misfortune** I never allowed to cross my mind. The one misfortune I wouldn't wish upon my worst enemy! This occurred when my son married an *odar* (a non-Armenian) in April 1954.

I had woven so many dreams and aspirations around him. From the time Mardig was born there had been a special bond between us.

Mardiros Chitjian (Los Angeles, 1952)

There was total assimilation into the *odar* world within one generation. We had managed to escape the bloody barbaric *charrt* of 1915. Now we were both left wounded emotionally by the "White *Charrt*"—assimilation! There is no escape from the *"White Charrt."* If allowed, the *"White Charrt"* will finally achieve the aspirations of the vicious barbaric Turk—**our youth must understand this!**

How many times had I heard the desperate words and fears my beloved mother instinctively knew about the hazards the young naive Armenian boys confronted in foreign lands by the *odar* women?

How could I now be accountable to my dear father's wishes when he emphatically repeated to instill into the conscience of his sons the fear of the *"White Charrt."* I can still hear my father's voice as he quietly sang to himself:

Lyre resonate your tunes for the whole world to hear,
about the persecuted Armenians, the mortally wounded.
Groan as you cry, with so much affliction, so much evil.
With so much blood, we have shed so many tears.
If our descendants should forget this much grief,
let the whole world dishonor the Armenians. . .

All my life I strove so hard to fulfill my father's aspirations and wishes. I fashioned my whole life to honor his aspirations. I wanted his soul to be proud of me. I still feel the pain we all felt when he quietly let go of Kaspar's hand, turned around and walked away from us forever. That was the moment I vowed to myself and to God that I would never let him down and up until now, I never had.

This was no longer in my power. I never understood how it happened. I had let my grandfather down, I had let my father down, but what hurts more, I had let my nation down!

The world no longer was mine. **Another part of my soul was eternally wounded.** The pain is not for my father, nor for me, but for my *Yergeer.* I have failed to do my part to bring justice to the grave injustice that was done to our nation. *There is no reconciliation for this wound.*

Now, I have only one avenue to pursue my lifelong commitment to my father. *That avenue is to support individuals and organizations that profess both unity and justice for our Armenian cause.* **Without unity, we will never achieve our goals and aspirations.** Day and night, I still hear my father, "If they don't unite, the Turks are going to eat our heads!"

Much to my regret, for the last eighty-eight years, our Armenian politicians and clergy don't seen to understand this.[*] What will it take to convince them? How many opportunities will we obliterate? *Their course of action is not fair to the millions of martyrs and survivors of the vicious sword of the enemy.* They act only to enhance themselves with self-proclaimed power or for monetary gains to the detriment of the silent majority. Justice for the Armenian cause waits in the background.

Those who do not understand that position did not personally experience the slaughter of innocent men, women and children. The Turks did not spare one particular group—Dashnag, Ramgavar, Hunchag, Loosavorchagan, Protestant, Catholic... young and old, children, babies still in the womb were all slaughtered alike!

---

[*]   It must be understood, I have greatly respected and supported those who have **unselfishly** served their people!

Back row: Michael Hagopian, Toni Hagopian, Ara Sarafian
Front row: Seta Maronyan, Hampartzoum and Zaruhy

A united front will be our only salvation. Haven't we experienced enough setbacks from our egomaniacs? I strongly feel that if all Armenians pooled their efforts together to expose the Armenian cause, the world will listen. Fortunately, in the beginning of this new millennium there are **glimmers of hope of international recognition of the Armenian Genocide.** Perhaps Peter Balakian is right. Perhaps, "this is the best time to be an Armenian." *I only wish I could see that day! I am one hundred and two years old.*

Only with the Grace of God will I be able to witness my one and only aspiration… when Turkey is made to address her crimes against humanity!

36. SEARCHING FOR SOLACE

MEXICO REVISITED

In 1957 to brighten up my life and to *search for encouragement* to lift up my spirits, I decided to take a trip back to Mexico City. I thought for sure that I would find some solace there. Hagop and his family were still there. He had come to Los Angeles and Fresno many times with the intention of remaining here, but was never able to come to grips with the general lifestyle in the United States and always returned to Mexico. His children Asdghig, Ara, and grandchildren are still in Mexico City. Only his daughter Anahid resides in New York.

With my daughter as my co-driver, we set out to drive to Mexico City. It took four days and three nights to drive the three thousand miles. The roads were at best second and third grade. Only God knew the quality of gasoline we pumped into my new "Ninety eight" Oldsmobile. We sped along with the car's smooth drive ignorant of the hazards we took. Again, God was with us!

We drove along the western border from Nogales and came back from El Paso, driving through the central part of Mexico.

We had a very delightful time visiting with family and friends we had made twenty-five years earlier. We also drove my Oldsmobile to visit dear friends in

Kerop, Kaspar, Hampartzoum, Mihran and Bedros. Photo taken shortly before Bedros passed away (Los Angeles, 1962)

Puebla on the eastern border of Mexico and to Acapulco on the southern border. Only in retrospect did we really realize the danger of the roads and the jungles.

Unfortunately the Mexico I remembered no longer existed. To my great sorrow, Gabriel Babayan had passed away. The charm and quaintness of that majestic city was no longer there. The population had grown from one and a half million to over ten million. Mexico City had changed much like Los Angeles, neither were the beautiful safe cities they once were thirty years earlier. The growth in population had really taken its toll in Mexico City—which was very disappointing!

BEDROS PASSES AWAY

Sometime in 1963 Bedros fell ill for a few months and went to the hospital. During a hospital visit, he revealed to Ovsanna he would never go home again. He died in the hospital shortly after, leaving behind his daughters Alice and Colleen and his son, Levon. Now we were four brothers.

FIRST ARMENIAN DAY SCHOOL

That same year the Armenian community in Los Angeles was taken by surprise with an unsuspecting announcement. A relative newcomer from Beirut announced he was going to open an Armenian day school in Los Angeles. The general reaction from the community was neither financially nor emotionally supportive. Such a school was considered *a crazy idea.* Twenty-five years earlier Mr. and Mrs. Matheos Ferrahian, a childless couple had the foresight to stipulate a will to intrigue an ambitious and dedicated Armenian to accept their convictions to open an Armenian day school up to the twelfth grade in Los Angeles. Gabriel Injejikian had the courage and tenacity to establish the first Armenian day school in America—Encino, California.

Gabriel Injejikian, a *Kessabtzee*, was an admirable pioneer in education. He paved the way for subsequent Armenian day schools. My hope is that these schools will negate the pace of assimilation in America, which is unbearable! I **also hoped** we would have fiery, high-spirited *dedicated* graduates defending our Armenian cause. This school gave me cause to rejoice![*]

---

[*]   Forty years have passed and I am still not aware of graduates from any one of "these" schools who have "productively" enlightened non-Armenians. Where are our journalists, reporters, newscasters in the public media?

   Armenians "continue" to talk among themselves in Armenian. Who knows how much support we could have had, if more Armenians and non-Armenians knew about the Armenians! *Meghk!*

> Ermaneeneen gunoo lakhlakh elan gehcher
> Hayoon oreh barab khossehlov gantsnee
> The Armenian day is spent with empty platitudes!

It also delighted me when my daughter volunteered the following year to teach a math class after her own school day in North Hollywood. I had high hopes she would improve her Armenian skills and learn how to read and write in Armenian.

Now in the year 2003, I hear we have more than forty Armenian day schools in the Western Hemisphere, twelve of which are in Los Angeles County. I am equally proud of Dr. Garabed Der Yeghiayan, possibly related to the Yeghoyan family I knew from Kharpert. He is the founder and president of the Mashdots College in Glendale, the only Armenian College in the Western Hemisphere. I wish him much success with all of his endeavors.

KEROP PASSES AWAY

In 1967, unexpectedly I lost Kerop, my younger brother, the brother with whom I shared a bed in Perri. We had a special bond. One evening after coming home from a social visit, Kerop didn't feel well. By the next day he had died of heart failure. He left behind his wife, Yeranouhi and fraternal twins; Garabed and Seeroon—the only other set of twins in our family.

This time Kerop had left me for the last time. When I sent him to America shortly after my marriage, I knew his life would only get better. Now I saw him laid to rest. I had already lost my eldest brother and now my younger brother. Only the three of us remained. We were once a family of thirteen. **I was only sixty-six years old.**

VISIT TO SOVIET ARMENIA: SHORT STOP ALONG THE WAY

By the year 1969, tourism in Soviet Armenia[*] was encouraged. I have never reconciled with the current status of our occupied historical homeland—we should never lose sight of this goal! However, the small Soviet Republic of Armenia now became the source of hope for the continuity of our people. For years we wanted to see and feel for ourselves the land we were now able to call our own.

We planned a special itinerary from New York to Yerevan, visiting relatives and friends along the way. In the fall of 1969, Ovsanna, Zaruhy and I flew to New York City. We visited with Ovsanna's younger sister Nevart and husband Nishan, and her son Avedis and wife Rosemary. In New Jersey we visited Ovsanna's older sister, Maritza, her daughter, Rose, and son Harry.

---

[*]   Although Soviet Armenia, which is part of eastern Armenia, suffered under the barbaric Stalin regime, it did not experience the horrific atrocities and losses of the Genocide perpetrated by the Turks in western Armenia also known as Greater Armenia.

For a few days we went to Montreal where there was a relatively large Malatyatzee community. From there we flew directly to France to visit with Ovsanna's half sister, Margarite's family. *Margarite and her two young sons escaped from Turkey with members of her husband's family.*

By 1969, Margarite had died; thus Ovsanna didn't have the opportunity to see her sister for one last time. However we had a most memorable and delightful visit with her two sons, Sarkis and Avedis, and their families. The two cousins had been Ovsanna's playmates in Malatya. They were very close in age and spent much time playing together with Khachadour's three children.

They had not seen each other since 1915. *For many years they had lost contact, and they did not know the ordeal each respective family endured during the chaos and tribulations of those terrifying days of the Genocide.* In two weeks the three had so much catching up to do. A half-century later, the three adults reflected on their lives when they were merely five to six years old. It was amazing to see how much they remembered the happy moments and experiences they shared with each other along with other family members during their unforgettable childhood.

Margarite and son Sarkis (France)

Despite the horrendous experiences they endured, they had basically kept their childhood characteristics. The same childhood personality traits were apparent in their adulthood. **It was amazing what each had remembered about the other.**

Both brothers had also been caught in the bloodshed of World War II in the French army. They both had battlefield scars fighting in the front lines, once again miraculously escaping death. Subsequently, they also led hard lives.

Sarkis Kepenekian settled in Romans with his wife Areknas and their two sons, Haroutune and Hovannes. Avedis settled in Lyon with his wife Sona and their daughter, Margarite and son, Kevork—both of whom became physicians.

Kevork Kepenekian became a prominent urologist and has volunteered his time in Yerevan since the horrific earthquake of 1988. Every year, in addition to taking medical supplies, he conducts many surgeries. Most recently we heard he has been promoted to a prominent administrative position in a hospital in Lyon.

While still in France we were also able to locate several close playmates Ovsanna cherished in her memories. Some were success stories and some were not. Among the many Malatyatzees in Valance and Paris, Ovsanna was fortunate to locate a few of her childhood friends.

It was heart wrenching to experience a common sense of loss—the painful yearning for our Yergeer wherever we went and with whomever we spoke. We all shared the same tragic grief regardless of the country we had immigrated. **Armenians around the world have a wound that will not heal until justice is achieved.** Where is God!

So far, our trip was very rewarding. It had brought back so many cherished memories of the wonderful life we all once shared in our youth. *Nostalgically we embraced the fleeting opportunity to once more relive the life (before the charrt!) we all yearned for.* Our shared memories both confirmed and enlightened what we once had. *Akh, akh* how we all missed our *Yergeer,* the congeniality of our people, the respect we had for each other, the soil, the water, the air, the fruit, the vegetables. *We missed it all!* Even though the lifestyle was harder and the present day conveniences were almost nil, the people were happier with whatever they had, putting aside the Turkish wrath and fear. It seems that the more we have here in America, the less happy we become. It took so little to make us feel happy and content in our *Yergeer.* We greatly appreciated what little happiness we did have.

From France we went to Bolis. Just because we were so close to our *Yergeer,* we both felt an inner pull telling us to stop there. We knew we never would have an

Mihran with his doctor and nurse in front of the hospital in Bolis, 1959

My Aunt Aghavni, her husband Levon and children (Perri, cir. 1930s)

opportunity to be this close again. Ovsanna had several childhood friends, who now lived in Bolis that she wanted to see once more. I had an inner drive to see what could have been the gateway out of hell for me. If only I had made that bus trip in 1917 when the Americans had provided the opportunity for my escape. I would have avoided a most treacherous year of my life. As my luck would have it, I went from one inferno into another inferno. *This trip to Bolis brought some kind of closure to all of those feelings.*

Now that we were so close to Kharpert and Malatya we had an urge to visit both cities. Rationally we knew we wouldn't be able to endure the pain of reviving the memories deep in our souls of our precious childhood. *Emotionally, we wouldn't be able to witness the ravages of rape and destruction of our Yergeer.* That pain would have killed us.

Some years earlier, in July of 1959, my brother Mihran *went back to Perri to see our Aunt Aghavni and to Ismiel, to see the house where he was born and the infamous toeneer where he was placed for safekeeping while the Kurds plundered the house. For years he knew of this incident. He was about seven years old when we moved from Ismiel to Perri.*

The Kurds occupying the house allowed him to enter. As he walked in he felt ill and passed out. How much he was able to recall remained a mystery. He was immediately hospitalized in Bolis where he remained for several months. When he felt well enough to leave the hospital, he went to Perri to visit with Aghavni and her family. Aghavni and her family were still living in the same subterranean house. He was saddened to learn Aghavni's circumstances had not improved

Gahmarr Aghpiur (Perri, 1950s)

much. She was still in a state of poverty. She was now called Hadiga. She and her husband Levon had four children. This was the destiny she had chosen for herself and as much as I know her grandchildren have remaind in Perri.

Mihran was devastated when he saw with his own eyes the complete destruction of our precious church and school—only the ruins of the foundation could be identified. The population of Perri at the time was only a fraction of what it once was, mostly Kurds.

While in Bolis it was recommended that we stay at the Park Hotel because the owner and employees were all Armenians. This turned out to be more of a disadvantage than an advantage. The hospitality was much to be desired. That was only the first of many disappointments we experienced in Bolis. Once we settled in our room, we wanted to telephone a few of the names we were given. To our surprise and misfortune there were *no* surnames ending with *'ian'* or *'yan'* in the telephone book. We later discovered all Armenian names had been changed to Turkish names. Thus, we were able to locate only the few friends whose addresses we had acquired along the way. In addition we learned that none of the existing Armenian churches and schools are permitted to be repaired or renovated *when needed*. Within time those institutions will become *inoperable*. All Armenian structures will no longer be replaced. All Armenian structures are gradually deteriorating under the auspices of the government's design—nothing has changed! It is disturbing the U.S. Government assumes the Turkish government is a **DEMOCRACY!**

With some difficulty and the aid of taxi drivers, we located and visited only a few families. As we were driven around the city, we were surprised to see the degree of poverty, even in Istanbul. The backwardness of the local people had remained

Levon and his grandchildren (Perri, 1959)

the same. . . nothing had changed. Our cab driver was puzzled when I read the Ottoman script engraved on the entrance of the St. Sophia Greek Cathedral. After admitting he couldn't, he inquired how I knew—*I didn't know how much I should reveal to him.* **With Mustafa Kemal's sly ploy, immediately adopting the Latin alphabet, in a short time the Turkish citizens were unable to read and learn about their barbaric past... the Armenian Genocide.**

Even though we were now traveling as American citizens with American passports, we still felt the intense foreboding fear of danger. Turks and their government still could not be trusted. *This was the only country where no one is allowed to speak Armenian in pubic.* We were always warned to control our speech while we were outdoors.

Although we had mixed emotions, we were glad to have made this stop—just to proclaim to the barbaric Turk *we had survived.* **Their attempt to obliterate all Armenians failed!** With God's will one day those heathens will be tried for the heinous crimes they perpetuated upon us. *Meghk. . .*

From Bolis we flew to Beirut, our gateway to freedom for Ovsanna and me. This time we were very impressed with the complete transformation the city had undergone from the small dusty town infested with mosquitoes to a magnificent city cluttered with beautiful high-rise buildings.

We found a few Malatyatzee and Perritzee families during our two to three day stopover. I found Kevork Yerevanian, a schoolmate who was a few years older than me. I used to play with him and his brothers during our recess breaks. I was happy to learn his brothers were all safe. We felt very proud to learn his son, Ara, was a member in the Lebanese Parliament and was held in high esteem throughout the country. We spent a wonderful afternoon at his home. Before leaving he gave me a letter to deliver to Hagop Holipigian in Soviet Armenia.

From Beirut we boarded an Aeroflot Soviet airplane to our final destination, Yerevan. While the flight was less than three hours, emotionally **it was a unique experience.** All the passengers were Armenians as were the crew and pilots. As we shortly flew over Mt. Ararat there was *a spontaneous burst of unanimous exhilaration with tears of joy. For one fleeting moment we all shared a feeling we were one. We were all aware that we bore the same scars inflicted by the vicious barbaric Turk. Now we were proof to ourselves and to the world we had survived and were not obliterated. Just like Mt. Ararat, we survived the test of time and will continue to do so. That was a moment I shall always cherish within my soul.*

Within a few minutes after the plane landed, we were walking towards the Yerevan airport. Suddenly we were perturbed that young Russian soldiers were guarding *our* airport. Our feelings of exhilaration faded just as rapidly as they had sprung up on us as we flew in full view of Mt. Ararat. There was a quick realization that we still were not in charge of our country, or of our destiny!

Going through customs was something else. Even though the three of us passed through within minutes with our simple luggage, we were detained along with others. It seemed to us those coming from Beirut were conducting a practice of *free enterprise* between the two countries. For six hours each piece of luggage was inspected. There were huge numbers of unusual items such as nylon clothing, plastic household items, toys and gold jewelry and who knows what else.

While waiting, we witnessed *a sad incident.* A cheerful man in his sixties proudly carried two small containers from the airport in Beirut, into the plane, one in each hand. Each container had a beautiful cedar seedling about ten inches tall that he was taking to his brother as a symbolic gift from one country to the other. Unfortunately they were taken away from him because they were not in "compliance" with custom regulations. Yet all the other *activities* were overlooked. . .

Topping off the list of things that went wrong, after the long wait at the airport, we were driven to the Arabkeer Youth Hostel instead of the Hotel Armenia where the Levon Travel Agency in Beirut had booked us and for which we paid for our two weeks' stay.

It took almost a whole week of complaining and demanding. It was only after we made an official complaint in the "Blue Book" when we were transferred to the Hotel Armenia which had been overbooked because it was the year of the *Mehron* Festivities—A special celebration which takes place every seven years, Blessing of baptism oil by the Catholicos. Tourists from all over the world had come to celebrate this holiday.

During those negotiations, I was able to locate my dear cousin Hmahyag whom I had not seen since our very sad and painful departure from Haleb in 1923 where he was left all alone and on his own. He was the only surviving member from twenty-eight families on his father's side. Leaving him behind was my gravest regret, but my brothers in America felt they couldn't sponsor *one more cousin*. They had been deceived so much by the other cousins! *Meghk. . .*

During several visits, Hmahyag and I tried to catch up on all that had transpired in our respective lives. At the same time, we relived the joyous days of our childhood along with the treacherous suffering we endured before our escape. Once again, our tears and nightmares overwhelmed us.

Of all the people I was fortunate enough to see once more during the span of eighty eight years, none was more heart wrenching and heart warming than my visit with my cousin, Hmahyag. Was it because we were closely related or was it because he was the only other person who, like myself, had suffered throughout our lives with the memories of the devastation, the personal losses, the personal pain and suffering? The memories were etched in his mind and soul as they were in mine. He, too, was never able to shed the pain from his daily life. He knew exactly how and what I felt.

During our brief encounter we relived our fright and fears of being captured. Hmahyag was the only person who *thanked* me for all the times I helped him. He realized the risks I took stealing bread from the *poorr* to provide a little more food for the orphans. No one else expressed their appreciation for the risks that I had taken for them. I shall always cherish his acknowledgment and appreciation for the times I was able to protect him during those most unforgettable heinous years. Both of us barely escaped alive.

We cried together more than we talked. We came to grips with what really had happened to us and the consequences it had on our present lives and the fate of our people. "Sev Sovgat" (Dark days of hunger). What a painful memory.

In addition, it pained me to learn his circumstances in Armenia were so similar to his situation in Kharpert. Even then he was barely making ends meet. Unwillingly, he was now dependent on his wife and sons. It was difficult to accept that he still needed to be protected. Tragically he was tied into a political system where he felt trapped. I felt so sorry for him.

Most of all, I shall never forget his display of respect and appreciation for my visit. Without hesitation before we entered his house in Nork, he sacrificed a lamb on his doorsteps in my honor, *mahdagh*. Amazingly, the lean meat and bones of the poor lamb were quickly converted into a variety of traditional Armenian dishes by his wife and daughters-in-laws. That was the first and last time I was given such an honor.

While I was very impressed with the manner he carefully beheaded and cleaned the animal, I was greatly taken aback by the poverty of his circumstances. Even though he passed away a few years after our visit, those feelings haunt me to this day.

Hmahyag was my only cousin (Soviet Armenia, cir. 1960s)

Did it have to be this way? Hmahyag's father and three uncles were well established in Perri. What a pity that a person with such a gentle and generous heart was not able to acquire a more serene life after the *charrt*. I greatly regret I wasn't able to have been more helpful for him.

During that same week, I also located my dear friend Hagop Holipigian. On several occasions in Kharpert, he had been very helpful too. Most of all I shall always be grateful to him for reuniting me with my brother Kerop during my most wretched years. Now, I had a letter to deliver to him from his dear classmate, Kevork Yerevanian in Beirut.

While my visit with Hagop was very cordial, I was keenly aware of his agitated posture. He was constantly surveying all corners of the public room where we were visiting. For many years he was a judge under the Communist Regime. Even though he was now retired, he still felt uneasy. While I was surprised he didn't spend more time with us, I didn't press the issue. I didn't want to jeopardize his position, as we had heard so many rumors of how citizens were under surveillance. However, from his posture and clothing, I knew he had been able to make a decent living for himself. He was able to take care of himself much like in Kharpert and for that I felt good.

During the second week we searched for Ovsanna's childhood friends. One day while we were in the center of Yerevan on Abovian Street, we walked into the Yerevan Hotel to use the phone. We had the number of one of her dear neighbors in Malatya. When we found a phone, we realized we didn't know how to dial the number. As we looked around for assistance, there was only one person in sight. He was standing there doing nothing, as if he was just waiting to help someone.

When we gave him our slip of paper with the number we were trying to reach, he looked up at us and broke out in laughter. It was his number! His sister whom we visited while we were in Romans, France, had given the note to us. Her family owned a renowned shoe factory that made and sold shoes to famous stores in Europe and the United States. This was Khosrov Vorperian, Ovsanna's next door neighbor in Malatya. Now he lived in Nor Malatya in the outskirts of Yerevan.

That day he took us to his house for a traditional Malatyatzee dinner. We were so happy to see some of our traditions had not changed in the Soviet regime. Two of Ovsanna's childhood friends, Varter and Lamon were also invited to the dinner. We all had a very delightful night.

The next day, Khosrov took us to the wool factory in Nor Malatya where he and his sons were primarily in charge. In one area we saw machines wash and process raw wool, in another area the wool was spun into yarn and dyed, then the yarn was woven on mechanical looms into beautiful woolen yardage, and finally sewn into beautiful costumes. This whole process was done under one roof. It was sad to learn those beautiful finished products were not available in Soviet Armenia. They were sent to Europe and Russia. The knits ranged from baby clothes to women's knit suits, which were comparable to Italian kits.

Most of our experiences visiting with friends in Soviet Armenia were similar to those we shared in the previous cities of our trip. Again we were overjoyed to see and learn about those who had survived, to learn how each escaped, and also to learn about their situation and achievements.

We felt very proud when we learned about success stories. In addition to Khosrov and his sons, we were proud of Davros Manooshagian who was the chief director of the Nor Malatya Hospital, one of the renowned hospitals in the Soviet Union. He was the son of one of Ovsanna's neighbors. We were friends with his uncle in Los Angeles. Ironically, when we went to meet him and to tour the hospital, he had gone to Los Angeles for a conference.

During our short visit in Armenia, we were not surprised to learn that there wasn't equality among the people after all. It was the same there as everywhere else. There were the haves and the have-nots. The Soviets were becoming capitalistic and America was going socialistic. Those who had achieved higher positions also led luxurious lives.

That was most noticeable at the home of Haigaz Jamgochian (another former Malatyatzee neighbor), a math professor at Yerevan University. While we were in his home, we felt we were in the home of a Western Armenian—they even spoke with the "Western dialect". However, Haigaz did surprise us when he discouraged us from searching for a bottle of red wine similar to what he had served us. We wanted to take home a bottle as a souvenir—*Hayasdanee Garmeer Keeneen* ("Red Wine of Armenia"). It was truly different. How he got the red wine remained his secret.

We were very fortunate to have had the generosity of Varter's son, Mardiros, who drove us to almost all of the prominent historical sites in Armenia. Each was memorable and breathtaking with its unique history. In addition, he took us to a couple of schools and the Science-Technological Exhibition Hall. In particular, I

Khosrov Vorperian's family with Malatyatzee friends
(Nor Malatya, Soviet Armenia, 1969)

was very impressed to learn how fiberglass was being made with the overabundance of Armenian stone.

As we were leaving, I felt very proud to have my picture taken with a uniformed policeman in front of the hall. I quickly admitted to him I sneaked out a piece of the fiberglass. His response made me feel even better. He suggested I should take and show it to my friends in America. I have done just that! I felt proud that we finally had officers in uniform!

As we were departing from Soviet Armenia, on our way to the airport, we were left with a glimpse of encouragement, a makeshift assembly line removing rocks from a particular field. A line of men and women were laboriously passing rocks and boulders, one to the other, until the rock reached the roadside where they were loaded onto a truck and hauled elsewhere for a more profitable use.

When we questioned this mode of clearing the area, the response was, *"Vocheench* (never mind)... Come back in fifteen years and you will see our beautiful healthy wheat fields swaying with the wind."

That feeling of accomplishment and hope left us with a very positive lasting impression. *Hayasdan* (Armenia) will prosper with that attitude and drive. I hoped at the time that I would be able to return in fifteen years to see those wheat fields. Only with the passage of time, will we be able to see what really happens. Again I remember my dear father's words, "Only with the will of God, do the leaves of a tree move!"

On the other hand who would have guessed in 1969, my dear *wife's perception* when we were no more than a couple of days in Armenia, "If they were to open

Ovsanna and I flanked by two Armenians in uniform who could stand up to Turkish gendarmes.

the doors, the people will flood out of Armenia. No one will remain." While she lived long enough to see Armenia gain its independence and achieve its initial steps to prosperity, she did not live long enough to witness how correct her omen was. In the year 2000, the exodus from Armenia was unnerving.

If we do not unite and act sincerely for the good of our nation, we will not survive. *The Turks understand our weaknesses more than we do!*

Nevertheless, Armenia itself is an open air museum. Our ancient historical monuments and artifacts reflect the wonders created by its people on this minute, barren land. We are proud of this part of our homeland and we should all strive to support and help to enhance our country. We, Armenians, have no other choice. It's a pity we do not have ownership of all of our accomplishments!

It was a godsend that we made that trip in 1969. Shortly thereafter, within a year or two, one by one, most of our dear relatives and friends whom we visited on our trip began to pass away. Most of them had not reached the age of seventy. **We were very happy to have made this final trip!**

37. THE GENESIS OF MY MEMOIRS

In the 1970s, the untimely death of our loved ones made a subdued impression upon our lives. This was another cruel misfortune we had to confront. Just when we all had established ourselves in our respective countries and were ready to make the best of our lives to enjoy and renew the company of relatives and friends, one by one Ovsanna and I began to lose those who were personally dear to us. However, we were both thankful for our good health and content with what we had. At this point, that was all that mattered.

The highlight of our week were Saturday evenings spent with a few remaining friends with whom we were still able to share our mutual past joys and sorrows. They were our sole comfort and *connection* with our *Yergeer*. The evenings were spent with the traditional cup of Armenian coffee and the customary *chorags* (pastries) and fruit after a lively game of *scambill,* a card game.

Our Sunday afternoons were shared with my dear son and his family. Ovsanna prepared his favorite dishes, *dolma* (stuffed grape leaves) in particular, and I spent a challenging afternoon playing *tavlee* (backgammon) with Mardig. Those moments were soon to become cherished moments as well.

GOD OPENED A NEW DOOR FOR ME

During this tranquil period of our lives, God opened a *very meaningful door* for me. Unexpectedly my daughter's classroom endeavors gave me the opportunity to have a whole new perspective on my inner conflict. She was a teacher for the Los Angeles Unified School District. This unforeseen opportunity began to unfold when Zaruhy initiated a mini-class on Armenian Culture within her school's extra-curriculum program.

These classes began in 1975 and for the following twenty years I became *keenly observant* of the various related activities she undertook in her classroom. I was greatly appreciative whenever I had the opportunity to directly or indirectly become involved with her classroom activities. As the years flew by, I was gradually becoming *alarmed* our case would never be heard and that the perpetrators would not be brought to trail. Armenians and non-Armenians *showed little interest* with the injustices suffered by the Armenians! This opportunity gave me a new *zest* for living because *the students assured me that **there were individuals who were both interested in our cultural history and gave credence to our efforts to have our case*** *heard. I strongly believe when these youngsters become adults they will have an open mind supportive of our case. This was the gift I was looking for to take to my father to reassure him we have not forgotten our obligations to our ancestors and to our martyrs.*

Zaruhy Chitjian, 1973

From more than one thousand students, grades fourth to sixth, eleven students were curious enough to attend the "Armenian Culture" class. In 1975, not one student really knew who the Armenians were. Yet, they had the curiosity to select a class from a long list of choices from sports, cooking, literature, music, art, crafts and so on.

Zaruhy shared her amazement that there were eleven students eager to learn about our Armenian history and culture. *At once, I felt the angels in heaven were rejoicing.* I felt proud and fortunate. Immediately, I volunteered to help her because I knew she wasn't fluent in reading and writing in Armenian. The next day, without her knowledge, I began to write each of the eleven names on individual slips of paper in Armenian script. All of the names were foreign to my ears. I too *appreciated* their willingness to learn about our culture and *Yergeer!* I felt they were my students as well.

During the week I lost no time and wrote a short poem about our precious alphabet and language for them. *I hoped they too would have the same kind of fun and fond memories with these words as I had when I was their age learning English phrases in my school in Perri:*

Hye Lehzoon

Khelatzeeutiune eh sorveel oureesh meg lehzoo
Parehgahmootiune guh hasdahdvee
Yerp khosees eer lehzoon
Nahkhundrehlee eh ahrahcheenuh uhla Hye Lehzoon
Vor lehtsoon eh Mesrobian Keerehrov
Tiurin eh sorveel Hye Lehzoon.

The Armenian Language

It is wise to learn other languages,
Friendship are made when you speak in someone else's tongue,
Armenian is preferred to be the main language,
Its many letters were formed by St. Mesrob,
It is easy to learn Armenian.

(Note: The same sentiment expressed by Margaret Meade, the prominent American anthropologist in the 1960's)

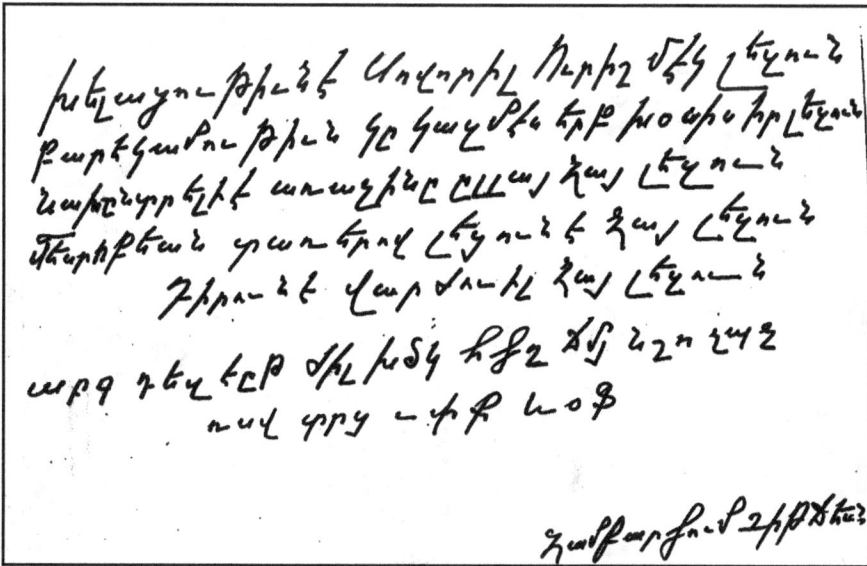

The poem and the Armenian alphabet I wrote especially for the students in 1975

For six weeks, Zaruhy kept the interest of her 11 students with a brief overview of highlights of our 3,000-year history. The fourth week, the week of April 24, Zaruhy took the *opportunity* to give a brief overview of the meaning of Genocide and how my brothers and I were separated from my father and family. Then they viewed the film, "The Armenian Case," the 43 minute version of Dr. J. Michael Hagopian's film on the Armenian Genocide. Because I appeared in three small segments in the film, the students were able to relate with me as a survivor of the genocide. I was only a couple of years older than they were when the barbaric Turks viciously snatched me away from my father. I was amazed when they personally related to this tragedy and to my pain. *They began to ask pertinent questions about my personal experiences and the atrocities afflicted upon the Armenians by the Turkish government. **They wanted to know more...***

As I became aware of their interests, I developed a special bond with them. They made me realize the importance of recording my personal experiences and

Student's art work and my poem

feelings. *Finally,* I had discovered individuals who showed an interest and wanted to know what happened to me during those six terrifying years!

What a gift my daughter had given to me! I shall always feel indebted to those precious students who had the compassion and intelligence to question how such outrageous governmental acts could go on without justice and redress, especially from the American government. From their own government! The children were bewildered, they had become aware of the contradiction of what they were being taught in their social studies classes. Those innocent minds couldn't understand how such horrific acts had not been addressed. These astute students were no more than ten to twelve years old!

At the end of the fifth session, a little blond Swiss student meekly asked if she could invite her mother on the last day the 6th lesson of the session. She wanted her mother to see all that they had learned.

Zaruhy didn't hesitate to say yes. With that in mind, within the last two weeks of the school year (when the classes were studying for their final tests), during their free time the students prepared a small program for parents and friends! They came in an hour before school, stayed in during recess, and an hour after school knowing full well they were not getting credit or a grade for all their effort and time.

All parents were invited, mothers, fathers, relatives and friends. In addition to the non-Armenians, Zaruhy invited her Armenian friends and of course Ovsanna and me to witness what those eleven students had accomplished in six weeks. The school's auditorium was packed.

Their program was solely devoted to our Armenian heritage. The skits, songs, and dances were in Armenian. The reports about historical events were in English. It was especially heart warming to observe that *the children's parents* were also impressed with this magical event as well! There were no more than three Armenian families enrolled in the school.

The most heartwarming moment for me was *when I finally was able to meet the eleven God given children.* To see and hear them perform. To hear them recite in Armenian the poem I had written for them. To be surprised at the end of the program when they dedicated this program to Ovsanna and me. *To feel the joy when they rushed towards me for hugs and kisses.*

This is the gift I will share with my father—Armenian descendants will not forget, even in a foreign country. This is the gift my daughter, Zaruhy, gave to me. A gift I hold dearly in my heart.

At the end of the year the fourth and fifth grade students requested that a similar class be held for the following year. Sure enough, thirty-seven students all elected to learn about Armenian culture and history. **That was when I finally sat down and started writing my memoirs. . . little did I know then, it would take over a quarter of a century to complete.**

Hampartzoum writing his memoirs in his back yard (1975)

Determined, I forced myself to unfold the layers of the nightmare preserved in my mind for 60 years—sixty years of excrutiating pain— pain that never subsides.

It all began with the poignant fear I experienced when my father ran to hide in the Kurdish village when there was no cause for him to run away to hide. That fear and confusion escalated when he returned home after he was beaten senslessly in jail and I saw him covered with blood from head to toe—beaten to a pulp! He was not guilty of a crime!

God gave me a way to cope with those painful memories. Each and every horrific experience was tucked away layer by layer, pressed tightly against each other much like cabbage leaves.

That was the only way I had "the will" to face the moment at hand. Each and every new day presented itself with a new and different terrifying experience. Each morning I had to convince myself I had the strength to survive and I had to discover the means to do so. Every morning upon awakening, I exclaimed, "It's a miracle that I am alive for yet another day!" Much like a bank vault, my mind guarded each and every horrific event.

The third year followed with the same popularity with more than forty students participating in this mini elective. That year's program had a segment presented especially in my honor. The children enacted a traditional custom observed solely by Armenians worldwide. That is the celebration of the Day of Ascension, *"Hampartzman Orr."* This day always falls on the fortieth day after Easter Sunday and it is always on a Thursday. This is *my name day*, Hampartzoum, the day I observe my birthday.

Traditionally on this day, the young village maidens came together on the hillside where the flowers are all in bloom. Each maiden gathers colorful flowers and makes a garland for her head. Then they sing, dance and rejoice that spring has arrived, since they have just recovered from a harsh winter.

The evening before the maidens gathered petals from seven different flowers and placed them in a vessel of water from seven different springs, as well as a personal trinket. The vessel was set under the light of the stars and the moon. It was believed that during the night nature's children came down and bestowed their charm and individual prophecies for each maiden. As the stars came down to earth the flowers and trees began to speak with each other, giving each their secrets. In turn, each one relates a remedy for an existing wish.

On the following morning as the maidens dance and sing around the vessel: "Hampartzoum ya la, ya la jan, ya la..." Shortly a younger child between the ages of three to five years old dressed in white, like a bride, plucks a trinket one by one from the vessel. As each maiden's trinket is picked, a poem relating her fortune is read. Each girl waits anxiously to hear what her fortune would be for that year. Would this be the year she will be betrothed and whatever else she might be hoping. The day continues with laughter and tears as each girl has her fortune read.

At the end of that program, two handsome boys approached me with candles and gave me a big hug. This was the first time I celebrated my name day with this personal celebration and joy. *I was seventy-six years old that year!*[*]

When I heard this group also recite the poem I had written for them, I knew my father's soul was rejoicing as much as I was, as those *odar* children voluntarily continued to embrace our language, history and customs. Each program included a significant event of our history—depending on who helped Zaruhy that year.

With each program Zaruhy took me to heaven and back. We were both very grateful to them. The sincere love and participation of the children assured me that when they grow up, they would have fond memories of this unique experience. I hope that they will be receptive to support our cause. I am sure many of the students will achieve influential positions in their chosen careers as adults. Let's hope some of them will follow the course Bob and Elizabeth Dole have taken for us.

A REQUEST GREATLY APPRECIATED

Coincidentally the following year, the school district required *all teachers* to enroll in an *ethnic studies class.* Because her mini class was so well received by the students, as well as their parents, a couple of the Dixie Canyon teachers convinced Zaruhy to present an Armenian ethnic class to meet that requirement *for teachers* at their school.

Zaruhy appreciated this request and accepted that unique opportunity. Unfortunately, she had not anticipated *the strong opposition taken by the district office.* She tried a variety of suggestions to convince the district to allow the requested Armenian ethnic class. None was accepted until in desperation she came up with the concept to *compare Armenian history with that of the American Indian.*

She pointed out that the two groups were brutally driven off their ancestral homelands where they had lived for thousands of years, with the expectation that neither group would survive. However, as history has proven, both groups had the tenacity and will to survive with great hardship *despite* their predator.

The district's attitude and denial was difficult for Zaruhy to understand because at this time hundreds of Armenian refugees from Beirut and Soviet Armenia were enrolling in the Los Angeles public schools. They were already establishing a pattern of problems unique to their culture and there was no one

---

[*]   I do not recall this or any other celebrations of merriment within our reserved and sombre atmosphere during my childhood. However, I do remember on a few occasions, during the last couple of years, a few of my classmates and I were allowed to celebrate—we would find a suitable place along the hillsides with an abundantly flowing spring to have a cook-out. Each boy brought something from home: bulghur, salt, "gavourmah," a pot. . . we built a fire, and cooked pilaf and we all agreed how tasty it was! What fun we did have!!

prepared to address their needs. With much reluctance, *for the first time* an official number was finally established for Armenian Ethnic Studies for the district at large in the Los Angeles Unified School District.

At this point, Zaruhy had the good fortune to have the most prominent educators and professionals in Los Angeles participate in the class as guest speakers. Even though most of them were not personally familiar with Zaruhy or me, without hesitation they all accepted her request.

The list of participants ran from Professor Avedis Sanjian, Dr. J. Michael Hagopian, Dr. Richard Hovannisian, Jiriar Libardian, Osheen Keshishian, Gia Aivazian, Edward Hosharian, Lucy Agbabian-Hubbard, Hrant Agbabian, Levon Marashlian, George Kooshian, Armine Sukiasian to Marilyn Arshagouni!

Without the time and effort of those participants, the course would not have been the success it was. We were fortunate the introduction of our Armenian history and culture was initiated in the Los Angeles Unified School District by our community's best. For once our professionals and educators worked together *in unison* for our cause. There was nothing more exhilarating and satisfying seeing them work with this spirit. It meant a great deal to me that the participants represented every faction of the Armenian community. That was a real success!

To everyone's surprise, from the first day she had fifty-four teachers enrolled in the class. That became *the highest number* for teacher workshop classes in the whole district at that time. There were a handful of Armenian teachers with the rest being non-Armenian teachers from the surrounding schools, including her home school Dixie Canyon. Most admitted they knew very little about Armenians and even a few said until now they had never met one.

Amazingly from the very first session to the last, the teachers were *riveted* to the speaker of the day. On the last day of the course, *the most rewarding comments the teachers expressed were what a rich and extraordinary cultural heritage we had and how unfortunate it was that so little was generally known about it.*

Zaruhy was greatly impressed when *they requested* a Part II of the same class with sixteen sessions instead of eight. You could imagine how sincere they were since they already had met the district's requirements with one class. Now the same teachers elected to continue with sixteen additional weeks for three hours a session after a hard, tiring day in their own classrooms! *That request could have reflected only their sincere desire to learn more about a people they knew so little about...*

This time the district did not hesitate to follow through with a Part II class that was listed solely as "Armenian Culture and Heritage Part II" in the brochure.

By the end of Part I, Dr. Armen Sarafian, President of La Verne College had offered three units of college credit for those teachers who needed the college credit. In addition, several schools in the Hollywood area were requesting a Part I

Los Angeles City Unified School District Area

ADMINISTRATIVE AREA F
644 WEST 17TH STREET, LOS ANGELES, CALIFORNIA 90015
TELEPHONE: 625-5507

William J. Johnston
Superintendent of Schools

John J. Lingel
Area Superintendent

Samuel F. Marchese
Administrative Consultant

January 27, 1977

Mrs. Sara Chitjian
Dixie Canyon

Dear Mrs. Chitjian:

Never in my experience on this job have I seen such unanimously
outstanding evaluations of any in-service given. There are always
some ratings in the average section. You're not even average!
I'm only sorry that I did not have an opportunity to come observe.
(As you probably knew, I was carrying another full-time load as
the secondary English consultant so that anytime that I went out
into the field, I usually was committed to observation of
English classes.)

But after seeing the consistently excellent evaluations from your
Armenian Heritage, Armenian Culture class, I just had to express
my admiration. You obviously put in a great deal of time and
energy, making this in-depth study a serious and meaningful
experience for your peer students. I will indeed recommend
your course to those interested in taking Part II.

Sincerely,

Kyoko Handler
Instructional Adviser

cc: Mrs. Teretta Terrell
     George Montes
     Sam Marchese

*The following year, Kyoko Handler's husband, Harry Handler, was the next
Superintendent of Schools and was a very close colleague of Dr. Vahakn
Mardirosian (the Director of the Hispanic Urban Center): another decisive
opportunity lost due to "ahn-meeoutiun."*

class to be taught at their schools for their teachers. By now the teachers in this area were experiencing the need for those classes. Most of them knew very little about the background of this new immigrant influx from Lebanon and Soviet Armenia.

It was enlightening to know there were people who were interested. I had always held on to my feelings and belief that it was imperative that *the world should know and understand what had happened to us and were concerned to redress the situation.*

It was not just the pain and losses we endured collectively—it was just as important for people to realize the barbaric, vicious acts that were perpetrated on innocent citizens in a subjugated country. We already lived as subjects under a tyrannical government. As much as I can remember, we lived our lives with fear in Perri. I never understood what provoked the bestial instincts of the Turk. Equally painful for the rest of my life, I can't understand the indifference or outright denial of the injustices we suffered in our homeland, our motherland where our basic essence was born and engraved. It was our sun, our air, our water, and our earth. That is what we have lost forever! *We have really lost the core of our essence forever.*

Every one of God's given creatures flourish best on the soil where it was created. Why is it so hard to realize and accept what we Armenians are yearning for when we yearn for our *Yergeer?* We have become an uprooted people and that is a crime and a pity. We can never be the same again. My heart and soul will never be at peace until the pain of this injustice and loss is understood!

> *Our soil is different*
> *Our water is different*
> *Our sun is different*
> *Our Yergeer is different*
> *It is ours!*

My dear reader, I hope you can understand why I appreciate *those* teachers, *those* students and *their* parents.

LOST OPPORTUNITIES

Armenians know the spoils of the *"White Charrt."* That is why they are so adamant about maintaining their ancestral traditions. In a free society they should not be forced to assimilate **so that they forget their roots.** That was the tactic the Turks used. Only the conditions and customs here are more subtle.

Most Armenians make excellent progress as Armenians and at the same time are productive and law abiding citizens of any country in the world in which they reside. In a *global world,* the *mosaic concept* is a more prudent concept than the *melting pot* concept.

Simultaneously as all of those activities were going on, Zaruhy realized the need for Armenian teachers to organize to develop the necessary programs and materials to address the existing issues and the emerging problems. . . to promote *that* interest in all of the schools!

Awareness of our Armenian culture and history was not enough in the public schools any more. Significant educational needs were emerging in great numbers because of the new immigrants. They were having difficulty adjusting in a new and different system both with the problems they confronted in their new schools along with the problems they brought with them.

Zaruhy founded the "Armenian Educators Association" with the sole objective to serve those needs. She collected the names of a hundred or more active Armenian teachers in Los Angeles and surrounding cities. Within a short period of time the main objectives of the organization were diverted by the new members who brought in *"personal priorities."* The main objective of the organization was totally lost.

Unfortunately this, as well as the Armenian Urban Center, never had a chance to achieve their prime objectives for the same reasons.

In the meantime, Zaruhy had approached Dr. Vahaken Mardirosian, founder of the Hispanic Urban Center for assistance. He was the only influential Armenian administrator in the district at that time.

He too was born and raised in Mexico, much like Gabriel Babayan. However, his heart and soul was Armenian, but unlike Babayan he still had command of the Armenian language.

Without wasting time, Dr. Mardirosian's lawyer drew up the necessary papers similar to the Hispanic Urban Center. Within a couple of months or so the Armenian Urban Center was established, a non-profit organization which was entitled to receive a grant for a quarter of a million dollars annually.[*]

From the very beginning those who became most actively involved were "again" concerned with *"other priorities"* than the specified objectives written in the grant. At this point Zaruhy decided to transfer over to the Hollywood area where by now the majority of refugees were pouring in from Soviet Armenia. This was where the Armenian students were having the most problems.

---

[*]   The objectives of the Armenian Urban Center was to meet the needs of the immigrant Armenian students. It was to develop the necessary programs and materials and to provide the necessary personnel to implement the objectives.

A FULL DAY OF GRATIFICATION

Before Zaruhy left Dixie Canyon, in Sherman Oaks, California, she surprised us again with a full day of activities. That was the first time I realized how much of an impact the saga of my excruciating years during my youth had made upon her mind and soul. Unconsciously, she too had become **a victim** by being confronted day in and day out listening about my losses and tribulations. *This experience prompted her to devote her time and effort to appease my pain with these significant endeavors, rather than wiping away my tears with a handkerchief and soothing words.*

On the morning of April 24, 1978 she took me to school for a short assembly on the schoolyard where the whole student body stood in lines with their respective teachers, in observance of the Armenian Genocide. Standing amidst the crowd of young children between the ages of *six, nine* and *thirteen* (the ages of my three brothers and myself) and listening to reports about what the vicious Turk had done to the Armenians was stirring my emotions—joy and pain mixed in together. As I looked upon their innocent faces I empathized with the happy and carefree feelings they projected. I *knew* their exact feelings. *There is something about a school setting that grips my soul even to this very day.*

The memories of the joy and serenity of my most cherished school days with my classmates were mixed with the unbearable, unforgettable impact of the moment we were standing in front of the Turkish school watching my father walking away without saying a word. Without one final hug, walking further and further away from us, he was leaving us all alone, forever...

Then suddenly the words of one of our patriotic songs drifted into my ears:

> *Mer Hayrenik tishvarr ander*
> *Mer tushnamyadz vodnagokh*
> *Eur vortvotz Sourp arieunov*
> *Beedee leenee azadvadz!*

> *Our ancestral homelands painfully*
> *left alone without help.*
> *Our enemy has treated us brutally*
> *under its bondage*
> *With her sons' sanctified bloodshed*
> *We will be freed!*

Did anyone understand how I felt at that moment? Did anyone notice how my legs were trembling? What tricks the mind could play on the body and soul. *Akh, akh,* to have lived through this tragedy. To have survived and now to remember so many years later. This is not easy. My mind won't stop and it won't let go.

The words and voices of these non-Armenian students were spinning my emotions into turmoil. My soul was back in Perri in my cherished classroom, singing with the same enthusiasm with my beloved classmates and teachers. Then I recalled my father's voice as he sang woefully pounding down with his *gaghabar*. . .

"*Lyre resonate your tunes for the entire world to hear...*"

Yet at the same time, I was engulfed with the emotions expressed on the students' faces reflecting a zest for life. Standing among them, I felt God telling me to cling on to my hopes and goals. We have no other choice... *It is these bittersweet memories that nourish me to live on.*

That whole day was spent with many fulfilling hours. From Dixie Canyon we went directly to UCLA and joined hundreds of college students, Armenian and non-Armenian, protesting a course taught by Professor Shaw who denied the Armenian Genocide in his classes. It was with real satisfaction to know that the Armenians, in due time, won their case against the professor.

From there we went to Hollywood where there was another gathering of Armenian men, women and children walking down the middle of Santa Monica Boulevard.

The combination of those events awakened me to feel more obligated to write about my experiences, a dog's life for six years witnessing a variety of the most inhumane atrocities perpetrated on mankind. *Was this the beginning? Had the Armenian offspring awakened to their obligation? God has left one door open for me so I can't complain.*

IT'S NOT THEIR FAULT, THEY WERE NOT TAUGHT

Zaruhy now kept her focus solely on her classroom. Her yearly programs continued to delight non-Armenians as well as Armenians. During her first year at Ramona, I *volunteered* to translate office notices that were sent home to the Armenian parents. I still made a point to attend class one day during the week of April 24 to reveal my experiences during the Genocide. I was now in *my eighties.* Ovsanna and I had difficulty climbing the two flights of stairs to her classroom. During these sessions it saddened me to realize the Armenian children were not informed of our tragic past. This was very disturbing to me. Had they forgotten so quickly? They had no thought that it was their obligation to hold on to our legacy, to continue our quest for justice. *Their lack of knowledge and interest was not their fault. **How were they to know if they were not taught?***

Each year I was affected by my interaction with these students. On the one hand, I saw the difficulties Armenian parents and teachers confronted. On the other hand, I realized if handled properly, our Armenian youth will be committed to assume the task bestowed upon their souls and shoulders by their forefathers.

In eighty-eight years I have realized how quickly our whole past could be completely forgotten within a couple of generations—if a *definite* effort is not made to keep it alive. Thus it is *imperative* that parents, teachers, Armenian schools, professionals and community leaders assume the responsibility to educate and instill upon our youth not only to seek justice for our Armenian cause, but also, to instill within their souls the glorious history, culture, traditions, of their ethnicity. ***It is never too late to address man's inhumanity to man.***

Determined, I forced myself to continue to unfold the layers of nightmares preserved in my mind for eighty-eight years—six years of excruciating pain—a pain that never subsides.

God gave me a way to cope with those painful memories. Each and every horrific experience was tucked away layer by layer much like cabbage leaves, pressed tightly against each other. That was the only way I had the will to face the day at hand. Each and every new day presented itself with a new and different terrifying experience. Each and every evening I had to convince myself I had the strength to survive and I had to discover the means upon waking. Every morning I expressed it was a *miracle* that I was alive for yet another day!

I would not exchange all the wealth in the world for my experiences with the children from the years **1975-1994**. With each visit I was taken to heaven and back every time I attended one of my daughter's programs and had the opportunities to participate in her classroom. The students gave me hope. With this young new blood, our cause will be heard. *We should never lose sight of justice of that which is rightfully ours.*

MY LAST VISIT

April 24, 1994 was the last year that I attended Zaruhy's classroom and her students. That was the year she retired. As God willed I was left with encouragement and a *surprise from Heaven.* Early in the morning, a young inquisitive student *Kaspar* embraced one hand. I sensed my twin's soul had just joined us. Within seconds another handsome student snuggled against my other side, his name was *Hampartzoum, "Hampig"* for short. What a miraculous climax for such a rewarding experience! My mind twirled with happiness as I clung on to them. *One on each side, they gave me strength to continue on with my painful saga for that day. After listening to my trials, the students understood the wounds and anguish in my heart—this, I hope they will never forget.*

Was this a sign from God reassuring me what Kaspar and I experienced would never be forgotten?

Kaspar was on my right and Hampig was on my left, 1994.

When I returned home from school, I wrote my last letter to the class. I customarily thanked each class by expressing my appreciation for their listening to my tribulations and assuring me they will *never* forget *their oath:*

My last visit to Zaruhy's class. Hollywood, April 1994.

To my dear sweet grandchildren, and to all those who follow,

I have described tragic and sad experiences I suffered during the brutal days under the vicious Ottoman Empire. I have to do this so this tragedy will never be forgotten. This responsibility will soon be yours. You are going to be the protectors of our future.

Instill within yourselves the suffering the survivors from Hell endured, much like myself. This is what we beseech from you.

Always keep within yourself the opportunity to alert and inform those who have assimilated and drifted away from our cause.

Work together and cooperate among yourselves. That is the most important stand you can take. You must realize much of what happened to us was prompted by the disunity among our politicians and clergy.

As April 24 approaches, newspapers are filled with ink but there is no real substance to what has been written about the Armenian Genocide.

You, my dear children, you be the instigators and establish unity among your peers and make a change in our destiny.

Hampartzoum Chitjian

Today I went to Ramona School. My precious daughter was the teacher. She has taught her students about our Armenian history and life. The twinkle in their eyes and their sweet smiles from the students gave me encouragement.

From their inquires and their desire to learn more, I knew they were proficient listeners and they understood exactly what I had to relate about the brutal acts of violence perpetrated on the Armenians in Kharpert.

We embraced each other with love and hugs. They had a good understanding of what I had suffered and all that the Armenians had lost. They understood the need for our fight to continue until we get justice.

Hampartzoum Chitjian

38. DREAMS LOST

A DREAM OR REALITY

On January 6, 1981, Kaspar and I celebrated our eightieth birthday. This was a very special and emotional day for the both of us because it was the first time we celebrated our birthday together on the *same day.* Previously, Kaspar has always *observed January 6th,* assuming we must have been born in January since he was named after one of the Wise Men. Likewise, I observed the fortieth day after Easter, the day of Ascension, since I was named Hampartzoum (He has risen). Neither one of us were certain of either day. We just knew for certain *we were born in 1901*—we will never know which one of us had the correct date.

Nevertheless, on that particular day we were very grateful that both of us had miraculously survived from the vicious Turk, the tribulations of life itself and that we were aging with relatively good health. During the black days of the *charrt,* we were both at the ages between fourteen and eighteen when *our escape from death dangled on a thread.* On this day, as we reflected on our past, we both knew our luck was based on the strength given to us by the intangible God. Was this day *a dream or reality?*

Kaspar and me, our last picture together
(Los Angeles, 1981)

In the twilight years of our lives, while we had relative satisfactory health, we were drawn closer together. Strangely at this late age and for the first time since coming to America, we began to reminisce "together" about our torturous past and how we both managed to escape. Kaspar was beginning to reflect upon "his" wounds. For the next two years, whenever we got together, Kaspar and I renewed our past.

Finally, we were attempting to bring closure of some sort to our tribulations. At the same time, we knew that was an impossible feat. A few months earlier, on September 16, 1980, we had lost our third brother, Mihran. Now we were the sole survivors of our family.

Despite the fact that we survived with different experiences, our painful memories and thoughts were similar. Sixty-six years had passed from those dark days, yet the tears streamed down our faces as we recalled each bloody memory— *the memories and pain that have remained in the marrow of our bones.* Even today, my body trembles when I hear the voices in my ears, shouting from the minarets, "Whoever harbors an Armenian will be jailed for five years with a chain around his neck!" *How* much I feared that I would be caught! In my nightmares, I break out in a cold sweat shouting out with fear. Torturing and killing Armenians never ceased. The Turks had but one goal and that was to completely annihilate every single Armenian. *How* many times did I witness Armenians rounded up and slaughtered? My mind was never able to comprehend how God allowed such heinous acts to occur. I never understood what was happening or why.

The confusion and reality was always bewildering. It was painful and incomprehensible to hear and to read that the American, English, French and German consulates and missionaries were continuously alerting their respective governments, both with reports and photographs in their daily newspapers about all that was transpiring in the innocent Armenian villages by the vicious barbaric Turk—and yet they allowed it to go on without redress. They were not sincere in their attempts to stop the slaughter until the Turks had reached their desired and well-planned intentions. Where was the Christian world at that time? **Where were those who fight for "human rights"?** Kaspar and I just couldn't come to grips with those conflicting feelings. . . what a conscienceless commentary on mankind. *Meghk!*

OUR FINAL SEPARATION

Shortly after, Kaspar began to have heart problems. We both had had cataract surgery. While I had a full set of dentures and thus experienced minor difficulties chewing certain foods, Kaspar still had his full set of teeth free of any cavities! I always teased him that he robbed me from having better teeth because my mother chose to nurse him. However, I still had a good amount of hair on my head while he had lost most of his. This I attribute to my grandfather who died with beautiful white hair at the age of ninety-two. By now our walk was much slower and Kaspar had begun to shuffle. That was the most noticeable difference between the two of us. Our hearing was still intact, but our voices had lost their strong resonance. We didn't look alike, but our voices sounded the same. It was difficult to distinguish between the two of us over the telephone.

Kaspar spent most of his time in the family market, where he had good rapport with his customers and that was a good pastime for him. I, on the other hand, spent most of my time in my garden and on my daily four-mile walk. During those walks my thoughts were always sprinkled with memories of the times I went from one village to another seeking a safe place to sleep and a job that would give me a piece of bread to sustain my body. However, while gardening, I brought to mind my successes. I always took pride in the success I had with raising fruit trees from bare seeds, so much like my life! My trees varied from apple, persimmons, apricot, peach, papaya, and avocado. I had beautiful flowers throughout the year for my beloved Ovsanna. At the same time I tried to keep abreast of what was happening in our Armenian community that was of particular interest to my family and me.

In my garden, 1999

It was on one of those days when I had just returned home from my walk when *I had a call from Nishan,* Mihran's youngest son. He calmly informed me that Kaspar had passed away, leaving behind his wife Ashkhen, daughter Viola and son, Kaspar Jr. Hearing that news out of the blue and over the phone made it even harder for me to accept what I had heard.

That became our final separation. We were first separated at birth, then at the tender age of fourteen, and finally at the age of eighty-two. Now I was the *sole survivor* of my family. Ironically, Ovsanna was also the sole survivor of her family. She was only seventy-six.

SURREAL PHENOMENON

Kaspar died in early May of 1983. As I tried to come to grips with my loss, I started having *strange sensations,* mostly when I was alone, especially during my daily walks. I kept feeling Kaspar's presence on my shoulder. It seemed he was beckoning me to join him. This went on for several months. It was very disturbing. No longer able to handle this sensation alone, I shared it with my wife and daughter. I thought if I talked about it, it would disappear—as I remembered Khanum's advice many years earlier. This time it did not go away, it continued. Now my wife and daughter were concerned. All that, however, came to an abrupt end during a nap one day after my daily walk. Unlike my usual nightmares, which always reflected my torturous past, on that day I dreamt my son was in some difficulty and I had to go to him. My nap became a horrifying experience, which I have no prior recollection of ever having before. While still asleep and in the darkened room, I got up and walked into the hallway. Instead of going straight into the den where my wife and daughter were sitting, I made a right turn and walked down the hallway. Instead of turning into the first door, which led into the back porch, a door that was always left open, for some reason, I passed that door and went another few steps to the door that leads to our basement. While we always kept this door locked, on that day the door must have been unlocked.

We will *never know* how I opened the door in my sleep and flew straight down ten steep stairs in the dark, head first, hitting my forehead on the cement floor. Miraculously, I didn't pass out. *Again, God was with me!*

When Zaruhy heard a noise caused by my fall, she rushed towards the living room, which is adjacent to the basement. Noticing that nothing had fallen, she walked back. She noticed the basement door was ajar. As she checked in to see why, she saw me sprawled on the floor, face down.

You can imagine her panic as she rushed down to me. She noticed I was conscious but oblivious to where I was. As she darted back up to call 911, Ovsanna rushed down to my side. She helped me up, compressed my wound with a handkerchief she always kept in the pocket of her apron and helped me up the stairs.

By the time Zaruhy came back to the basement, Ovsanna and I were almost up to the door. The paramedics had instructed Zaruhy not to move me from the basement floor and to place a compress on the wound.

Now there were two miracles. Only God knows how Ovsanna *herself* came down the narrow steep stairs, got me on my feet and helped me climb up the steep steps without the use of a railing. For over thirty years she had been afraid to go down those steep steps. You can imagine Zaruhy's concern and bewilderment. Where did Ovsanna get the courage and strength? She was seventy-six years old.

While waiting for the paramedics, I was sitting on the sofa in the den and questioned whose pajamas I was wearing. I remembered nothing and felt no pain.

Kaspar in his market, 1980

When the paramedics saw me on the sofa, they reprimanded my wife and daughter for moving me from the basement. I was taken to the emergency ward, where I was given eighteen stitches on my forehead and x-rays were taken of my shoulders and ribs. The doctors instructed Zaruhy to listen carefully to the coherence of my speech for the next two days in order to detect abnormalities. They were not sure of the extent of my head injuries. They wanted to wait three weeks to see if there were any changes in my speech before taking head x-rays.

Ironically, my stitches were exactly on the same spot where I had injured myself playing hide-and-seek at my home in Perri when I was six years old. Had I taken the fall in the same position? Ever since my first fall I had a noticeable indentation, about the size of my palm, on my forehead right above my left eye. Now I have a negligible liner scar on the indentation where my stitches were made. Considering all that I had gone through, it is remarkable these are the only two physical scars on my body!

It took about three weeks before I slowly regained my strength, confidence and mental alertness. During those three weeks I went in for several check-up visits. The doctor was still waiting before he took x-rays of my head.

By the beginning of the third week, I resumed some of my daily tasks. I never remembered the fall or how I fell. All that I was able to remember from that night was that I had a *dream* Mardig was in some kind of trouble, and I felt I should go to him. During those three weeks, we didn't want to inform him of my fall until I had my head x-rays and felt I was all right. *I didn't want to burden him.*

On Thursday of the third week, Zaruhy had just returned from school and I was feeling somewhat better and was leaving the house to go for a short walk. Suddenly, I heard her calling me back. Nishan was on the phone again. As I walked back, I wondered why he was calling me *this* time. There was no one left on whom to report.

Again, in his calm, cold manner, he informed me that my precious son, Mardig, had passed away from a heart attack. All three of us went into *shock and disbelief.* My son had always been in good health. He had never had any kind of a health problem of which we were aware. It literally took us a couple of days to come to grips with that reality. He was only fifty-two years old and the youngest person in our family to die—that was a day I never thought I would experience. Once again, there was no preparation for a fate such as this!

October 27, 1983 was a Thursday, exactly three weeks to the day since my fall. Subsequently, we learned that he was experiencing chest pains for three weeks. He, too, refrained from calling us during those three weeks *not to alarm us.*

Now I had lost my *angelic* son, who from the day he was born had a special place in my heart, as he bore my dear father's name. As a father I had never felt such pain. Understandably, Ovsanna was affected as well. Mother and son had their unique bond.

I had two tragedies within six months. My wife and I suffered much during our lifetime. Yet neither one of us were prepared for such a fate. Although, we supported each other by managing the best we could, *the effect of this loss took its toll on the both of us forever...*

From the day of his birth, I had bestowed upon my son the expectations of his grandfather. I felt so sure that *my son* would honor my father's aspirations. From the day he got married, we became *victims* of the white *charrt.* The pain on that day was more intense because it didn't have to be. I cried more at his wedding than at his funeral, *that* was the day I lost my son. . . *I was no longer able to keep my promise to my father.* His fear that if our offspring forget our cause, Armenians would be annihilated forever. . . fulfilling the Turk's desire! **Do you realize how difficult it is for a father to make this admission?**

The pain from the loss of my son superseded my head injury. We completely forgot to go back for my head x-ray. As I slowly resumed my daily walk, I suddenly realized Kaspar's beckoning calls over my shoulder *no longer spooked me.* Now, I realized what Kaspar was trying to alert me about. *It was my son who was being called and not me.* It should not have been in that order. The son should not be called before the father. *My sorrow and pain is inexplicable. . .*

OBITUARIES

Mardig and Me, Me and Mardig

In Mexico City, God's gift a beautiful angel was born on a Friday, on February 20, 1931 at 8:30 p.m. This precious treasure was bestowed to Ovsanna and Hampartzoum Chitjian. He was named Mardiros in honor of his paternal grandfather.

The name Mardiros is greatly revered in remembrance of all the Armenian martyrs throughout our history. This newborn was extremely beautiful and healthy. Because he was treasured so much, I called him the "White Horseman, Mardig." I wove upon him vindicative ideals while remembering the words my father used to sing in despair, recalling the Turkish massacres of 1895. . ."With this much bloodshed and tears, if this much baseness should be forgotten by the younger generation, let the whole world become outraged towards the Armenians." So, with these feelings, I vowed upon my father's name that his grandson would forever be a true Armenian and struggle for our cause.

And with our cherished doting, he developed into a fortunate and successful youth. During his first three and a half years in Mexico city he was loved by his maternal grandfather, Sarkis Piloyan and grandmother, Hripsime, Piloyan, his Uncle Hagop, Aunt Nevart, and paternal uncle Kerop. Loved and caressed by all, he enjoyed a happy childhood. Three years later, a new member to the family was born, his sister, Zarouhy. She was named Zaruhy in honor of my older sister.

In 1935, we moved to America to unite with my brothers Pete, Mike, Kerop, and twin, Kasper in Los Angeles; and with his maternal uncles in Fresno, Setrak and Manoog.

Mardig graduated from Garfield High School with the highest scholastic record for which he was offered a full-tuition free scholarship for Stanford University for four years. But because he preferred to be near home, he completed a 5 year pre-med course at UCLA. But in 1952 he studies were interrupted and he was drafted into the army. He was stationed in Japan for over a year. during this time, he was trained in computer science. Upon returning he pursued this skill professionally. He married Barbara and established a family; he had a daughter, Cathy, and a son, Mark.

As the events in his life began to change, an untimely and unexpected heart attack snatched our beloved Mardig from us on October 27, 1983, leaving his father, mother and sister in intense grief. . . especially me.

A survivor of the heinous Armenian Genocide. At the age of fourteen, I witnessed the terrifying slaughter and wretched tribulations. Not one day goes by that I do not relive these unforgettable memories with anguish. Why was this done to my family, my people, my country? And now this, this unconsolable fate. Is God so merciless that first he allowed the Turks to slaughter my father and now he has snatched my precious angel from me?

39. LETTERS CONFIRM THE PAST

MOST CHERISHED POSSESSION

In 1990 when all of my brothers were gone, Levon, my eldest brother's son gave me a cigar box filled with letters. There were more than three hundred letters! While most of the letters were those that I had written, there were many written by Kaspar, a few by Kerop, Dickran Amo, and by my brothers and their aquaintances who are unknown to me. However, that wasn't a complete set, nor were all of the letters intact. I knew Kaspar had as much, if not more, in his possession.

I wrote many of those letters in the old Ottoman dialect with Arabic script whenever I was plagued with fear of being caught. Today, however, much to my surprise, I am no longer able to read my own letters, even though I had written them. I was even more surprised and discouraged when I couldn't find anyone else to read or decipher them. I tried every resource I could think of. Even the Zoryan Institute, who had originally microfilmed the whole set, was not able to find someone.[*]

Whenever there was a subtle feeling of calm with the "awareness" of the American presence, I wrote my letters in Armenian. Also there are several letters written in Perri dating from 1914-1915 before the *Charrt*. Those letters were my father's letters (handwritten by Kaspar). On many occassions my father dictated his letters to Kaspar. There were a few that my father wrote himself, the last of those being dated February 25, 1915. . . pleading for financial help from his sons in America because the circumstances were deteriorating in Perri and he was concerned with the welfare of the family for the coming year. Those are the only possessions I have that once belonged to my father and *I cherish them dearly.*

INSIGHT TO UNKNOWN EVENTS

While reading these letters, I not only relived the pain they reflect, they also gave me insight into events unknown to me previously and confirmed most of what has been etched on my soul. The most poignant letters for me were those written by Kaspar when he found his freedom. It was most touching to discover

---

[*]   Again it was only by chance in 2000, when we encountered a history scholar who was able to find someone in Turkey to transliterate the extinct Ottoman into modern Turkish.

Reading these letters today (February, 2002) intensifies and confirms the
terror I experienced for six years

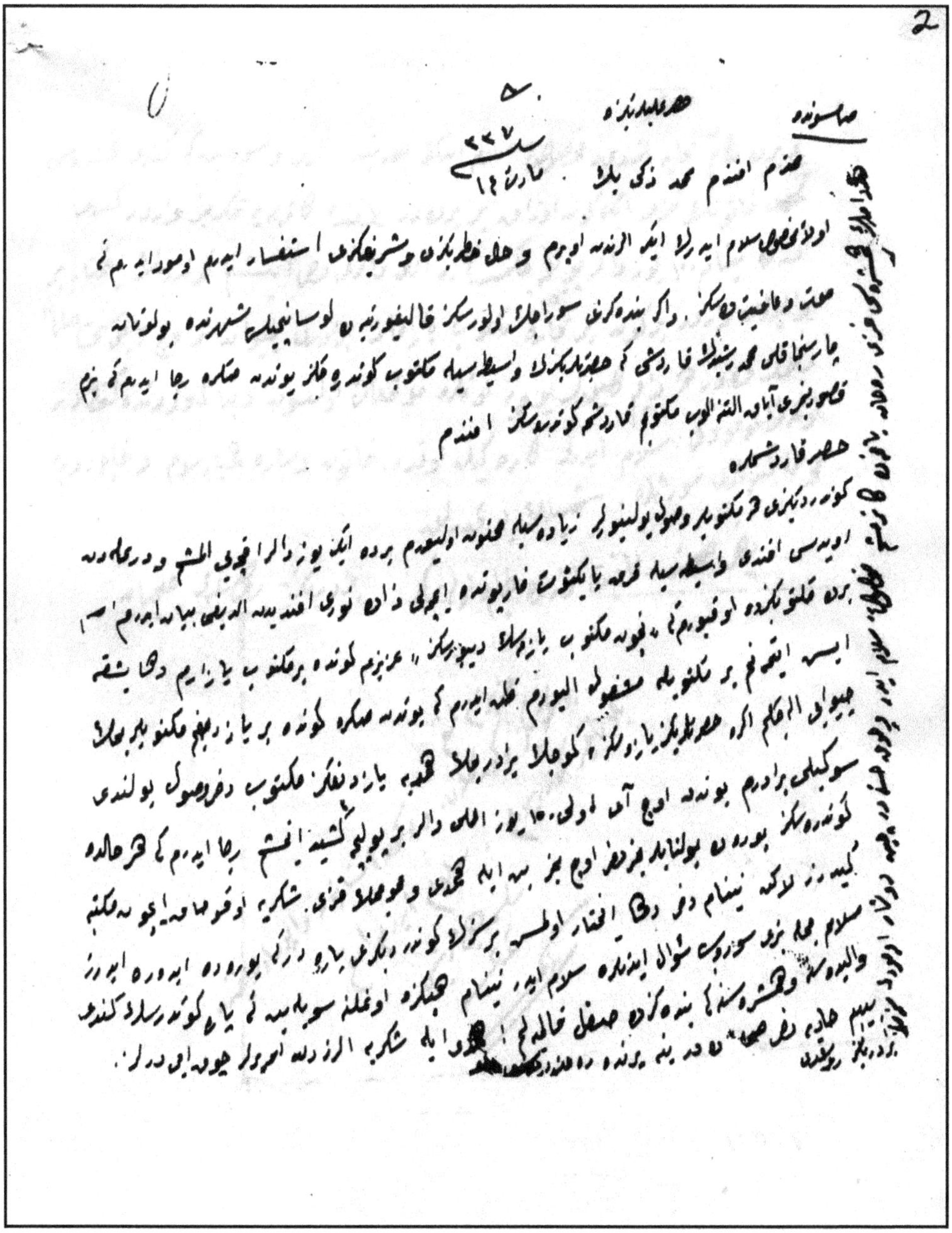

A copy of the Turkish letters

598 S. Indiana St., Los Angeles, California.
(How I wished I could have gone with these letters to this address!)

Excerpt of a letter written in Armenian

how much he was concerned about my welfare. He knew I was in more danger than he was. It is only now when I read the letters, that I am able to learn about his trials and tribulations that were unknown to me previously.

As I look back, sadly, I cannot understand why Kaspar and I weren't able to share in greater length the horrific experiences we endured from 1915-1922 when we had the opportunity. Since we lived relatively near one another, we allowed so much to slip by. . . *meghk*!

I was always aware that my older brothers never wanted to pry into our ordeals. I never knew if they were being protective of us and didn't want to subject us to relive our terrifying experiences. Was it that they could not conceive or understand the horrors and **finality of what took place?** Therefore, they did not grasp what I related to them. Annihilation of a nation was not the same as the sporadic massacres Armenians had historically suffered on their homelands throughout the ages when they rebounded and rebuilt. *How could they have understood what the innocent citizens endured at the hands of the crazed Turkish government—the annihilation of a nation!*

I also learned that Bedros actually had thoughts about returning back to Turkey when the situation permitted. How could he have grasped the enormity of the atrocities with that frame of mind? *This confirms the fact that the Turk's viciousness was a well planned and* **deliberately concealed crime** *that only the victims, perpetrators and a handful of foreign witnesses really knew what took place.*

Kaspar's ordeals were not as life threatening as mine. Even though throughout his captivity he lived with the same Turk, he still lived with some fear of being cruelly disciplined if for whatever reason the Turk was displeased with him. Since Kaspar was smart enough not to provoke the Turk, his fears were less life threatening. *Maybe* that is what made it easier for him to suppress his feelings within himself.

After I read the letters and discovered how much Kaspar struggled to rescue Kerop and me, when he was in Zonguldak, I was greatly saddened because I was not able to show him how touched I was. I would have liked to have thanked him personally. *Akh*. . .

I could only thank Kaspar now when I go to *his gravesite* in Whittier, California. With tears in my heart and the hope he hears me, can I express my gratitude for his sincere concern for my rescue.

1915-1920: KASPAR'S ENSLAVEMENT

It was only through his letters that I learned specifically about his trials and tribulations during his enslavement.

In 1915 right after I was cruelly separated from him and my other two younger brothers in the Turkish school, the Turks used the remaining larger boys to continue to plunder and loot the abandoned Armenian homes. During that time the district attorney of Perri, Meudayee Oomoomee, had noticed Kaspar's diligent behavior and took him for his slave. As he approached Kaspar, Kaspar pleaded with him to also take Nishan. At that point the Turk assured Kaspar he would come back after Nishan in a day or two.

The very next day his *Effendi* sent Kaspar (along with his wife and children) to Baghnee, a village a short distance from Perri, for eight days. Upon their return, when Kaspar immediately inquired about his baby brother, he was quickly and brutally silenced and warned never to ask about Nishan or his whereabouts again.

During the Kurdish attack from the Derseem, which was the last time I saw Kaspar until we were reunited in Los Angeles, they escaped to Hoshay. After staying there for five days, they started their trek towards Kharpert in heavy rain and winds. That was *exactly* the same day I escaped from Korr-Mamoe and ran off with the Kurdish caravan, *also* in the wind and rain. They made one stop in Pahloo. From there they walked six more days in the rain until they reached Kharpert. Once in Kharpert, Kaspar searched for Aghavni and us but we were not to be found.

Shortly after a month, they went to Bursa, which was not too far from Bolis. While Kaspar remained there with his *Effendi's* family for the next two and a half years, his *Effendi* returned to Perri because of his work. The carnage was more low key in Bursa because it was a seaport with foreign commercial activity. However, Armenians were in danger even there.

Kaspar worked laboriously in his *Effendi's* rice fields. He worked from sunrise to sunset. He wasn't expected to go home each day because it was quite a distance. When it got dark, he just fell asleep in the fields with nothing else but his lightweight clothing. He was lucky if someone brought him food. If not, he spent days with nothing to eat.

When his work in the rice fields was done, he had other jobs. Mainly he drove a donkey laden down with tobacco a distance of twenty five to thirty hours walking on his bare feet. He was forbidden to ride on the donkey on the return trip. This walk was very hard on Kaspar. Kaspar laments in his letters it wasn't the physical work that disturbed him the most, but the thought of how hard his father labored to provide a good education for his sons so they wouldn't be subjected to hard labor. He too yearned for our father's love and protection.

Kaspar felt he had no alternative. He knew if he eased up with his work, he would have been beaten or worse. If he attempted to escape, he could have been easily caught and killed. He did his best to cope. Within days of his enslavement, *he was brutally circumcised and forced to go to the mosque every day for prayers*. At one point, he described himself much like an alley cat or dog. "If you're good to

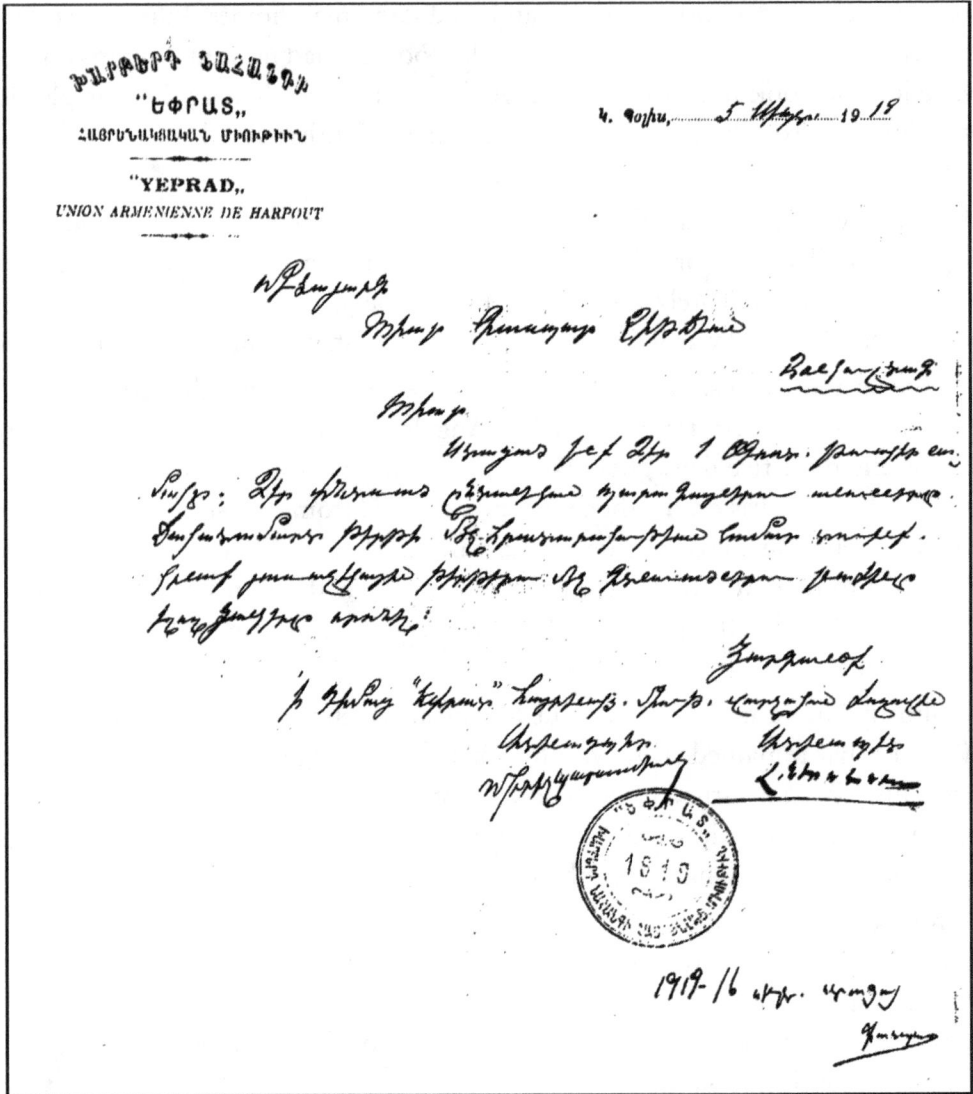

Response from "Yeprad Union" informing Kaspar they had received his letter and had printed his notice in the newspaper, 1919

your keeper, they keep you. Once in a while they throw a bone at you. If you're not, they just kick and beat you several times or even kill you."

Two and a half years later his *Effendi* returned to Bursa and moved his family and Kaspar to Devreck. Kaspar's workload remained the same. The turbulence in Turkey had calmed down slightly. The Americans had arrived and were rounding up the Armenian women and children who were enslaved by Turks and Kurds.

For a time Kaspar became aware of an Armenian merchant, Mr. Hrant Mooradian, who was watching him from a distance for some time. At first Kaspar was afraid to reveal to him that he was an Armenian. One day he cautiously decided to take the chance, approached Mooradian, and acknowledged that he too was an Armenian. Mooradian quickly informed Kaspar that all Armenian slaves were being rounded up and released from their bondage.

At first Mooradian had a difficult time releasing Kaspar from the clutches of the Turk who didn't want to release Kaspar, *claiming he was a Muslim.* Initially, Kaspar himself was cautious and reluctant to completely surrender his true identity. He knew nothing about Mooradian or his intentions. Mooradian had to apply to the Yeprahd Compatriotic Union of Kharpert for assistance. They suggested that Mooradian should take Kaspar to the local church hoping the priest could convince Kaspar to trust Mooradian. . . that turned out to be Kaspar's most terrifying day.

Kaspar   Markar
Bolis, 1920

When the priest began to ask Kaspar his name and related questions, Kaspar replied in Turkish, the only language he knew. He, too, had forgotten his mother tongue. The insensitive priest angrily pointed to a pistol hidden in his robe and yelled at Kaspar, "If you repeat one more word in Turkish, I will blow your head off!"

On the spot Kaspar felt he had been tricked and was now going to be killed. Mooradian immediately realized the situation and reminded the priest that Kaspar had lived with the Turk for five years and was forbidden to speak Armenian, thus he had forgotten his Armenian.

Immediately Kaspar began to diligently practice writing down, "My name is Kaspar, I am an Armenian and I want to speak Armenian, my mother tongue." Eventually Kaspar felt that the priest probably used shock treatment on him to help him quickly recall his Armenian. After all it was under shock that we all quickly forgot our Armenian in the first place!

Soon after, Mooradian took Kaspar to Zonguldak, which was a seaport east of Bolis, and gave Kaspar a job in his business so that he could provide for his personal keep. Mooradian's business partner, Khachig Yeheyan traded supplies from Zonguldak to Bolis. *As soon as Kaspar felt safe, he actively started to search for Kerop and me, even though he didn't know if we were dead or alive.*

He now had the opportunity to go back and forth to Bolis where he began using the facilities of the Yeprahd Compatriotic Union's head office. When he didn't receive replies from his letters, he began to put notices in the *"Jagadamard"* newspaper, which circulated in major cities around the world, including Chicago.

From this paper he discovered the name of Gegham Chitjian, a Yersangatzee who was living in New York, and used the paper to search for his wife. Kaspar wrote to Gegham in New York and asked if he would try to locate Bedros or Mihran Chitjian in Chicago. Gegham was not familiar with the Chitjians in Chicago but he obliged Kaspar's plea. He was able to find Dickran Amo and forwarded Kaspar's letter to him. Dickran Amo, in turn, gave the letter to Bedros who had moved to a new address in Chicago. *It was this change of address that caused so much confusion both for Kaspar and me.*

In the meantime Kaspar continued his search for me using the *"Jagadamard"* (Frontline) newspaper that also circulated in Kharpert. In the article *he wrote only what he knew.* He was looking for his twin brother, Hampartzoum, who was alive in 1916 using the name Mahmed Rooshdee and was living with a blind man named Korr- Mamoe. Hampartzoum also had an Aunt Aghavni who had married an Armenian who had converted to Islam and was now called Hadiga.

Instead of spending his hard-earned money on clothing and his other personal needs, Kaspar spent most of his earnings on paper, ink, postage, and phone calls. Kaspar tried desperately to find me. He continued writing letters to my brothers, to the Yeprahd Compatriotic Union and to Mr. Riggs' office. The longer Kaspar didn't receive a response, the more he worried and tried even harder to locate us. *At this precise time in Kharpert,* I was searching for my brothers in America, and also using the facilities in Mr. Riggs' office.

Finally, when Kaspar received a letter from my brothers, he learned that my brothers had moved to a new address in Chicago.

Zonguldak was twelve hours away from Bolis and under French control. The fear of the Turks was still prominent. He gave an example of an incident he witnessed. It happened one night in an Armenian coffee shop. Turkish policemen stormed in and began shouting at the Armenians who were enjoying the evening. "You have no right to be happy and laughing. You should feel thankful you are still alive!" The next morning this whole group was ordered to court. *Kaspar alerted our brothers that Armenians were not safe even in Zonguldak.*

The letters also revealed that Kaspar always lived with the knowledge that it was *his Effendi who ordered the young Armenian boys in the Turkish school to be taken to Pertahk to be killed.* Those children who couldn't keep up with the difficult trek perished along the way and those who did survive were dumped into the rivers. Kaspar lived with that knowledge for five years while he lived with his *Effendi*.

I WISH I DIDN'T KNOW

That was all happening to Kaspar in Zonguldak at the same time that I had discovered that only Markar was chosen to go to Bolis on the bulletin board in Mr. Riggs' office, and that it was Dickran Amo, his father, who had responded to the notice in the paper that I had written, listing all of our names. However, unknown to my brothers, Dickran Amo had only chosen his son, Markar. Kaspar continued his relentless search for me by sending letters and telegrams to Mr. Riggs' office. When Dickran Amo arrived in Bolis, he called Kaspar to join him. Kaspar immediately left his job in Zonguldak and with the small amount of money he had saved from his job and went to Bolis.

As soon as he arrived in Bolis, Dickran Amo advised Kaspar to ask for additional financial assistance from Bedros because life in Bolis was very expensive and he was now left without a job.

Along with the financial aid they sent to Kaspar, my other brothers also informed him it was their time to get married. They asked him to look around for suitable prospective wives. Kaspar was furious. He couldn't understand how his older brothers were thinking of marriage while their younger brothers were still in the inferno.

Once in Bolis, Kaspar discovered all roads going in and out of Kharpert were closed. This also meant letters and telegrams were no longer going through. Those restrictions aggravated Kaspar's fears about our welfare. What would become of us! He had no way to search for us or to contact us.

Markar had taken the last American bus out of Kharpert. As soon as he arrived in Bolis, Dickran Amo convinced Kaspar to leave with Markar. Kaspar couldn't understand why we weren't rescued along with Markar. My brothers had written to Kaspar that we were *all* living at the *Loosavorchagan* orphanage together. Markar confirmed the same thing when he arrived in Bolis. Kaspar didn't want to leave without us. Dikran Amo reassured him we would follow shortly after they left. Kaspar arrived in Chicago on May 23, 1920.

As it turned out, that was about the time I was released from the hospital and had made Mr. Riggs my first stop to see if anyone had responded to my second notice in the Chicago newspaper. Now I realize how close Kerop and I were to being rescued along with Markar! **What a cruel hoax...**

That was the day Mr. Riggs gave us **five** Turkish bank notes, barely enough money to buy bread for a few days. . . much less than 25 American dollars!

40. DISAPPOINTED BY THE CLERGY

EXPECTATIONS NOT MET

Attending church services everyday after school with my father as my role model left a profound effect on me. I have never relinquished the particular reverence and expectation from our clergy who have been entrusted the position to uphold and promote our traditional values and lifestyles. Therefore, I expect all those who have taken their oath, to *sincerely uphold* the ideals of the church and all that the responsibilities their followers have bestowed upon them.

Unfortunately, I have been generally disappointed with the role the church has or has not played in fostering our "scared" traditional values, customs and culture, particularly in Los Angeles. Thus you will be able to understand the devastation I have experienced not once, but on several occasions when I have been brushed aside by clerics with shameless, unwarranted rudeness. In reality, it didn't matter who I was or if they knew me personally—a particular degree of respect is warranted. Respect towards the elderly was one of the first values we were taught: to respect and to obey on all occasions. To do otherwise was considered a sin. . . as young boys we were punished.

In all instances it was obvious I was a survivor, both from my age and the specific purpose of those occurrences.

If our clergy do not assume the role to show an appreciation and understand the plight of our elders, the survivors, then who else should we expect to do so? Who else should assume the role to understand what this generation of Armenian elders has suffered—their heinous physical and emotional pain of losing their family, *Yergeer,* and historical lands! They have suffered it all. . . but if you have not personally experienced those atrocities, then you can not understand.

While rudeness is uncalled for from anyone, it is totally offensive from our clergy—especially *our* clergy. Do they realize how they hurt and effect those who they have offended? Do they even care? Unfortunately, I have been greatly disappointed by the clergy who have fallen short of the nostalgic expectations deeply embedded in my soul.

HIS HOLINESS VASKEN I'S VISIT

In 1968, our most revered Catholicos of All Armenians, His Holiness Vasken I made his first visit to the United States from Etchmiadzin, the seat of the Armenian Church in Soviet Armenia. Even though religious practice was forbidden under the Soviet regime, he was serving Armenian churches in the diaspora.

Catholicos of All Armenians, Vasken I

Extensive arrangements had been made to hold his main service in the Shrine Auditorium, at that time the largest auditorium in Los Angeles. Upon his arrival, he was ushered into the auditorium by an entourage of prominent dignitaries. As he approached the entrance of the auditorium he quickly noticed the crescent and the star. Ironically, the symbol used by the Shriners also is the Turkish emblem. Without hesitation or apologies, he abruptly stopped, refused to enter and exclaimed, "I will not enter *that* building!" He followed his heart and honored his basic convictions! His reaction was worth a million. He was the first cleric I knew to publicly call for retribution for his people from the Turks.

The auditorium was packed. We had all entered from the same entrance oblivious to what we had passed and were sitting with great anticipation, waiting for his arrival when we heard the announcement of what had taken place.

Suddenly, my mind flashed back to the entrance of the Turkish school where my father unwillingly abandoned his four sons and walked away without turning back—*he had no choice.* The beloved Catholicos had a choice—he made the right decision without hesitation! He refused to enter!

I had a sudden revelation. After decades of searching, finally I had found a man of the church who honored and respected the souls of the one and a half million martyrs—the horrific, brutal suffering of our survivors and the grave destruction of our homelands, our Yergeer.

The service was quickly transferred to our St. James Church's hall. I remember he was greatly revered by everyone for honoring his convictions. Everyone was gratified for the opportunity to be in his presence, to have the opportunity to *kiss his right hand and receive his blessing.*

I was awestruck. I felt this cleric was truly holy. Likewise, his words were holy. His actions and intentions came from my heart. There was no other like him. Once again, within my soul, I felt this was the same faith my father professed with our daily prayers, the *"Havadov Khostovaneem." That was genuine faith.* That was what I was searching for fifty-two years. *A faith that is true* and pure, not just empty platitudes and falsehoods. . . It still pains me to remember my father, grandfather, mother, the ravines filled with corpses, the hillsides covered with bones scattered around as far as the eye could see and Perri all in flames. *Akh, akh* this is how a *survivor's memory* torments him for the rest of his life. . . *images and feelings keep breaking his heart!*

HIS HOLINESS VASKEN I'S SECOND VISIT

In 1987, our Holiness Catholicos Vasken I was to make his second visit to Los Angeles. Within the lapse of time from his first visit, *I had spun an elaborate yearning for him.* I valued this pending encounter more than going to paradise. This time I yearned for the opportunity to squeeze his hand while embracing him—pressing my heart against his heart to hear his blessing. Would there be a possibility that he would *open up my heart* to learn about the painful, unconscionable tribulations that I had harbored, festering in my soul? Would he give me a *few words of solace?* Could he alleviate my pains and grief? Would I then experience some peace? *At this time of my life, this was the one and only wish I wanted granted before closing my eyes.*

The schedule for his second visit was for a longer period of time. Several social events were planned. The first evening, which was the main program, took place in the Los Angeles Convention Center, free of any affiliations. The following morning, church services were held in the Hollywood Bowl. Since both of these events attracted a huge crowd, I didn't feel comfortable to approach him for my personal wish.

The following evening however there was a reception in his honor where Hagopig had personally arranged for an opportune moment for me to be introduced. I was standing directly in front of the Catholicos, my hand stretched out waiting for his grasp, when suddenly I was pulled aside by the hand of a prominent local cleric. *Suddenly my mind zeroed in on the marches in the Der Zor where the vicious Turks pointing their swords prevented a parched soul thirsty for one sip from the rushing river to quench his thirst before taking his last breath. . . that's as cruel as a human can be!*

Perhaps I was to fault for yielding and allowing myself to be pulled back. I was a victim of my upbringing. I did not want to cause the slightest disturbance. Thus I denied myself from my most coveted wish. What were the chances I would be able to find a better gift to take to my father and all of the other martyrs? *That would have been the finest gift of all!*

I am not a pretentious person, but when I remember my past and take into account that I have lived in Los Angeles for fifty two years, I have yet to meet a cleric that is dear to my heart, to my ideals that were ingrained into my soul since birth. This saintly holy man held the same Christian faith held my by precious father. *Much like my father, he also preached for unity among his people. That prayer is Godly. Unfortunately, it falls on deaf ears in a divided church.*

There was one more event to attend. I hadn't given up my dream. I was still yearning. I knew what I wanted to say to him, *"I offer my life to you, Your Holiness. I am ten years older than you are and I have suffered ten fold a variety of punishments. Beneath the cross lying upon your chest is your heart. Place your hand upon your heart and ask your conscience, is it possible that you can talk to me? Look deeply into my heart to console me and give me your revelation for me to take to my father and all of the other martyrs."*

To appease my spirits, my daughter took us to the Armenian convalescent home in Mission Hills the following day. This gathering was more informal with fewer people. I was still hoping I would have an opportunity to have my wish granted. Even though there were many good-hearted people, *my luck was not to be.* Everything seemed to be a lie. . .

Although I was ten years older than our beloved Catholicos Vasken I, he passed away leaving my cherished wishes unfulfilled! Nonetheless, *to this very day, that most venerable and worthy Catholicos holds a very special place in my heart! He preached unity among his people!. . . a cleric to be honored!*

PULLED AWAY A THIRD TIME

A year before, Hagopig had invited the oldest living Armenian survivor, Krikor Derderian who was one hundred and ten years old, as a special guest from the East Coast to an advance showing of his latest film, "Witnesses." Although Derderian was healthy, the years had taken their toll on his frail body and memory.

The night before the gala event, I spent some time talking with him. At first, he had some difficulty remembering his past. We carried on a fair conversation about his life. Gradually, he began to remember images of his youth in Kharpert. He was able to talk about this mother who was born in Perri—his memory was coming back and he was beginning to unfold all that was tucked firmly in his soul. Noticing he showed signs of fatigue, I refrained from further questioning that night. I knew we would see each other the following evening at the banquet.

I was very optimistic and hopeful that I had finally found someone who was old enough in 1915 who would have some knowledge about the fate of my precious father, my family, and the other eight hundred Armenian families living in Perri.

The following evening at the banquet we shared a table and resumed our conversation. Just as he was beginning to shed light on Altoon Bahgee's husband, *(Alexan Amo who was a fedayee and was last seen a few years before the charrt)*, the same cleric swept him away from me. I was no longer able to find out any more of what was sheltered in his memory. I often wonder what else he would have been able to reveal. How did he escape? Who was he with?. . .

Ovsanna, me, 110 year old Krikor Derderian, his son and Michael Hagopian

THEY SPOKE WITH A SPLIT TONGUE

On January 22, 1994, I attended a program in the Arshag Dickranian School's auditorium to hear a proclamation of unity by our Archbishop and our new Catholicos, His Holiness Karekin I. With some skepticism, I listened to every word spoken from their *sincere* heart anticipating words of unity within the church.

Sitting directly in front of me were one Catholicos, one archbishop, and four other clerics. And with my faith in God, I waited for their blessed expressions of unity to heal our bleeding wounds. . .

Instead this setting brought to mind our church meetings in Perri in 1915. For five days, our two priests, one Vartabed, six teachers and ten to fifteen community leaders met to resolve the problem that confronted them—should the Armenians surrender all of their weapons of self defense or should they hold on to them? My father had sent me to serve as an errand boy and when I returned home each night, he cautiously questioned me about what had transpired. What did this priest say? What did that teacher say? Upon listening to my replies and understanding their stance, my father would solemnly exclaim, "they are going to eat our heads, they are going to destroy us, they are not united. . . " and that they did!

On this particular day, ostensibly, the Archbishop and the Catholicos represented unity. I was so excited when I heard they were going to proclaim unity. I felt *I had to witness that coveted moment.* I made sure I had a front seat to witness their sincerity, their honesty—another sham, another disappointment. Their utterance reminded me of the boy whose mother sent him to invite their in-laws for dinner and instructed him not to insist too much, just to speak with a "half mouth," *"Gess Pehrahnov."* When the boy began to speak, he covered half of his mouth with his fingers. The in-laws were puzzled with his gesture. The boy explained, "My mother instructed me to speak with half a mouth (tongue in cheek)."

I say, my dear Catholicos and Archbishop, if there is a *will* you *can* place your healing hands upon the bleeding wounds of your congregation. Yet physically they did not acknowledge each other, *neither one looked at the other, not a word was spoken between the two. Meghk* **and they were preaching unity!**

Are they not the same people who with the leaders of our political parties have splintered the Armenian community? What else can I say?

A UNIQUE OPPORTUNITY LOST

In 1985 the seventieth commemoration of the Armenian Genocide took place in Washington, DC where Armenians from around the world gathered in great numbers. I have not been aware of *any similar* event anywhere else or at any other time.

For months the Armenian press made announcements and coverage encouraging survivors, relatives, and friends to attend. This was to be an event with great magnitude and a purposeful agenda.

Even though emotionally and physically we were no longer fit to attend such a rigorous undertaking, I convinced Ovsanna to make this final attempt. She, too, was compelled to attend since she realized that this could be an extraordinary opportunity to encounter long lost neighbors and friends from our *Yergeer*. She also felt strongly that we were *obligated* to show the world *we did survive and we bore witness* to the horrible crimes perpetrated upon us by the Turks!

When we purchased our airline tickets from Sidon Travel, we were assured the needs of the survivors would be addressed. We had nothing to worry about with the assumption that our needs would be met. That was our first misconception.

To our dismay, upon our arrival at the Washington Hilton hotel we learned that the survivors *were dispersed* among four different hotels—none of which were within walking distance from each other for the elderly. Neither was there a roster of names of the survivors attending or the particular village they represented. Finally, we discovered there wasn't even one scheduled event to recognize and honor all of the survivors in one area who had made every effort to attend.[*] *Why did we go?*

There will never be another opportunity to attract worldwide Armenian survivors of the Genocide who are physically and mentally capable of attending such a convention and who are old enough to have significant firsthand memories of the *charrt* or of our traditions from our *Yergeer*.

What an opportunity that event could have been. Who knows what revelations might have been discovered? With the *huge* turnout, the potential for a productive outcome was lost forever. Those Armenians were *unique. Within their minds and souls they each possessed a wealth of crucial data and emotions to be shared. As much as I know, nobody took the trouble to ask for it. . . to record it!*

A HUNGER TO CONNECT: FOUR TREASURES

Despite all of the hardships and disappointments we endured, this trip was worth our while. The highlights for us were the few countrymen we did see. Ovsanna encountered a few Malatyatzees with whom she shared mutual memories.

Only survivors could have felt the mutual exhilaration filtering into the atmosphere throughout the foyer as he or she mingled, laughed, cried, and rubbed shoulder to shoulder wondering within their hearts, "could this person standing next to me have been a neighbor, a relative, or a lost family member?" The emotions amongst the

[*]   Survivors attended with stretchers, wheelchairs, canes!

Der Krikor's daughter and her husband with Ovsanna and me
(Washington DC, 1985)

survivor reflected a hunger to connect. Their pensive stares were asking "Vor dehghahtzee es?" ("Which village are you from?") "Do I know you?" "Did you know my brother?" At the same time, they collectively recognized they defied the Turk's plan to annihilate all Armenians—to annihilate them! **A victorious essence permeated in the air!**

By chance and through my own effort, I found four treasures. While mingling around and seeking Perritzees, I found the daughter of our beloved priest, Der Krikor, who advocated that the Armenians should not surrender their weapons to the Turks. My father respected him as our clergyman. I was very happy to know someone in his family had survived. Next, I found my dear classmate, Bedros Yermoian. We ran into each other in front of the hotel while waiting for a bus to take us somewhere. He was the boy who brought *Crayolas* from America to our school. There was no time to find out any more from him. I never found out what happened to his father and family. It seemed he had made a success for himself and this too made me happy.

The one treasure that touched my soul the most was the elderly woman sitting next to me while we were on a bus being shuttled from one place to another. She seemed to be older than I was, frail and very soft-spoken. The ride was a short one. By the time I found out who she was, we had to depart from the bus.

While I was trying to get her name and the name of her hotel, the archbishop who was in charge of our bus cruelly hustled me on. When I tried to explain to him what I had found and wanted a chance to get her name and address, *he*

Me, Der Hayer Dervishian and Dekmejian (Washington DC, 1985)

promised me he would make a special effort to bring us back together that very evening in the banquet hall. *Did I believe him?* Emotionally, I hoped, but my mind told me otherwise. I had the sinking feeling I would never see her again.

My frustration was aggravated more that evening when I was brushed aside for the second time when the archbishop didn't show any intention to help me to locate that woman. He showed no compassion nor did he understand the essence of my quest. All I asked from him was courtesy, the slight chance of *consoling one of my eternal pains.* How could he be so heartless? Did he have any understanding what the survivors experienced in 1915? *Did he even care?*

I had just discovered that this woman had come all the way from France to attend this event and the air travel and the arrangements were too exhausting for her. Once I found out she was from Perri, I began to delve into her family background. *She was Kevork Noroian's relative. . .* my best friend! She reacted to my excitement and tears I couldn't hold back. She was just beginning to tell me what had happened on that bestial day when Kevork, along with hundreds of other Perritzees were tortured, slain and dumped in the river. I still *tremble* when I recall the image of his stare looking straight at me with his one eye, the other gouged out by a beast or a Turk. It's as if he was trying to ask me why? The pain he and the others had endured on that infamous day when Korr-Mamoe and I were walking towards his friend's house.

I searched in vain to find her. My heart was wounded once more because I knew I wouldn't see her again. *I resigned to hopelessness. I have often wondered what this frail woman would have been able to reveal to me.* It pains me even more when I remember how much faith and respect my father had in the church. I have never met a person who believed more than he has. *Meghk...*

The fourth person I saw was Hovannes Dekmejian. We readily recognized each other because we had previously encountered each other in Los Angeles. He had now moved to Washington, DC to be closer to his daughter. We saw each other on the last day of the program at the Arlington Cemetery for the Armenian Genocide memorial services. Thousands were in attendance.

In all I met survivors from India, Australia, Europe and South America. *With what expectations had they all come?* This convention surely was a once in a lifetime experience for all of us. Yet again we survivors were let down by those who planned and organized the event. . . *Meghk!* Was this a result of their disunity? It was a pity we lost the potential of a monumental, once in a lifetime opportunity. *I never did learn the main purpose of the convention.*

41. REFLECTIONS AND APPRECIATION

From every harrowing experience, every torturous tragedy and atrocity my eyes and ears witnessed during my six years of persecution, I led a dog's life. From the moment my father left the four of us in front of the Turkish *maktab* (school) till I reached Haleb, I felt every Armenian that crossed my path was mine and I was theirs. In other words *I felt I had to support and help any Armenian in need as best as I could and likewise I would be helped in the same manner. We had to help each other.*

Feigning to be a Turk, as we walked in the streets of Kharpert amongst ourselves, we recognized each other with a glance from our eyes. Within our souls we knew and felt each other's pain and suffering. Again, with our eyes, we reassured each other that we would stick together and protect one another.

You, my dear reader, if you were there, you would have felt exactly the same, and in the same way you would have helped with your heart, mind and soul. Those feelings have always remained with me. They will never leave my soul.

By the 1960s Armenian professionals had gradually began to emerge in various fields such as medicine, science, education, film, and politics. They made us feel very proud we were Armenians. We had rejuvenated. We wished each and every one of them success and hoped they would achieve even higher goals and stature. *If we are to realize our Armenian Case, we must all encourage and support those individuals so that we can present a united force throughout the world.*

I greatly admire the Alex Manoogian family, Kirk Krikorian, the Hovnanian brothers—some of our benevolent benefactors. I am aware there are many others but unfortunately these are the only names I can now recall.

FILM PRODUCER

By chance, in the mid-sixties, *Hagopig,* Dr. Mikahil's son came back into my life. I felt so proud when I discovered he had pursued his beloved father's endeavors. He too has devoted his life where his father had left off.

During those Black Days, I hadn't realized the impact of the doting unconditional affection *Hagopig* and his sister generously gave to me when they were still babies.

Dr. J. Michael Hagopian

I was no more than sixteen to seventeen years old at that time, still an adolescent. I was lost in a quandary of questions about what was happening. By then my eyes and ears had witnessed so many atrocities. I was in complete despair. Not a day went by when I wasn't tormented, wondering and worrying about my father, sisters, and brothers.

I have always felt a deep appreciation for Dr. Mikahil in retrospect. *I had no idea what that particular day would mean to me for the rest of my life.* That special day when my Aunt Zaruhy walked me to the doctor's house hoping he could use me for menial chores—dark became light.

It was God's will that I have that gift during the most turbulent, trying years of my life, my transition from a youth to adulthood. *Now, I had found Hagopig, or Michael the name he now uses, in the prime of his adulthood. The son of the most benevolent person I have known.

As Michael grew up in America, he went to the university, pursued two fields, International Relations and Cinema, that enabled him to devote the rest of his life to the cause that had *pained his heart forever.*

In the 1960s he spear headed the establishment of the UCLA Narekatsi Chair of Armenian Studies. In 1979, he was also a founding member of the Armenian Film Foundation. Most recently in the year 2000, he was the founding chairman of the Friends of the UCLA Armenian Language and Culture Studies.

Michael has devoted his time researching, writing and producing educational and documentary films. *Most of his time and effort, however, has been spent documenting the carnage and destruction perpetrated by the Turks upon the*

Armenians from 1915-1923. The fruit of his work will enhance the quest for justice for the Armenian case—he had followed his father's footsteps.

His latest and most prominent undertaking has covered more than twenty years of research and filming of Armenian survivors living on almost every continent in the world. *With over three hundred and fifty interviews he has developed a project called "The Witness," a trilogy—documenting the truth. . . the horrors of the Armenian Genocide.*

Whenever I hug Michael, one hug is for him and another is for his father, a man who selflessly helped Armenians in need. An Armenian son, like the rays of the sun, May God be his protector. May He bless him, his wife, Antoinette, and children.

A DEDICATED HISTORIAN

Shortly after my unexpected encounter with *Hagopig*, I became acquainted with Richard Hovannisian, a professor of Armenian History at the University of California at Los Angeles. He has dedicated his life to research documenting our turbulent past.[*] Both of his parents were Kharpertzees. His mother was from Buzmehshen; the same village where I joined a group of boys to help an American soldier search for large and suitable houses to be converted into orphanages for the hundreds of Armenian orphans whose parents had been brutally slaughtered. *Akh, akh*—what a heart wrenching day that was. Whenever I see Richard Hovannisian or his mother, those images and feelings well up in my mind. His parents are to be commended. May God bless him, his supportive wife Vartiter and children.

[*]   With great enthusiasm Ovsanna and I participated in the UCLA project and poured our souls out to be audio-taped with the expectation, finally, the "voices" of our survivors were to be recorded! All that we suffered and all that we lost would **now** "be heard" . . . Almost 30 years have gone by and I have been waiting and wondering **what has been done** with our input? Sadly the voices of 800 survivors **remain silent** in the UCLA archives! *Meghk, meghk!*

I am equally proud of his son, Raffi Hovannisian, who has a large space in my heart. Like his father, he has devoted himself to our cause. May God's watch always be over this family, his gracious wife Armenouhi, who likewise is actively devoted in these endeavors and may their children follow the aspirations of their parents, grandparents and great grandparents.

GOVERNOR GEORGE DEUKMEJIAN

Governor George Deukmejian and me
(Los Angeles, 1980s)

Our first pioneer in American political life to hold a high office was George Deukmejian. Deukmejian came from a noble family. He was born to be an upright son. Upon taking his oath of office, he became an honorable political pioneer for Armenians. Deukmejian reached out to the Armenian community and provided leadership elevating and strengthening them and their issues. First he served as a California State Senator for sixteen years, then as a District Attorney for eight years, and finally as the Governor of California, the largest state in the United States, for two terms. *His words were not empty platitudes and promises.* The Armenian legacy of blind faith and betrayal changed! The faith of the Armenians in *this* honorable man was a new beginning of hope! This was a divine moment for all Armenians.

As much as he was able, he was concerned with Armenian issues. In addition to enhancing the quality of life in California, Deukmejian provided career opportunities for many qualified Armenians seeking high positions. Within a

Senator Chuck Poochigian, his wife Debbie, Zaruhy, and me, 1999

short period, they too proved to be successful and productive in their respective posts, serving the State and their community.

May God increase and support individuals like this worthy Armenian son who took the burden upon his shoulders to be at the helm for eight years as the thirty fifth Governor of the most populated state of the strongest country in the world. That is another gift I will take to my father, a miracle we should not take for granted. May God bless and protect him, his lovely wife, Gloria, and their children.

SENATOR CHARLES "CHUCK" POOCHIGIAN

I feel extremely fortunate to have lived long enough to witness and to personally have become acquainted with *a great grandson from Perri successfully engaged in political life and for that he has a unique place in my heart.*

With much acclaim Chuck Poochigian is a source of light for all of us. As a California State Senator, he is serving his constituency as well as his own people. Since his time in office, he has been responsible for many improvements for the people of California. He worked equally hard for the passage of a law waiving the statute of limitations on life insurance policies held by victims of the Armenian Genocide. He was also responsible for the statute allowing April 24, the Armenian Day of Commemoration for the victims of the 1915 Genocide to be officially observed in the State of California.

In the prime of his life, he is greatly respected by his peers because of his past accomplishments. At the same time he shows much promise for the future.

Chuck Poochigian has brought honor and pride to all Armenians. With his charm, endearing smile and the twinkle in his eyes, I cannot resist giving him a big hug whenever I see him. *That hug is not only for me, but also for all of our martyrs from Perri.* He also comes from an honorable family and has a sincere heart. May God bless him, his partner in life, Deborah, and their family, most especially his dear parents, grandparents and great grandparents who raised sons who have *upheld our eternal commitments.* May God bless them all and show them the light to continue our pursuit. May he bless this family with love and good health and may they receive the support and kindness they have given to others.

VOICES THAT COUNT

Another offspring from a village in Charsanjak, Levon Katerjian must be commended not only for his unique voice, but more so for many of his songs reflecting the pain and suffering endured by his parents under the Turkish wrath! May he too have a long life and his dream fulfilled—*returning to his parent's house in the foothills of Charsanjak to sing his swan song.*

I am equally appreciative of Charles Aznavour who has not forgotten his roots even though he is recognized world wide for his distinctive voice and self-written songs. *He touches my heart with his devotion to Armenia and the Armenian cause—*as well for his loyalty to France, the country of his birth.

May God enhance the brilliant steps these Armenians have undertaken to inspire our youth to follow in their footsteps!

TRUE FRIENDS OF THE ARMENIANS

We can no longer be content to rely only on our children and grandchildren to support and defend our Armenian Case. We must also strive to impress non-Armenians to become involved with our efforts to achieve our goals.

We were alone during the dark days of the Genocide, unlike the Turks, who from the very beginning **sought foreign involvement to carry out their sinister plot to annihilate all of the Armenians living on their indigenous homelands.** We have been too slow in that respect.

It was only by *sheer chance* that we received the first genuine support from a very honorable and influential figure with political clout. In his humble manner he showed his personal appreciation for the Armenian physician, Dr. Hampar Kelikian, who skillfully treated his World War II battlefield wounds and enabled him to lead a normal productive life—a bond was created between Senator Bob Dole and the Armenian community. *No other non-Armenian political figure has* *been so sincerely supportive with all of our Armenian issues extending over so many years.*[*]

US Senator Bob and Elizabeth Dole, 2002

We are additionally blessed *that Elizabeth Dole has equally been supportive of our cause.* Armenians worldwide acknowledge this couple for their devotion. *I extend my personal respect and appreciation to this very special couple. May God bless them and may they, in turn, receive the support and kindness they have given to others worldwide.*

Elizabeth Dole has a *unique* and very special place in my heart and soul for which I will always be grateful. This chance meeting first took place at the Armenian Martyr's Memorial Monument in Montebello, California where she had come to campaign for her husband's presidential elections in 1996.

By the 1990s, Ovsanna and I were physically frail and had our doubts about our ability to attend. The monument is set upon a hilltop and the upward climb was not going to be easy for us this time. However, we were both determined to make an effort for this special opportunity, *to show our respects and appreciation.*

From our past experiences we knew we had to get there early enough to find a suitable place so we could hear and see her.

Going early and waiting an hour or two was not the problem. Our physical

---

[*]   In the year 1998, I would like to express my sincere appreciation and gratitude for all the **current** and subsequent legislators who are genuinely concerned and supportive of our plight—I have prayed 88 years for this effort and involvement! May God be with them and with us!

stamina was the issue. Would we be able to make it? I now had a numbing sensation in my feet while sitting or standing in one place for a long period of time—poor circulation caused an unbearable throbbing sensation in both legs—and Ovsanna was now frail and weak. We did our best and made the effort.

Luckily, going early helped. We got a seat at the end of the front row. Finally, after a couple of hours of waiting Elizabeth Dole was introduced. From our angle we didn't have a clear view of her, but we were able to hear and understand her very well. I was not sure if she looked towards us or if she saw us. Nevertheless, I was deeply touched when I heard her voice repeat several times, "Bob Dole is a true friend of the Armenians and he will always do his best to support and help the Armenian Case."

I was completely overwhelmed at the conclusion of Elizabeth Dole's heart-warming speech. I wanted to personally shake her hand and thank her and her husband for their sincere support. I wanted to reveal to her what their commitment meant to a survivor. **How much we appreciated that a U.S. Senator had the integrity to acknowledge the atrocities committed by the Ottoman Turks upon the Armenians and that this crime must be addressed in an international court.**

Instinctively, I got up and started to shuffle up towards her as quickly as my feet would move. My feet were numb. I did my best to advance holding firmly onto my cane. I knew I had to get up there before she was whisked away. Suddenly, I felt Ovsanna tugging on my jacket attempting to bring me back, but I pulled away and got loose causing an awkward moment in view of everyone. This time I wasn't going to allow *anyone* to stop me. I knew Ovsanna was only trying to protect me from another disappointment. She knew the *well-trained* scouts would rush over and stop me from approaching Elizabeth Dole.

No one was going to stop me. I continued to shuffle, the weakness in my legs became a disadvantage. I was inches away from Elizabeth Dole when I suddenly felt two strong arms stopping and turning me away—like a criminal I bowed my head and started back. Again, the insensitivity and indifference to my aching soul thwarted my ambitions and dreams.

Much to my surprise, within seconds the scouts stopped as we all heard, *"Oh, please do bring the gentleman back!"* I was quickly led back. I shall never forget the hug and thank you Elizabeth Dole bestowed upon me. I shall never forget her smile and delightful reaction embracing a survivor! How could I ever forget this honor from such a grand and worthy person? *She understood why I had gone up there. It was her humility and respect for the elderly, a survivor of the Turkish atrocities.*

In my opinion, from its inception when the Armenian community considered to establish a monument it wanted a permanent site where Armenians could commemorate their martyrs, survivors, and the loss of their homelands. A site where Armenians could congregate on April 24 to listen to the accounts of the few remaining survivors who miraculously escaped. To learn what happened to them and the horrific means used by the Turks.

If you don't know what the survivors experienced and saw, what they lost and how they suffered, how could you pursue the Armenian Cause? **If you don't appreciate the personal accounts revealed by the few remaining survivors, still physically and mentally capable, who are the only living authentic witnesses, how could you justify your case by only seeking lost documentation?**

Unfortunately, at this time in the year 2003 we have already lost this *precious opportunity*. What a *critical* loss that has been. For now, you can only count on your fingers the number of survivors capable of relating those torturous accounts that transpired during those dark days.

In addition this site was to provide the opportunity for survivors to gather together to share with one another the pains and grief locked within their souls and memories. *There was hope perhaps this opportunity would bring consolation and psychological closure before their eyes were closed.*

Only these witnesses and the predator Turks knew the severity the heinous crimes that transpired during the methodically well concealed atrocities committed by the Turks. **All their deeds and actions were well planned and executed deliberately to obliterate recriminating evidence.**

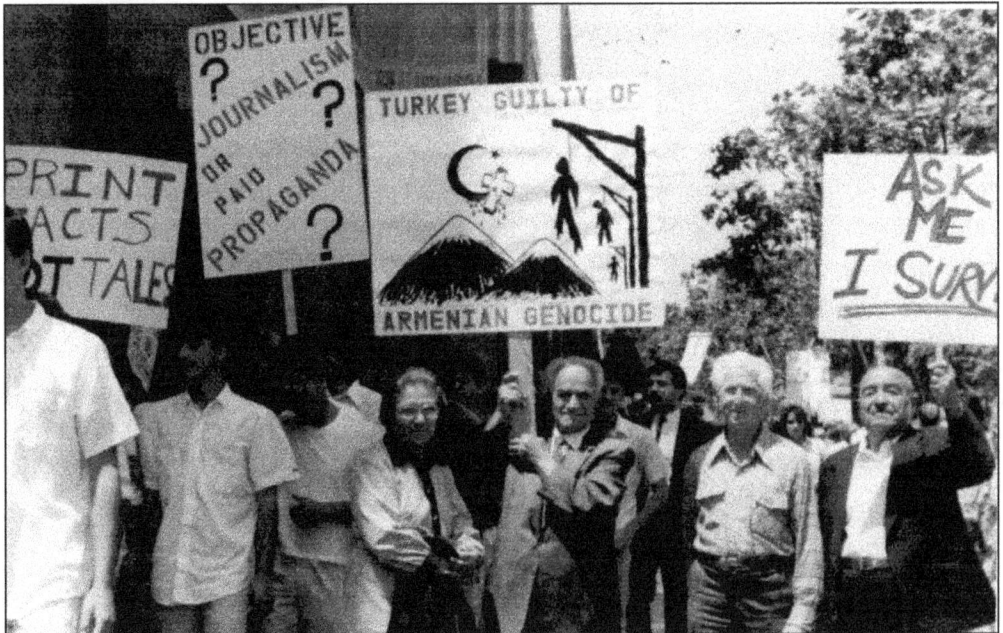

Who will carry the Torch after I am gone?

By the late 1950s, we knew the world powers would not take the initiative to help us in addressing our Cause. In the 1960's, we knew we had to rely solely on our own strength. We organized many significant marches proclaiming our rights and demands with the hope our cause would be heard and addressed. These marches were more than three miles long with five to ten thousand participants, including young and old, the wheelchair bound and baby strollers. The Armenian population in Southern California was not more than 30,000 at the time! *There was the spirit of unity among the organizers and the participants.* The marches concluded at the monument where a program followed. *Initially, these programs were meaningful and encouraging. Prominent speakers and dignitaries took part. We came home feeling optimistic with the hope our long held aspirations were coming true.*

Gradually, within a few years, little by little it became apparent our initial aspirations were not to materialize. Little by little, the scope of participation dwindled. Ironically, as the number of Armenians in the area was increasing, the number of survivors dramatically began to wane. The purpose and objectives of the programs began to lose its meaningful intent. The lack of unity of purpose among those conducting the programs was sensed in the atmosphere. *Now we came home disenchanted with feelings of despair and hopelessness that the struggle for our cause was mishandled and abused.*

Even our basic values and traditions were corrupted. The mood of the occasion, a memorial service, became one of a picnic—depicted by the attire of the participants, the boisterous laughter and play, the inattentiveness of the congregation. *Gone was the solemn mood and purpose honoring and respecting our martyrs, survivors and lost homelands. . .*

One of the images that has not left my soul is that of an elderly woman bent from the waist almost at a ninety degree angle, struggling alone to ascend the slope of the hillside. Where were the well-trained scouts to assist her? Whose great-grandmother was she? *What memories and feelings had she harbored that compelled her to make this pilgrimage to pay her respect to our martyrs?* As she approached the top of the hill, she gave a deep sigh of relief when she found a chair to sit. The chairs were set up under a canopy providing protection from the blazing sun. She was unaware the chairs were not provided for her or the rest of the congregation. I felt so sad when a scout rushed over and exclaimed, "*Mayrig,* you can't sit in this area, these chairs are for *our special guests,*" insinuating she was not "a special guest." Without a word but with an exhausted and weary expression she got up and stood side by side with the rest of us under the hot sun. My thoughts crumbled into pieces, I was completely disheartened. *What has happened to our traditional values, our religious upbringing?*

The sole purpose of our monument to honor and respect our martyrs and survivors was completely disgraced. The program lasted more than two to three hours, if not

Elizabeth Dole honoring an Armenian survivor of the Genocide, Hampartzoum Chitjian
(Los Angeles, 2001)

more. I don't remember if the elderly woman remained to the end of the program but I cannot forget that one to two hundred chairs remained empty throughout the program. *My soul was crushed. Was this the discipline our scouts are being taught? Meghk! What more can I say. . .*

Even though I had lost hope during the last few years when Ovsanna and I barely had the physical stamina to fulfill our responsibility to honor and respect our martyrs we continued to attend. To our dismay, the programs had lost *their sincere intent* since there was obvious discord among the leaders and between the clergy. Ovsanna and I gave our private respects and sincere prayers prevailing within our hearts and returned home *disenchanted!*

Now you can understand more fully my appreciation for Elizabeth Dole's response to my request—within one moment she recognized and understood the pain of a survivor!

Fortunately, since this episode, I have had three to four occasions to personally thank Elizabeth Dole, along with her husband, for their support of the Armenian community. I doubt she remembers me, but each time I am given a humble hug and recognition as a survivor. *I could only wish our leaders would recognize her grace and humility as an example to emulate and to educate our youth.*

It saddens me to recall this in public, but I hope our leaders take note. *My prime concern is that we do not lose our dignity, our traditions. Our ancestral traditions could shine above those of any nation. Was this not one of the reasons the Ottoman Turk* wanted to finish us off? What is our ultimate goal but to preserve and enhance our traditions, culture and values. . . all what it means to be Armenian.

The following is a translation of some thoughts I had written in Armenian immediately following my visit to the Armenian Martyrs' Monument in Montebello on April 24, 1996:

In my old age, it was hard to believe it. I wish my eyes were blind so that I would not have seen nor read about it. It was unbelievable but it is true.

I have always been present at this monument on April 24th from the time the monument was constructed. The crowds have been measured in the tens of thousands. Political figures, clergymen, independent people, laity and all of them yell that they want retribution from the Turks, and they want to retaliate against the Turks. But no one hears their words. Their words don't hold any measure. In Turkish they say, "The day of the Armenians passes with chatter." Or, "The dog barks and our caravan continues to roll."

This year, I went to the monument but there weren't many people there. At this gathering I heard the voice of the splendid wife of Bob Dole. In her voice, I received the world. In a loud voice she said that Bob Dole would represent the needs of the Armenian people. This Senator gave us hope. God's voice, the events of the Genocide, all moved me to walk towards the angelic wife of Bob Dole. I wanted to tell her that I am ninety-five years old and a survivor of the Genocide and to shake her hand. They motioned for me to go away. Then one of her bodyguards came over and motioned for me to come back. She hugged me and kissed me. In my entire life, I had never felt this way. God was with me. I have endured much pain. I remembered father, mother, brother, sister, relatives, bodies and bones.

Armenians… come together! Unite! Speak well! Hold faithful to your principles! Don't alienate those who have been saved from the evil Turks! My age is old. My pains are many. I am a disappointed survivor.

Hampartzoum Chitjian

42. EXPECTATIONS FROM THE ARMENIAN YOUTH

From the 1960s to the mid-1990s, I attended many of the events and programs that concerned the Armenian cause. From a select few, I began to sense a glimmer of hope. These young men and women had assumed the **monumental task pursuing justice.**

Perhaps there was a Divine plan for Armenians to be scattered in all corners of the world. Armenian youth in all of their respective countries are seeking to resolve our case in the international arena. *Without the will of God, the leaves on the trees do not move.*

May they never forget the recorded accounts our survivors witnessed, the heinous, brutal acts perpetrated by the Turks in 1915 upon innocent Armenian citizens:

> . . . *the beautiful strands of hair, some still braided, clinging onto the tree branches along the banks of the rivers, or on the brush in ravines—loosely tangled locks of brown, blond, and black hair waving in the wind.*
>
> . . . *and the butchered, mutilated corpses strewn wherever the unfortunate victims took their last breath—corpses not only victimized by the barbaric Turk, but also by the crazed dogs roaming the desolate lands, perhaps the pets who once had long lost their masters.*
>
> . . . *and the pile of bones in mounds here and there, or maybe scattered over the hillsides, some half buried and some staring straight at you—bones and bodies of newborn infants, the hardest to witness.*
>
> . . . *or the screams and cries of those silenced by a whip or sword— the same screams and cries of those forced to witness the demise of his or her loved ones.*
>
> . . . *or the stench that revealed an earlier carnage—different from the stench of the more recent carnage.*
>
> . . . *or encountering the living dead, with bodies so badly mutilated, their hands, feet, tongues, or ears chopped off—eyes gouged out, dangling from their sockets, feet tied to a branch, with heads dangling downward, all left alive just barely enough to suffer the pain.*

. . . multitudes trapped in their churches and set afire to finish what the sword didn't accomplish.

. . . and the simple crazed, most likely a witness to one or more of the above, allowed to roam the streets, no longer in control of themselves.

This list can go on and on. . .

Again, I repeat: survivors who have seen this partial list of beastial acts appreciates the young, vibrant youth who chose to devote their lives to redress our case.

NAMES NOT TO BE FORGOTTEN

I mostly admired Gourken Yanikian for his ideals and courage, when he justifiably took revenge for the murder of his father, mother, and countrymen. He was himself arrested. He was tried, convicted, imprisoned. In the twilight years of his life, he closed his eyes knowing *he had impressed upon the youth that our cause is just and has yet to be addressed.*

Thereafter, I followed Hampig Sassoonian's case. I attended several of his court hearings, as I did with Yanikian's. While I understand his motives, I truly believe he wasn't guilty and is wrongfully imprisoned—only to appease the Turks.

With the same admiration, I am proud and appreciative of the Lisbon Commandos, Sarkis Aprahamian, Setrag Ajemian, Vache Daghlian, Simon Yahneian, and Ara Keyelian. . . and equally proud of those "few" whose names have not been mentioned!

I was equally proud of Mr. and Mrs. Ajemian, when they said, "As proud patriots of our country, we wouldn't stop any one of our other children!" They truly express how I feel.

Death is the same everywhere. A man dies only once. *Fortunate is the man who dies for his country.* All of those individuals are our heroes. My only wish and plea is that we speak with one voice so that their sacrifices will not have been made in vain. **All men have the right to defend themselves and their nation.** That is the truth and the only truth. My only wish is that I had been a strand of hair on the heads of those fathers and that I had made the sacrifice for our cause in the place of their sons.

When I die, I am going to take my father this gift, which would have been close to his heart. May God increase the shining stars like these boys, who gave us hope so we could rejoice and have a better future.

May we all remember and never forget Soghomon Tehlirian, who bravely assassinated one of the chief Turkish perpetrators, Talaat Pasha the most instrumental culprit, in revenge of the atrocities committed against the

Armenians. He was tried in a German court of law and acquitted. He had the right to do what he did. Unfortunately, that was not enough. Thousands of culprits were not convicted and tried for the crimes they committed against the Armenian nation. *Thus, our "case" is still pending.*

I cannot repeat enough that our offspring must always remember that they are the children of the innocent martyrs of the attempted annihilation by the barbaric Turk! Those martyrs and survivors expect from them only one thing— that they never give up our drive for complete justice.

Likewise, every bit that each survivor contributes will be a cumulative, indispensable testimony. Each one of us, with our effort and our own brief message, can provide the truth of what was done to us. *We can bear witness for the world to understand what really took place in Turkey from 1915-1923. The Turkish attempts to deny their heinous plot to annihilate an entire nation under its subjugation only aggravates their crime against the civil law of mankind throughout this world!*

It is with this hope that whenever the last gray haired survivor closes his eyes, he will know *this beacon of light provided by past heroes* will be the torch to guide our offspring and their descendants toward the redemption of our cause. The restoration of our nation and the glory of our historical achievements is the goal— regardless of how long this takes.

Our children should always remember the unburied bones of our innocent martyrs remain scattered all over our historical motherland, waiting for their souls to rest in peace.

My dear reader, if you haven't witnessed atrocities such as these, then read what all of the innocent surviving victims have written. Please listen to what they have said and then try to understand what they have experienced. *They have revealed what their eyes have seen, what their ears have heard, and what their bodies and minds have been subjected to.* They could only relate the genuine truth. What they experienced was too incomprehensible to be fabricated!

I repeat, let us not bury with us all that we have suffered. Let the voices of the white haired survivors be seen with the action of the devoted youth! **Let us back up and support all those who bring our cause before the international court to bring justice for the wrong that was perpetrated on the Armenians by the barbaric Turk.** May they finally address disciplinary action! If we unite our voices, we will be heard! This is the truth!

43. TWO EXPERIENCES: ONE OF JOY, ONE OF SORROW

In the latter part of 1996, by chance I discovered Isahak Yerevanian while reading particular articles in the Armenian weekly, *Nor Gyank.* Suspecting he might be related to Kevork Yerevanian, I obtained his phone number from the editor.

My hunch was right. He was Kevork's youngest brother. The minute we spoke over the phone, there was a mutual feeling of kinship. Within days, we went to visit him and his wife. He and his family had recently immigrated to the United States from Beirut because of the civil war in Lebanon.

Isahak was born in 1915. Thus, he didn't have personal memories of the *charrt.* *Vicariously,* he lived the atrocities through the related experiences of his family, his mother, brothers and sisters. Therefore, he can empathize and relate to my feelings and experiences. He is familiar with our life in Perri. *Even at this age,* we developed a very special bond and became as close as brothers. Finally, I had discovered a kinship from Perri.

During our first visit, he informed me of his only living brother, Khosrov. He was living in Dubai, United Arab Emirates, with his daughter. Isahak felt Khosrov

Isahak and me

would have a lot to share with me since he was older. The very next day, I wrote a letter to Khosrov introducing myself and my experiences.

In 1997, during my second visit with Isahak, he gave me a second gift, a copy of his brother Kevork's book, *A History of the Armenians of Charsanjak. This was a treasure for me.*

Kevork Yerevanian

Kevork was one of my schoolmates in Perri. He was one or two years older than me. His book is very impressive. I highly recommend it to anyone who is interested to learn more about that region. In 700 pages, Yerevanian brought light to history of an era of highly developed people whose history has been ignored. His inclusion of maps and photographs enhances the credence of his text. He sought research both from Armenian and non-Armenians. He minutely illustrated the borders and landscape of that area. Kevork describes the landscape, water sources, vegetation, animals, climate, and natural resources. He discusses the past history of the people and their lifestyle and their relationship with the Kurds.

The history goes back before the subjugation by the Ottoman Empire. Armenians had lived on that land for centuries. From stories handed down, it has been said that a notable priest named Simon lived in the area. Thus, throughout the centuries, the name Derseem emerged. *Der* means 'priest' and *seem* came from his name, Simon.*

Within a few months, I received a very emotional response to my letter from Khosrov. I discovered he was one of the younger boys taken to Pertahk. Unfortunately, he didn't remember my brothers Kerop and Nishan.

---

* This book, as well as many other books harboring our past, written in Armenian should be translated—we must reach those who do not read in Armenian.

The best part of his letter, however was that he was planning a trip to Los Angeles in 1998 to visit his son who had recently immigrated to the United States from Beirut.

I was so happy to have *finally* found a Perritizee to exchange sweet memories of our *yergeer*. As fate would have it, Khosrov passed away shortly before the date of his planned visit for the spring of 1998. We only had the opportunity to correspond with each other with one letter apiece. With those two letters, we shared tears of pain and suffering. That fate was also the will of God.

Celebrating our 65th anniversary

On May 2, 1998, I lost my most beloved partner in life of 69 years, my wife Ovsanna. I would not have been able to endure the two experiences simultaneously, one of joy, *one of sorrow and grief. I had now lost everything. Life was no longer meaningful for me. . .*

44. EPILOGUE

Even though so much of our three thousand year old noble past with its magnificent edifices, glorious manuscripts, artifacts, and traditions have been cruelly destroyed forever, I feel we still have a chance to rebuild on our historical homeland once again and become the distinctive and productive nation that God intended for us from the very beginning.[*]

We should never lose sight that we have endured horrific historical injustices throughout our existence because of **our tenacious determination to maintain our ethnicity and traditions that have produced extraordinary accomplishments throughout our past and present.**

What we must not forget is that *these characteristics are carried only in our offspring,* who are our most valuable possessions—*they are our resources and our weapons.*

That was the one mistake the Turks made. They underestimated **the Armenian will** to resolve the injustices they have suffered throughout their history because the love they have for their *Yergeer* is in their blood (genes).

> *This is what makes an Armenian an Armenian.*
> *This is what makes an Armenian different.*
> *It is* **this** *difference that makes us remain Armenian.*
> *Hampartzoum Chitjian*

As I have come to the last chapter of my memoirs, nothing could have made me happier than to hear the pledge from enthusiastic college students, both men and women on April 24, 2001. The United Armenian Students spoke sincerely as they represented students from all of the local universities, colleges, and high schools in Southern California. I was told their sole objective is to **unite** our communities at large to resolve the Armenian case with *one voice!*

May God be with them and their followers. May He give them strength and the light to achieve our goal. May the clergy and political organizations have the **will and foresight to allow** them to follow their course. May these two cohorts grasp the spark of the genuine enthusiasm these devoted students have undertaken and give them the **opportunity and respect to unite with one voice.**

---

[*] The lines and names on maps are constantly changing, history is not fixed, and our right to return to our homeland could still be realized one day.

Let us not lose this momentum in the new millennium, now that the major European governments are following the French to recognize our case. In addition to this movement, we must be appreciative of the prominent historical scholars from England, Germany, Israel, and even Turkey who are producing materials that reiterates the truth.

Governments without an ax to grind have no difficulty understanding or accepting our claims and supporting our efforts. I am hoping we are gradually approaching the day when the Turks could no longer shrewdly use deception and collusion as a means to promote their denial of their brutish crimes against their *innocent citizens. Time is on our side...*

Unfortunately, I have become confused, disenchanted, and gravely saddened with the American position on human rights. Has the strongest military power in the world lost sight of **its most honorable and coveted past?** Basic ideals that America once stood for? *Faith in the American ideals of freedom and justice for ALL, under God*—the ideals that refugees worldwide are seeking.

These were the reasons my father and many other fathers sent their sons to America. This is why I chose this as my adopted country. These ideals meant everything to me. The Fourth of July was the only day out of the year that I closed my market so that I could show my appreciation and faith in these *"ideals."*

Now it is difficult for me to understand how the United States professes to be the champion and guardian of human rights, justice, personal dignity, and expects and insists that the nations of the world follow the code of "Human Rights," when it has different rules and standards for different countries and for itself! **These inalienable rights cannot be compromised for political and corporate motives.**

On June 28, 2001, on the national television program, "Night Line," General Wesley Clark declared, "Sovereignty is not absolute. No leader in the world can abuse its own people and get away with it." The same night, in the evening news coverage, former Serbian President Milosevic, was turned over by his own people to be tried for international war crimes in the Hague. He was labeled "the Butcher of the Balkans."

I say, *the Ottoman Turks were the vicious barbaric butchers,* who slaughtered one and a half million innocent, defenseless Armenian civilians, citizens of the Ottoman Empire. These Turkish atrocities can no longer be denied or ignored. *Let us all support those who bring our case to the forefront of the international court so that justice for all that was perpetrated on the Armenians by the Turk will finally be settled. Finally, the Turks will face disciplinary action.*

Only then will the souls of the one and a half million martyrs, who remain scattered over the landscape of their historic homeland and the souls of the thousands of victims who survived and have now closed their eyes, buried, scattered in various countries all over the world, after their escape, be allowed to rest in peace. *This will be the moment they have all been waiting for.*

Eighty-eight years have passed since our last defeat. Now, we are just beginning our fight. As Peter Balakian has said, "This truly is the best time to be an Armenian."

The most important truth all Armenians must understand is that *no one* person or *one* organization can achieve our most coveted goal alone. May God give the Armenians the will and the wisdom to accept this fact. This is the one characteristic God has been seeking from the Armenians before He offers us solace. When they do unite, they will succeed and if they don't, we will continue to fail!

> *Turkish: "Gavouroun son akle behndeh ollsah."*
> *Armenian: "Hyeen vercheen khelkeh eendzee uhlahr."*
> *English: "If only I had the Armenians' final wisdom!"*
> **(Be afraid when they unite!)**

That is, don't be afraid of the Armenians now. Be afraid when they unite! The Turks understood us better than we understand ourselves!

Before I close my eyes eternally, my ultimate aspiration is to see this genuine unity among Armenians and the final victory of our Armenian Case. Unfortunately, I am consumed with a sense of fear and hopelessness that the essence of the following tale will prevail. . .

> *One day the Turkish beg warned his slave not to go home until he completed his job tilling the soil, otherwise, he would be beaten to a pulp.*
>
> *Just before the slave had completed his job, a friend ran up to the slave and informed him that his mother was dying and wanted him to go to her before she died.*
>
> *The slave responded, "Please tell my mother to wait, not to die until I complete my work so that I won't be punished."*
>
> *Moral: Man goes on with his own **selfish agenda** completely ignoring the poignant pleas from his ailing nation.*

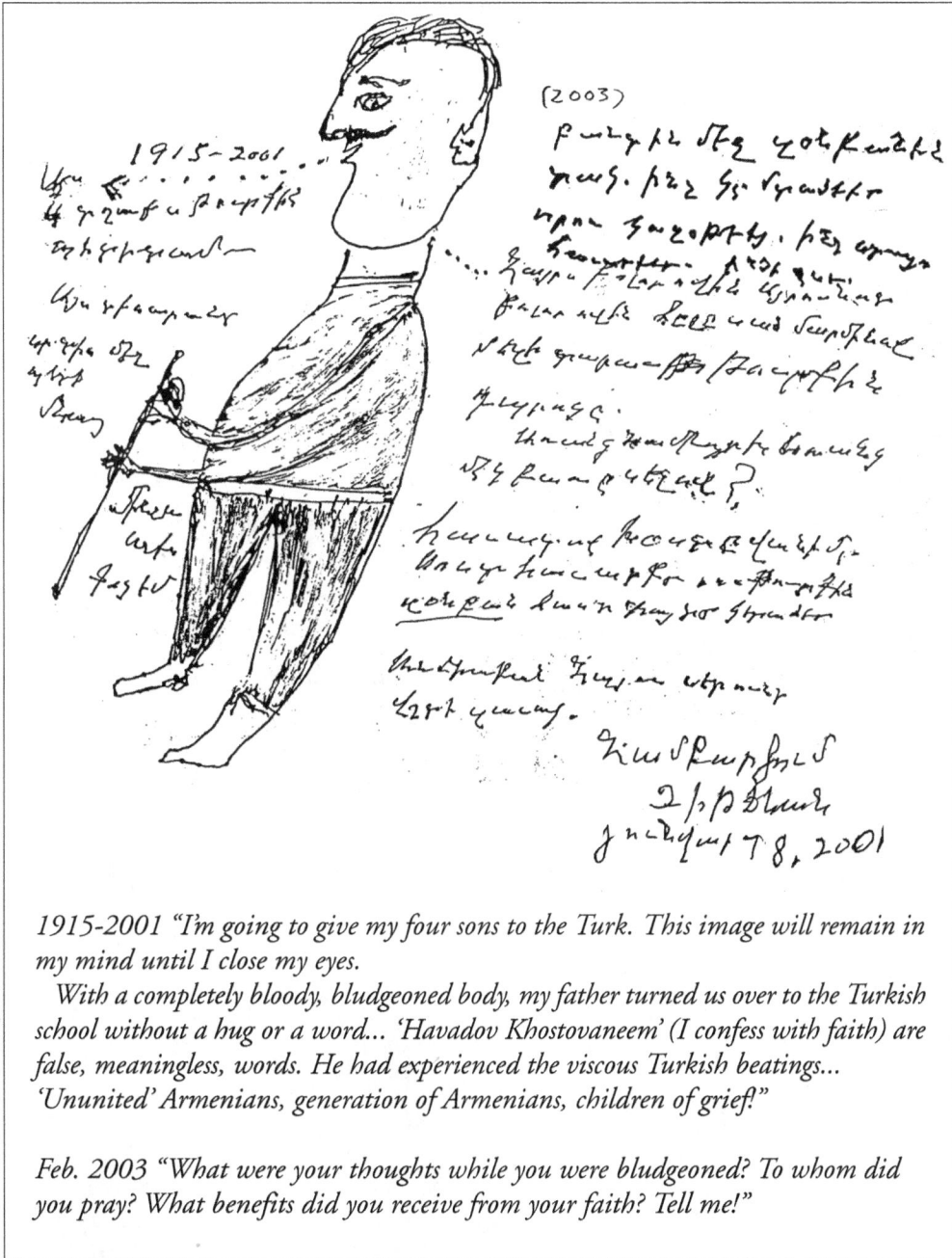

1915-2001 *"I'm going to give my four sons to the Turk. This image will remain in my mind until I close my eyes.*

With a completely bloody, bludgeoned body, my father turned us over to the Turkish school without a hug or a word... 'Havadov Khostovaneem' (I confess with faith) are false, meaningless, words. He had experienced the viscous Turkish beatings... 'Ununited' Armenians, generation of Armenians, children of grief!"

Feb. 2003 "What were your thoughts while you were bludgeoned? To whom did you pray? What benefits did you receive from your faith? Tell me!"

FINAL WORDS

A sketch first made by Hampartzoum Chitjian at the age of 100 in 2001, one day when he found himself alone. It expresses the pain and grief still festering in his mind and soul. . . recalling the last images of his father.

Up to his final days in 2003, he kept "talking" to his father, searching for solace; he kept questioning his father's faith for "revelation" for himself. This is the only sketch he has ever made.

To My Dear Reader:

With the difficulties of being one hundred and two years old, and with the loss of Ovsanna, my life companion of 69 years, I have encountered many hardships in rushing to complete my testimony to you. I now make my final plea that my candle remain lit until the Genocide of Armenians committed by the Turks from 1890-1923 be brought to the International Court and that the Armenians receive their redemption to have sovereignty of their beloved homelands and Ararat.

If you have read what I have shared with you, then I am sure you have understood what took place in 1915 and the significance of the consequence of those losses for the Armenians.

Please accept my gratitude and appreciation for your devoted time and understanding.

Hampartzoum Mardiros Chitjian (2003)

Hampartzoum Chitjian, Los Angeles, 2001

APPENDIX

1915   իմ Սիրուն Հարսնարիանէ   1994

վերապրողնե․ յուշերու և վկայութեր․
Դատժեզ այն նկղպաական և աղջատ․դի
որաատ Ֆարձիք օրրածատ ելատն հայ
Դապթանհերուն

1. ․ Ճատքնրժ․   երե նիզայեն Հայգժեատ
    ննեա Գատհգել․ ութ եերա ատմեժ․
1915 ժաժի օրերաժ․վաց Թարբեն ատատեղ
վարե իր վեցե․ Բրուաա իրաժեժրա ֆրեզա,
և ժիերաժաատ այ օժել․՝ Հաժթ ջ Թարֆեր ա ր
վերապրագ ևաղ ժե ապայեր․․ 13ֆապքֆեմ զ զաժ

2. ․ Ճատքնրժ․ ․ Գիատ ար․ եաթա-Մեթ Թար
    1917 1923․ Դատրատթատ․ հատթաղ
    Գ թա 2500 ֆա ատեժ հատ Հատե Հատեժ Ժ ժատ

3. Թատքե․ Եերա նեզ Հա թ ժ․Մեթ Ճատե
    20 հատա Աատ Հա թ Հատ հայ ատ ատ․
    Բատե ատ Հատատ Թատ Գե վ ատ ․

4. Մեգ թատ ատ զ․ Գատ թ ատ զ ատա ատ
    15․․ որ ե ատ Գատ Ժ ատ․ հայ ատ
    ատ ատ ատ ատ ․ ․ ․ ․ ․

THESE FOUR MEN SHOULD ALWAYS BE REMEMBERED

My Name is Hampartzoum

A survivor. From my memories and feelings the most humanitarian, benevolent, altruistic men who helped survivors and deportees are:

1. Kharpert—Dr. Mikahil Hagopian: a most esteemed, self-sacrificing doctor during the most terrifying days of the 1915 Genocide. While fearing for his own life and that of his family, he still tended to the gravely ill, gave money to the needy and did his best to help those fleeing from the claws of the barbaric Turk.

2. Kharpert—Kude Archbishop Mekhitarian 1917-1923. With much difficulty found a way to locate and rescue more than 2,500 orphans from hell and led them to safety in Haleb (Aleppo).

3. Tabriz—Nerses Melik Tankian 1922. Tried his best to help 20,000 starving soldiers fleeing from Bolshevic Armenia and the survivors from Turkey.

4. Mexico City—Gabriel Babayan who was the first Armenian in Mexico City who welcomed and helped Armenian refugees to establish themselves with jobs and homes in Mexico, 1923.

(*Top*) J. Dr. Mikahil Hagopian
(*Middle*) Archbishop Melik Tankian
(*Bottom*) Kiud Mekhitarian, wife Lucia, daughter Shakeh, and son Manoog. Brazil, 1936.

Between my two parents who
shared different inherent qualities,
I acquired a unique impression of
what makes the Renaissance Armenian

Being their daughter
is truly an honor,

Zaruhy,
2003

A Note from Sara Chitjian: Mishmeeshian Story

Shortly before this book was ready to go to press (October 2002) with the astute input of Lena Kaimian (my typist), we learned there was a Mishmeeshian family listed in the Chicago Armenian telephone directory.

With our telephone call, we learned Levon (Leon) Mishmeeshian and an older sister, Havas, had survived. Their father was Abraham Mishmeeshian (shoe maker). But as misfortune would have it, we were informed by Mary (Levon's widow), that Levon had just passed away at the age of ninety-five. That was 40 days prior to our phone call—once again we were "cheated" of the opportunity to have a personal exchange of mutual recollections and heartaches.

However, Mary was able to furnish us with a copy of Levon's memoirs which was published in the *Armenian Weekly* on April 25, 1981 in Chicago.

While it was unnerving to read Levon's account (about how much he suffered and lost), it was not surprising to read about the similarities of the basic brutalities at the onset of the "charrt" which took place in Perri starting with the closing of the school, the rounding up, imprisonment and torture of the local men. His mother, also, was led to believe the government was allowing all those who had relatives in America the safety to join them.

Their ordeal reveals the carnage that took place on the deportations throughout the Der Zor desert. At the onset there were 700 members in their group—primarily women and children—the men were all killed, including his father. Levon was left with his mother, his 18 year old sister, Havas (Hakalmazian); her three year old daughter, Araxie; Boghos, his eldest sister's son; and Zarman, his cousin Sarkis' wife (Sarkis was in America with his brother Kevork, Havas' husband).* The women and girls disguised their appearances making themselves

---

* Sarkis eventually remarried and had two daughters with his second wife.

less appealing to ward off the vicious brutalities inflicted by the wanton beastly Turks.

Several months later, only 35 deportees had survived when they finally reached Haleb (Aleppo). Along the way Levon and Havas witnessed their mother, Araxie, Boghos and Zarman "perish" with the others—that is a memory never to be forgotten! At the age of seven, Levon remembered:

> *Very vividly I remember it was a day after Easter, in the school during class, when Turkish police appeared, and soon after, the class was dismissed.*
>
> *A few days later, the stores in Perry were closed. (The city of Perry is located in the province of Kharpert) and my father with neighbor Hagop Apar and my cousin Ohan Apar were at our house conversing, and I was playing on a nearby roof top of a neighbor's house. I noticed two Turkish policemen entering our house. Terrified, I ran in and saw the police asking questions and my mother was crying. A few minutes later, the three of them were tied together, and were taken to prison.*
>
> *One day my mother and sister suggested that I take some food to my father in prison. While in prison, I saw my father and many other depressed people, tears in their eyes but silent. None of them said a word to me. My father embraced me and told me to go home.*
>
> *The Turkish police would invade the homes to search for guns. They would beat the man of the house in the presence of his family demanding his gun. If he surrendered his only gun, they would demand another one. If he swore that he never saw a gun in his life, they would suggest that he get one from somewhere and take it to the police. They had one thing in their mind: with some excuse to arrest them and take them to prison.*
>
> *At the prison, they submitted them to unimaginable tortures. They pulled their fingernails, put nails to their hands and feet, and at night tied them together and took them to a nearby river, killed them and threw their bodies in the river.*
>
> *A few weeks after these terrifying days, the town crier began informing the Armenians, that any person who has relatives in America should be prepared. In two days, they will start their journey going there.*
>
> *Most of Perry's families had some relative in America. The cunning government thought to massacre the whole Armenian population of the city wasn't an easy task to perform in the city, so the best way was to take them out of the city, and annihilate them with some means.*
>
> *The government gave us permission to take with us our belongings, as much as we could carry.*
>
> *Early in the morning, hundreds of us who had relatives in America, gathered at the outskirts of the city, and we began our journey.*
>
> *The caravan was escorted with Turkish soldiers carrying guns with bayonets on them. . .*

*Back row left to right: Leon Mishmeeshian, his sister Havas Hakalmazian,
who was with him in the Armenian Genocide, and her husband Nishan.
Front row: Leon's nephew Harry Hakalmazian and niece Araxie
Hakalmazian. Chicago, Illinois, 1928.*

After three days of walking under the blazing sun, we came to a city that was called Palu. Soldiers commanded us to gather in the field, not far from the city.

In the city of Palu, or in the vicinity, we didn't see any people, either they were deported from the city before us or all had been massacred.

We were there not very long when the Kurds from the villages came to pillage the caravan. Some of the mothers remembering the shocking sights on the road—mothers being killed and the children besides them crying—were begging the Kurds to take their children, so if they are killed, at least their children will have a chance to live. . .

As we were passing the bridge on the Palu River, we heard gun shots. A woman had thrown herself in the river. The woman was Perry's minister's wife. She wanted to commit suicide, before she would be submitted to unthinkable suffering. The soldiers didn't want her to take her own life, they wanted to kill her; that was the reason they were shooting at her.

Three days after we left Palu, the soldiers commanded us to walk to the top of the mountain and wait there for their command. A few minutes later they ordered all men to separate from women and children, and forced them down in the valley. They were the forty men who were released from the prison to go to America.

The helpless people could hear gun shots from the valley, and they knew what was going on, but what could they do? Nothing but cry and pray silently.

In less than half an hour, soldiers returned and arrogantly told the mournful people that their loved ones were so terrified that not much blood flew from their wounds.

I saw one of the soldiers carrying the rug that my father was carrying. I swiftly ran to him and demanded the rug. Immediately, the soldier raised his sword to nullify me. My sister ran to him and begged for mercy, explaining to him that I was only a child, I didn't know what I was doing.

After days of walking, careful not to step on dead bodies that were everywhere on the road, we came to a city called Gumish Madan.

We didn't see any Armenians. We thought they all must have been massacred, as we were expecting the same thing would happen to us soon. We passed the night on the outskirts of the city. In the morning we began our journey. . . .

Levon's account was so similar to my father's up to that point—it really was *unbelievable*—two different people, different ages, from different places, remembering almost the same situation!

We also learned from Mary that Levon had a cousin living in Lincoln, Massachusetts with her daughter Mariam Felegian. We were surprised to learn his cousin, Olga Mishmeeshian Kuludjian is Zaruhy Mishmeeshian's daughter. Her father was Kevork, Ohan Mishmeeshian's (shoemaker in Perri) eldest son. Ohan had three sons, Kevork, Stephan, and Sarkis.[*]

In 1909 Kevork, his wife Zaruhy and Sarkis, the youngest son, went to Chicago, most likely to avoid conscription into the Turkish army. This was the same year Bedros went to Chicago.

In 1914 Zaruhy returned to Perri with her daughter Olga (about five years old) to visit with her extended family. Most likely they were oblivious to the political situation in that part of the world. And again, as fate would have it, she was caught in the throes of the Genocide, much like the Yermoians when they returned to Perri from America.

While Zaruhy was a "Myreeg" at the Euphrates Orphanage, she was, also, Dr. Mikahil's washer-woman. In 1922 with the American Consulate's assistance in Kharpert, Zaruhy and Olga returned to America via Bolis (Constantinople). Zaruhy died at the age of 76.[†]

---

[*] Ohan's middle son, Stephan, remained in Perri and perished with the other Peritzees. There is no word about the other two brothers, Marsoub or Garabed, nor of their off springs.

[†] The Mishmeeshians were related to my father by his great grandmother's lineage!

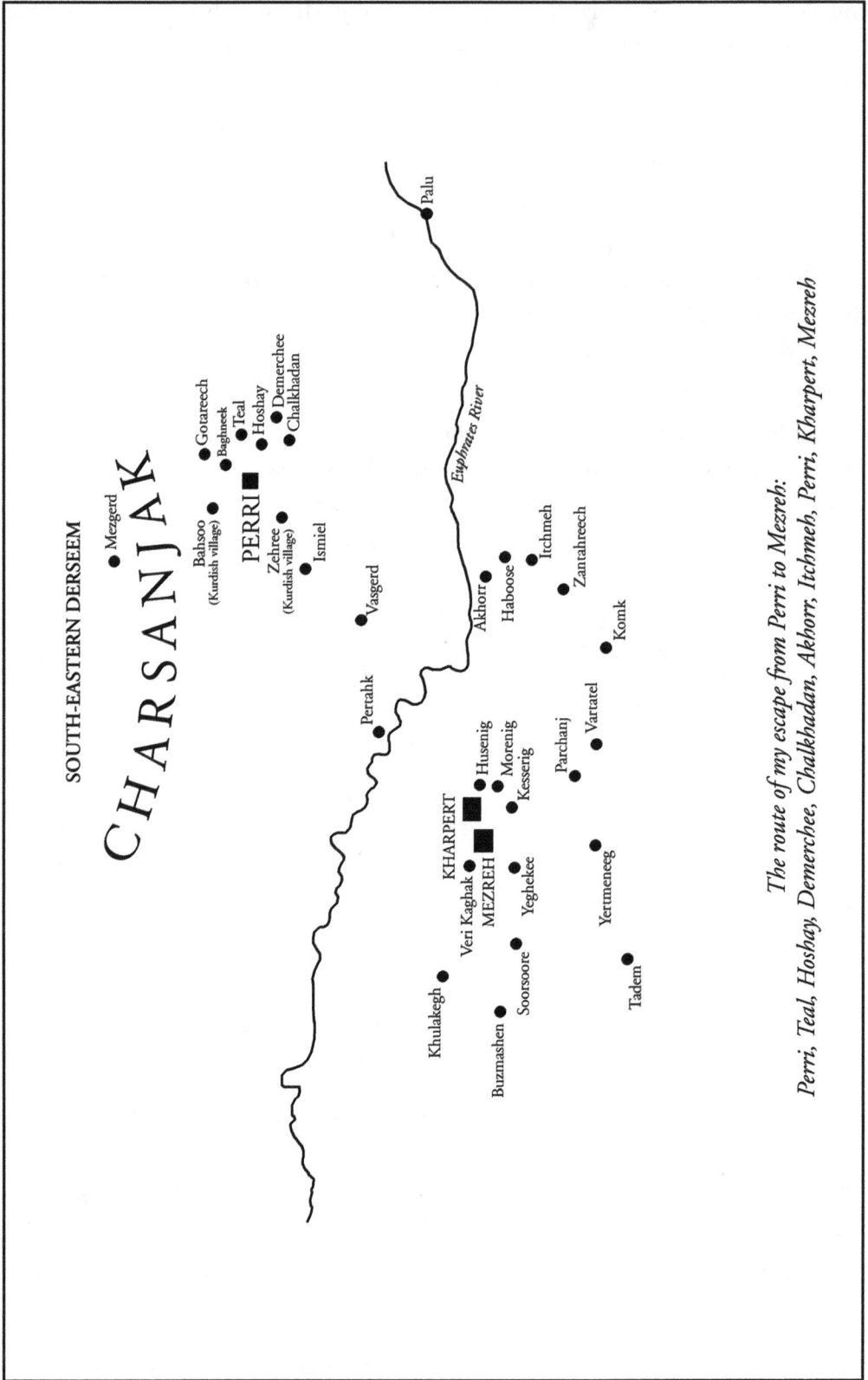

SOUTH-EASTERN DERSEEM

CHARSANJAK

Palu

Euphrates River

Mezgerd

Gotareech
Baghneek
Teal
Hoshay
Demerchee
Chalkhadan

Bahsoo
(Kurdish village)
PERRI
Zehree
(Kurdish village)
Ismiel

Vasgerd

Itchmeh
Zantahreech

Akhorr
Haboose

Komk

Perrahk

Husenig
Morenig
Kesserig

Parchanj
Vartatel

KHARPERT
Veri Kaghak
MEZREH
Yeghekee

Yermeneeg

Khulakegh

Soorsoore

Buzmashen

Tadem

The route of my escape from Perri to Mezreh:

Perri, Teal, Hoshay, Demerchee, Chalkhadan, Akhorr, Itchmeh, Perri, Kharpert, Mezreh

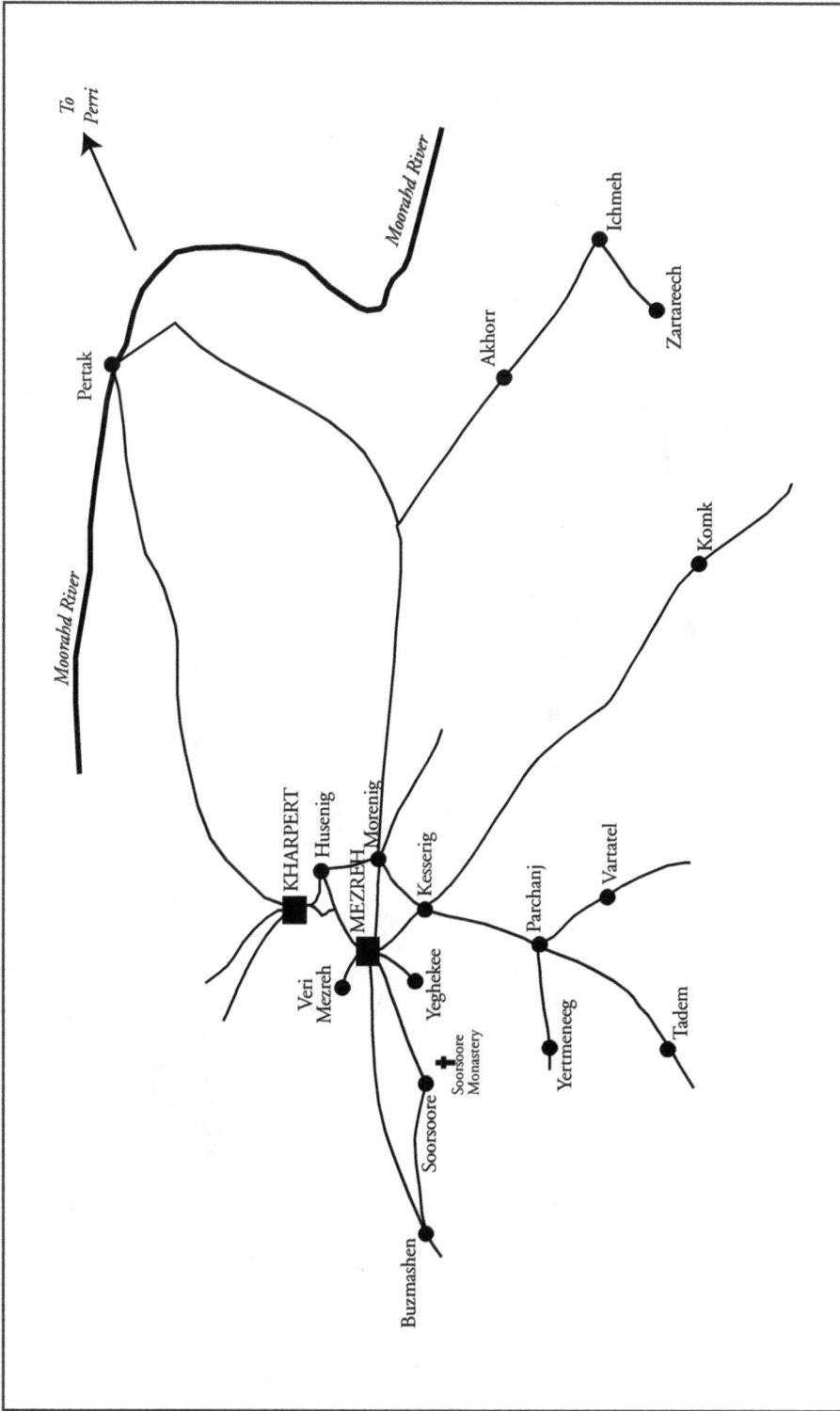

The various villages where I aimlessly wondered six years escaping from death.

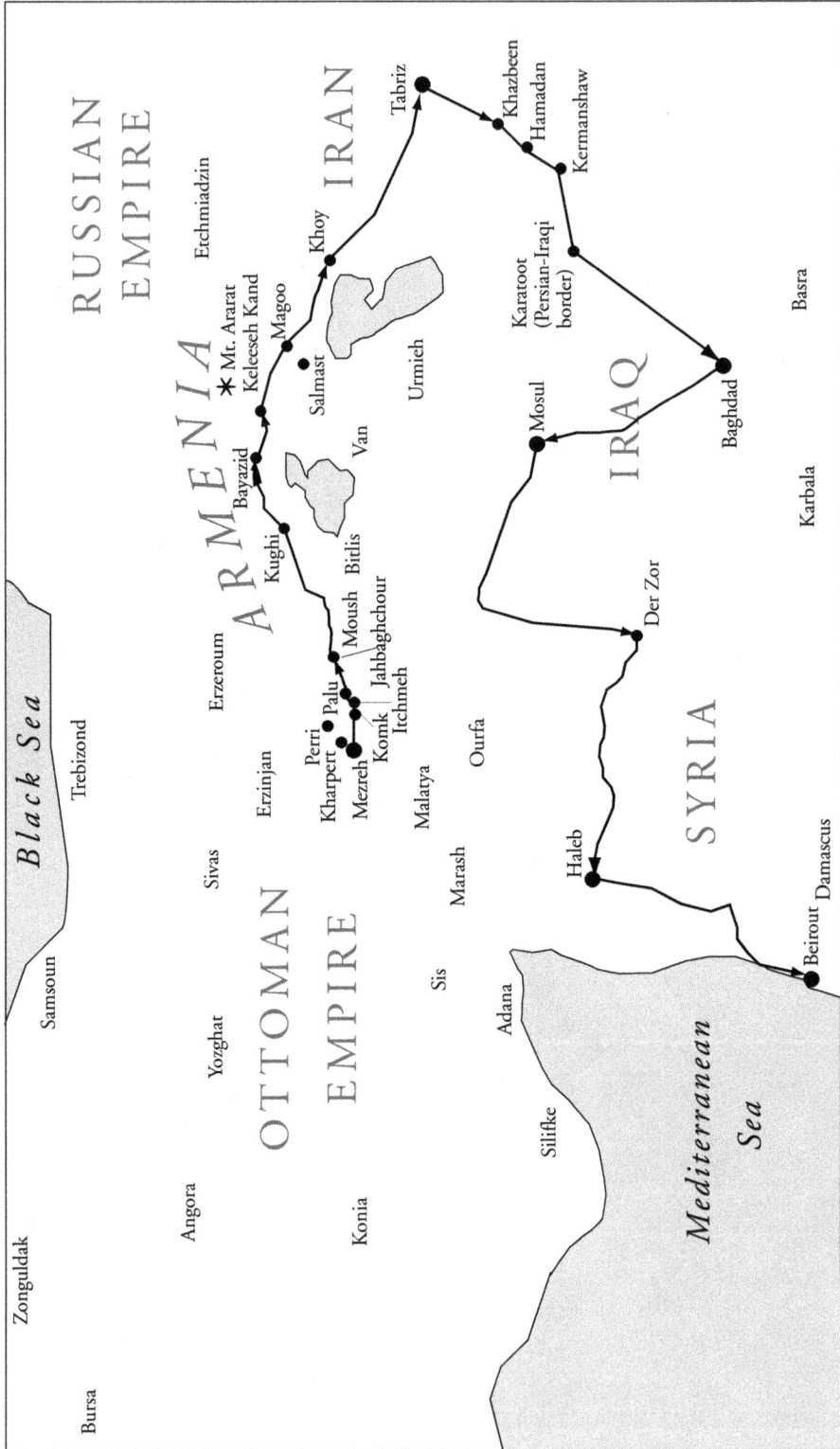

Route to Freedom. 1. From Mezreh to Keleeseh Kand: Mezreh, Komk, Itchmeh, Palu, Jabaghchour, Kughi, Bayazid, Keleeseh Kand. 2. From Keleeseh Kand to Tabriz: Magoo, Khoy, Tabriz. 3. From Tabriz: Khasbeen, Hamadan, Kermanshaw, Baghdad, Mosul, Der Zor, Haleb, Beirout.

Armenian, Kurdish and Turkish Words and Phrases as Used by Hampartzoum Chitjian

Ach guhbook (Game of hide and seek)

Agha (Title for a rich Kurd)

Aghpiur (Fountain)

Ahroo (Channel)

Akh, akh (How unfortunate! too bad!)

Aksor (Deportation, exile)

Akhor (Stable)

Aljack (A thick pad made of a soft material)

Angogheen (Comforter)

Arkhaj Baghchah (Mulberry grove)

Asorie (Assyrian)

Bag (A king, master, landowner)

Baghbanjee (Overseer of the garden)

Baghchah (Garden)

Bastegh (A preserve)

Byoosahg (Bag)

Bahgee (Sister)

Bardahkhanah (The kiln)

Baron (Mister)

Baumbohzz (Type of grass)

Beat-bazaree (Flea market)

Beg (A Turkish Lord, position of respect)

Bighintz (Copper)

Bin Bahshee (Commandant)

Beeleek (Bread, a thicker and softer type)

Centavos (Mexican currency). 100 = 1 peso)

Chaghahts (Flourmill)

Chahghahlah (Green almonds)

Chargee (Vendor)

Charroughs (Sandals)

Charrt (Massacre)

Charshahf (Sheets)

Chettehs (Turkish or Kurdish thugs)

Chooval (Burlap sack)

Chorags (Pastries)

Chorr hatz (Dry, cracker bread)

Chorrbah (Soup or broth)

Chortahn (Dried yogurt)

Chour (Water)

Chughuns (A square muslin to wrap goods)

Dashnag (Armenian Revolutionary Federation political party)

Deeg (Hollowed skin container)

Dehlee-Teefoh (Typhoid)

"Der Voghormia" ("Lord Have Mercy")

Doebrahgs (Bag)

Doeshag (Mattress)

Dolma (Stuffed grape leaves)

Doo-dook (Armenian flute)

Doon (House)

Dundess (Custodian of a place)

Eeleeg (Spindle)

Effendi (Sir)

Eolchek (Bushel)

Esh (Jackass)

Fahnos (Candleholder)

Fahroon (Bakery)

Fedayee (A freedom fighter)

Gaghabar (A wood block)

Gaghgee (White powdery clay)

Gahn (Wooden board)

Gahrep (Hemp)

Gahrahs (Terra cotta)

Gahveej (Chalk)

Galls (Threshing area)

"Gavour Boghee" ("Armenian filth")

Gavours (Infidels)

Gendarme (Policeman)

Godoradz (Massacre)

Gogeskraw (Large black grapes)

Gohl (Base of the waterfall)

Goosh (Water jug)

Gouvach (A Persian soup)

Guhdav (Cotton muslin)

Gunkahayr (Godfather)

Gunkamayr (Godmother)

"Havadov Khostovaneem" ("I Confess With Faith")

Hayasdan (Armenia)

Hayrig (Father)

Hereesah or Kashkahg (A dish made with whole grain wheat)

Herrt (Chaff)

Hoja (Teacher)

Horr (Loom)

Hye Tad (Armenian Case or Cause)

Karrehtaghdagh (Blackboard)

Kaylahg (River raft)

Keervah (Reliable Kurdish friend)

Kehree (Maternal uncle)

Kertasdan (Extended family, distant relative)

Khach (Cross)

Khahzahn (Large cauldron)

Khajakhgee (A man who secretly rescued refugees)

Khan (Small inn)

Khanum (Madam)

Khashahvoo (Special brush)

Khezh (Resin, glue)

Khnotzee (Churn)

Khooroosh (Coin, Turkish currency)

Khran (Persian currency)

Khuseer (A straw mat)

Khuzehn (Pantry)

Koemesh (Water buffalo)

Kodee (Belt)

Kogh (A thief)

Kondagh (Swaddling clothes)

Konedourahs (A pump with a two to three inch heel)

Kooshkurr (Square brick made from animal dung and wheat chaff)

Krahj Baghchah (Mulberry grove)

Kughatzi (Peasant)

Lahgode (Turkish punk)

Logh (Stone roller)

Loosavorchagan (A member of the Armenian Apostolic Church)

Magtab (Turkish school)

Mahdzoon (Yogurt)

Mahee (death)

Mahdzoon abour (Yogurt soup)

Mahjeed (A Turkish silver coin)

Mahlahmat (Embarrassment)

Mahlez (Paste)

Mahs (Special sock)

Mahsoosah (Long stick with a sharp nail at the end)

Mairig (Mother)

Maktab (School)

Maz (Hair)

Meeltahn (Coat)

Meghk! (A sigh of sorrow, pity)

Mehsheh (Poplar)

Mode (Near)

Moonehdeek (Town crier)

Muhrrdahl (Untouchables)

Mullah (Islamic priest)

Naghergee (Shepherd)

Nahmah hahrahm (Punishable crime)

Nahmat (Sinful)

Nerrgah (Present)

Odars (Non-Armenians)

Ohcheel (Lice)

Ojahk (Fireplace)

Olcheg (Bushel)

Ooleeg (Kid)

Ouree (Willow)

Pabooj (Slipper)

Pahlahs (Woven mats)

Para (A minor Turkish currency)

Parch (Water pitcher)

Peenehche (Shoe repair)

Pehtahks (Containers)

Poorr (Oven, Bakery)

Rojeeg (A preserve)

Sahkoosee (A wooden deck in a stable)

Sahls (Two flat, hard stones)

Sapat (Basket)

Serr (Cream)

Serrgahn (Clay floor)

Shalvahr (Pants)

Shoogah (Market place)

Shooshmah (Sesame)

Shuroob (Syrup)
Sobah (Wooden stove)
Sov (Starvation)
Tagh (Neighborhood, district)
Tahn (Yogurt drink)
Tahn ahbour (Yogurt soup)
Tapzee (Tray)
Tavlee (Backgammon)
Tayag (Mid-wife)
Tohrr (Net)
Toneer (Cooking pit)
Toot (Mulberries)
Torrtah (Courtyard)
Tsiavor (Horseman)
Tuhmagh (A fat pouch that hung from a lamb's rear)
Tumahn (A Persian currency)
Tzeetzeeyank (Millstone)
Vartabed (Celibate priest)

"Vagh, vagh" (Exclamation, "Too bad!")
Veri mailah (Uptown shopping area)
"Vocheench" ("Never mind")
"Vooroun!" ("Beat him!")
Vosb (Lentils)
Voskeruch (Goldsmith)
Yahzmah (Scarf)
Yeghpayr (Brother)
"Yehgav" ("Here he comes")
Yehmahnee (Men's shoes)
Yergahnk (Small millstone)
Yergeer (Homeland, country)
Yergeeratzee (Countryman)
Zehmehlee (Small pocketknife)
Zehzahts (Whole-wheat grain)
Zhoghovahran (Armenian Protestant church hall)
Zuhboons (Dress)

ԿԻ

GOMIDAS INSTITUTE ARMENIAN GENOCIDE DOCUMENTATION SERIES

Child Survivors

Hampartzoum Mardiros Chitjian, *A Hair's Breadth from Death,* London: Gomidas Institute, 2021 (2nd ed).

Misak Khralian, *Palahovid : An Ancestral Memoir,* translated from Armenian by Simon Beugekian; ed. and intro. by Ara Sarafian, London: Gomidas Institute, 2021.

Vahram Dadrian, *To the Desert: Pages from My Diary,* translated from Armenian by Agop Hacikyan; ed. and intro. by Ara Sarafian, London: Gomidas Institute, 2020 (3rd ed).

Souren H. Hanessian, *Through The Depths: A True Life Story,* London: Gomidas Institute, 2017.

Papken Injarabian, *Azo the Slave Boy and his Road to Freedom,* translated from French by Elisabeth Eaker, London: Gomidas Institute, 2015.

Jean V. Gureghian, *My Father's Destiny: The Golgotha of Armenia Minor,* translated from French by Diran Meghreblian with a preface by Yves Ternon, London: Gomidas Institute, 2015.

Avedis Albert Abrahamian, *Avedis' Story: An Armenian Boy's Journey,* edited with an introduction by Carolann Najarian, London: Gomidas Institute, 2014.

Levon Shahoian, *On the Banks of the Tigris* (Youth edition), transl. by Garabet K. Moumdjian, London: Gomidas Institute, 2014.

Euphornia Halebian Meymarian, *Housher: My Life in the Aftermath of the Armenian Genocide,* with a foreword by Stephen Sheehi, London: Taderon Press, 2005.

The Gomidas Institute Armenian Genocide Documentation Series includes other seminal works consisting of memoirs, diaries and documentary collections by eye-witnesses who recorded what they saw of the Armenian Genocide in 1915.

For more information about our books on the Armenian Genocide

and the modern Armenian experience please visit

www.gomidas.org or contact *info@gomidas.org*

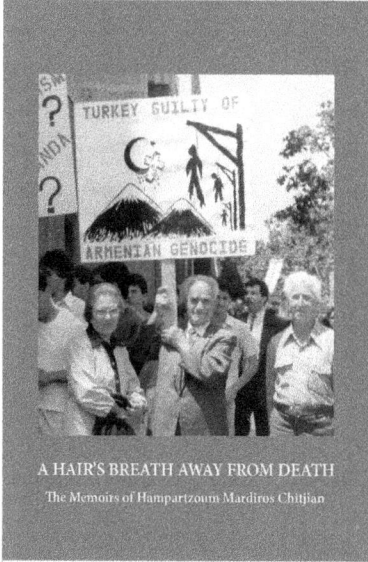

A HAIR'S BREATH AWAY FROM DEATH

The Memoirs of Hampartzoum Mardiros Chitjian

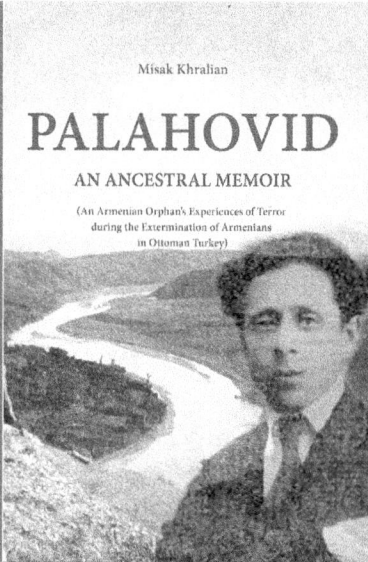

Misak Khralian

PALAHOVID

AN ANCESTRAL MEMOIR

(An Armenian Orphan's Experiences of Terror
during the Extermination of Armenians
in Ottoman Turkey)

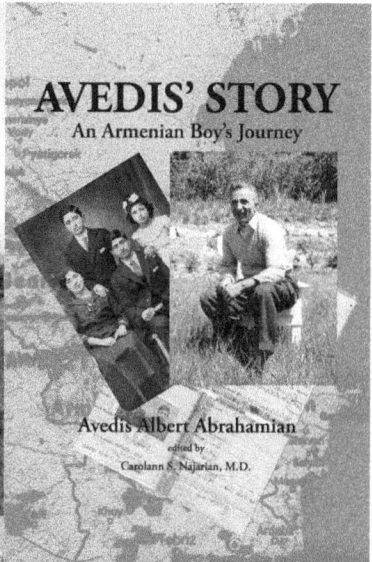

AVEDIS' STORY

An Armenian Boy's Journey

Avedis Albert Abrahamian

edited by
Carolann S. Najarian, M.D.

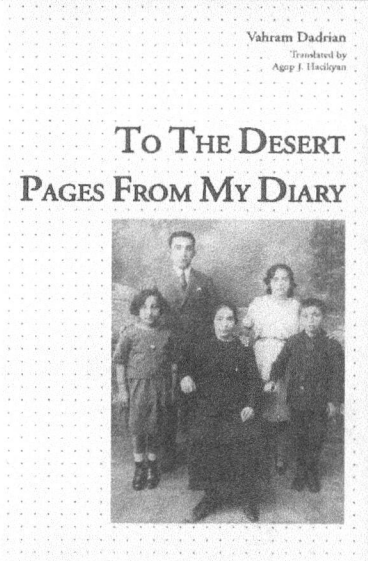

Vahram Dadrian
Translated by
Agop J. Hacikyan

TO THE DESERT
PAGES FROM MY DIARY

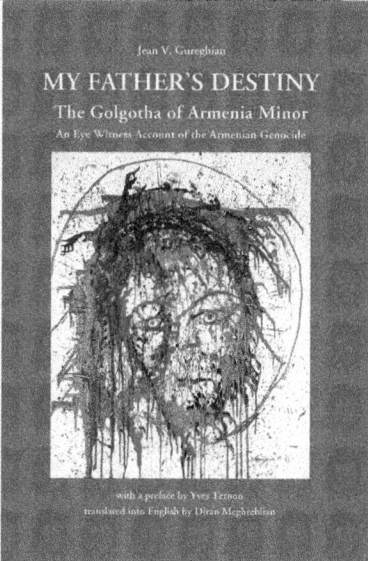

Jean V. Gureghian

MY FATHER'S DESTINY

The Golgotha of Armenia Minor
An Eye Witness Account of the Armenian Genocide

with a preface by Yves Ternon
translated into English by Diran Meghrehlian

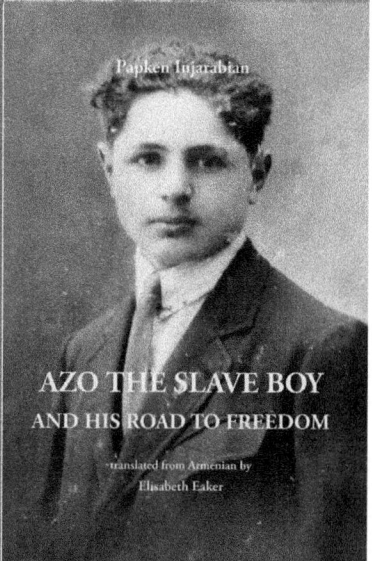

Papken Injarabian

AZO THE SLAVE BOY

AND HIS ROAD TO FREEDOM

translated from Armenian by
Elisabeth Eaker

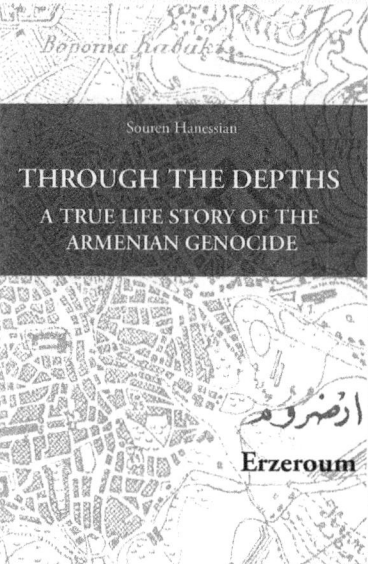

Souren Hanessian

THROUGH THE DEPTHS

A TRUE LIFE STORY OF THE
ARMENIAN GENOCIDE

Erzeroum

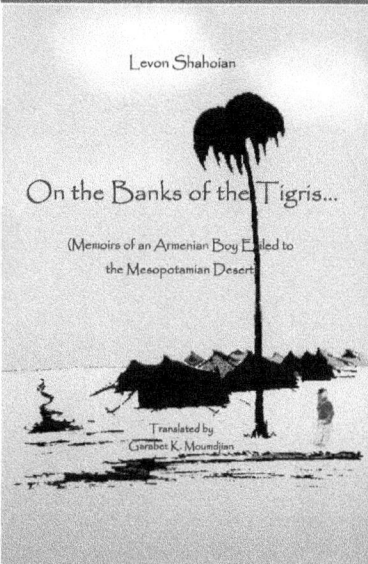

Levon Shahoian

On the Banks of the Tigris...

(Memoirs of an Armenian Boy Exiled to
the Mesopotamian Desert)

Translated by
Garabet K. Moumdjian

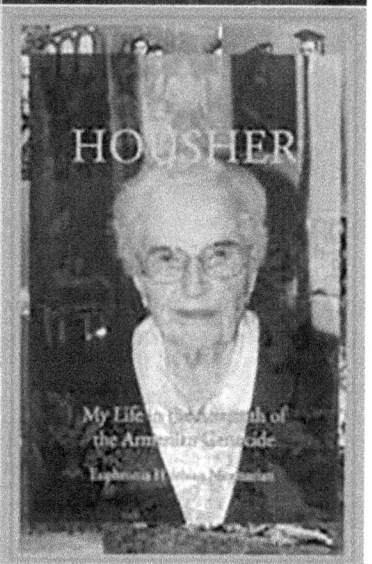

HOUSHER

My Life in the Aftermath of
the Armenian Genocide

www.ingramcontent.com/pod-product-compliance
Lightning Source LLC
Chambersburg PA
CBHW080242030426
42334CB00023BA/2670